Harry Potter a
the Classical W(

Harry Potter and the Classical World

Greek and Roman Allusions in J.K. Rowling's Modern Epic

RICHARD A. SPENCER

McFarland & Company, Inc., Publishers

Jefferson, North Carolina

LIBRARY OF CONGRESS CATALOGUING-IN-PUBLICATION DATA

Spencer, Richard A. (Richard Albert)
    Harry Potter and the classical world : Greek and Roman allusions in J.K. Rowling's modern epic / Richard A. Spencer.
        p.   cm.
    Includes bibliographical references and index.

    ISBN 978-0-7864-9921-2 (softcover : acid free paper) ∞
    ISBN 978-1-4766-2141-8 (ebook)

    1. Rowling, J.K.—Criticism and interpretation.   2. Rowling, J.K.—Characters—Harry Potter.   3. Classical literature—Influence.   4. Mythology, Greek, in literature.   5. Mythology, Roman, in literature.   6. Children's stories, English—History and criticism.   7. Fantasy fiction, English—History and criticism.   8. Civilization, Classical—Influence.   I. Title.
    PR6068.O93Z8874 2015
    823'.914—dc23   2015023929

BRITISH LIBRARY CATALOGUING DATA ARE AVAILABLE

Printed in the United States of America

McFarland & Company, Inc., Publishers
    Box 611, Jefferson, North Carolina 28640
    www.mcfarlandpub.com

To Libby

vitae meae felicitas atque adeo domus meae animae

Table of Contents

Acknowledgments

I am indebted to the administration of Appalachian State University and to my department chairs Dr. Jesse Taylor and Dr. Conrad Ostwalt for their encouragement and support in allowing me to offer an experimental special topics course entitled "Classical Mythology and Classical Culture in the *Harry Potter* Novels" in addition to my usual courses in biblical studies, Latin, classical mythology, and Greek.

Sincere thanks are owed to the many students who brought to the classroom a phenomenal level of personal engagement with the subject and whose unique insights into imaginative literature made the classes a joyful learning experience. Their enthusiasm for the appearance of this volume has provided me with constant motivation to bring it to completion.

Anonymous peer reviewers have offered much-appreciated critique and advisement, which have made the end product much better. I am grateful for their close reading of the text, their insights, and their encouragement.

I wish to express deep personal appreciation to Janet Palmer, who proof-read the manuscript so remarkably well. Her excellent literary skills, technical expertise, and diligence refined the presentation significantly. She took a vigorous and busy manuscript and healed it of many of its ailments and imperfections which had begun to elude my sight the more I read the manuscript. For any inadequacies which may remain, I alone am responsible.

Abbreviations

In order to avoid unpleasant repetition of the names "Harry," "Hermione," and "Ron" who are cited together so frequently, the abbreviation HH&R designates the set. References to specific pages in the *Harry Potter* novels are indicated by the abbreviations for the novels listed below along with the page number of the book. For example, page 653 of *Harry Potter and the Goblet of Fire* is cited as (*GF* 653). The pagination cited is to the editions indicated below and in bibliography. I have tried to avoid over-use of such references except where necessary and where direct quotations are cited because readers may have access to other editions of the novels than those used here.

Aen.   Vergil, *Aeneid*
AFr   Anglo-French: used in medieval England
Argonautica   Apollonius of Rhodes, *Argonautica*
A.U.C.   Livy, *Ab Urbe Condita*
BCE   "Before the Common Era," the period formerly designated as BC ("Before Christ")
CE   "Common Era," the period formerly designated as AD (Anno Domini, "In the Year of Our Lord")
e.g.   Latin, *exemplī gratiā*, "for (the sake of an) example"
Epit.   Apollodorus, *Epitome*
et al.   Latin, *et alii*, "and others"
Fr   the French language
Gk   the Greek language
Heb   the Hebrew language
HH&R   Harry, Hermione and Ron
Fab.   Hyginus, *Fabulae*
i.e.   Latin, *id est*, "that is"
Il.   Homer, *Iliad*
It   the Italian language
L   Latin language of the classical period (third century BCE to the second century CE)
Libr.   Apollodorus, *The Library of Greek Mythology*
LL   Late Latin: the Latin used from the late second to the fifth centuries CE, known as the Patristic Period, because the major works of the period were done by the

1

church fathers, who developed a formal style for distinctively Christian purposes

l., ll.   line, lines

LSJ   *A Greek-English Lexicon.* Ninth ed. Henry George Liddell, and Robert Scott, eds.; rev. by Henry Stuart James. Oxford: Clarendon Press, 1940; repr. 1968.

ME   Middle English: the English language of the period 1100–1500 CE. All Middle English definitions given in this book are taken from the *Middle English Dictionary* (Hans Kurath, Sherman M. Kuhn, and Robert Lewis, eds.), unless otherwise noted.

Met.   Ovid, *Metamorphoses*

ML   Medieval Latin: the Latin used throughout Europe from the sixth to the fourteenth centuries CE

ModL   Modern Latin: the Latin used from the fifteenth century until today, mainly in academic and scientific contexts

n.   note (footnote or endnote)

NRSV   The New Revised Standard Version of the Holy Bible

Od.   Homer, *Odyssey*

OLD   *Oxford Latin Dictionary.* P.G.W. Glare, ed. Oxford: Clarendon Press, 1983.

OED   *The Oxford English Dictionary*

OFr   Old French: the French language in use during the ninth to the thirteenth centuries

OHG   Old High German: the German language of the eighth to the twelfth centuries

OL   Old Latin: the Latin language prior to 75 BCE

repr.   reprint

Theog.   Hesiod, *Theogony*

trans.   translation by; translator

VL   Vulgar Latin: the Latin used by the common people. Elements of this occur from the earliest periods of Latin through the fifth century CE.

Works   Hesiod, *Works and Days*

All abbreviations of books of the Bible follow the system used by Sakenfield 2006–2009. All translations of ancient sources are my own, unless otherwise indicated. Citations to the novels will use the following abbreviations, followed by a page number.

SS   *Harry Potter and the Sorcerer's Stone.* New York: Scholastic Inc., 1997.

CS   *Harry Potter and the Chamber of Secrets.* New York: Scholastic Inc., 1999.

PA   *Harry Potter and the Prisoner of Azkaban.* New York: Scholastic Inc., 1999.

GF   *Harry Potter and the Goblet of Fire.* New York: Scholastic Inc., 2000.

OP   *Harry Potter and the Order of the Phoenix.* New York: Scholastic Inc., 2003.

HBP   *Harry Potter and the Half-Blood Prince.* New York: Scholastic Inc., 2005.

DH   *Harry Potter and the Deathly Hallows.* New York: Scholastic Inc., 2007.

Symbols (used in etymologies):

> \>   becomes or influences the development of the following
> \<   is derived from or influenced in its development from the following

Preface

Having taught Greek, Latin, classical mythology, and biblical studies for forty-three years, I have a passion for the world of the ancient Greeks and Romans. Their stories have encoded and immortalized rich expressions, perspectives, and experiences of life which have come to be the cultural DNA of much of our western civilization. When I first encountered the *Potter* novels, I was so amazed at the presence of classical gems at every turn that I saw this as a great opportunity to advance the cause of education in classics. For three years I offered a course on classical culture and classical mythology in *Harry Potter* at Appalachian State University. Students were sorted into the Hogwarts Houses using a Sorting Hat, and were required to take O.W.L.s and N.E.W.T.s in place of mid-terms and final exams. The enthusiasm of the students was inspiring and addictive. Most of the students were already quite devoted to the *Potter* books. In fact, many of the students said they "grew up with *Harry Potter*." By engaging in a concentrated study of the novels at the specific points where Rowling has drawn so deeply from this ancient resource, the students' admiration for her genius as a writer, and their understanding of the undying legacy and value of our common classical resources were greatly enhanced.

This book focuses on the ancient tradition and literature from the Greek and Roman worlds to which Rowling often alludes in her novels. It is obvious to all readers that she uses the pool of classical resources to inform and color her writing, which is natural, as she is an accomplished student of classics. Today, many people have some acquaintance with classical mythology, either from school or by its frequent reprise in modern fantasy literature, science fiction, or movies. Not so many know exactly who Clytemnestra or Meleager are, or the source and purpose of their stories. And yet, when classic predecessors are revitalized, and the themes, motifs, and issues which they employ are part of the art and literature of our time, there is something deep within us which responds to them as if we know them in advance and embrace the new as if there is something there of the "of course," or the "naturally." And the new presentation draws our sense of discovery, even as it ties what is original to something ancient and familiar. The roots of the classical tradition, which live deep within us, respond to her stories as if we know already something of the unspoken meaning or "music" of her narrative, permitting us, almost, to hum along with her, being enlightened by the novel treatment of a common heritage.

This work presumes that the readers will have a significant degree of familiarity with all seven novels and some basic knowledge of the classical referents. Its thesis is that the reading of *Harry Potter* is illumined and enhanced if we consider the novels as beneficiaries of classical predecessors, if we become more familiar with those ancient sources, and if we apply what can be known of those predecessors to the novels.

In order to consider some of the ways in which classical tradition is used in the *Potter* novels, we adopt the following approach. In the first chapters, we consider the over-arching type of hero story which is at work (the quest story), the principal types of hero which are used to create the character Harry Potter (Seeker and Savior), and the main figures whose roles offer the most frequent echoes of antiquity (Harry, Dumbledore and Voldemort). Next, we turn to other important characters who present suggestive classical connections (Draco Malfoy, Ginny Weasley, et al.). Then, we examine a number of other supporting characters who have linguistic or typological predecessors in the Greek and Roman world. The two remaining chapters deal with the function and craft of magic which is common to the classical world and the Wizarding world, and Rowling's various uses of the classical languages. A concluding chapter summarizes our findings.

Introduction

The widespread appreciation of J.K. Rowling's *Harry Potter* novels has generated a number of popular books for devoted general readers, as well as numerous scholarly volumes and articles which view the literature from an increasingly wide range of perspectives. And as time passes, the production of specialist studies on the novels increases. Today, there are articles and books which examine the *Potter* books from the viewpoint of issues and disciplines such as these: the law (Thomas and Snyder), sociology and politics (Barratt, Gupta), history (DuPree, Reagin), education and teaching (Belcher and Stephenson, Frankel), adolescent psychological and social development (Grimes, Mulholland, Saxena), magic and science (Highfield), therapy for grieving children and adolescents (Markell), philosophy (Baggett, Bassham), gender issues (Dresang, Mayes-Elma), career development (Morris), political themes (Bryfonski), international relations (Nexon), Christian theological parallels (Luke Bell, Dickerson, Garrett, Granger 2008, Killinger, Neal 2008), ethics, morality, and moral development (Guttfield, Kern, Neal 2007), fictional heroism in twenty-first century heroism (Berndt), comparative literature (Granger 2007, 2008, 2009, Nel, Prinzi), and theories of myth and (post) structuralist methodology (Flotmann). In addition, some volumes of collected studies emphasize critical, multli-disciplinary and multi-national scholarship: Anatol, Christopher Bell, Bice, Fenske, Hallett (2005, 2012), Heilman, Lackey, Patterson, and Whited. This list is only a small representation of the vast body of materials now available on the *Harry Potter* novels. Since 2004, Cornelia Rémi has maintained an up-to-date and marvelously informative website of international scholarship, symposia, sources, the "Harry Potter Bibliography" at http://www.eulenfeder.de/hpliteratur.html, which attests to the ever-growing, worldwide attention being given to this literature and the vast sea of literary productions emerging from that attention.

It is evident to all readers that Rowling has drawn very deeply from the pool of classical resources to inform and color her writing, which is natural, given that she is a devoted student of classics. Her allusion to those resources ranges from the most obvious to the most obscure. The vicious three-headed dog which Hagrid posts as guard over the door leading to the chamber in which the Sorcerer's Stone is hidden is clearly a re-packaging of Cerberus, the vicious three-headed dog which guards the Underworld. What Rowling does with this borrowed image, however, is as charming as the image is arresting, for she has Hagrid name this vicious dog "Fluffy." This is a humorous and playful reversal of the image of the dog, and a revelation of the character of Hagrid, who, in his innocence and kind-spiritedness, sees the cuddly and attractive even in bizarre and vicious creatures. The significance of her quotation from Aeschylus in the frontispiece of *Harry Potter and the Deathly Hallows* is a matter of speculation.

This volume focuses on J.K. Rowling's drawing from the bank of timeless materials which have come down to us from the era of the Greeks and Romans. Many writers have commented on the fact that classical imagery is abundant in *Harry Potter*. Usually, the topic is mentioned briefly, or, at best, in studies of specific themes or topics. In Adney and Hassel's work covering the life and work of J.K. Rowling, the authors give very informative and suggestive comments on a few characters and creatures in the magical world which are reminiscent of figures or mythical motifs of antiquity (2011). M. Katherine Grimes studies some motifs from antiquity which are found in the novels: archetypal child heroes who are threatened by a father-figure or malicious adult male enemy (Romulus and Remus by a king; Harry by Voldemort); abandoned children who are rescued by animals or shepherds (Oedipus by a shepherd; Harry by Hagrid). Peggy J. Huey offers observations on some of the magical beasts—the basilisk, centaur, hippogriff, phoenix, and unicorn. She comments briefly on the role of these figures and cites the other scholars' comments on the figures in recent sources. Her aim is not to give detailed information and tradition about the classical parallels themselves. Her observations are very insightful, though they are not always developed at length. Roni Natov focuses on Rowling's episode of the Mirror of Erised as a reimagining of Odysseus' test of the Sirens for children, as an example to hear but not act on a calling (134). Philip Nel's analysis of the genre of the novels offers observations on the importance of prime numbers in the series (2001). He does not develop any connection between the numbers and the original source of number mysticism, the ancient world. Mary Pharr makes brief and specific connections between the stories and the classical world. One of her more developed contributions is her linking of Harry and Achilles, as heroes who experience the significant loss of a dear friend, and are forced to deal with the reality of mortality (2002). Vandana Saxena's book on adolescent rebellion and containment in the series gives extensive analysis of the hero and savior figures, with an in-depth comparison of Harry and Oedipus, and the themes common to both (2012). Holly Blackford explores the myth of Persephone and its frequent use in fantasy literature for girls, giving substantial attention to that model for the experiences of Ginny Weasley in the *Chamber of Secrets* (2012). Thury and Devinney devote an entire chapter of their text on classical and world mythology to a psychological study of the themes of father-figures, mother-figures, birth and rebirth in hero tales and in Rowling's novels, using the theories of C.G. Jung, Sigmund Freud, and especially Otto Rank (2013).

Students of Latin (present or potential) may be excited to discover Rowling's abundant use of the language, whether it is actual, grammatically correct Latin, or creatively playful inventions using the language. Activating the language of dead poets, imperial politicians, and medieval scholars and wizards brings to the stories the tone and atmosphere of the magical, the mysterious, the ancient and the forbidden. Many of the incantations or special phrases used in the magical world are genuine Latin words and phrases—e.g., *Accio!, Caput Draconis!, Nox!, Ferula!, Sonorus!* Others are playful alterations of Latin words—e.g., *Alohomora!, Wingardium Leviosa!, Expelliarmus!, Animagi, Lumos!, Densaugeo!* Many names are genuine Latin names or are invented from genuine Latin bases—e.g., *Minerva, Lucius, Draco, Rubeus, Albus, Severus, Ambrosius, Ludo, Nigellus, Phyllida, Sanguini.* And some words derive from classical language which has been playfully transformed for magical applications—e.g., *Amortentia, Incarcerous, Obliviate, Rictussempra.*

Rowling's use of Latin has been noted in occasional papers and within groups of local classical associations, but not enough has been published on the topic. M.G. DuPree's book on history and *Harry Potter* explores the novels from a variety of historical angles, such as the making of medieval manuscripts (2011). Her own article, however, "Severus Snape and the Standard Book of Spells: Ancient Tongues in the Wizarding World," is the only entry which deals with the classical tradition. She studies Rowling's use of Latin and Greek in her magical spells, and comments, briefly, on how the author often toys with the language. Alleen P. Nilsen and Don L.F. Nilsen have published an article on how teachers can take advantage of the vocabulary in *Harry Potter* to aid in the teaching of Latin, making connections between Rowling and Latin (2006). It is obvious that the subject of the present book is widely recognized as significant and worthy of investigation. At present, however, there appears to be no work which aims to collect and assess the wide range of classical resources and allusions which exist between the *Harry Potter* novels and the language, literature, history and culture of the ancient world of Greece and Rome.

In most of the works mentioned above, the writers are concerned with tracing themes or allusions to exhibit connections between Rowling's novels and possible, classical antecedents. They do not explore a wide range of parallels or classical allusions very extensively. This book intends to take a serious look at the ancient tradition and literature from the Greek and Roman worlds which are so frequently employed in Rowling's stories, based on the thesis that much of the richness, distinctiveness, and attraction of the novels derive from the force and uniqueness of the preceding tradition and her variations on it. It is my hope that by engaging in an extensive comparison of the parallels and by exploring the distinctiveness of the ancient predecessors, this book will increase our appreciation for the brilliance of the author and her novels, and create a renewed appreciation for the timeless treasury from which she draws.

Several disclaimers need to be presented at the outset. I do not aim to read J.K. Rowling's mind or claim to have discovered precisely how she intends for readers to take her classical allusions. She may at times rely on much more recent literature or sources than she relies on the Greeks and Romans. Perhaps some of her names, types, or motifs have come to her from their presence in later and western literature. Her particular uses of the classics may be merely casual, or inspired, or purposeful. Whatever her intentions are, the abundance of her allusions which have ancient correspondences demands investigation. Sometimes, the allusions are bold and undeniable, demanding readers to recall the ancient referent and to transfer something of the original to the present application. At other times the similarities are subtle, suggestive implications, allowing for reasonable inferences. Not every detail of the predecessor has to be known and applied to its successor in order to "get" the significance of its recycling in *Harry Potter*. For example, in order to get the effect of the three headed dog Fluffy's being a Cerberus look-alike, it is not necessary to know that when the newly deceased arrived in Hades, Cerberus wagged his tail, but if they tried to escape, he ate them (Henrichs "Hades," 2012, 640). But the more we know about Cerberus, the more our conception of the Hound of Hogwarts is enhanced. Some readers may think that the parallels, similarities, or associations which I offer are a "stretch." And they may be. As the Roman playwright Terence wrote, "There are as many opinions as there are people, and each has his own way" [quod hominēs tot sententiae suōs quoique mōs est, *Phormio* 454].[1] I press the comparisons for readers to consider on their own. In addition, the information which has come down to us from antiquity offers a wide variety of options and variations on characters and their stories, which are often contradictory. I cannot possibly include all details about all the referents being cited, only those aspects which reflect some parallels to features in the seven novels.

This volume is not a *Harry Potter* encyclopedia. The items which I mention are limited to those which have some place in the arena of our investigation. For general information about all aspects of the series, readers should consult Vander Ark (2009) and the Harry Potter Lexicon online at http://www.hp-lexicon.org/help/lexicon.html.

Why is this work important? First of all, the subject has not yet been given the extensive treatment it deserves. Second, it will provide new light on an under-emphasized aspect of Rowling's genius as a writer and the nature of her novels. Third, it will create for readers an enhanced awareness of Rowling's appropriation of the classical legacy, and will lead them to appreciate more than ever their own indebtedness to this treasury of classical lore, and, hopefully, to pursue the ancient material more deeply. Fourth, I have found that *Harry Potter* is such a fixed part of the canon for many readers, especially those who are younger, that sound and substantial courses on the subject are still being offered in colleges and schools. This book, then, may serve as an incentive for classicists and readers with interest in classics to take the ideas offered here, and to go even further with them in their own thinking, teaching, and research.

Throughout this study, I have appreciated the assessment of Peggy J. Huey, that Rowling "introduces today's readers to a world grounded in mythology that dates back to the ancient Greeks" and her contention that "making the classical allusions that she does, Rowling moves her books into th[e] realm of 'elegant literature' ... a new epic for the twenty-first century" (65). Rowling has created a brand-new, and at the same time, timeless epic work. The hopes and expectations listed in the previous paragraph are very realistic aims for readers, because I have experienced them myself and they are rewarding.

I have chosen to rely on the seven novels themselves, not on the *Harry Potter* movies, interviews with or press releases by J.K. Rowling. While such resources surely could add new dimensions to this study, I limit my primary sources almost exclusively the novels themselves.[2] The novels speak for themselves, as does all good art, engaging the reader or viewer apart from insider commentary or circumstantial information. For all I know, many of the names and characters may have come to Rowling from the people she knows or to whom she is related. But for me, if the name of a character, or the character's story or action or personality has any type of parallel in the classical era, I

consider what the nature and extent of the parallel may be, and attempt to
suggest what it may add to the reading of *Harry Potter*.

An *allusion* is a reference in a literary text to some person, place, event
or character outside the text, which the author presumes the reader will
understand and appreciate. Morner points out that the power of allusions
"lies in suggestion and connotation. They serve to evoke emotions, convey
information concisely, and establish character, mood, and setting" (Morner
5–6; see also Quinn 13). An allusion may be direct or indirect. And it relies
on the familiarity of the readers with the original to which they are being
directed. In this book the term is used to cover many kinds of parallels which
are drawn together for comparison between the novels and the ancient world
and its resources.

By employing timeless referents, Rowling introduces into the series a
quality of the epic, of an "other" but familiar world, and an aura of timelessness. When she borrows from and applies ancient themes, terms and situations to modern times, she provides variation on the originals, while infusing
the present with the uniqueness of the past. This yields two results. First, the
reader comes to intuit more fully something about who the novels' characters
are and how their situations and actions are to be viewed. This is similar to
our gaining greater understanding of people by learning their family name,
origin, heritage and background. Second, when the themes or characters are
presented in light of their ancient depiction, Rowling's creative variation on
those predecessors stands out even more strikingly.

For example, does it make any difference that Professor McGonagall's
name is "Minerva"? Would she come across to readers just the same if her
name were "Sally McGonagall"? By Rowling's giving the Professor of Transfiguration this name, she not only invites us, she *compels* us to bring to this
character some of the tradition and identity associated with the goddess Minerva, and to view Harry's teacher as performing a role which transcends the
words and actions of the magical Scottish woman. Minerva was Jupiter's
right-hand assistant, the only one to whom he ever surrendered his thunderbolt, the symbol of his divine power, as Ms. McGonagall is Dumbledore's
Assistant Deputy Headmistress, the only one to whom he ever surrenders
his office and power. The goddess was the Roman protectress of schoolchild-
ren, as McGonagall is the protectress of students at Hogwarts. Both goddess
and professor transfigure themselves into other forms by magical power. And,
on the grandest level of a hero's quest, the professor is a powerful supporter,
sponsor, and enabler of Harry the Seeker in his quest for identity, family and
destiny, just as Athena (whom the Romans called Minerva) was the protector

and helper of the most famous ancient hero who was on his own ten-year-long quest for home and hearth, Odysseus. Please note, in making these types of comparisons, I am not claiming that the characters in the novels are allegorical figures—Dumbledore is not Zeus disguised as a Headmaster, and McGonagall is not Minerva the goddess incognito as a teacher. But the point stands that if the professor at Hogwarts were named "Sally," or anything other than what J.K. Rowling has chosen to name her, all the associations pointed out above would not be nearly as apparent or purposeful as they are because of the mythological name she bears.

Rowling draws on the classical fund in her creation of many personal names—Hermione, Dedalus, Agrippa, Ptolemy, Circe, Draco, Regulus, Remus, Sibyll, Lucius, Narcissa, Amycus, Alecto, Merope and the Greek and Roman gods Minerva, Mulciber, Luna, Hestia, Hermes, Janus, and Pomona, to name just a few. Even if we do not recall immediately or completely the stories behind those names, their presence contributes to the stories a particular kind of timelessness and historical grandeur. When she creates characters with these names, she subtly directs us to pick up a lens which was created long ago and which has served us well for millennia, and look through it in order to get an image of the people we meet in her books. This is an ingenious way of helping us to link both worlds of the natural and supernatural, of the past and the present, of the timely and the timeless. The more we know about these ancient referents, the more we can appreciate the creativity and artistry of J.K. Rowling.

Sometimes, she adopts classical names which influence our intuition, affect our attitude, and give us signals concerning the nature and probable character of the named persons or creatures. For example, Harry's fellow student and enemy at Hogwarts is named "Draco" Malfoy. His personal name is a fitting title for the kind of person we find this snake-in-the-grass to be. The Greek word for "dragon" or "serpent" is *drakōn*. What parents would name their baby boy "the snake"? Only someone for whom snakes are very attractive and esteemed symbols—as we find them to be for the Malfoys. The name also has a very negative significance, historically. Draco was the name of the first lawgiver in ancient Athens (7th century, BCE), who instituted laws so unbelievably cruel (for example, the death penalty for laziness), that since his time, his name has been used to identify unconscionable and unreasonable laws— "Draconian." Even before we read much about young Malfoy, we get the feeling that this will be a sinister and rigidly self-righteous young wizard.

By "classical," I am referring to the period of history, literature, and culture of ancient Greece and Rome. I do not mean the classic western literary tradition. I am not including all of antiquity (e.g., ancient Sumer, Babylon, Egypt). I am limiting the range of investigation to Greek and Roman data, but including a few biblical resources, because my teaching and research areas for over four decades have been classics and biblical studies. I include a few biblical allusions, also, because the trend in recent years, in "classical" studies, has been to collaborate with Near Eastern studies and not to guard the barriers between the two disciplines. As Carolina López-Ruiz has noted, "Historical scholarship has ... removed some of the barriers that had been erected around classical culture to keep it free of contamination by the 'Other,' such as the Semitic cultures of the Near East" (xvii). I have omitted many biblical parallels from this volume because there are excellent books on religion/theology/and biblical parallels in *Harry Potter* already. The few which I have kept are so clearly pertinent to the *Potter* characters, and so similar in their parallelism to Rowling's use of Greek and Roman models, that I just could not pass them up.

In this work, we shall be giving attention to materials which derive from mythology, legend, saga, folklore, and ancient poetical and historical record. They include allusions to imagery, types of characters, specific names, themes and motifs, terminology, roles, type-scenes, values and significant cultural features of and other cultural aspects from the world of the ancient Greeks and Romans. In short, the focus of this book is on any and all aspects of the classical tradition which are either obviously alluded to in the narratives or which, by some type of similarity, invite comparison to elements of Rowling's writing.

A number of those materials come from mythology. But they can be found in a much wider array of sources than mythology alone. We find them in the writings of mythographers (Apollodorus, Hyginus, Ovid), historians (Herodotus, Ctesias, Strabo), playwrights (Terence, Aeschylus, Aristophanes, Sophocles, Euripides), philosophers (Socrates, Plato, Aristotle, Seneca, Theophrastus, Cicero), physicians (Hippocrates, Sammonicus), poets and their verses (Apollonius of Rhodes, Callimachus, Cleanthes, Hesiod, Homer, the Homeric Hymns, Horace, Juvenal, Lucius Accius, Lucretius, Pindar, Stesichorus, Theocritus, Valerius Flaccus, Vergil), authors of works on a variety of subjects, including animals (Pliny the Elder, Aelian), biblical names and stories (Adonai, Eliphaz, Hephzibah, Miriam, Phinehas, Tobiah, YHWH, Zechariah). There are historical figures who add to the search for her allusions (Agrippa, Antiochus, Augusta, Draco, Ennius, Hannibal, Maeceneas, Nero, Octavian, Regulus, Septimius Severus, and Quintus Fabius Maximus). Specific personalities in the novels are comparable to classical predecessors with respect to their character types, roles, characteristics, or nature (gods, semi-divine beings, heroes, humans, and marvelous or bizarre creatures). Resources for investigating the allusions can be found in literary models and type scenes (the *nekuia* or visitation with the dead, the *nostoi* or homecoming tales, one-on-one duels between singular champions of opposing sides, an embassy to recruit a withdrawn leader back into battle, abduction and rescue from the Underworld), cultural rituals of burial, emancipation of slaves, coming of age rites for youth, superstition and magical craft (techniques, materials, mysterious language, symbolism of animals, powerful numerical symbolism, amulets and talismans, hexes, curses, incantations), ancient stagecraft (*deus ex māchinā*), standard epic elements (*in mediās rēs*, the working out of the will of the gods/fate), religion (oracles, prophecies, sacrifice, blood), techniques of rhetoric and writing (Socratic method of dialogue, depiction of transformations in process, ring composition), common world-conceptions (the Cycle of the Ages), proverbial wisdom and principles of value (*sōphrosynē*—moderation or the Golden Mean for avoiding excess, avoidance of hubris or overweening pride). Names used in antiquity or derived from Latin, Greek, and Hebrew sources shed light on the characters in the *Harry Potter* novels who bear the same or similar names. Innumerable themes and motifs in the seven novels are common to the ancient stories.

Anthropologists, scholars of linguistics and literature, and psychologists have laid the outlines of modern study of myths, legends, folktales and the like. This work builds on their findings.

The type of story which we propose here as the matrix of the *Potter* series is the "Quest" type of folktale. Anthropologists and students of ancient stories have observed for over a hundred years now that particular stories have distinctive contents and features. There are "legends" of heroic or tragic people who have endured great challenges, which one ought to read, or which deserve to be read (as the Latin word *legendum* means). These give us models of characters who prove to be greater or more powerful, or more overwhelmed by rage, revenge or kindness than we, who face greater problems than ours. Their stories serve as cues for us in dealing with our life situations. "Sagas" relate the fortunes of entire families or dynasties which experience, one generation after another, their interconnected glories and misfortunes. "Fairy tales" appeal to our magical, fanciful, wishful desires for simplicity and order. And "myths" are the vehicles of the full array of expressions of life for those who tell or transmit them. They instill in the recipients how they came to be, who they are and are not, and give impressively-told and easy-to-remember examples of values and common wisdom.

Folktales represent a variety of stories, usually about an ordinary person, who becomes heroic by overcoming great obstacles through wit and courage. Antti Aarne classified the types of folktales first in 1910, in a multi-volume work which was translated and enlarged by Stith Thompson (1928). Vladimir Propp studied hundreds of Russian folktales and found that they all employed thirty-one essential elements, always in the same order; not all stories included all thirty-one, but the elements which were used of the set of thirty-one always came in the same order (1928). Thompson developed the work further in 1946 with his book *The Folktale*. He distinguished between "Folk-Tale Types" (e.g., "the monster [animal] as bridegroom") and "Motifs" (such as "animal languages learned by having ears licked by serpent"). The structuralist scholar A.-J. Greimas applied the findings of Propp to other kinds of tales, and established a pattern for what he called a "Quest," including the series of tests which a hero undergoes in his heroic adventure (1966=1983).

The expert on world mythology whose work developed during the latter half of the twentieth century was Joseph Campbell. It was he who added to the mythic story of the hero the term "monomyth," based on his belief that this particular story was a universal type of myth found in many races of humans (*The Hero with a Thousand Faces* 1968). He posited that the master story has three fundamental stages (Departure, Initiation, and Return) which comprise the overall structure of seventeen specific stages which the hero undergoes, testing, proving, and confirming him as a hero (1968).

Psychologists have proposed theories which help us understand "why" our stories and dreams affect us as they do. Sigmund Freud considered dreams and myths to be related, in that both come from human psychological factors, particularly those which relate to one's earliest sexual awakenings, and the features of dreams or myths are symbolic of everyday life. Naturally, he gave great attention to the story of Oedipus who was fated to kill his father and marry his mother (1900). His concept was that "myths are the collective and recurrent dreams of the race" (according to Powell 703). The symbols of myths and dreams arise from psycho-sexual constraints which people experience and they serve to deal with repressed desires. The concept of an individual's inheriting both the psychological and sociological constructs of a person's race was developed further by Carl G. Jung. He maintained that the dreams and myths of people were common possessions of a race, which he called the "collective unconscious" (1968). Otto Rank focused on the individual's relations and conflicts within the family as the source of the basic story of the development of the hero (1959, 1990).

While I do not approach the present subject from the angle of psychological analysis, I have an appreciation for the Jungian conception of the structural and psychological fundamentals which are at work in us far below the patent levels of observation, and for the belief that stories reach down into and produce echoes within us. The contents of the literary treasuries which are mined here, whether they are names, types, situations, or responses to situations, seem familiar to us, because they exhibit patterns and resources and elements which we have encountered before. They have been passed down to us from time immemorial and are part of our being, as much as is our marrow.

An "archetype" is an essential component of the monomyth, proposed by Jung and followed by other psychoanalysts and students of myth, folktales and rituals. By definition, it is "a basic apprehension of, or response to, an aspect of life embedded within the collective unconscious of every human being" (Quinn 208). Examples of the archetype "are evident in certain myths and rituals that underlie the forms of narrative literature and are the source of our profound response to certain stories and plays" (208). They find their way into the unconscious of members of a race through the almost primordial life experiences of their group, not by means of their unique life discoveries. Archetypes, then, are the presupposed "givens" of all members of a common race.

In recent years, world mythology scholars and literary critics have chafed against the notion that many races possess in common a singular mythic template, a "monomyth." Critics disagree with the universalizing theory, which, they claim, popularizes the study of mythology, fails to give proper recognition to the ethnographic contexts of myths, underestimates cultural differences by thinking in terms of "races," and ignores women in the theorizing, except when it introduces them in masculine models. The criticism is leveled, also, that the common factors of the myth which Campbell has assembled may derive from common cultural factors rather than from the common human experience itself.[3] Several scholars have proposed two basic patterns of essential myth, the "Laurasian" model and a second mythological giant, the "Gondwana" model which preceded the Laurasian (Leeming 2003, Witzel 2012).[4] The study of archetypes and motifs of international folktales is still receiving great attention in the work of Thompson (1993), Uther (2004), and Jane Garry (2005).

In the hero's search, the monomyth, a heroic person, usually born under difficult or miraculous circumstances, and rescued miraculously, becomes the only one of his race who can cure the malady of his people. Each of his exploits increases in danger, and he is regularly beset with disabling circumstances as well as unforeseen assistance by strangers. In the end the hero defeats his people's enemy, risks his life, and becomes their celebrated savior. On Rowling's use of Campbell's monomyth, see the informative, though brief article by Antoinette Winstead (2005).

The two terms "theme" and "motif" are used for studying folk literature and are often employed interchangeably. What one person may call a theme another might designate a motif. More properly speaking, though, themes are important ideas or concepts which form the main message of a narrative. Examples of themes are death, mortality, the futility of striving for perfection, "love never fails," "no good deed ever goes unpunished," or the like, the truth of which is illustrated again and again in the larger narrative, in order to make the point clearly.

A motif is a particular or "concrete example of a theme" (Quinn 202). It is repeated in order to help with the development of a theme. There are many more folktale motifs in *Harry Potter* which are commonly found in the classical sources than we can entertain in this work. For example, the motif of the dragon which guards a treasure or a golden egg (Jason and the Golden Fleece; Heracles and the Apples of the Hesperides; the first task in the Tri-wizard contest).[5]

This work presumes that the readers will have a significant degree of familiarity with all seven novels. It is prepared with an informed reader in mind. It has been carefully researched and presented both for the generalist reader and for those with extraordinary interest in the *Harry Potter* novels and the classical tradition. It is intended to be an "ancilla" [L *ancilla, -ae*, "female servant"], a help or aid for increasing readers' delight in the two worlds of "stories" in focus here. The work can be read straight through. Or, it can be read selectively, beginning at the start of any chapter. I have tried to make the book readable, but also serviceable as a reference book for use after a first reading. The chapter on Latin may be of interest to fewer readers than the preceding chapters. Nonetheless, if readers who do not delight in the language, per se, will read the English of that chapter, with a quick eye, they will derive an appreciation for Rowling's use of Latin without having to wrestle with the intricacies of the Latin language.

For this exercise I presume the correctness of the Jungian concept of the collective unconscious, the theory of archetypes in human myth and history, and the adequacy of the monomyth or hero's journey as the normative form of the quest folktale or myth which is common to *Harry Potter* and much of our classical resources. I do not attempt to create new theories or defend or find fault with any particular, current approach with respect to psychological analysis, structural analysis, form and function, or categorization of literary terms, though I do borrow terms which are generally accepted for this particular type of literary study. The terms and approaches used here are tools, not masters, for our study. Detailed critique of distinctions between scholarly proposals is not necessary for this study. And commitment to any one theory alone is not necessary for gaining fully what this book offers.

Chapter I

Harry Potter as Seeker

As the main character in these novels, Harry is endowed with more numerous and varied types of association with classical characters, culture and mythology than any other. He appears to be characterized by two types of heroes. First, he is depicted as a clever hero of folktale, a hero on a quest (in the tradition of Odysseus). Second, he is presented as a savior figure (reminiscent of Heracles, Achilles, Theseus, Oedipus, and Aeneas). In this chapter, we shall consider the first type, Harry as a Seeker.

Harry Potter *and the Quest Folktale*

There are many interwoven stories in the seven *Harry Potter* novels, which represent different literary types (genres). And the entire series is a singular literary composition. The series has been categorized in a variety of ways as to its literary type(s). Philip Nel refers to the stories in the series as a "wide range of genres synthesized by her [Rowling's] imagination" (51), including the boarding school coming of age story, an epic fantasy, a mystery quest, fairy tales, the Young Adult novel and the Bilsdungsroman (novel of formation).[1] He calls the series "an epic fantasy" (36) and "a mystery quest" (38). Anne Alton thinks that Rowling incorporates many genres: elements of pulp fiction, mystery, gothic and horror stories, detective fiction, the school story, the sports story, series books, fantasy, adventure, quest romance, and myth (141). Vandana Saxena refers to the series as an "eclectic mix of popular genres—fantasy and adventure, the hero myth, schoolboy fiction and the story of a savior" (167). These proposals work within the arena of general comparative literature, comparing *Harry Potter* to other recent types of western literature. There is unquestioned merit to all these assessments, which attests, once more, to the marvelous nature of Rowling's literary achievement. The focus of this book, however, is not the place of Rowling's work in recent literature. Rather, it centers on the relationship between her work and the ancient tradition of the Greek and Roman era to which she so often alludes. The marvelous subjects, themes, plots, devices, characters, stories, and powerfully effective motifs which have shaped subsequent literature were already at work in that ancient era. Consequently, we shall consider the over-arching literary genre of *Harry Potter* in light of the factors which link it to that ancient and earliest tradition.

The *Harry Potter* stories belong to the type of traditional material known as "folktales," stories about the adventures of a person who represents the common people, but whose ingenuity and daring in the face of extraordinary trials—often involving fantastic beasts or enormous odds—make his stories worthy to be passed along to teach others about bravery, character and intellect. More specifically, the *Potter* stories are folktales of the "quest" type. These are tales about a person who goes in search of his rightful place or true home, or sets out to secure some birthright that is his. In the process, the person on a quest is aided by friends or other companions and impeded by obstacles or enemies.

The most influential analysis of the quest type folktale has been done by Vladimir Propp, who studied more than one hundred Russian folktales of that type. He isolated thirty-one elements or "functions," which are the structural components of the tales. Not all stories possess every single one of the thirty-one elements, but all stories contain only the elements which are part of the set, and they always occur in the same order. Jann Lacoss notes that one reason the *Harry Potter* novels are so easy for children to relate to is that the pattern, plot, and structure of folktales which are found here have been ingrained in them from their infancy by other folktales (85). She analyzes several of the *Harry Potter* books and concludes that both the individual books and the overall plot of the series follow the pattern described by Propp. She even creates a table listing in order the elements of *Sorcerer's Stone* and *Goblet of Fire* which fit Propp's elements (86). I do not intend to do a structuralist analysis of the quest; but I do maintain, as does Lacoss, that the quest folktale is a very prominent pattern in the books.

Stith Thompson built on the pioneering work of Antti Aarne to develop the typology of the folk tale, distinguishing between themes and motifs. This work greatly illumined the essential as well as the ingenious make-up of the folk tales. Joseph Campbell, who researched world mythologies, proposed that behind many of the world's races is a universal type of hero-story, the "monomyth," which narrates the sequence of a series of tests and trials through which a person seeks, is tested in the seeking, and reaches his heroic goal. The psychologists and psychoanalysts Sigmund Freud, Carl G. Jung, and Otto Rank drew the connections not only between our dreams and myths, but also between our deeply inset patterns of perceived reality, the "collective unconscious," and how we develop individuality in the family group.

Not only the structure and pattern of the hero folk-tale are ingrained in us from time immemorial. The themes and motifs of the stories which serve to give expression to these archetypes or unconscious "givens" of our race follow distinct patterns. The terms "theme" and "motif" are often used interchangeably, but not always. Themes are significant ideas, concepts, or beliefs which form the larger message of a story. The list of themes treated in Peter Barta's work on themes and motifs includes the following: adolescence, alienation, anti-hero, cave, death and the individual, divine tutor, escape, evil, family, jealousy, Labyrinth, love, mirror, monsters, name and naming, noble criminal, parents and children, pride, rebellion, responsibility, search for father, Siren, social status of the hero, spy, stupidity, terror, time, tower, union, and werewolf (1988). All of these universal themes are present in the seven novels of Rowling.

Forty-two years ago, G. S. Kirk, in his brilliant book *Myth: Its Meaning and Function in Ancient and Other Cultures*, listed and exemplified the broad themes which occur regularly in classical mythology: structural creation of drama and suspense; creating and resolution of dilemmas; the seemingly limitless and extraordinary achievements of humans; fate and individual freedom; social concerns of family dynamics, particularly the child-parent relationship. Some of the more specific themes which are the regular material of those ancient myths, according to Kirk, are these: fire as a powerful force over life and death, the testing of life and death through visits to the Underworld, the weight of the fear of mortality and its opposite, the tragedy of attempting to avoid it, the succession of generations, and the displacement of elders (172–205).

Kirk listed the following as some of the most common themes in Greek myths about heroes: tricks, riddles, ingenious solutions to dilemmas, transformations, accidental killing of a relative or lover or friend, giants, monsters (centaurs, a sphinx, satyrs), snakes, attempts to get rid of a rival by setting impossible and dangerous tasks, fulfilling a task or quest (killing a monster, gaining an inaccessible object, freeing and sometimes marrying a princess), contests for honor, punishment for impiety, displacement of elders or parents (actual or feared displacement, often in accordance with an oracle), killing or attempting to kill one's own child (often in accordance with an oracle or prophecy), revenge, sons avenging their mothers, disputes within the family, special weapons (needed to overthrow a particular enemy, cure a wound), prophets and seers (who understand the language of animals, propound riddles, reveal a way out of an impasse), perils of immortality as a gift to humans, external soul or life-token (the life of a hero depends on a hair, a firebrand, etc.), enclosure or imprisonment (187–89). To anyone who has read *Harry Potter*, Kirk's lists almost appear to be descriptions of Rowling's novels.

Motifs are used to give examples of the themes in order to keep the themes alive in the minds of readers or hearers (Quinn 202). It is repeated in order to help with the development of a theme. For example, one theme in *Harry Potter* is obviously, "eyes as the windows of the soul." The motifs which serve that theme are the instances in which seeing a character's eyes or the color of the eyes calls forth a response by the reader to the nature of the figure. Harry's reincarnation of his beloved mother is repeatedly signaled when people tell him he has his mother's green eyes. Voldemort's cruel eyes are red; the deadly sphinx in the maze has sexy, seductive eyes (*GF* 658). Nosy Mrs. Norris has "bulging, lamplike eyes just like Filch's" (*SS* 132). The thestrals have white, haunting, and piercing eyes. The killer basilisk has large, yellow eyes, the last thing Moaning Myrtle can recall from the moment of her death. Severus Snape's black eyes cause Harry's scar to burn the first time he sees the professor eye-to-eye. Snape's eyes glow fanatically when he believes he has captured his enemies in the Shrieking Shack. And, in perhaps the most poignant scene of the seven novels, when Harry and Snape see each other for the last time, and really for the first time actually "see" each other, Rowling writes, "The green eyes found the black" (*DH* 658), with the professor's eyes no longer causing Harry's scar to burn.

In *Classical Mythology*, Mark Morford points out that in Greek sagas, specific motifs function quite similarly to the thirty-one essential elements of the folktale which Vladimir Propp isolated. He lists ten recurrent motifs, all of which pertain to the hero of the story: (1) his birth or youth is characterized by very unusual circumstances; (2) he is compelled to face increasingly greater tests to prove himself; (3) his enemy sets up the critical situations in which he shows himself to be successful; (4) he is aided by an assistant, either human or divine; (5) the contests which he faces are virtually impossible; (6) he faces extraordinary opponents which put him through a range of challenges; (7) he has to observe taboos or restrictions on his behavior; (8) his contests may be life-threatening, particularly the task of visiting the Underworld; (9) when he succeeds in his heroic quest, he is rewarded with personal, social, and political benefits such as "marriage, political security, or wealth and power" (409); (10) through the journey of the hero, he gains "knowledge through suffering and more lasting spiritual enlightenment (literal or symbolic)—entailing purification, rebirth, redemption, and even deification" (409).[2] All ten of these motifs are employed in the *Harry Potter* series.

Throughout this book, we shall refer to the over-arching story as Harry's quest. The classic model of quest stories in mythology is Homer's *Odyssey*, the tale of Odysseus' ten-year-long journey home to his kingdom of Ithaca after the Trojan War. Harry is comparable to Odysseus in several ways. First, Odysseus has been away from his rightful kingdom for ten years during the Trojan War. Harry endures ten years of agony with the Dursleys before he can begin to seek his rightful home, place, and destiny (recall the second-by-second countdown to his eleventh birthday, as a dramatization of the new beginning, [*SS* 45]). Both characters face a singular, formidable enemy during their quests. Voldemort, the Dark Lord, works against Harry and is intent on killing him, and Odysseus is impeded from getting home by the efforts of the angry sea god Poseidon, who is enraged at him for blinding his son, the Cyclops named Polyphemus. In the end, each hero reaches the goal of his search.

Of course, the story of Harry Potter is not an epic of the magnitude of Odysseus' quest or a reprise of all the epic elements. There are no invocations to Muses. The writer does not presume to tell the tale from the vantage of omniscience. There is no catalogue of ships or armies to dramatize the crucial battle. We read no set speeches by towering figures. The language in which the story is told is neither poetry nor grand rhetoric. There are not similes to characterize actions or epic epithets to reiterate the principal feature of the characters. The absence of these stock epic features makes this a creative and inspired epic-like quest, not a slavish re-cycling of the established form.

At the same time, the quest does appear to introduce itself to us in the epic fashion, by jumping into the story "in the middle (of) things" [L *in mediās rēs*]. In this way, the hearer or reader is thrown immediately into the action, rather than having to suffer through a lengthy prelude. With this epic form of opening, the events which have led up to the action are given by flashbacks, or by the hero's telling them to interested listeners. The *Iliad* opens in the ninth year of the Trojan War, at a moment of great crisis and activity, when a plague threatens the Greek encampment, and Achilles, the main figure of the epic and the greatest of the Greek warriors, harbors deadly hatred for another formidable leader, Agamemnon. Though Achilles remains the central figure of the entire story, Homer "removes him for two-thirds of the poem" (Tracy 3). The *Odyssey* begins late in Odysseus' pilgrimage toward home, when his son, Telemachus, having come to maturity during the absence of his father, takes steps to find Odysseus, while the suitors who court the king's wife plot to kill the young man.[3] Odysseus himself comes into the story only in Book 5, and he begins to recount his travels to the Phaeacian king Alcinoüs only in Book 9. Vergil's *Aeneid* opens seven years after the fall of Troy, when Aeneas has arrived at Carthage, where he narrates to Dido, the queen, all that happened during those seven years to bring him to Carthage (Books 2 and 3). In Chapter One of *Harry Potter and the Sorcerer's Stone*, we encounter the Wizarding world on the night which alters the future of the entire population and which welds together the unique opponents whose lives form the template of the entire series. But the backdrop or lead-up to the first lines of the series begins to appear only in Chapter Four with the appearance of Hagrid.

Rowling also adds standard components of classical epic to the novels. The canvas on which the story is presented is grand, including the entire Wizarding world and, eventually, the entire Muggle world. The hero, as The Boy Who Lived, the most famous of all wizards, is head and shoulders above all other characters (though humanized and made accessible by his rather undistinguished physical and personal characteristics). In his quest, Harry undergoes a number of separate dangerous and trying episodes which require exceptional courage and commitment to a grand goal. Supernatural powers affect, assist, and impede some of the characters and their actions. The story begins "*in mediās rēs.*" There are encounters with the dead. The hero has to undergo journeys into and out of an "Underworld." Baleful prophecy provides an over-arching pattern to the drama. The prevailing crisis becomes a universal competition of good versus evil, which is reduced, for dramatization, to duels between individual representatives of the warring sides (the *mano-a-mano*–type scenes). There are adventures of super-human beings, heroes and average people.

Rowling's obvious and quite numerous uses of or allusions to classical parallels and antecedents beg comparison with her characters, scenes, adventures, motifs, and themes. There are ancient witches, seers and prophet-types: Medea, Circe, and Calypso, Tiresias, the Sibyl, the Pythia, Cassandra, Kalchas, Melampus, augurs, Helenus. As well, there are heroes and demi-gods: Aeneas, Odysseus, Anchises, Perseus, Heracles, Achilles, Helen of Troy, Andromeda, Phaëthon and Meleager. Monsters from long ago seem to reappear or shed useful light by comparison: Scylla, Charybdis, Cerberus, centaurs, sphinxes, satyrs, the Hydra, the Minotaur, Chimaeras, the Gorgons, the Harpies, the basilisk, the Graiai, Sirens, the hundred-handed giant Briareus, manticores, Geryon, and Centaurus. Of course, an array of gods suggest themselves: Minerva/Athena, Poseidon, Rhea, Zeus/Jupiter, Hera/Juno, Thetis, Artemis/Diana, Cephisus, Themis, Nemesis, Asopus, Cronus, Mars/Ares, Demeter/Ceres, Hermes/Mercury, Hades, Atlas, Prometheus, Persephone/Proserpina, Helios, Apollo, Styx, Aphrodite/Venus, Luna, Dionysus/Bacchus, Oceanus and Tethys, Earth/Gaia, the Furies, the Fates, Hephaestus/Vulcan, Peneus, Janus, Hestia, Phorcys, Oceanus, Murcia, Pomona, Leto, Asclepius, Hypnos,

Aeolus, Enipeus, Vertumnus, Proteus, Hecate, and Nympha. Specifically named characters and particular character types found in the classical tradition resurface in the novels, to characterize Rowling's cast either for their similarity to or difference from the ancient predecessors. Some specific, archetypal scenes from mythology are used with variation or even reinvention: the Battle of the Lapiths and the Centaurs; the Embassy to Achilles; the Riddle of the Sphinx, the Song of the Sirens and the attack of the Harpies, the Twelve Labors of Heracles, the Abduction of Persephone, the story of Narcissus, for example. Ancient motifs employed in the novels provide imagery, tone, and drama: birds which mirror or represent the character of their owners, wands and curses, poisons and potions, mysterious and esoteric numbers, articles of invisibility, amulets and talismans.

Harry and Odysseus

In his poetic episodes about Odysseus, Homer uses a variety of epithets for the hero. The first occurs in the very first line of the *Odyssey*, "much-turned," "much wandering," "versatile of mind" [Gk *polytropos* < *poly* "much, many" + *trepō*, "turn, direction," > "of many devices, resourceful" (LSJ 1444; Cunliffe 338, 389)]. The numerous and varied experiences which the hero has in this epic are summed up in this one word, a man of vast experience and cleverness. The most frequently used epithets are "much enduring" (*polytlas*), "much conniving/versatile" (*polymēchanos*), and "of many wiles" (*polymētis*) (Hexter 4). The epithets highlight the two most important aspects of the legendary Odysseus: his having endured numerous and varied challenges during his ten-year journey home to Ithaca after the Trojan War, and his unfailing quality of crafty inventiveness. The name of Homer's hero is significant as a clue to his life. While there is no certain history as to what the name "Odysseus" meant originally, a mythic tradition links his name to Poseidon's hatred for Odysseus, because he blinded the god's son, the Cyclops Polyphemus. The sea god's vengeance was the cause of all the hero's sufferings and trials [Gk *Odusseus* < *odussomai/oduiomai*, "to hate, be angry with," meaning "hated by gods and men" (LSJ 1199–1200)].

Rowling's novels read like a chronicle of "much-enduring Harry," or "Harry of the many turns." The books recount the boy's trials, contests, and life-threatening adventures, all of which come his way because of the malice toward him by a supernaturally powerful enemy—Lord Voldemort. The two heroes struggle in their quests under the malicious ill-will of a supernaturally powerful enemy. And both show remarkable ingenuity and cleverness. Consequently, it is here, at the point of their similarities, that we begin our own quest of the two heroes.

Odysseus of the Many Wiles

One of the standard qualities of heroes in folktales is their cleverness and ingenuity. It may well be that this common factor derives from the characteristics of the model hero himself, Odysseus. In virtually all ancient memory of Odysseus, he is depicted as Homer presents him, as a man of *mētis*, "wisdom, cleverness, skill," and with the epithet *polymētis*, "of many counsels, devices," "very crafty, 'of the many wiles,' full of shrewdness" (see Jones 120; Tracy 61). He is renowned in mythology for these mental powers.

The strongest personal link between these two heroes is their common ingenuity. Harry is ahead of others in his skill at putting things together, getting the big picture, knowing how to succeed, drawing conclusions which elude everyone else. That is, he is able to "cotton on," to use Rowling's phrase. To begin, we shall view some of the details from ancient lore about Odysseus, then present similar examples of Harry's unique cleverness, and finally, compare the two.

In the *Iliad*

In the *Iliad*, Odysseus is depicted as being superlative in statesmanship, strategy and warfare. When Agamemnon tests the Greek soldiers to see whether they have the will to fight to the end of their prolonged war, he offers them the opportunity to return to Greece and be done with their toiling and dying. Odysseus, with his impressive presence and rhetorical skill, convinces the armies not to retreat, but to remain in Troy (2.169–335).[4] Homer describes Odysseus as "equal to Zeus in wisdom" [*Diī mētin atalanton*], "noble/brilliant/marvelous" [*dīos*], and "immortal, divine, godlike" [*theios*]. In a military strategy, Odysseus, accompanied by Diomedes, plots and successfully executes a daring night-time foray into the camp of the enemy to size up their ranks and discover their placement. Malcolm Willcock comments that while Diomedes functions as "the perfectly efficient soldier," Odysseus is "the man of sense and foresight" (117). In his recitation of this "Doloneia," as it is called, Homer depicts Odysseus' courage and resourcefulness with the terms given above, and adds that he is *polymēchanos*, "resourceful" (10.137, 144, 148).

In the *Odyssey*

In the *Odyssey*, Athena tells the gods that Odysseus is *polyphrōn*, "inventive, ingenious, highly intelligent," as if to say that he possesses much in the vault of his faculties (1.83). Menelaus says of him, "In my time I have studied the wit and counsel of many men who were heroes and I have been over much of the world, yet nowhere have I seen with my own eyes anyone like him nor known an inward heart like the heart of enduring Odysseus" (4.267–70).[5] Odysseus is self-aware of his talent of inventiveness, as he says that he is known as a master of *dolos*, "trickery, deception, contrivance" (9.19–20). The following are some instances of his gift of craftiness. He designs the ploy of the wooden horse, filled with Greek soldiers (4.271–89, 8.494ff.).[6] He contrives the plan for himself and his crewmen to escape, unharmed, from the cave of Polyphemus, the Cyclops, by telling the giant that his name is "Outis" [Gk for "nobody"], by blinding their drunken captor, and by strapping his men and himself to the underside of Polyphemus' huge rams (9.318–566).[7] When he arrives at his homeland of Ithaca, bedraggled and disoriented, he makes up an interesting yarn about himself, rather than speaking truthfully to Athena, who meets him in disguise (13.250–86). To this trick, she responds that he is devious, never tiring of deceptions (*dolē*), that he is the best of all human beings for his counsel and stories, and that she is able to recognize these characteristics in him because she, herself, is famous for her wit and keenness, *mētis* (13.297–9). When he has to do battle with the more than one hundred suitors of his wife and claimants to his throne, Odysseus has his son Telemachus remove from the palace great hall all the weapons of the suitors, as a crafty prelude to the slaughter of his rivals. He does this under the pretense of keeping the weapons in a safe place, so that if any of the suitors becomes drunk and fighting breaks out, the suitors will not have the means to do each other any real harm (19.1–52). And before he reveals to the suitors who he is, he devises the ingenious contest of stringing his bow, and shooting an arrow through twelve axeheads (21.386–434). He alone is able to make the bow ready and perform the phenomenal shot. His enemies are beaten because they are out-thought.

In Other Classical Lore

In subsequent tradition, Odysseus' legendary craftiness and skill at deception are played up, at times turning him into a liar and unprincipled manipulator. From these numerous depictions of Odysseus, the following two are illustrative. In Pindar's *Nemea* 8, the poet says that in the contest with Ajax over the divine armor of Achilles, the prize is awarded to Odysseus, the devious liar [Gk *aiolō pseudei*, 8.25]. And in Sophocles' play *Philoctetes*, Odysseus acts on the principle that the end justifies the means, and in so doing, shocks the innocent young son of Achilles, Neoptolemus. The young man winces at Odysseus' directions to lie, sharpen his wits, and become a thief. He prefers to use persuasion, honor, and truth to persuade the aged and sick man, Philoctetes. But Odysseus pressures him to tell whatever lie he must, to deceive their target with craft (*dolō*), to "ensnare the soul of Philoctetes with ... words" (54–55),[8] and to outwit the sick and marooned warrior, in order to get from him the bow and arrows of Heracles which are necessary to win the war with the Trojans.

HARRY OF THE MANY WILES

Rowling portrays Harry as talented at "spotting things other people didn't" (*SS* 280). In this sense, the boy's clever observations and exploits are comparable to the numerous ingenious insights, plans, and actions taken by Odysseus. The following are some examples. When HH&R encounter Fluffy, Ron fixates on the dog's menacing heads, and logical Hermione observes that the dog is guarding a trap door beneath its feet. Harry, however, draws much more far-reaching and specific conclusions concerning what is being guarded. When Harry encounters the centaurs Ronan and Bane in the Forbidden Forest, they obliquely comment on the brightness of the planet Mars (named for the Roman god of war). He understands, however, that it is a prophecy about himself and the danger in which he exists. He forms an insightful decision as to how Snape received a wound on his leg. And from Firenze's leading and vague questions to Harry, he identifies the mysterious figure who was drinking the blood of a unicorn in the forest.

Harry, alone, comes up with the identity of the mysterious stranger at the pub, who manipulates Hagrid into revealing important secrets about Fluffy. By studying the stamp which is affixed to T. M. Riddle's diary, which names the shop where the diary was bought, he deduces the owner not to be a pure-blood wizard. When he works out why the victims of the basilisk are petrified but not killed, and how the monster enters the school, Ron is so surprised that his jaw drops. When Dumbledore and Hagrid are removed from Hagrid's hut by Fudge and Lucius Malfoy, they want to deliver messages to HH&R, who are hiding under the Invisibility Cloak. But they do not want to reveal the content of their messages to Fudge and Malfoy or to expose the students. So, trusting in Harry's quickness and insightfulness to figure out what they mean, they deliver their messages in cryptic generalities. While HH&R all look for evidence of an access to the Chamber of Secrets in Moaning Myrtle's bathroom, only Harry sees the clue that leads them to the opening. When Harry battles the basilisk and confronts Tom Riddle in the Chamber of Secrets, he hits upon an ingenious way to solve the problem of the power of Riddle's diary. He spontaneously contrives a trick to play on Lucius Malfoy which greatly benefits Dobby. When Harry solves the mystery of the basilisk, Hermione screams in delight.[9] Although Hermione is able to transport herself and Harry back in time, it is Harry, not she, who devises a plan for using that skill to save two innocent lives, and devise an escape plan for Sirius. When Hermione tries to deceive Professor Umbridge by faking an emotional collapse and surrender, Harry notices the tell-tale traces of her ruse.

He draws a conclusion about the changes which have occurred in Draco and what they indicate regarding his relationship to his father and the Dark Lord's circle of followers. Hermione disbelieves him and Ron laughs at his judgment, which proves to be accurate. He alone surmises that the strange girls who accompany Draco are actually Crabbe and Goyle, disguised by taking Polyjuice Potion. He connects the Vanishing Cabinet and the two deadly gifts of a cursed necklace and poisoned mead, and can put his finger on the culprit who is behind the gifts, even in the face of almost overwhelming evidence to the contrary. While the faculty and staff of Hogwarts do not know how the Death Eaters can enter Hogwarts, Harry makes a correct speculation and explains it to them. His suspicions about a possible romantic connection between Argus Filch and Madam Pince are confirmed. When HH&R release two Death Eaters and the diner waitress from the spells they are under, Harry devises a scheme that will make it appear as if the whole event never occurred. He deduces the identity of the person who switched Voldemort's locket for a fake locket. His theory that there must be a Horcrux at Hogwarts receives disagreement and complaints from Hermione and Ron, though he is proved correct in the end.

At one point, Harry becomes anxious that Dumbledore left him with practically nothing to go on to deal with the Horcruxes. But the Headmaster's reticence clearly shows how much he trusts Harry's cleverness to fulfill the task. And Harry does not disappoint that trust, for when he begins to connect the clues concerning Horcruxes and Hallows, Harry even amazes himself at his discoveries. His method of gathering evidence by questioning Griphook and Ollivander separately (confusing Ron and Hermione as to why he does this), shows the cunning of an Odysseus. When Hermione overhears Harry and Mr. Ollivander discussing wands, she is dumbstruck at how much Harry knows and how he has put clues together. Harry comes to a mature and self-aware realization, which he explains to Ron and Hermione, regarding what Dumbledore thought was most important for him to do regarding the Horcruxes and the Hallows. When he recalls that Professor Flitwick told him that no one had seen the diadem of Rowena Ravenclaw "in living memory" (*DH* 601), Harry realizes to whom he must go to find directions in his search for the heirloom. He judges rightly why Tom Riddle came to Hogwarts to ask Dumbledore for a job teaching there, when he knew that the Headmaster would not hire him. And when Harry opens the snitch which he has inherited and sees the Resurrection Stone, he understands what it is without even having to think.

Of course, not all of Harry's assessments and conclusions are correct. He is completely surprised when Professor Quirrell spells out the things which he did, which Harry believed Snape to have done. But Harry is more crafty, resourceful, and prone to see things more accurately than most others. Cleverness does not rest in having the right answers, but in the processes of creatively assessing available information, learning on one's own, by taking chances and gaining first-hand knowledge. And at this, Harry excels.

The Similarities of the Heroes

Both characters spend ten years away from their "home" (Odysseus at Troy engaged in battle for ten years; Harry struggling to survive in a hostile adoptive family). Both begin their homecoming-pilgrimage with their eleventh year of absence.[10] During the journeys to their rightful "homes" (Ithaca, the Wizarding world), both endure hardships and life-threatening trials. Each has a super-human, formidable enemy (Poseidon, who assails Odysseus because he blinded the Cyclops Polyphemus, Poseidon's son; Voldemort, who seeks kill Harry, because Harry and a prophecy stand in the way of his becoming immortal). Both have scars which identify their true identity. They both have encounters with the dead. And both are assisted in their pilgrimages by a powerful patroness.

The Scarred Hero

Students of the *Odyssey* will see a parallel between Harry and Odysseus in their both having unique scars which they received in their youth. The scars are significant details in both stories. When Harry was about one year old, Voldemort tried to kill him. His mother's love protected him and made the assailant's Killing Curse rebound, weakening the Dark Lord severely and leaving a permanent scar on Harry's forehead in the shape of a lightning bolt. Several characters identify Harry by the scar as The Boy Who Lived: Professor Dumbledore and Professor McGonagall, Mr. Ollivander, the Weasley twins, and Ron. The scar grows in its significance with the advancement of Harry's story. The scarring of a hero occurs often in folktales, marking him as destined for or engaging in heroic conflict. When the wounding occurs in his youth, it increases sympathy for the hero and endears the victim to the readers because of his vulnerability.

When Odysseus returns to his kingdom, he has to rid his palace of more than a hundred suitors who daily occupy his home in their attempt to force the queen, Penelope, to choose one of them to replace the long-absent king. Athena helps Odysseus by tapping him with her wand and transforming him into a haggard, unrecognizable old beggar, so that he can enter the palace undetected (*Od.* 13.429ff.). Despite his disguise, he is recognized by the elderly family nurse, Eurycleia, who breast-fed him as a child. As she performs the welcoming duty of washing his feet, she recognizes a scar on his thigh. She had treated Odysseus for such a scar, when, as a young man, he was wounded by a boar during a hunt (19.386ff.). The recognition scene is the first of three episodes which identify the beggar as the returning king in disguise. It is one of the classic pieces of ancient literature.

The Siren Song

A timeless metaphor for the temptation of a good man to yield to the seductive lure of something or someone is the "Siren song." The origin of this image is the temptation of Odysseus by vixens who use their enchanting music and song to lure sailors onto the rocks and to their death. While they dwell in a lovely and inviting meadow, they are surrounded by the bones of their previous victims. Odysseus is warned about the Sirens by the sorceress Circe, who directs him to escape their deadly enticement by having the crewmen's ears filled with wax so that they cannot hear the song or any commands he may shout out when he comes under their influence. She charges him to have himself strapped to the ship's mast so that he can hear and enjoy their music, but not be able to follow their call as they row past the women (*Od.* 12.39–54, 153–200). He follows these instructions and makes the passage successfully. Their name, even in antiquity was used as a metaphor for deceitful women (LSJ 1588).[11]

Harry's brush with a Siren song is the taunting behavior of the veela at the Quidditch World Cup match. The veela are the mascots for the Belgian Quidditch Team. They are not ordinary human females, but the most beautiful female nymphs or fairy-like beings whose seductive dancing and alluring appearance cause males to become totally fixated on them, to disregard anything else, and to make fools of themselves by trying to impress these women (*GF* 103ff.). When the Belgian team scores, Mr. Weasley warns everyone to protect themselves by calling out, "Fingers in your ears!" (*GF* 108).

As beautiful as they are, the veela have an equally repulsive and detestable side. When they become angry, their appearance and nature change completely. Their heads produce sharp beaks and they take on scaly wings—which makes

Arthur Weasley warn the boys, "And that, boys … is why you should never go for looks alone" (*GF* 111–12). The veelas' combination of beauty and treachery appears to be a creative hybrid of the mythological Sirens and the Harpies. The mythological Harpies, whose name means "snatchers," have faces like women and bodies of birds [Gk *harpē*, "bird of prey" > *harpazein*, "to seize" > L *Harpyia*, "the Harpies"]. To harass anyone who comes to their islands, they spoil every attempt of the visitors to eat food, either by snatching it away or by pooping on it. The two famous tales of this behavior depict their harassing the Thracian king, Phineus (*Argonautica* 2.177ff.), and Aeneas and his crewmen (*Aen.* 3.209–77). Rowling has amplified the drama of the temptation by indicating that there were a hundred veela. According to most of the ancient sources, there were as few as two or three Sirens, and as few as one Harpy (*Il.* 16.149), or two (*Theog.* 267). Altogether, those who are called "Harpies" in the ancient sources add up to at most thirteen, but most of the authors name only three.[12] Rowling has greatly magnified an image of seductive trouble by the huge number of the Belgian team's mascots.

Two other incidents may also beg comparison with the Siren song—the Mirror of Erised and the veiled arch in the Department of Mysteries in the Ministry of Magic. Roni Natov writes that Harry gazes into the mirror at the objects of his deepest longings, yearning for an alternate reality; but he lets it go and avoids being ruined by its attraction. The mirror's dangerous and hypnotizing power seems to captivate Harry, who is rescued by Professor Dumbledore's warning and intervention. Like Odysseus, he hears but does not yield to a seductive call. In effect, Natov says, "Rowling has essentially taken the great test of Odysseus, who must hear the song of the Sirens but not act on that calling, and reimagined it for children" (130, 134). In the Department of Mysteries, Harry is spellbound by voices he hears beyond a veiled arch, and is released from this Siren song of mystery only by Hermione's intervention.

The Nekuia

On several occasions, Harry has encounters with the dead (e.g., Tom Riddle, Sirius Black, Remus Lupin, James and Lily Potter). All of these, except Tom Riddle, are either his parents or parental figures who die while trying to save or protect him, and from whom he receives help in time of trouble. Of course, the climactic and most dramatic encounter with the dead is at "King's Cross Station." One might consider his experience with the Mirror of Erised to be an encounter with the dead; however, there is a difference between that visual experience and the others in which he actually can communicate with the deceased.

Encounter with or a visit with the dead is a standard motif in ancient literature and lore. When Aeneas flees from falling Troy with his father on his shoulder and his son in hand, he loses track of his wife, and returns to the chaotic, embattled city to find her. What he meets there is her ghost or spirit. He tries three times to embrace her, but feels only empty air. His departed wife, Creusa, helps him by prophesying what lies ahead for him, and dismisses him to his fated journey (*Aen.* 2.736–804). Much later, he goes to the Underworld to learn from his father, Anchises, the coming course of Roman history. Three times, he attempts unsuccessfully to embrace his father, and, like before, catches only empty air. But he receives a major prophecy of Rome's coming greatness (6.700–892).

The model for Aeneas' visit to the house of Hades is Odysseus' encounter with the shades of the dead, including his own mother, in Book 11 of the *Odyssey*. In that episode, the deceased appear to have bodies, which are neither truly physical nor simply ghostly—as Odysseus can identify and talk with the dead, but cannot embrace them. The scene in Homer's poem is called a "nekuia," a summoning of ghosts [Gk *nekuia*, "magical rite by which ghosts are called up and questioned about the future" < *nekus*, a dead person or the spirits of the dead]. Odysseus approaches the deceased, blind prophet Tiresias, to learn how to return to his home of Ithaca. In the process, he speaks not only with the prophet, but also with Trojan war heroes, and his mother, Anticleia, whom he attempts three times to embrace, though unable to touch her (*Od.* 11. 204ff.).

In these encounters with the dead, the visitor (Aeneas, Odysseus) either seeks or is given direction and aid to move forward in his quest. The same is true of Harry's experience with the dead. The experience at King's Cross Station provides Harry with a "prophecy," as it were, and aids the boy in making his greatest decision.

The Embassy to a Withdrawn Warrior

In Book 9 of the *Iliad*, an embassy of three Greek leaders (Odysseus, Phoenix, and Ajax) is sent to the hero of the epic, Achilles, who has absented himself from the battle, because of being deprived of his "honor" by Agamemnon. The purpose of the mission is to convince him to return to battle. He refuses to rejoin until he has been appropriately honored once more. Each emissary makes his appeal to Achilles in turn, and Achilles counters each appeal. Aged and wise Phoenix appeals to Achilles as his teacher, mentor, and father-figure, emphasizing personal, moral obligation, claiming, "I made you all that you are now" and "it was you, godlike Achilles, I made my own child" (*Il.* 9.485, 494–95; Lattimore 1951, 211). Finally, Ajax, sensing the futility of the mission, tells Achilles that there is a code of honor to respect, and that now he should do his duty.

Wily Odysseus tries a four-pronged approach to sway him. First, he reminds him of the words of Achilles' father, making it personal. Second, he summons him to do his duty to the gods, making it a religious and ethical issue. Third, he appeals to the man's ego by offering him the opportunity to fulfill his ambition and attain much honor (i.e., to seize a glorious future). And, finally, he appeals to the tangible kind of esteem which is being offered to him in their honor-driven society, telling him that Agamemnon will offer him many gifts of great value if he will return (*Il.* 9.223–306). Unfortunately for the trio, their exhortation is unsuccessful.

The parallel to this in the *Harry Potter* novels takes place in the village of Budleigh Babberton. Dumbledore apparates with Harry to this place in order to coax out of "retirement" Horace Slughorn, the former teacher of Potions at Hogwarts and former Head of Slytherin House. He is hiding and on the run from the Death Eaters. Dumbledore needs the professor for more than just another individual companion in the fight with the Dark Side. He needs a special kind of help in dealing with the Horcruxes which only Slughorn can provide. While the "retiree" is not the greatest warrior to oppose the Dark Side, as Achilles is the greatest of the Greek warriors, he is indispensable to the plan to defeat Voldemort. Two options are set before Slughorn, to continue to live in fear and hiding or to return to his office of shaping young leaders of the magical world, leaders with whom he can associate himself and whom he can collect as part of his circle of "friends." In short, he is offered a choice of a life of depraved fear or a life of resolute honor and opportunity in the face of difficulty.

Although Slughorn concedes and agrees to return to Hogwarts, and Achilles does not re-enter the battle as the result of the embassy, there is a similarity between the Greek heroes' mission and Dumbledore's and Harry's mission to draw back into battle a jaded and resolutely drawn leader. An element of irony surfaces in the difference between the subjects who are being urged to come back into the fray. One is a battle-weary and honor-driven warrior while the other is a terrified old man who is on the run and disguising himself in the form of an easy chair.

With all these similarities between Harry and Odysseus, there is one way in which Harry is quite different from Odysseus, at least the Odysseus who is represented in an odd and singular ancient tale. The unflattering story goes that at the beginning of the Trojan War, when the Greeks came to take Odysseus with them, he tried to avoid leaving home and taking on the responsibility of his destiny by pretending to be insane. However, he was tricked into revealing that he was, in fact, quite rational. He yoked an ox and an ass and plowed salt into a field, pretending to be a fool. One of the Greeks, a man by the name of Palamedes (whose name, in Greek, connotes cleverness), tricked Odysseus into revealing his ploy by placing Odysseus' baby, Telemachus, directly in front of the plow. Odysseus steered around the boy and was discovered (*Fab.* 95.2). Thus, the great hero was taken off to the Trojan War unwillingly. Harry, on the other hand, when offered the opportunity by Hagrid to venture into a completely unknown and potentially dangerous world on a quest for his destiny, leaps at the chance. Of course, Odysseus faced leaving a kingdom and family, a considerable deprivation, while Harry is given the opportunity to leave deprivation and the hateful Dursleys, a considerable gain.

The Protectress Athena-Minerva

Not only is Harry like Odysseus in search of his home and destiny. He is like the epic hero, also, in having a patroness on his quest. In the *Odyssey*, the goddess of war, wisdom, intelligence and tactile arts, Athena (known as Minerva to the Romans) takes unique interest in protecting and helping Odysseus. On his way, Harry is supported and aided by another "Minerva," this one belonging to a family named "McGonagall."

Athena as Protectress of Odysseus

The goddess who sprang from Zeus's own head, Athena, appeals to Zeus for Odysseus' release from Calypso, the sorceress who detains him from his homecoming for seven years (*Od.* 1.44–62, 80–87).[13] When Poseidon causes him to shipwreck in a storm, and he drifts on the waves, she calms all the winds except for the North Wind, to drive him safely toward land (5.382ff.). When he approaches land of Scheria, the coast of the Phaeacians, he fears that Poseidon will kill him before he can get ashore. Athena intervenes and gives him the notion to cling to the rocks until the waves go out. And she gives him forethought as to how to approach the shore at the safest place, thus avoiding death (5.427ff., 437ff.). She then puts sleep on his eyes to ease him after his ordeal (5.491ff.). Disguised as a young woman, she inspires Nausikaä to go to the river and wash clothes, in order for the young woman to discover Odysseus (6.1–126). To make Odysseus' presence more impressive and respectable, even immortal, several times she makes him appear more handsome, taller and huskier, and his hair curly (6.227–37; 23.156ff.). So that he will not be seen and mistreated as a stranger among the Phaeacians, she hides him within a heavy mist and, with herself in disguise as a young maiden, leads him safely to the palace of Alcinoüs (7.14–77). To ensure that he will get a respectful hearing by the Phaeacians, Athena disguises herself as the messenger of Alcinoüs, approaches individuals and causes them to assemble to hear and warmly to receive Odysseus, whom she, again, makes taller and broader and more striking than normal (8.7–23).[14] She convinces the Phaeacians to present numerous gifts of great value to her hero which will help him on his way (13.121).

When Odysseus awakes in his homeland of Ithaca, Athena hides him and the land in a mist, so that he will not be recognized, and so that he will not yet recognize his homeland (13.190ff.). She approaches him in the disguise of a young shepherd and informs him that he is indeed in Ithaca. Not knowing who this shepherd is, he spins yarns to the stranger. She smiles at him and at his lies, and approaches him in another disguise, the form of a statuesque woman (13.221ff.). She tells him that she will be at his side and that the two of them will deal with the suitors. In order to set the plan in motion, she transforms his appearance into that of an old beggar (13.372–440). Odysseus tells Athena that her counsel is the only thing which prevents him from being killed in his own palace at his homecoming, as Agamemnon was murdered in his own palace when he returned to Mycenae after the Trojan War (13.392–96). On the night before the battle, he is unsettled about whether he will be successful. Athena comes to him to assure him (20.30–55).

As the battle proceeds, she draws near to Odysseus in the likeness of aged Mentor, his friend to whom he had entrusted the care of his household while he was away at war. She chides him for not fighting with the valor which he showed at Troy (22.205–40). Then she transforms herself into a sparrow and flies to a beam to watch Odysseus and his son Telemachus re-take their home and country (22.241ff.). To assist Odysseus in routing the suitors, Athena waves the aegis and drives the suitors into panic (22.297ff.). When Odysseus and his wife Penelope are reunited and share their bed for the first time in twenty years, Athena makes the night last longer than normal (23.241ff., 344ff.). In the morning, when Odysseus and his men leave the city, she hides them in darkness and leads them safely away (23.372–73). In these adventures, most of the time Odysseus is not aware of Athena's help. She tells him, "you never recognized Pallas Athena, daughter of Zeus, the one who is always standing beside you and guarding you in every endeavor" (13.299–301).[15]

Minerva McGonagall as
Protectress of Harry Potter

Professor McGonagall is a type of helper and guard for Harry in his adventures. She gives him unique care and attention, as Athena assisted her favorite, Odysseus. After Voldemort's attack on the boy as an infant, McGonagall is concerned about the boy's welfare among the Dursleys. Early in his first year at Hogwarts, she comes to Harry's aid. When he disregards Madam Hooch's threat of expulsion from school for anyone who flies on a broomstick during her absence, McGonagall does not have him expelled. Rather, she introduces him to the captain of the Quidditch team as a Seeker, and takes it upon herself to see if Professor Dumbledore will bend the rule and allow Harry to play Quidditch, even though he is a first-year student.[16] She provides him with a state-of-the-art broom, the Nimbus Two Thousand, to help him succeed as a Seeker. She rewards Gryffindor five points for taking on the troll in the girls' toilet, despite her anger and disappointment at Harry's careless and unwise behavior. Most of all, however, Professor McGonagall functions as a mother-figure to Harry, when she gives him the gift of knowledge about his father, that he was an excellent Quidditch player. This not only enhances his knowledge of his family; it gives him another way of relating to them ... through his inherited skills at Quidditch. As a mother-figure, she is the opposite of the mother-substitute found in Petunia Dursley. The Dursleys try their best to stamp out Harry's wizard ways, making sure he never finds out who and what he is. Minerva McGonagall (stern and stiff and rule-oriented as she is), seems intent on seeing Harry grow and develop to fulfill his potential. Katherine Grimes says, "It is she who tells Harry that, even as a first-year student, he can play Quidditch. Symbolically, this is Harry's permission to fly, to seek, to aim for his reward, represented by the golden snitch" (96).

The name which the Greeks gave to the goddess, "Athena" [*Athēnaiē/ Athēnē*], appears to be an appropriate description of her protecting nature. She is, of course, associated with the city of Athens as its protector and defender. An ancient explanation of her name is that she was known as "the immortal virgin" [*hē athanatē parthenos*], and that her name connotes her immortality (Maltby 61). Adrian Room notes that her name is found in Linear B tablets from Knossos as *a-ta-na*, and that "the meaning of the Mycenaean name ... could be 'protectress'" (69).[17] He suggests that the name "Minerva" may mean something like "mindful" [Gk *mnēmōn*, "remembering" < *mimnēskō*, "to remember" > L *meminī*, "to remember" (205)]. It also was said in antiquity that she is called "Minerva" [L *Meminerva*] because "she warns (or advises) well" [L *bene moneat*] (Maltby 385). It is certainly an appropriate name for the mother-figure Minerva McGonagall, who fosters and nurtures Harry Potter with such care.

Chapter II

Harry Potter as Savior

The second major characterization of Harry as a hero on a quest is that of a savior figure. He possesses an irrepressible drive to set things right and to rescue people. The word "savior" may seem to be an exaggerated term to use for Harry. But the terminology of "saving-savior-rescue" is too prevalent in the novels to shrink from that word choice. The frequent refrain of Harry's functioning as a noble rescuer cannot be side-stepped. As Hermione puts it, Harry has a *"saving-people-thing"* (*OP* 733–34). Ginny Weasley comments to Harry, "you've been too busy saving the Wizarding world" (*HBP* 647). He is a kind of savior figure, not because of his marvelous, super-human abilities, but because of his extraordinary character. His selfless surrender of his own life for the sake of others certainly elicits the image of a heroic savior.[1] Perhaps his being reared as an unwanted orphan, never knowing any real love or affirmation, gives him an inner drive to make life good for others. But speculation about the psychological nature of a literary character is not our task.

As Harry grows older and the crises intensify which he and the Wizarding world face, his actions and aims are referred to, increasingly, in terms of savior-activity. For example, when he and his friends arrive at the Ministry of Magic to rescue Sirius Black from Voldemort, the telephone box which allows entrance to the Ministry asks him to state their business, and he replies that they are there "to save someone," and the machine issues badges with the wording, "Harry Potter Rescue Mission." When Harry rescues Ron from being poisoned, Mrs. Weasley tells Harry that he has rescued three of her family: "You saved Ginny ... you saved Arthur ... now you've saved Ron..." (*HBP* 403). And at the end of the last volume, on the morning after the duel between Harry and Voldemort, Harry's community "wanted him there with them, their leader and symbol, their savior and their guide" (*DH* 744). This public outcry forms the climax of the theme of Harry as a savior figure.

The following partial list of his activities illustrates some of his rescuing activity. In his first year, he saves Hermione from a troll, and the Sorcerer's Stone from Voldemort.[2] In his second year, he rescues Justin Finch-Fletchley from Draco's serpent, Ginny from the Chamber of Secrets and from Tom Riddle, and Hagrid's name and reputation which are jeopardized by untrue rumors, and finds a way to liberate the House-Elf Dobby. In his third year, he saves Wormtail from Sirius and Lupin, Sirius and Buckbeak from death or worse. When he uses his Patronus to dispel Dementors at the lake, protecting himself, Hermione and Sirius, he exclaims, "I've just saved all our lives" (*PA* 412). In his fourth year, he saves Gabrielle Delacour, Hermione, and Ron from drowning.[3] He also saves his own life during the challenge with a sphinx. In his fifth year, he saves Dudley from a Dementor, Arthur Weasley from an attack at the Department of Mysteries, and engages in a heated battle with Death Eaters to rescue Sirius Black in the Department of Mysteries. In his sixth year, he saves Ron from the poisoning, and Dumbledore from the Inferi and almost certain death in the seaside cave. In his last year, Harry saves Draco Malfoy from the fire in the Room of Requirement, and attempts to save the whole Wizarding world by his unstinting and unflagging leadership in the war against Voldemort.

Harry and Heracles

In these rescuing acts, Harry is comparable to the Greek hero, Heracles (Hercules to the Romans), whose legacy, in large part, depicts him as a rescuer and savior. At first glance, the two heroes may not seem to be very similar. Heracles is always depicted in story and art as an enormously powerful and muscular figure. The image we get of Harry is quite the opposite—not a physically powerful young man with a stunning presence. But the similarities are there, nonetheless, which can be cited in at least six ways.

DUAL NATURE

Both Harry and his predecessor have dual nature, as is common in the case of heroes of folktales and legends. Although Harry is a half-blood magical person (his mother was the daughter of Muggles, like Hermione), he has both Muggle and magical pedigree. Consequently, he can draw on the resources of both his non-magical nature and his magical nature. Heracles is a semi-divine being, the son of the king of the gods, Zeus, and a human mother, Alcmena.[4] Deceived into having an affair with Zeus because he comes to her disguised as her husband, Amphitryon, she gives birth to a son who is half immortal, half mortal. Many years later, when Heracles dies, he is consumed by fire, which burns away his mortality. Hence, he is unique in mythology, in that though mortal, he is made immortal and elevated to share the company of the gods.

SURVIVORS OF
MURDEROUS ASSAULT

The heroes share a cluster of connections which have their settings in the boys' cribs: infancy, murder, survival, fame, heroism in battle and life lived under the burden of prophecy. When Harry and Heracles are infants, each is assaulted by his own greatest enemy. Miraculously, however, both boys survive, and the fame that comes to them may well make both of them deserving of the title, The Boy Who Lived. Voldemort's attack on the Potters kills Harry's parents but leaves him only wounded and changed. The uniqueness of Harry's surviving and his weakening the Dark Lord makes the boy famous throughout the magical world, even before he comes to know that he is a wizard. He grows up to play a unique role in the battle against this enemy. And a prophecy concerning his fate becomes a major factor in his quest, especially in the *Order of the Phoenix*.

In the case of Heracles, Zeus's wife and queen of the gods (Hera) is jealous and irate because her husband fathers a son with another woman. She sends two powerful serpents to kill the baby who is cradled in his father's huge shield. To everyone's surprise, the infant kills the serpents with his powerful grip. Astonished by this portent and marvelous feat, Heracles' human "father" consults the blind prophet Tiresias, who delivers a prophecy of the future of the child, that he will kill many wild beasts, be a formidable force in the Battle of the Gods and the Giants, be chosen to be made immortal because of all his labors, allowed to dwell on Olympus, and have as his bride Hebe, the goddess of eternal youth.[5]

LIFE UNDER PARENTAL THREAT

Both Harry and Heracles labor under the threat of a parent or step-parent who can terminate their lives. This is a common motif in classical mythology, of a parent or parent substitute (step-parent, godparent) who holds the power of death over the child. A famous classical example is the myth of Meleager, the son of Ares and Althaea, who lives his life only so long as his mother desires. At the time of his birth, the Fates decree that he will live, as long as a log which is burning in the hearth does not burn up completely. Althaea extinguishes the log, preserving his life; but, she keeps the log in a chest. Years later, in a fit of anger over Meleager's killing her brothers in a fight, she takes the log from the chest and throws it onto the fire, bringing an end to the life of her son. Meleager lives his entire life under the oppressive weight of his mother's retaining the means and power to annihilate him.

In the stories of both heroes, step-parents are the threat to the heroes. Heracles' step-mother, Hera, holds such an unquenchable hatred for him that, during his whole life, she attempts repeatedly to annihilate him. Harry's threatening mother-substitute, Petunia Dursley, would be glad to see Harry disappear. She does all she can to make him feel unwanted and detested. But the "parent" figure who holds a more realistic threat of death over Harry appears to be Sirius Black, a crazed killer, an escapee from Azkaban, who betrayed his best friend and was an accomplice in Voldemort's attack on Harry when he was a baby.

In Harry's case, there is a turn-around or cancellation of this motif, when he learns the truth, that Sirius Black is not the traitorous enemy Harry thought him to be. Nonetheless, for a while, Harry lives under the burden of fearing an evil parent who can and intends to extinguish his life at will. This motif helps to create dramatic tension in the story. It does not culminate in the death of the child (as with Meleager). The model is used and reversed for a radically different resolution—the reconciliation of the child and the parent substitute.

Life Under a
Dreaded Arch-Enemy

Another aspect of the motif just mentioned is the similarity that Harry and Heracles both live out their lives in conflict with a powerful and malevolent enemy. In fact, neither Heracles nor Harry would be memorable apart from their antagonists. Heracles, whose name means "the glory of Hera," undergoes a number of life-threatening contests, all of which are really Hera's attempts to kill him.[6] Consequently, his legendary achievements are testimony to his powers, but also to the famous ("glorious") animosity of his arch-enemy Hera. If his life were not endangered constantly by the most powerful of the goddesses, Heracles would not be famous and immortal. The challenges his hateful step-mother puts him through show how mighty she is, and his achievements reveal his unique powers. In the same way, without the unrelenting assaults on Harry by Voldemort (the chief of the dark wizards), Harry would be just another male member of the Wizarding community. The lives, fates, and fame of both boys are inextricably entwined with their respective arch-enemies. Both owe their fame, in part, to the grandeur of their opponents.

Herculean Contests

The most widely known of Heracles' feats are his Twelve Labors, tests which require super human strength and which can cost the hero his life.[7] Behind this set of contests (the Greek for these "Labors" is *athloi*, "contests") lies the vengeance of Hera. She causes Heracles to go insane and kill his wife and children. As punishment for this act, the Delphic Oracle requires him to serve Eurystheus, the king of Tiryns, for twelve years. The king imposes on him one tremendous contest each year, a number of which are calculated, surely, to endanger his life. If Heracles succeeds in all of them, he can become immortal. Fortunately for him, Athena assists him on a number of occasions. Ancient visitors to the Temple of Olympian Zeus at Olympia in southern Greece (the Peloponnese) could see sculptures high on the temple depicting Heracles engaged in these Labors. In several of the metopes which have survived and are partially intact, Athena is shown working along with the hero. In one, she helps him to hold up the sky, while Atlas is away, securing the Apples of the Hesperides for Heracles. In another, she collaborates with him in cleansing the stables of Augeas. And in a third, she receives the man-eating Stymphalian Birds which Heracles has killed.

The trials which Harry Potter endures are similar to those of Heracles, in that they come to him because of a powerful master, Lord Voldemort, who sets him up to defend his life. In these struggles, Harry can continue to live only if he succeeds in each of them. And he always has the support of two powerful sponsors, Dumbledore—even when he perceives that the Headmaster is creating distance between himself and Harry—and Professor Minerva McGonagall.

Two classic tales of journeys to and from the Underworld and a simile derived from the legend of Heracles are re-cycled in the *Potter* series. The first story has to do with the conquering of the guardian of Hades, the three-headed hound, Cerberus. Within the first few months of Harry's life at Hogwarts, he has to deal with a vicious, three-headed dog which stands guard over an underground realm. HH&R encounter the animal by accident, barely escaping its jaws. They learn from Hagrid that the beast is his pet, which he calls "Fluffy," and that it can be put to sleep with music. Harry uses this information, and by playing on a wooden flute, he gains access to the lower regions.[8]

In Greek and Roman mythology, only a select few ever make it down to the Underworld and back alive, past the three-headed guard-dog of Hades. Heracles is required to overcome Cerberus somehow, bring him to the upper world to show to King Eurystheus, and return the beast to the Underworld.

In both Heracles' and Harry's situations, they have to subdue a three-headed (i.e., "all-threatening," as it were) guard-dog. Their means are different, and their tasks differ (Harry only has to get past Fluffy). But their heroic, life-endangering descents to worlds below, to face enormous perils, bear similarities which encourage us to bring to Harry's contest the colors and tones of the contest of Heracles (who declares that this was the worst of all his labors), and that he could accomplish it only by the help of Athena and Hermes (*Il.* 11.617–26).[9]

The second story has Heracles, again, visiting the Underworld, this time to save Theseus, the king of Athens. Theseus and the king of the Lapiths (Pirithoüs) make a pact to help each other find a suitable wife. Theseus abducts Helen from Sparta, though she is only ten or twelve years old, and she is eventually rescued and taken back to her home. Pirithoüs' desire for a wife is even more difficult to satisfy, for he wants Persephone, queen of the Underworld. The two adventurers go to Hades, are captured and made to sit on the Chair of Forgetfulness, to which they become bound. Though Pirithoüs never escapes, Heracles pleads the case for Theseus and secures his release. In this contest, Heracles once again faces and conquers death and the Underworld, this time for someone whom he esteems highly (*Epit.*1.23–24).

The striking simile is introduced by Professor Snape, when he warns the students that battling with the Dark Arts is "like fighting a many-headed monster, which, each time a neck is severed, sprouts a head even fiercer and cleverer than before" (*HBP* 177). His analogy depicts fighting the Dark Arts as a task as difficult at those of Heracles. The allusion here is to the mythical Hydra, a poisonous water snake with many heads which inhabits the marshes near Lerna. The task of killing the Hydra is another of Heracles' Twelve Labors. The monster has nine heads (only one of which is immortal). Every time Heracles removes a head, two magically replace the one cut off. He succeeds only because his nephew, Iolaüs, helps him. The boy uses a torch to burn the stump of each of the eight mortal heads as it is severed, preventing its regeneration. Then Heracles buries the immortal head under a huge rock (*Libr.* 2.5.2).

THE CHOICE OF HERACLES

A timeless theme has to do with the relationship between characteristics or behavior and character. In discussing the nature of the soul, Socrates crafted a myth of the charioteer and his horses. As the myth goes, the horses are very different, one very beautiful and noble, the other bred from low and mean stock. Controlling the two is a strenuous effort, as the horses strain in opposite directions for their desired goals. This analogy applies to managing the soul, which is pulled in opposing directions, requiring one to make constant decisions and choices in light of one's values (Plato, *Phaedrus* 246aff.).

This same topic is one of the constant themes in Rowling's novels. At Cedric Diggory's memorial service, Dumbledore tells the students that they all face "dark and difficult times," and advises them that when they have to choose between what is right and what is easy, they should remember Cedric (*GF* 724). Harry, himself, is constantly called upon to make choices of great importance. And he never shrinks from them. The challenges he faces often offer him the options of electing to face mortal danger or to choose a path which will more likely ensure his safety and well-being. His natural tendency is to think of others, to avoid self-protective options, to choose trust rather than doubt. When he is tested as to whether to trust Dumbledore and follow the path on which he started, he takes the brave route. When he has to choose between the Horcruxes and the Hallows, he selects the unselfish option, exactly the opposite of Voldemort's choice. He takes the risk of losing his life for the well-being of others, whereas Voldemort uses or disposes of anyone in order to gain immortality for himself. And at King's Cross Station, when Harry is offered peace and freedom from an existence of hostility and conflict, he chooses to take the hard option, for the good of others. He tends to choose nobly and courageously, rather than selfishly. His choices show him to be a figure not unlike the hero Heracles, whose unselfish choices to help others caused him to be very frequently called upon as "the universal helper" (Howatson 284).

Perhaps Harry's greatest self-identity crisis occurs when he begins to realize that he and Tom Riddle have much in common in their appearance, family history, rearing among Muggles, gift of Parseltongue, and personality traits. He fears that he is doomed to be like Voldemort. With these fears whirling about inside him, Harry fails to take account of the ways in which they differ. Dumbledore guides him to see clearly that his fears are unfounded, that despite their similarities, the two are not the same, assuring him that it is not traits or circumstances which make people who they are, but the choices which they make. He recalls the choices that both Harry and Voldemort have made, which reveal how truly different they are. They are as different as their choices.

There is a famous story told about Heracles as a young man, when he has to weigh his future options and decide about the direction of his life. It is referred to as the "Choice of Heracles." He is faced with two options which appear in the form of women who come to him—Pleasure, who offers him an easy and desirable life, and Virtue, who can offer him only toil and glory.

Heracles chooses Virtue, which sets the course of his life and his contests with Fate. For his courage and character he comes to be thought of as the ideal human.[10] Harry's brave choice made at King's Cross Station, made not for his own advantage but for the good of others, is perhaps the most dramatic testimony to his likeness to Heracles.

Harry and Achilles

In several ways there are connecting links between Harry Potter and Achilles, the main figure of the *Iliad*. The ancient hero's name probably derives from a word which means "grief," "sorrow," "trouble," or distress" [Gk *Achilleus* < *achos* (LSJ 297; Cunliffe 65; Room 23)]. The personal anger of the greatest of the Greeks, at his having been dishonored by his fellow generals, initiates the major theme of the epic and sets in motion waves of grief and trouble which are the poem's dramatic materials.[11] Both Harry and Achilles are the leading heroes in their respective conflicts. While there are certainly differences between the two (e.g., Achilles acts on the basis of proud self-interest, while Harry characteristically acts on the basis of his personality trait as a "savior" figure), there are important similarities. We shall take a look at three ways in which they and their stories are alike: (1) they both are sons of mothers who would do anything to save and protect them, though each is left with a point of vulnerability which makes them virtually helpless to defend themselves; (2) they are models of fast and true friendship; and (3) they both engage in one-on-one duels with their greatest enemy in epic fashion.

A MOTHER'S LOVE AND
THE VULNERABILITY OF HER CHILD

The love of a mother trying to protect her child from harm and death is an age-old motif. Achilles' mother, Thetis, tries to cover her son with supernatural, protective power by anointing him with ambrosia during the day and holding him in purifying fire at night,[12] or by dipping him in the river Styx in the Underworld.[13] Since she holds him by his heels during the protective process, that part of his body is not made immortal, leaving him vulnerable to injury there. Years later, during the battle at Troy, the Trojan prince, Paris, wounds Achilles by shooting him in his heel with an arrow. From this myth, we get the metaphor of an "Achilles' heel."[14] There is a certain kind of irony in an immortal demi-god being killed by what seems to be a rather insignificant injury (not a blow to the head or a spear through his chest, but an arrow in his heel). That irony itself is part of the message of the myth. If a soldier is enfeebled and crippled in battle, he cannot fight effectively or run away … leaving him quite exposed and easily killed. So, the greatest of the Greek warriors is eliminated by injury to this one, seemingly unimportant spot on his body.

In the case of Harry, Lily Potter throws herself between Voldemort and her child, giving her life for her son. However, from that moment on, Harry is plagued by the scar on his head, a remnant of Voldemort himself, which gives the Dark Lord a level of control over the boy's thoughts and actions. For both Achilles and Harry, their vulnerable spot (Achilles' heel, Harry's scar), is created because of someone's quest for immortality—Thetis' loving effort to make her child immortal, and Voldemort's blind passion to gain immortality for himself, no matter who has to suffer in order for him to get it. Despite the most sincere efforts of a mother to save her child, nothing can protect her child from everything … as every mother knows.

Early in his life, Achilles learns that he has to choose between a short and glorious life and a long and inglorious life. He chooses the former, and years later, after a hiatus in his participation in the battle at Troy, he fights unreservedly, knowing that he is destined to die young. For his choice and his bravery, his name has been celebrated for aeons. Harry, too, has to choose whether to throw himself into the fight against Voldemort or sidestep the dreadful task. And he, like Achilles, devotes himself to a fight from which only he or his opponent can emerge alive. Both heroes choose honorably and courageously. In these ways, Harry resembles Achilles, and, consequently, Lily resembles Thetis, the loving mother of the ancient Greek hero.[15]

The Bond of True Friendship

In Cicero's dialogue "On Friendship," Gaius Laelius the Wise claims that in all of history, true and lasting friendships are so rare that only three or four pairs of such friends are readily remembered as models of loyalty and courage (*De Amicitia*, 4.46–50). The four are Achilles and Patroclus, Orestes and Pylades, Theseus and Pirithoüs, and Damon and Phintias.[16] To this set we add a fifth pair, from the *Aeneid*, Nisus and Euryalus.

Achilles and Patroclus

These friends grow up together and study medicine together. When Patroclus is wounded in battle, Achilles treats his friend's injuries. In preparation for re-entering the battle, Patroclus asks to wear his friend's glorious armor. On the battlefield, however, he is mistaken for Achilles and is killed by Hector. Achilles, enraged by the killing of his dear friend, enters the battle wearing no armor, and with his fierce war cry, drives the Trojans away from Patroclus' body. His fighting to avenge the death of his friend is a major element of the last part of the *Iliad*.[17]

Orestes and Pylades

Another famous pair of friends who grow up together is Orestes and Pylades. When the king of Mycenae, Agamemnon, returns from a ten-year absence in the Trojan War, his wife, Clytemnestra, murders him. For a decade, she had nursed her hatred for him, because he sacrificed their daughter, Iphigenia, to the goddess Artemis in order to satisfy that goddess' wrath. Artemis had made the winds and seas unfavorable for sailing to Troy. With Iphigenia's sacrifice, the goddess relented, and the Greeks sailed away. After Agamemnon's return from Troy and his murder, his son, Orestes, with the help of his friend, Pylades, kills his mother for blood vengeance. Orestes is put on trial at Areopagus ("Mars Hill") for the vendetta. When he is called to stand forth, his friend Pylades steps forward to take his friend's place, claiming that he is Orestes. Orestes does not let Pylades complete the selfless substitution, and takes his own chances with the court. Orestes is vindicated, and later, Pylades marries Orestes' sister, Electra.

Theseus and Pirithoüs

These two legendary kings make an agreement to help each other obtain an appropriate wife. They abduct young Helen of Sparta for Theseus of Athens, who eventually loses her when she returns to her home. Then, they go to the Underworld to get Persephone, queen of the Hades, to be the bride of the Lapith king, Pirithoüs. The companions are caught and forced to sit in the Chair of Forgetfulness. Heracles ventures to Hades to rescue them. He is able to secure the release of Theseus, but has to leave Pirithoüs there forever (*Epit.* 1.23–24). The extent to which the kings went for each other, even risking their lives, has made their friendship a timeless tale.

Damon and Phintias

According to Cicero's story, Dionysius, the tyrant of Syracuse in Sicily, condemns Phintias to death (for some crime). To get his affairs in order, the accused departs from Syracuse. This is permitted because his friend, Damon, stands as the guarantor of his return and appearance. When Phintias appears exactly on time for his execution, Damon is freed from his pledge which has put his own life in jeopardy. Although Dionysius has suspected that Phintias will betray his friend, thus saving his own life at the cost of his friend's, he is so impressed by the mutual loyalty of these two students of Pythagoras that he pardons Phintias and says, "Would that I were accounted a third friend to you (two)" (*Tusculan Disputations* 5.63).

Nisus and Euryalus

In Vergil's *Aeneid*, we read of two young men who share with each other in athletic competition and military expedition. They run together in a foot-race during the memorial games which Aeneas holds in honor of his father, Anchises. When Nisus is about to win, he slips in animal gore and falls out of the race. Nisus, in order to help his dear friend Euryalus, who is in third place, trips the only runner ahead of Euryalus, who then wins the race (5.315–61). From an ethical point of view, this "act of Fortune," as Nisus explains it, is quite questionable; but it was considered a gift given to help a friend become victorious. The friendship of the two is praised, also, for their proposing and executing a heroic and risky night mission against their enemies, the Rutuli. When they engage the enemy, Nisus escapes, but Euryalus is captured and killed. Nisus cannot save his friend, but he dies trying to avenge his friend's death (9.176–449).

When we look at these pairs of friends, we notice that in three of the five sets, one of the friends comes into the life of the other from exile or is born in exile (Pylades, Phintias, and Nisus). All five pairs face contests or dangers together. And in each instance, there is an act of selfless daring undertaken for the sake of the other member of the pair.

Harry Potter and Cedric Diggory

These two Triwizard Champions bear some likeness to the ancient pairs of friends. They are examples of devotion and willingness to seek the advantage and well-being of the other, even if it means death. Unlike the classical pairs, they are not lifelong friends. Harry is an outsider to the Wizarding community during his growing years, and is received into the Wizarding world. There may be a common motif at work here, of an outsider becoming an exemplary friend, just as in the cases of Pylades, Phintias, and Nisus who are received into the circles of Orestes, Damon, and Euryalus. In their common trials of the Third Task, Harry helps Cedric in the maze, when he is disabled by a curse. Both boys help each other bring down a giant spider. And, rather than beat the other out of first place, they agree to share the victory, showing tremendous mutual respect.

It All Comes Down to Two

One of the standard elements of epics is the *mano-a-mano*, hand-to-hand single combat between the most formidable heroes of the opposing sides. After long scenes of general battle, a storyteller narrows the field of vision to just two warriors, the most avid, or most able, or most inimical of the competing armies. This change in the action gives the hearer or reader a pause from the collective mayhem of pitched battle. And in these paired contests, the dynamics are both political and personal. This motif is at the heart of what is probably the most widely known literary duel, the biblical story of David and Goliath. In the Greek tradition, Achilles does single combat with and kills the Trojan warrior and prince, Hector. In the Roman tradition, Aeneas, the progenitor of the Roman race, does battle with Turnus the king of the Italic tribe, the Rutuli. There is hatred between the two, as Turnus' bride-to-be, Lavinia, has been given in marriage to Aeneas. Also, Turnus is the leader of the faction which wants Aeneas and his fellow foreigners to leave Italy. In battle, Aeneas kills Turnus and sets in motion the development of the future for Romans in Italy. Harry Potter faces off with Voldemort on several occasions, and reenacts this famous type of epic battle.[18] And, just as with their epic forebears, the motives for duel between the combatants are both social and personal.

Harry and Theseus

Harry Potter grows up in a home which is completely removed from his rightful society and place. He endures not only humble circumstances but also malevolent and spirit-crushing treatment by a female parent figure, Petunia Dursley, who gives preference to her own natural son, Dudley. When Harry becomes old enough to attend Hogwarts, he is finally released from this existence, and is able to begin his quest to discover and embrace the life of fame that is deservedly his own in the magical world. His story is not unique. The motif of a child sent away or kept away from home and reared by foster parents, because of the likelihood of a terrible destiny or of death, combined with the threat of death by a female parent, is a major element of the stories of heroes and mythical figures such as Theseus, Oedipus, and Orestes. These three and Harry Potter are reared away from their proper homes and as adolescents begin to live out their destinies. Since we have mentioned Orestes previously, here we shall focus on Theseus and Oedipus.

The tale of Theseus' youth and coming of age has interesting parallels to Harry Potter. His story is this. Aegeus, the king of Athens, is anxious to have a son as his successor; but he remains childless. He goes to Delphi to consult the oracle as to why he cannot sire a son. The oracle gives him a puzzling answer, as it is accustomed to do, not to "open the mouth of the wineskin" until he returns to Athens. On the way home, he visits Pittheus, the king of Troezen and relates the prophecy to him. Pittheus gets Aegeus drunk and has his daughter, Aethra, sleep with his guest. Sometime later, when Aegeus discovers that the princess is pregnant, he orders her to rear the boy in Troezen, not knowing who his father is, or his real identity, or that he is next in line to be the king of Athens.

Aegeus places a sword and a pair of sandals beneath a huge boulder and tells Aethra that when the boy is old enough to move the rock and secure those items, he should bring them with him to Athens. When Theseus comes of age, he moves the rock, secures the equipment, and begins his quest to obtain the legacy which has been his all along. On his way to his father, he undergoes many dangerous contests (similar to those faced by Heracles), in all of which he is successful, owing primarily to his craftiness and his skill. When he arrives in Athens, his jealous step-mother, Medea, tries to kill him, so that Medus (her own natural son by Aegeus) will ascend to the throne. Aegeus, fortunately, saves his son, recognizing him in time, when he sees him cutting food at the dining table with the very sword which the king had placed under the boulder years earlier.

Eventually, Theseus becomes a savior-figure, rescuing the Athenians from subservience to king Minos of Crete and from their obligatory human sacrifices to the Minotaur. In order to do this, he has to enter the winding, labyrinthine maze of rooms and dark paths, which are said, traditionally, to be beneath the palace at Knossos. There, he must kill the man-eating, half-human, half-bull monster. He is assisted in this contest by Minos' daughter, Ariadne, who falls in love with him. He completes his task successfully, becomes involved with Ariadne, and sails safely from Crete (*Epit.* 1.9–11).

The basic pattern of the stories of Theseus and Harry offers suggestive echoes. Some of the particular features of their stories, however, call for attention as well. For example, the circumstances of the early years are different for the two boys. From Harry's birth, he has an enemy, of whom he does not even know, who would kill him if he could. But Harry lives outside the Wizarding world, among Muggles, protected from being discovered because of the spell which Dumbledore created to keep him safe until he should come of age. This spell saves him from Voldemort and from the prophecy that he would kill or be killed by the Dark Lord, so long as he spends some time with the Dursleys every year. Theseus is born as the result of a transgression of

Apollo's oracle and reared away from his rightful family and people. Thus, he is reared in a very dangerous condition, and protected only by the facts that he is not known and does not know his real identity.

When both young men come to early adulthood and enter upon their respective quests, they face and succeed in life-threatening battles and contests with evil. On several occasions Harry ventures into an "Underworld," of sorts (the Chamber of Secrets and the black lake of the merpeople), to rescue someone dear to him. Theseus also ventures into an "Underworld" during his life-and-death contest with the Minotaur in the subterranean maze, in order to save his people and Ariadne. In their challenges with the mazes, both do more than survive personally. As savior-figures, they make their worlds safer for their people. And both heroes prevail because they are furnished with swords by their father or father-figure.

Harry and Oedipus

Oedipus is another hero who comes to mind, in thinking about Harry and his quest. Three items suggest themselves: the heroes both are identified by physical markings which came from brushes with death; both lived under the inescapable decrees of fate, of which they are not fully aware; and both have a common deadly run-in with a murderous, mythical being.

IDENTITY BY PHYSICAL MARKINGS

First, there are physical scars which each has received when they were infants, as the result of someone's attempt to kill them, a standard motif in hero stories. Naturally, Harry's lightning-bolt scar plays a continuing role in the novels. He is frequently recognized by the mark or is asked to show the mark, as if to signify that he really is The Boy Who Lived. Oedipus' mark is so essential to his identity, that to speak his name is to speak of his ill-fortuned experience. The name creates an atmosphere which hangs over his entire life. In the tradition about his childhood trauma, another motif is also at work, the tale of the child who is exposed or set adrift in order to eliminate the misfortune his survival will bring.

When Oedipus was an infant, his father, Laius, the king of Thebes, feared an oracle that the boy would grow up to kill him. To try to avert this dreadful fate, Laius had the boy exposed on a mountainside, with his ankles pinned with a spike, so that he would die in the wilderness.[19] The child was rescued, however, and reared in Corinth. His adoptive parents named him "Oedipus," which means "swell-foot" [Gk *Oidipous* < *oideō*, "to swell" + *pous*, "foot"]. Apparently, the injuries the child sustained by the staking of his ankles had some effect on his feet or on the way he walked. The name is a very unhappy or depressing one, as is his fate. In a similar way, Harry is everywhere known for and by the mark he bears from Voldemort's attempt to kill him in Godric's Hollow.

An Impending Oracular Curse

Second, both boys spend their lives under the overhanging curse of a dreadful prophecy. Oedipus is prophesied to kill his father and marry his mother. Harry is prophesied to have to do mortal battle with Voldemort, in which only one will survive. In both cases, the prophecies are unchangeable scripts by which they have to live their lives. And no matter what precautions they or their loved ones may take to avoid the fulfillment of the prophecies, their fates seem to be fixed. Elizabeth Ernst notes that "One of the most compelling critical readings of the Greek myth of Oedipus ... sees it as the conflict of free will versus fate" (326). That conflict is a very powerful dynamic in the life of Harry Potter.

Contest with a Sphinx

And third, both heroes confront a sphinx, the winged creature with the head of a woman and the body of a lion. In a famous mythological story told in Sophocles' play, *Oedipus the King,* a sphinx plagues ancient Thebes by killing and eating anyone who cannot solve a riddle which she proposes. Her riddle asks, "What it is that walks on four legs in the morning, two at noon, and three in the evening?" The correct answer is "the human being," who as a child crawls on all fours, as an adult walks upright on two feet, and in old age walks with a cane or walking stick as a kind of third foot. Oedipus answers the riddle correctly and saves the city from its plague and suffering, though he comes to a horrible end for other reasons. The Thebans hail him as their savior [Gk *sōtēra*].

During the Third Task of the Triwizard Tournament, Harry encounters a sphinx in the winding maze. She will allow him to pass only if he can answer correctly the riddle put to him. If he succeeds, he can proceed. If he answers incorrectly, she will pounce—a life-and-death contest. Intelligence and cleverness are the weapons for their duel. And, in Oedipus-fashion, Harry saves the day by his quickness and ingenuity, even amazing himself at his brilliance.

This parallelism does not ask the reader to see Harry as the original

Oedipus himself, in magical-folk disguise. It recalls the atmosphere of the original story and the characteristics of both the wise savior-hero Oedipus and his sphinx, in order to color Harry's story with classic imagery of danger and heroism.[20]

Harry and Aeneas

Another ancient hero comes to mind as having similarities to Harry in their character, behavior and experiences, Vergil's hero, Aeneas. The two are comparable in their sense of duty, their epic duels, and their visiting the "Underworld."

PIETAS AND HUMAN FRAILTY

Throughout the *Aeneid*, the adjective used very frequently to describe the hero's main personality trait is *pius*, "dutiful." The attribute of "duty" [L *pietās, -ātis*, "devotion, sense of duty"] underlies the epic poem, and Aeneas best exemplifies it. R.D. Williams writes that *pietas* in the *Aeneid* is "an attitude of responsibility towards gods and men, an attitude which may involve the subjugation of individual passions (like the desire for glorious death at Troy, or the love of Dido) to the demands of duty" (xxiii). Aeneas is symbolic or characteristic of what a Roman man should be, one who does what is honorable and dutiful and expected, in relation to his family, his country, his ancestors, and the gods. His name depicts his character: [Gk *Aineias* < *aineō*, "to approve, consent" > L *Aenēas* (Room 28)].

Aeneas' greatest virtue certainly matches the character of Harry Potter, as well. He has an unfailing sense of duty and responsibility. He never chooses for himself and against others in difficult matters. He is loyal to his friends and to Gryffindor. He can be counted on as a leader to help and rescue others. He even protects those he loves by distancing himself from them, a practice sometimes employed, unselfishly, by his Headmaster, to protect those whom he holds dear.

But what makes these two models of selfless loyalty even more similar is that both are imperfect human beings, with natural shortcomings. Harry can be quick to judge. As he advances in his adolescence, he grows increasingly sassy and unkind to the Dursleys and even to Albus Dumbledore. Sometimes he exhibits adolescent self-centeredness. Aeneas has his shortcomings as well. He is truly the hero of his quest, but he is not an Achilles or an Odysseus, in the sense of being virtually unfailing as a paradigm of greatness.[21]

He can be cocky and impetuous and self-serving. His abandoning Dido, the queen of Carthage, after their intense relationship, leads to her suicide. Vergil depicts the hero as calculating and totally unfeeling when he tells Dido that he has to fulfill his fated duty and sail away. These human traits make both Harry and Aeneas accessible to readers, having about them a degree of reality and human weakness.

Hero Faces Enemy

As we pointed out when we compared Harry and Achilles, one of the features of classical epics is that they end with a one-on-one duel between the leaders of the opposing sides: Achilles and Hector (i.e., the Greeks versus the Trojans) in the *Iliad*, Aeneas and Turnus (i.e., the Romans and the Rutuli) in the *Aeneid*. While Harry and the Dark Lord face off several times, their conflict comes to a climax, finally in singular combat between The Boy Who Lived and the Lord of the Death Eaters. Rowling gives the epic type-scene of Aeneas and Turnus a new rendering in her epic of the magical world.

Visit to an Underworld

In classical mythology, a hero is sometimes required to descend into the Underworld, to fulfill some mission there among the dead, and to return alive. There are not many lengthy classical stories about this radical challenge. The one most pertinent to Rowling's books, perhaps, is Aeneas' Journey to the Underworld in the *Aeneid*, Book 6. He descends to the Underworld under the guidance of a prophetess, the Sibyl. He needs direction and guidance as to how to continue on the odyssey which has been mandated by prophecy. He enters a world populated by violent, forbidding, and strange-bodied monsters. From his father, Aeneas gains an overview of the future founding of Rome and its rise to world power and glory, which is one of the major prophecies in the entire epic poem. And he receives the commission of Fate for all Romans. At length, he emerges from the Underworld alive and blessed with hope for the future.[22]

A close parallel to this dangerous adventure of Aeneas is the Second Task of the Triwizard Tournament. In that task, the contestants enter another world (the magical underwater world of the merpeople) to rescue something they love dearly—which has been taken from them and is being held captive in the underwater world—and return to their natural world safe and sound. Death and loss are the apparent costs of failure, but life and return home are the rewards for achievement. Of course, the adventure within the alien world will forever shape and inform the minds and characters of the champions as human beings, but the ultimate challenge is life or death and the test is a test of character and creativity. Harry undergoes the challenge because of his true friendship with Ron.

Both Aeneas and Harry emerge from their respective murky worlds of peril and death victorious and changed by their experiences. Both show devotion to those dear to them. Both are saviors, of friends and/or of their people. Harry joins the ranks of those who have entered and returned from an Underworld, as Heracles, Theseus, and Aeneas. John Granger and Travis Prinzi point out that in all seven novels, Harry descends into an "Underworld" of sorts: through the trapdoor to an Underworld, to battle with Voldemort (*SS*), through the bathroom chute down into an Underworld of the Chamber of Secrets to battle with the basilisk and Tom Riddle (*CS*), down into the subterranean tunnel beneath the Whomping Willow and into the black lake to rescue Ron (*PA*), into the gruesome graveyard where he duels with the revitalized Voldemort (*GF*), into the Department of Mysteries deep in the Ministry of Magic to battle with the Death Eaters and Voldemort (*OP*), into the cave where he battles the Inferi who attempt to drown him (*HBP*), and into the Forbidden Forest to duel with Voldemort, and into the other-worldly King's Cross Station (*DH*) (Granger *How Harry Cast His Spell*, 2008, 22f.; Prinzi 108–10).

Chapter III

Harry Potter and Narcissus: "Know Thyself"

An essential component of a hero's quest is the task of acquiring self-understanding. A quest leads the hero through various experiences and trials, coming to its end when the seeker arrives "home" and attains self-understanding, knows where and to whom he belongs, and discovers what is to be prized most highly. In the end, the seeker may be in the same place where the quest began (for Odysseus, it is Ithaca); but the self-awareness and self-understanding of the seeker have been transformed by the rigors of the journey. A freshman or first-year student away from home and at a new school soon encounters unaccustomed ways and ideas, and unfamiliar personalities, just as Harry does. Toward the end of his first semester at Hogwarts, he makes a discovery which opens a new and greater stage of self-understanding and value, the Mirror of Erised.

An ancient literary antecedent to this episode may very well be the mythological story of Narcissus, who has an amorous fixation on what he sees in a crystal clear pool, and which leads to his ruin (*Met.* 3.339–510).[1] In this myth, a river god, Cephisus, forces himself on a nymph named Liriope, who gives birth to a handsome son, Narcissus. The mother consults the blind prophet Tiresias as to whether the child will have a long life. The seer answers in the enigmatic language of an oracle, that he will live a long life, "if he does not come to know himself." When Narcissus reaches middle adolescence, he is so attractive that both girls and boys are drawn to him; but he is extremely proud of himself, unwilling to open up any of himself to anyone. A young man whom Narcissus has scorned prays to the gods for a curse to come upon the handsome young man. He asks that Narcissus will come to love someone deeply and not be able to win the affections of the one he loves.

The goddess of divine punishment (Nemesis or Themis) responds to the request of the rejected young man. The curse takes effect this way. Once, when Narcissus is tired and thirsty from hunting, he is lured to a pool of water so perfect that its surface had never known a ripple from a falling leaf. As he bends down to drink from the pool, another desire takes him, a passion for what he sees in the pool ... himself. The person he sees is perfect, divine, worthy of all desire. A longing for the boy whom he sees inflames him. He even tries to touch, converse with, and kiss the person who is just beyond the thin film of water which he thinks is separating them. The poet who tells us this story, Ovid, breaks into his own narration to address Narcissus and warn him of the vanity of his actions. But Narcissus persists, heedless. He stops eating and resting, and he wastes away with longing. He thinks that the person whom he sees in the pool desires him with equal desire, for the image seems to talk to him (though no words can be heard). His beloved returns his attempts to kiss him, and weeps at the frustrating situation, just as Narcissus weeps. At last, Narcissus comes to the shattering realization, "I am that person.... I burn with love for myself." In anguish, he wishes to escape from his body, and says, "And now grief takes away my strength, and long spans of life do not remain for me. I am extinguished in my early youth." In his madness he beats himself. In his affliction, his body slowly wastes away. He dies beside the pool, so close to, yet so far from his beloved. He is so infatuated with himself that even after his death, as he is punted across the river Styx to the Underworld, he leans over the edge of the boat to see himself in the foul waters of that river. At the place where he dies, a pretty flower, yellow with white petals, takes his place to commemorate his fate, the Narcissus flower.

Tiresias prophesied that Narcissus would live to a ripe old age if he did not come to know himself. Unfortunately for Narcissus, he does not come to know himself in the Socratic way of mature, self-understanding. He discovers only the tragic state of his incurable plight—that he is imprisoned by and fixed on love for no one and nothing other than an image of himself. Manfred Weidhorn says that with Narcissus, "self-contemplation turns into self-adoration rather than self-knowledge" (852).

The name "Narcissus" may derive from Gk *narkē*, "numbness, deadness" and L *narcē, -ēs*, "numbness, torpor" (LSJ 1160; OLD 1155). Room offers several options on the etymology of his name, building on Pliny's opinion that the name of the flower came first, and the name was applied to Narcissus because of the stuporous effect the flower had on people. He proposes that the name should mean "benumbed," describing the state of the boy as he wasted away (210).

In the episode of the Mirror of Erised, Harry comes upon a magical mirror which does not reflect what is presented before it, but what the viewer wants most of all to see—a reflection of one's deepest desire. Harry sees ten members of his family—all deceased. Since he has been reared as an orphan by his aunt and uncle who despise him, having a real family and a sense of belonging are more important to him than anything else in the world. He becomes obsessed with this image and returns nightly to view his projected wish again. He sees likenesses of himself in his father's hair and his mother's eyes. He feels that he has found his home, the place where he belongs, his family. He begins to lose himself, to act strangely, and to care about nothing else besides being there before the mirror. Eventually, he is rescued from this emotional whirlpool by Professor Dumbledore, who warns the enchanted young wizard that what he sees is not truth. It is only the projection of his deepest desires, the things for which he wishes most. And it can be destructive and is not itself life. With this corrective advice, Professor Dumbledore takes a further step than simply offering words of wisdom to Harry. He removes the mirror, making it impossible for Harry to continue this behavior.

There are so many possible parallels between the two stories, that it is instructive to observe them side-by-side.

Narcissus	*Harry*
1. is a youth of sixteen	1. is a youth of eleven
2. by chance, separated from his comrades	2. alone, having fled from Mr. Filch
3. comes to an isolated pool so pristine that its surface had never been disturbed	3. comes to an isolated classroom with a unique, magnificent mirror
4. is tired from the hunt and the chase	4. his heart pounds from Filch's chasing him
5. is attracted to the pool	5. is attracted to the mirror
6. while he drinks, another thirst arises	6. stares hungrily at the family image
7. is overcome by the form of his image	7. is astonished by what he sees
8. thinks the image is only a shadow	8. wonders about the invisible people
9. is speechless with wonder	9. covers his mouth to prevent screaming
10. gazes at his eyes and hair	10. sees that the eyes of all the family are like his; his father's hair sticks up like his
11. blushing reddens his snowy white face	11. his reflection is white and scarred
12. does not know what he sees	12. questions what the mirror is doing, reaches behind himself to see if they are real
13. his image has no substance of its own	13. the mirror gives neither knowledge nor truth

14. his image comes with him and does not stay	14. each viewer brings the image desired which leaves when the viewer leaves
15. has no desire to eat or rest	15. cannot eat, he is restless until he returns to the mirror
16. begins to waste away	16. Ron tells Harry he looks odd; men have wasted away before the mirror
17. feels affixed to the spot	17. has one thought, to get back in front of the mirror
18. cannot get his eyes full	18. returns persistently to view the mirror; on the second night, he pushes Ron aside to see
19. speaks to the image	19. speaks to the family, tells them he will be back
20. the image makes facial responses, no words	20. the family nod, smile, but cannot talk to him
21. touches and kisses the surface of the pool	21. presses his hands on the glass, hoping to touch the family
22. feels joy and sadness	22. feels joy and sadness
23. grief saps his strength	23. becomes pale and weak
24. Ovid addresses Narcissus with a warning	24. Dumbledore addresses Harry to guide him away from dreams and back to his life

Of course, there are many differences between these two stories which share the common theme of reality and appearance, but these similarities are not to be ignored. When Harry finds the Mirror of Erised, he is tempted in much the same way as is Narcissus. Both become inordinately obsessed with the deepest longing of their hearts. In both cases, a reflective vision becomes the means by which they are attracted and tormented. And the reflection is not the real thing, but only an image. Both boys deal with a danger much greater than they can realize, and are "blind" to what looks so perfectly good. And both are in peril of losing themselves entirely in the process, even wasting away to death and losing life. And in a real sense each comes to "know" himself more fully.

The great difference between the two stories, their conclusions, is what makes this variation on the motif so striking. The boys are opposites in their personal character. Narcissus is incapable of growth or movement and separation from his deepest selfish desire, and he spirals down to death, alone. When he comes to "know himself," he discovers the bankruptcy of his psychotic self-preoccupation, and a self which cannot move forward.[2] Harry, on the other hand, is able to pull himself away from his deepest, most personal longing, to go forward in his quest, to progress in learning what his life is all about, and to find his place in the social network of a much larger world.

The two stories diverge, crucially, with the intrusion of Albus Dumbledore. He intervenes and tells Harry the truth about the mirror which many have not learned, that it can rob one of life and allow a selfish substitute to ruin its viewers. In this way, Dumbledore shows himself to be a father-substitute and a kind of Zeus-figure, who rescues the boy from his crisis. Narcissus allows no room in his soul for any other person; Harry is open to the fatherly guidance of Dumbledore. In short, he passes the test, does not become a "narcissist," but advances in coming to know himself.[3]

Chapter IV

Albus Dumbledore:
A Warlock of Many Aspects

Besides Harry Potter himself, perhaps the character who offers the most numerous parallels to classical figures is Albus Percival Wulfric Brian Dumbledore (*OP* 139), the Headmaster of Hogwarts School of Witchcraft and Wizardry. A giant of a person and a major force in the entire series, he is praised for his brilliance, considered to be the greatest of wizards, and respected by all the previous Headmasters of Hogwarts. His leadership style and skills are famous, as he has been offered the post of Minister of Magic repeatedly, and been the Chief Warlock of the Wizengamot. Not only his administrative abilities but also his courage and commitment to oppose the Dark Lord place him above all other wizards. He is the leader of the forces who oppose Voldemort and the only wizard (besides Harry) who can face the Dark Lord alone in single combat.

Dumbledore's praiseworthy ability and power are complemented by his singularly fair and generous treatment of others, especially of those who have been mistreated or mistrusted. He stands up for and gives service opportunities at Hogwarts to marginal characters who are the objects of ridicule and suspicion, such as Hagrid and Sibyll Trelawney. He alone places genuine trust in the suspicious Potions teacher, Severus Snape. When Dumbledore faces the Death Eaters on the tower, he shows concern for Draco Malfoy, who is among the assailants, and protects Harry and not himself, risking his life for others. It is quite correct, then, that such an imposing and celebrated wizard be named "Albus," which is Latin [*albus, -a, -um*] for "white with age, auspicious." Rowling mentions his habit of humming several times (*SS* 298, *HBP* 54), which is an endearing quality of the wizard, and which is a manifestation of his family name, Dumbledore, which means the humming or buzzing insect, the bumblebee.[1]

In a variety of ways, Dumbledore elicits images which have similarities to classical predecessors: a practitioner of a superior level of cultic magic, a victim of epic torment, a wise and aged advisor, a celebrated national hero, and even a type of Zeus-figure. These features give unique and timeless color to his illustrious nature and his wise and helpful generosity.

Practitioner of Extraordinarily Mysterious Magic

Although the world of magical people in these novels abounds with the mysterious and the unexpected, Dumbledore seems to possess heightened exotic powers which set him apart from and above all witches and wizards. He sometimes uses strange and mysterious languages to ponder a situation deeply, as when he examines Argus Filch's petrified cat, Mrs. Norris. He employs unintelligible utterance to make his incantations work, as when he cancels the protective spells which Voldemort placed on the seaside cave, and when he removes the defensive spells which he himself set in place around the school.[2] His Pensieve is surrounded with "runes and symbols" unfamiliar to Harry (*HBP* 198). All this adds to the astonishing aura of the Headmaster's powers. Magical incantations or languages which are alien to most people are part of the ancient mystique of divination, prophecy and discerning the unknown. And it is precisely the oddness and unnerving "otherness" that strengthens the power which curses and magical texts have on people.

In the Greek and Roman world, people were known to speak in ecstatic or indecipherable sounds or "tongues," other than normal human language, to try to influence the gods or the forces of nature. Frenzied shouts and cries and gibberish chants were known in Dionysiac worship and common cultural religion. In his correspondence with the church at Corinth, the apostle Paul had to address a problem with speaking in unknown utterances. Almost certainly the recipients of his correction were converts from their worship of Dionysus or Demeter at nearby Eleusis, who brought their indecipherable speaking with them into their new religion.

Victim of Epic Torment

In the episode where Harry and Dumbledore enter the cave at the shore to get the locket which is one of Voldemort's Horcruxes, one danger follows another and gravely threatens the Headmaster. The two cross the dark, forbidding lake in an enchanted boat, through waters which contain the animated dead (the Inferi), to the knoll in the middle of the lake, a scene quite reminiscent of Charon's crossing the river Styx in his small boat in the Underworld. Dumbledore is overcome by a spell which creates in him a dangerous, unquenchable thirst. Harry tries to give him water, but the crystal goblet with which he scoops up drinkable water empties before Dumbledore can drink it, making him beg for more water. All Harry's magic cannot save the situation. The only way to save his friend is to risk his own life once more.

The scene has parallels to stories from Greek mythology regarding the Underworld, and the torments of Tantalus and the Danaïds, who, because of the horrible evils they have committed, are mercilessly and endlessly tormented in Tartarus, the lowest regions of the Underworld. Tantalus incurs the anger of the gods, either because he tries to feed his son Pelops to the gods, or by breaking the rules of hospitality and stealing the food that keeps the gods immortal—nectar and ambrosia—or by enjoying the invitation of the gods to dine with them and later telling his friends the secrets of the gods which he has heard (*Met.* 6.172–73; *Epit.* 1.2). He is condemned to stand in a pool of water which recedes from him every time he bends to drink from it, thus making him endure insatiable thirst forever (*Met.* 4.458–59).[3] The forty-nine daughters of Danaüs (called the Danaïds) are condemned to the aggravating task of eternally trying to fill leaky jars with water, because they killed their husbands on their wedding night with knives furnished to them by their father.

In the case of Dumbledore's tortures, there is a strong element of irony. Tantalus, whose name may mean "most wretched" [Gk *Tantalos* < *talantatos*, "most wretched" (LSJ 1755)], engaged in the most outrageous offenses against the most powerful gods who had shown him kindness.[4] Dumbledore experiences his torment not because of some evil abuse of divine hospitality, but because he falls under the curses of the most evil of wizards, in his attempt to rid the world of its main source of dread, misery, and hopelessness. So, like Tantalus, he offends a most powerful force, a "god," as it were. But this time, a good man is punished for noble efforts, rather than an evil man being punished for the most immoral acts. Consequently, it is ironic that the sort of hellish and cruel torment reserved in mythology for the worst of sinners appears to be inflicted, here, on the most innocent and decent of men. This makes Dumbledore's torture all the more horrific, as it is absolutely undeserved and unjustified. These allusions to ancient thematic precedents add color and pathos to the Headmaster's torment by placing him in a set of legendary sufferers whom we already know, and by their ironic re-invention.

Philosophical Sage and Aged Advisor

The Headmaster is presented to us as an advisor, tutor, and guide, who helps others with his wisdom and manner. His language appears to be formal, sometimes stilted, philosophical and proverbial, and even cryptic. Because of Dumbledore's keen mind and verbal brilliance, Ron Weasley cannot appreciate the Headmaster's manner, and he considers him to be quite intelligent, but "mental," "cracked," and not altogether sane (*DH* 133).

He speaks in impressive truisms drawn from long experience. For example, he warns Harry that dwelling on dreams too much can cause a person to ignore the business of living one's life. He says of death that, if one understands it correctly, death should be seen as yet another great adventure. Regarding the truth, he calls it both beautiful and terrible, and holds that it ought to be treated with caution. He speaks thoughtfully about how departed loved ones can still be present with the living. He advises that one's curiosity should be used with caution. About forgiveness, he says, "people find it far easier to forgive others for being wrong than for being right" (*HBP* 96).

Albus' way of advising often appears to suggest that he is something of a Socratic philosopher. This is not to say that he is Socrates in magical disguise, but that his way of dealing with Harry's questions is strikingly similar to the way of the philosopher. The Socratic method of dialogue raises a series of questions which disprove or remove proposed ideas or solutions which are wrong, unacceptable or less likely to be adequate, so as to elicit judgments which are more acceptable or more likely accurate. Often, when Harry asks questions of the Headmaster, he does not answer them directly; rather, he leads the boy to draw his own conclusions. This method is called "maieutic" [Gk *maieutikos, -ē, -on,* "skilled in midwifery, delivery"], because it assists a people in "delivering" or "giving birth to" what they have in their minds, without the leader having to make the concluding step for them (LSJ 1072).

Dumbledore does this when Harry anxiously inquires as to how and to what extent he and Tom Riddle are similar, fearing that the Sorting Hat made a mistake by placing him in Gryffindor. The Headmaster wants Harry to figure it out for himself: "You know why that was. Think" (*CS* 333). When Harry inquires about why Voldemort returned to Hogwarts to seek employment, Dumbledore leads him to the right conclusion without simply telling him. And at King's Cross Station, Dumbledore does not answer Harry's questions about death and the future. Rather, he leads him to his own opinions, urging him with cues such as, "you already know" and "Go on" (*DH* 707ff.). These are only a few of many examples. Travis Prinzi mentions "the fourteen times that Harry asks Dumbledore a question and Dumbledore replies with some form of 'you know' and then waits for Harry to work it out" (36).[5]

Underlying much of Dumbledore's advice and wisdom is the ancient Greek principle and virtue of moderation [Gk *sōphrosynē*, "avoiding excess"; *mēden agan*, "nothing too much"; L *nē quid nimis*]. Known as the Mean or Golden Mean, this piece of wisdom representing the best way of living wisely is cited or developed by such famous writers as Aeschylus, Pindar, Aristotle, and the Roman poet Horace.

One particular episode adds another element to the characterization of the Headmaster as a counselor and sage advisor—his visit to Horace Slughorn, which we mentioned previously. The retired teacher of Potions at Hogwarts is in hiding from Voldemort and the Death Eaters. Dumbledore takes Harry along with him to urge the former teacher to return to Hogwarts and to re-enter the battle against Voldemort. The visit to re-enlist Slughorn has similarities to the mission of three leaders of the Greek armies (Odysseus, Phoenix and Ajax) to appeal to Achilles to return to battle (*Il.* 9).

Dumbledore appears to function in his visit to Slughorn the same way aged and wise Phoenix did in his appeal to Achilles. Phoenix urges Achilles, as his teacher, mentor, and father-figure, to re-enter the war because of his moral obligation.[6] He tells him a myth about Meleager, who likewise was angered and withdrew from his charge, but for the sake of saving his city, rejoined the battle. Phoenix then warns that apologies have now been made to him, and if he refuses to accept them, he will be at fault for not honoring Agamemnon's repentance. Both Achilles and Slughorn are crucial to their respective wars—the Greeks need their most excellent warrior and his resources, and Dumbledore needs true and full information about a crucial conversation Horace once had with Tom Riddle about Horcruxes. Both "warriors" are confronted with ambassadors offering different appeals. Of course, there are many differences between these two appeals, not the least of which is that Achilles refuses to concede to his friends, while Slughorn yields. Nonetheless, the similarities at least deserve consideration. On a light note, Rowling introduces some comedy to this serious scene when she has Dumbledore bide his time in the bathroom, reading Muggle magazines, so that Slughorn will have to engage Harry ... which engagement eventually convinces him to yield—not exactly a Homeric tactic.

Superlative National Hero

Some of the most formal features of Dumbledore's funeral call to mind suggestive motifs, topics, and rituals from antiquity—particularly the presence and deportment of the centaurs, and the details of the funeral ceremony. The participation of the centaurs and their behavior at this solemn ceremony introduces an element of anxiety for the reader, as their species is generally hostile to humans. They are presented as frightening, wild and dangerous, all except for the centaur named Firenze. One might wonder if they have come to the funeral to gloat, or mock. They arrive armed, which seems out of place at a funeral. Will they engage in an uncivilized display at a sacred moment? This scene begs comparison with one of the most famous scenes of classical mythology, art and literature—the Battle of the Lapiths and the Centaurs. According to literary and artistic depictions of that battle which can be traced as far back as Homer, Pirithoüs, king of the Lapiths, invites the centaurs to attend his wedding to Hippodamia (a ceremony as sacred as a funeral). During the wedding, the uncivilized centaurs become drunk and try to abduct the bride and rape the Lapith women. The ensuing battle symbolizes for Greeks the conflict between civilization (Greek culture) and barbarism. The tale becomes so famous that a sculptural depiction of it adorns the west pediment of the Temple of Zeus at Olympia (one of the seven wonders of the ancient world).

Although the centaurs of the Forbidden Forest are by nature wild and untamed creatures, hostile to humans, because of the greatness of Albus Dumbledore and the enormous respect in which the Headmaster is held by all, they participate with all the other mourners in respectful observance of his funeral. They even launch a volley of arrows to salute the fallen Headmaster, and quietly return to their forest. This dramatic variation on the tale of the ancient centaurs, a breaking of the mold which shapes the mythological story, is a significant creative accomplishment.

The Headmaster's memorial service and interment are carried out with grand ceremony and impressive ritual. At the very dramatic end of the funeral, a sudden burst of flames surrounds the body of Dumbledore, and Harry catches a glimpse of a phoenix, flying joyously into the blue sky and disappearing, leaving a white marble tomb (*HBP* 645). The pomp and ceremony and these spectacular occurrences are remarkably similar to the manner in which the Romans would deify a deceased Emperor and send his soul on to be with the gods. Legend has it that this ritual goes all the way back to the time of Romulus, Rome's founder. The historian Herodian offers an account of the funeral of Emperor Septimius Severus (from the early third century CE) in the following manner. The body is taken to the open field of the Campus Martius outside the city of Rome. Officials attend from many regions and parade around a funeral pyre on which the Emperor's body is cremated by a fire lit by the Emperor's successor. After the fire burns out, an eagle is released to transport his soul from earth to his place among the gods, and he is then honored along with those gods.[7] There are additional evidences from antiquity which testify to the "resurrection" and "deification" of a deceased heroic figure. C.R. Whittaker notes that some Roman coins depict the Emperor being carried on the back of the eagle, which clutches a lightning bolt in its talons (383, n. 3). Ancient mythographers also tell of the heroic death of Caeneus, one of the Lapiths who battles with the centaurs. Unable to wound him in battle, the animals bury him beneath an avalanche of oak trees and boulders, pressing him down to Tartarus. To their surprise, they see a bird with gold wings rising from the mound and soaring upward into the sky, the Lapith hero transformed (*Met.* 12.459–535).

Divine or Zeus-Figure

Another image which emerges from the characterization of Albus Dumbledore is that of Olympian Zeus.[8] The father of the gods is known to assist, guide, inform, sponsor, help, provide, protect and even rescue other gods and/or humans, but also to punish, harass and annihilate people. Adney remarks that the Headmaster appears to be "an all-powerful but kindlier version of the king of the gods, Zeus..." and that "like Mount Olympus, the home of the Greek gods, Hogwarts serves as a foundation for the great thinkers and sorcerers of the wizarding world" (349).

Of the various aspects of Zeus (god of the sky, heavens, storms; overseer of justice and right; administrator of order; protector of the family), his role as father is unique. He does not beget or create all the other gods, and he does not create the human race after his own image. He is more like the principal figure in a patriarchal system (Graf 1589). The image given of Zeus in the *Iliad* is a combination of the supreme head of the gods, a god of sky and weather, and "the father of a large family, who has difficulty exerting his authority, especially over his wife (Willcock 14). An epithet which is used for Zeus, in both the *Iliad* and the *Odyssey* is "father Zeus," or "Zeus, father of gods and of humans" (Gk *Zeū pater, patros Dīos; pater andrōn te theōn te*).[9] He is referred to as father, also, in the writings of Aeschylus, Aristophanes, Pindar, and Sophocles, to name a few. During the Hellenistic Age (fourth-third centuries BCE), the Stoic Cleanthes produced a "Hymn to Zeus," which refers to all humans as his "children." Among the Romans, Jupiter (the adopted and revised Zeus) is the supreme god, known as the "Greatest and Best" of all the gods (L *optimus maximus*). He is referred to as Jupiter the father of the gods in the *Aeneid* (L *pater ille deum*, 10.875), as well as in the writings of Accius, Ennius, Horace, Livy, Seneca, Statius, Lucretius and others.

The similarities between Dumbledore and Zeus are numerous. Both Albus and Zeus are represented by bird messengers—Dumbledore's phoenix (Fawkes), and Zeus's eagle. Both also have flying "personal" messengers whom they keep close at hand—the Headmaster's Hagrid and Zeus's Hermes. Both have very personal and singularly trusted associates named "Minerva." Both intrude into the lives of others when they see fit, in order to work out their own plans or to assist fate, working behind the scenes as divine forces in the lives of those people. Both are known to make important appearances, near the end of dramatic episodes, stories, myths, or tragedies, to make things right or at least to make a way forward out of impossible circumstances— known as the *deus ex māchinā*, the "god from the machine."

This is not to say that Dumbledore is Zeus in disguise as the Headmaster. He is an Olympian sort of figure, but very human as well, which makes him accessible to the reader. A good man with altruistic designs, he humbly admits his limitations and mistakes to Harry. And human weakness, with which Harry himself has to battle, finally takes its toll on Albus.

DUMBLEDORE AND HIS
REPRESENTATIVE BIRD, FAWKES

Both the Headmaster and the king of the gods are noted for their bird companions, which symbolize the character of their masters and serve them importantly on their assigned missions. Zeus is fabled for his power, bringing order to the creation, after generations of violent battles among the gods, and is appropriately represented by the powerful raptor, the eagle. The ancients had a legend that when Zeus wanted to pinpoint the exact center of the world, where the oracle of Apollo would be established, he released two eagles from the farthest points east and west, flying toward each other. They met at Delphi, where an "omphalos," or stone in the shape of a navel was placed to mark the temple of Apollo. Throughout history, the eagle has been adopted by emperors and nations to communicate ruling power. The king of the gods was said to have even transformed himself into an eagle at times.

Dumbledore is known for his genuine compassion, fairness, wisdom, and protective nature. He is represented and symbolized by the legendary phoenix, which is gifted with power in flight, and tears which can heal. This mythological gold and crimson bird originated in Phoenicia (hence, the name "phoenix"). According to ancient legend, it dies every five hundred years, to be reborn as a new bird from its own ashes. Rowling has amplified the phoenix in the figure of Fawkes, for he is incinerated and reborn more frequently than the legendary bird. He is made into a "super-mythological" bird.

The phoenix is both Dumbledore's sacred bird and his Patronus. Fawkes serves Dumbledore; but he also serves as an extension of the Headmaster, to help others. The phoenix's song is heard as a notice of help on the way for Harry and Ginny in the Chamber of Secrets, and signals the presence of invisible help at hand for Harry when he and Voldemort, enclosed in a web-dome, face each other in the Little Hangleton cemetery. And, when Dumbledore presses Harry to give details of his terrible experience in the cemetery at Little Hangleton, and Harry so dreads going back over it all, a single note from Fawkes deeply steadies the boy, "warming him, and strengthening him" (*GF* 695). The final appearance of the phoenix offers Harry hope for immortality in the midst of an unimaginable loss.

DUMBLEDORE AND HIS "HERMES," HAGRID

The first time we meet Rubeus Hagrid, he comes flying to Privet Drive on a borrowed motorcycle to deliver the infant Harry Potter to Albus Dumbledore, who sent the Gamekeeper to rescue the child from Godrick's Hollow. The boy survived Lord Voldemort's fiery curse, which killed his parents and has scarred him for life. These details are variations on a motif of hero tales. The essentials of the motif are that an august or divine figure rescues the infant hero who has been attacked or hurt, turns the child over to a supernatural assistant to take the child far away and deliver him to appointed foster-parents to be reared in safety.

The classical myth is the following. When Zeus has an affair with a human named Semele, she brags of the relationship. The god's wife, Hera, vengeful toward Semele and the child she carries, tricks the mortal into asking Zeus to reveal his full power to her (since he only shows up for her in disguise as a human, but gives his full and divine glory to his wife, Hera). When Zeus accommodates to Semele's jealous request, the powerful lightning blast consumes the woman. But Zeus rescues from her ashes the fetus of their child, Dionysus. He sews the child into his thigh until its birth, at which time he calls upon his messenger Hermes to fly the boy to Mount Nysa, where nymphs attend to the rearing of the semi-divine child who has survived the fiery assault. The famous sculpture by Praxiteles (about 330 BCE), found in the Temple of Hera at Olympia, recreates Hermes' carrying the child Dionysus. A humorous twist to the parallelism of Hermes and Hagrid here, is that Hagrid flies in swiftly on a motorcycle.[10]

Dumbledore and His "Minerva," McGonagall

Both the king of the gods and the incomparable leader of the magical world rely on very close assistants named "Minerva." And there is more similarity between the two than just a name. When we first open the pages of *The Sorcerer's Stone*, Albus and Minerva come to life for us. Dumbledore engineers the rescue of The Chosen One, and McGonagall transfigures herself from her Animagus form as a tabby cat back into her human form, to support the Headmaster's work. Professor McGonagall is more than just her title, Assistant Deputy Headmistress of Hogwarts. She is Dumbledore's right-hand colleague. When the Headmaster has to surrender his office, it is to Minerva, alone, that he surrenders his authority. She is the strongest female character at Hogwarts, and a fearless protector and guide of students in their educational journey.

In the classical tradition, the ruler of the gods, Jupiter (as Zeus was known to the Romans) relies uniquely on his closest assistant, Minerva (known as Athena to the Romans, the goddess who at her birth springs from Zeus's own head, fully armed for battle, also the goddess of wisdom). She, too, as Professor McGonagall, can transform herself in order to disguise her real identity. Zeus entrusts his protective aegis to Athena, alone, and allows her, only, to wield his thunderbolt—i.e., to exercise his authority. What is more, the Roman god Minerva was the protectress of Roman school children, very similarly to McGonagall's being the trusted matron of students at Hogwarts.

Dumbledore as Divine Father-Figure

Owing to his age and his character, Dumbledore possesses more perspective and insight into significant events and destiny than anyone else. He intrudes himself into the lives of other characters, especially Harry, in order to guide or protect them, helping to advance in their destined lives. He is Harry's most powerful (perhaps even divine) sponsor in his quest (Grimes 114). Twice, he sees to it, secretly, that Harry comes into possession of his father's Invisibility Cloak, on both occasions leaving anonymous notes with the cloak about its use. He breaks Harry's fixation on the Mirror of Erised and hints to him that although he will make the mirror inaccessible, Harry's experience with it may come in handy in the future. Eventually, Dumbledore places the Mirror of Erised as a protective charm around the Sorcerer's Stone, providing godly "prevenient" help for Harry. The Headmaster grants allowances to Harry and his friends canceling their penalties for rule-breaking. He covertly assigns Mrs. Figg the task of keeping watch over Harry while he is at the Dursleys' house. He provides private lessons in Occlumency to protect Harry from being manipulated by Voldemort. He subtly advises Hermione to use the Time-Turner, to enable her and Harry to rescue two innocents. He protects Harry and Hermione from accusations by Cornelius Fudge that they had something to do with the escape of Sirius Black. Dumbledore "predicts" to Harry that one day he may be glad that he saved Peter Pettigrew's life, again, showing his divine foresight. He expounds to Harry that even though those whom we love are deceased, they are within us, and in Harry's case, the father lives on in the son. There are many other ways in which Dumbledore has a hand in Harry's quest. These are only a few examples of his working subtly and secretly to arrange for Harry to face his destiny. Like Zeus, Dumbledore appears to nudge his human (Harry) along and to affirm his adventure as he seeks to fulfill a destiny which only Albus seems to know.

As Harry's quest advances, so does his discontent with Dumbledore's piece-meal disclosures and his increasing personal distance. In the end, Harry comes to realize that Dumbledore always knows more about the circumstances of his life and destiny than he reveals, and that the Headmaster prefers for Harry to discover things on his own, by taking chances, rather than by simply being told. His method of teaching Harry resonates with the ancient Greek proverbial wisdom cited by Aeschylus, that Zeus has ordained that all learning comes through suffering [Gk *pathei mathos*] (*Agamemnon* l.174–83). Albus employs whatever ways he thinks best, to guide Harry forward safely, for as long as he is able, as a divine father or sponsor, an Olympian force in the boy's life, and as one who knows that the chosen boy will finally learn only through his crises.

The climactic revelation which Dumbledore delivers to Harry is served up to readers in the marvelously artistic scene in the Headmaster's office after the battle at the Department of Mysteries (*OP* 820–44). Here, Harry is perhaps at his lowest point, filled with anger, rage, and emptiness over the loss of the last vestige of a "family." Dumbledore exercises "tough love," locks Harry in his office, and does not permit him to leave until he has heard the full story of his fate. He compels the belligerent boy to hear the full truth concerning his past, and gives a full explanation of how he has tried to handle both informing him and shielding him for the past five years. He delivers the most complete explanation yet concerning Harry's destiny, the trustworthiness of Severus Snape, the force of Lily Potter's self-sacrificial love, and the surpassing power of love over other magical forces. He does not allow the guilt-ridden and angry boy to leave his office until he has set things right. In this episode, Dumbledore combines his philosophical nature and his "god-like" role, counseling and rescuing Harry.

There are two parallel progressions in this scene. The first is Harry's moving through stages in this "therapy session," from rage to a kind of numb resignation to the truth about Voldemort and himself. The conversation includes Harry's delivering outbursts at the Headmaster and a tantrum in which he acts out his pain by smashing some of Albus' personal items in the office. The second progression is a depiction of the rays of daylight advancing in the office, which occurs in tandem with Harry's successive states, from first light to full sunlight. Glory and the cost of glory are contrasted by Rowling's use of the shining symbol of the founder of Gryffindor House (the sword) and the shattered wreckage Harry has caused by the anger he feels in his misery (the broken instruments). A ray of hope is held out, however, even among the debris of Harry's rage, as the sunshine causes the broken pieces to sparkle "like raindrops" (*OP* 840). Albus has "illumined" Harry as his most reliable father-figure.

The epic tradition set the pattern for the chief of the gods as a director and influencer on humans and their destinies. At the beginning of the first book of the *Iliad* (1.5), the poet extols the powerfully effective providence of Zeus with the words "and the will of Zeus was accomplished" (Lattimore 1951, 59). Also, in the *Odyssey*, after the prologue, and Athena's appeal to Zeus for Odysseus, Zeus promises to see to it that the weary traveler will make it home safe to Ithaca (*Od* 1.76–77). And in the *Aeneid*, there are three major prophecies which deal with the destiny and the future of Rome, the first of which comes in the first book, and is spoken by Jupiter (1.257–96). In all three epics, while the king of the gods cannot control the Fates, his direction sets the program for the poems. He does not micro-manage human affairs, but he is enormously commanding in the lives of humans.[11]

Dumbledore is not a Zeus-figure in the sense that he works out his will in the lives of others. But he does seem to be endowed with a super-human awareness or knowledge of Harry's fate. All that Harry comes to know about himself and his destiny, he learns from the Headmaster's words and actions. Virtually "Olympian" in power and image, Albus knows Harry's destiny but only reveals it to him in fragments and over a number of years, directing Harry's experiences to assist him to face that destiny. And his involvement always stems from his love for Harry. This is similar to the pre-plan or foreknown direction of the hero.

DUMBLEDORE AS DIVINE DELIVERER

As a beneficent Zeus-type, the Headmaster is an agent of rescue. He often appears as a surprising help from beyond, just at the fateful moment. He rescues Harry from the attack on his family in Godric's Hollow, from his

fixation on the Mirror of Erised, from Professor Quirrell, from Tom Riddle
and the basilisk,[12] from Barty Crouch, Jr. (a.k.a. "Moody"), and from the
Death Eaters in the Ministry of Magic. He also engineers a rescue of Buckbeak, Sirius and Harry.

One rescue, in particular, the saving of Ginny Weasley from the Chamber
of Secrets, has a number of points in common with the myth of the Abduction
of Persephone by the god Hades, which is told in the *Homeric Hymn to Demeter*.[13] The story is that Hades receives permission from his brother Zeus to
capture his own niece, Persephone, the daughter of Zeus and Demeter, and
to make her his bride, queen of the Underworld. He sets a trap in order to
abduct the girl. While she is out gathering flowers, Earth (in collusion with
Hades) produces a marvelous narcissus flower which sprouts a hundred blos-
soms from its stem. As she reaches for the flower, Earth opens up for Hades
to kidnap her in his chariot, and to take the unwilling and terrified girl down
to the realm of the Dead. Her disappearance drives Demeter to despair and
wrath. In her fury, the goddess of grain withholds her benefits (grain food)
from humans, persuades Zeus to intervene on her behalf and to have the girl
returned from below. The king of the gods sends his messenger god Hermes,
who wears the petasus (winged, traveling hat), to Hades with orders to allow
the girl to return to the earth above. Hades concedes to the request. But he
tricks his "bride" into eating some pomegranate (thereby making her have a
"taste" of the Underworld). The result of this seemingly innocent act is that
Persephone is not granted complete freedom from the lord of the dead. From
that moment on, she has to spend eight months of each year with her mother
in the world above, and return to Hades every year for four months, where
she reigns as Hades' queen of the dead.[14] Demeter fears that conniving Hades
may have done something evil to ruin the rescue, and interrogates the girl,
who relates all of her experiences to her mother.

The similarities between the stories are obvious: two charming, young
females of super-human pedigree (divine/magical) are enchanted by lords of
death (Hades, Tom Riddle), who employ alluring devices (the flower, a diary),
to abduct the unwilling girls to underground realms of death (the Underworld, the Chamber of Secrets), where terrible monsters dwell (the monstrous
creatures such as Cerberus, Chimaeras, the Gorgons, the Harpies, the
basilisk), and from where their captors intend them never to leave. Each is
rescued by a flying messenger (Hermes, Fawkes), who is under the command
of a kindly and powerful master (Zeus, Dumbledore). On return, they narrate
their entire experience to their mothers (Demeter/Molly Weasley). While
there are intermediary rescuing figures in these stories [Hermes, Fawkes (and
Harry)], the ultimate deliverers are Zeus and Albus Dumbledore.

In addition to these basic narrative parallels to the story of Persephone which appear to be at work in Ginny's abduction story, there are echoes of other mythological models as well, which relate to Odysseus' escape from the sorceress Circe and the adventures of Perseus. First, Ginny's immediate savior, Harry, draws the sword of Godric Gryffindor from the Sorting Hat, strikes the head of the basilisk with it, is poisoned by the fang of the snake, and is healed by the tears of Dumbledore's messenger, Fawkes, whom he has dispatched to the Chamber of Secrets. In the *Odyssey*, Odysseus learns that some of his crewmen have been transformed into pigs by the magic of the sorceress Circe, and he hastens to rescue them. He is enabled to escape her power himself only by means the antidote "moly," which is provided to him by Hermes (*Od.* 10.274ff.). The messengers of Zeus and Dumbledore supply the devices needed for rescue.

Second, an oracle decrees that Perseus, the son of Zeus and Danaë, is fated to kill his maternal grandfather, Acrisius. The fated victim seeks to thwart fate by imprisoning his daughter in a bronze chamber, then by setting her and her semi-divine child adrift on the sea in a box, which floats to Seriphus. The two are rescued and become associated with the household of Polydectes, the king of that land. Years later, when Perseus is a young man, Polydectes falls in love with Perseus' mother, Danaë, and attempts to rid himself of her son. He requires the young man to deliver to him the head of the Gorgon Medusa, which is ringed with snakes. Her power over others is that she turns to stone anyone who looks directly into her eyes. Hermes intervenes and supplies Perseus with a sword which allows him to complete his deadly task. Athena assists him by providing him with a mirror or shiny shield, so that he can see his victim indirectly and safely. He succeeds at beheading the monster. On his way home, Perseus rescues a young woman named Andromeda from a horrible death. Because a sea-monster has been ravaging his land, the girl's father, Polydectes, has tied her up by the sea as a sacrifice to the monster, following the advice of an oracle. The oracle decreed that such a sacrifice was the only thing that would satisfy Poseidon's beast and prevent further ravaging of the land. Perseus saves her by exposing the head of Medusa to the monster, turning it to stone. He falls in love with Andromeda, and marries her.[15]

Although they may already seem obvious, the similarities between Perseus and Harry are the following: both heroes live under a curse or the oracular threat of doom; both survive murderous attempts on their mothers and themselves by a powerful predecessor and enemy; both engage in mortal combat with an opponent who can turn to stone anyone who makes eye contact with it; both are unexpectedly supplied with a sword by "divine/magical" intervention of a winged messenger, in order to do the impossible and kill monstrous creatures which petrify anyone making eye-contact with them (Medusa, the basilisk); both rescue a young maiden from a monstrous serpent; and both fall in love with and eventually win the maidens whom they rescue (Andromeda, Ginny).

Dumbledore as *Deus ex Māchinā*

In ancient Greek tragedies, the plots and characters are sometimes presented in such a way as to make the play virtually grind to a halt, without the possibility of any satisfactory or reasonable resolution. A theatrical vehicle for breaking up this log-jam and moving the story forward is known as the "god from the machine" [L *deus ex māchinā*]. In this way, a playwright suddenly introduces into the play a god or hero, who resolves the crisis. This god (L *deus, -ī*) is brought onto the stage by a mechanical device similar to a crane (L *māchina, -ae*), which lowers into place the actor who is portraying the god or hero. Sometimes this feature is effective, meaningful, and didactic. Sometimes (especially in the plays of Euripides) it is just a silly way to end a play or to deride the view that when life gets too complicated, trusting in religion or the gods is senseless. The superhuman status and unquestioned authority of these divine resolvers are supposed to have a compelling effect on the characters in the drama and their audience, inviting them to consider their "supernatural" instruction.

Dumbledore's pattern of turning up toward the end of the novels, to help Harry get things in perspective and see some meaning or purpose in his trials and misfortunes, makes Albus something of a *deus ex māchinā*. In the *Sorcerer's Stone*, he arrives in the nick of time to pull Quirrell off Harry, saving him. Then he explains to Harry how his mother's love has protected him, and reveals that he is the person who gave Harry the Cloak of Invisibility. In the *Chamber of Secrets*, he saves Ginny from any blame which the Weasleys might feel toward her for being taken in by Voldemort by giving his perspective on the affair. He helps Harry get the right perspective on the similarities between Voldemort and himself, so that the novel will not end with Harry tormented by his fears. And he reveals to Lucius Malfoy the entire plot which he knows Malfoy hatched regarding Ginny Weasley and Tom Riddle's diary. Although Lucius refuses to admit that Dumbledore is correct, the function of this late synopsis is to give readers a review of the story up to that point, to pronounce Ginny Weasley innocent, and to give a "Dumbledorian" take on all the events preceding—i.e., to give readers the correct understanding of it all, as a playwright would with his *deus ex māchinā*. In the *Prisoner of Azk-*

aban, he covers for Hermione when suspicions arise about her and Harry's possible complicity in the disappearance of Buckbeak and Sirius. In the *Goblet of Fire*, he arrives at Moody's office to rescue Harry, subdue Barty Crouch, Jr., and to reveal the truth by using Veritaserum. In the *Order of the Phoenix*, he arrives at the Ministry to turn the tide of battle, to rout Voldemort and rescue Harry.

A novel twist on this device occurs in the *Half Blood Prince.* The usual *deus ex māchinā* is complemented and preceded by a touching depiction of the reversal of roles of the old man and the boy by means of a device called "ring composition." This literary and rhetorical device presents an idea, event, action or motif and later introduces repetition or echo of the original to frame the events or material enclosed. The device invites the reader or hearer to consider the difference between the initiation and the completion of the ring, and, thereby, to apply the essence of the development to one's understanding of the material or events which are framed. The ring here has to do with the strength and authority of Dumbledore as a Zeus figure undergoing a transition and transfer. It occurs in Albus' and Harry's visit to the cave by the sea. Early in the volume, when Dumbledore escorts Harry away from the Dursleys, he provides the Apparition, with Harry as his Side-Along, and he tells the boy that he will not have to worry about being attacked that night, because "you are with me" (*HBP* 57–58). Much later in the book, after their experience in the cave, Dumbledore is so weakened that he has to lean on Harry for support. Their roles have reversed, and Harry tries to encourage the Headmaster by saying that he is able to Apparate both of them. He tells the Headmaster, "Don't worry," to which the old man responds, "I am not worried, Harry … I am with you" (*HBP* 578). Dumbledore had rescued Harry, and later Harry rescues his father-figure. The boy who relied on him as his mentor comes to the fore and assumes the care-taking of his Headmaster. The ring is complete … the motif of the transfer of power and responsibility has come to a close.

It is important to notice that Rowling puts both of these declarations in the mouth of Dumbledore—the first when he tells Harry that he should not worry, and the last, when the master says he knows that he does not have to worry, because he is with Harry. He volunteers both the initiation and the closure of the ring. If it were otherwise, Dumbledore promising safety to Harry, and then Harry promising safety to Dumbledore, it could appear that Harry takes over his Headmaster's place in order to subordinate him. As Rowling presents it, Dumbledore yields leadership to the future, to the person who can solve the problem of Voldemort. This scene signals the resolution of Harry's growth and his own decline. The ring can be visualized this way:

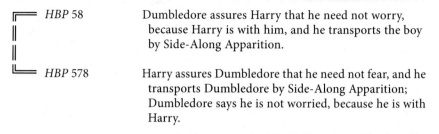

HBP 58   Dumbledore assures Harry that he need not worry, because Harry is with him, and he transports the boy by Side-Along Apparition.

HBP 578   Harry assures Dumbledore that he need not fear, and he transports Dumbledore by Side-Along Apparition; Dumbledore says he is not worried, because he is with Harry.

In this surrender of age and wisdom to youth and vision, one is reminded of the famous scene of Aeneas' escape from burning Troy. Aeneas carries on his shoulder his weak and aged father, Anchises, who is clutching the family's household gods tightly. With his other hand, Aeneas holds his young son, Iulus. Age has yielded to youth, but only after Anchises has received approving signs from the gods. Aeneas, the hero and savior of the people, has been handed the duty of leading his family and people forward to fulfill their destiny, to found what will become the Roman people and nation (*Aen.* 2.624–804).

The *Half-Blood Prince* has its own *deus ex māchinā*, of course. On the tower, with Harry hidden beneath the Invisibility Cloak and therefore invisible to Draco, the Headmaster leads Draco to confess to all the events of the year which have led up to this dramatic confrontation. The disclosure which Dumbledore engineers draws together many threads, and reveals many mysteries for the readers. Now, many things become clear to readers, things which even Harry himself had no way of figuring out.

And, of course, in the *Deathly Hallows*, we have the most significant example of the "god from the machine" resolutions: Dumbledore's time with Harry at King's Cross Station. In that scene, the widest of rings brings to a close one of the most familiar of motifs, Harry's scar. In Chapter One of *Sorcerer's Stone*, Dumbledore and Professor McGonagall detect on little Harry's forehead "a curiously shaped cut, like a bolt of lightning" (*SS* 15). This cut and the scar which it leaves affect all of Harry's life. It identifies Harry as a victimized hero. In the King's Cross Station episode, Harry feels his forehead and the scar is gone. The appearance and disappearance of this identifying scar mark the beginning and end of the motif of a curse over the life of Harry Potter.

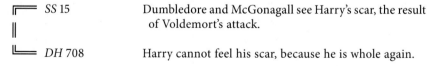

SS 15   Dumbledore and McGonagall see Harry's scar, the result of Voldemort's attack.

DH 708   Harry cannot feel his scar, because he is whole again.

One of the differences between the episodes in the *Potter* novels and classic examples of the *deus ex māchinā* is that in Greek tragedies, the device brings the play to its conclusion. In the majority of these novels, the rescuing episode is followed by Harry's conversations with Dumbledore and the necessary closing out of the stories by Harry's leaving Hogwarts and returning to his Muggle home. Nonetheless, in a way, the Headmaster's significant presence at the end of the novels is something of a *deus ex māchinā*.

Chapter V

Lord Voldemort: Evil, Even on His Best Behavior

The figure of unrelenting evil and unparalleled narcissism, Tom Riddle/ Lord Voldemort, is depicted with a variety of features drawn from literary predecessors, some of whom have much in common with the Olympian and high-profile mythological characters Cronus, Hades, Medea, Prometheus, and Zeus.

Voldemort and Cronus

After Voldemort's rejuvenation, when he and Harry duel and their wands form an arc, the Priori Incantatem spell comes into effect. The Dark Lord's victims begin to emerge from his wand in reverse order of their death, from the most recent to the first. Cedric appears, then Frank Bryce and Bertha Jorkins. This procession reminds one of a horrifying tale in the mythology surrounding the Greek god Cronus.

In the earliest times of creation, the supreme god Cronus becomes an accomplice with his own mother (Gaia) in castrating his father Uranus, and in taking over his position. Eventually, Cronus learns that he, too, is destined to be overthrown by one of his own divine offspring. In an attempt to avoid destiny, he swallows each of his own newborn children when they are delivered by their mother (Rhea). But Rhea tricks him when she delivers her last son, Zeus, by hiding the child and handing over to Cronus a stone wrapped up as a baby. Years later, when Zeus is grown, he and his grandmother (Gaia) cause Cronus to regurgitate the children whom he has swallowed. When Cronus gives up his victims, the first thing brought up is the stone which he swallowed in the place of Zeus, then the other divine children, who, together, unseat their murderous father (*Theog.* 453ff.; Evelyn-White 112–17). Voldemort has a predecessor in Cronus, in that both try to eliminate their enemies who are destined to overthrow them. And the imaginative, dramatic reappearance of their murdered victims in reverse order links their stories.

The larger motif of the story of Cronus is that of the ruler who, fearing for his power, attempts to eliminate future claimants to his position, but who, finally, is unseated by the victim(s) whom he intends to eliminate. This type of evasive action is a familiar motif in ancient mythology.[1]

Voldemort and Hades

Naturally, we should suspect that Voldemort has a lot in common with the original master of death, darkness, and cruelty, the lord of the Underworld, Hades.[2] Both are pitiless and severe, and both are associated, principally and ultimately, with death. In the preceding chapter we noted the similarities between the episode of Ginny Weasley's abduction to the Chamber of Secrets and the myth of the Abduction of Persephone. The focus there was on the role of Dumbledore as the Divine Deliverer. Here, our focus is on the role of He-Who-Must-Not-Be-Named. Voldemort (Tom Riddle) is like Hades in that these two lords of death abduct impressionable young women by putting before them attractive devices which enchant or distract them (the narcissus flower, Tom Riddle's diary). The two villains take the girls, against their will, to subterranean realms of death (the Underworld, the Chamber of Secrets) populated by vicious beasts, from which neither abductor intends his victim ever to depart. Voldemort appears to be a dead ringer for a Hades figure.

Another aspect of Voldemort's likeness to Hades is the element of fear associated with their names. It is suggestive that both Voldemort and the god Hades are figures whose names are fearfully avoided. In the *Harry Potter* novels, all but a few characters (principally Harry himself and Professor Dumbledore) refuse to speak the name of the Dark Lord. Speaking aloud the name of one's greatest enemy is an act of daring and courage. Voldemort is usually called "He-Who-Must-Not-Be-Named," "You-Know-Who," or "The Dark Lord." Mr. Ollivander fears to speak the name, and he claims that the Dark Lord's actions are "terrible ... but great" (*SS* 85). He seems to be afraid that he may incur Voldemort's wrath, so he adds a word of guarded praise ("great"). The Death Eaters are submissive to, but terrified of, their master. In the *Deathly Hallows*, the Dark Lord instigates a new curse by jinxing his name, as a means of detecting the location of any enemies who have the courage to speak it aloud.[3]

The name "Voldemort" is a combination of French words, meaning "flight from death" [Fr *vol*, "flight" + *de*, "from" + *mort*, "death"]. True to his name, Voldemort declares that his goal is "to conquer death" (*GF* 653). Ironically, while Voldemort boasts that he has outdistanced all others in gaining immortality, he has been at death's door for thirteen years, not exulting in vigorous life. Death is the point of contact between Hades and Voldemort, but with the former, it is the realm of his power, the arena in which he traffics; for the latter, it is his singular and most terrifying enemy. His followers are called "Death Eaters," who are summoned by the incantation "Morsmordre" [a playful and creative use of L *mors, mortis*, "death" + *mordēre*, "to bite" > Fr *mordre*, "to bite, eat into"].

In ancient Greek mythology the god of the Underworld, Hades, whose name means "the Invisible One," is often unnamed, or is addressed by a variety of circumlocutions and epithets, to avoid speaking directly about the final, dreaded, and inescapable power over life. His name is used for the god of the dead, for death itself and for the Underworld. He is called Aidoneus ("the unseen one"), "chthonian Zeus," "the chthonian god," "king of those below," "lord of the dead," "the god below," "Zeus of the departed," "the other Zeus," or "lord."[4] In the *Homeric Hymn to Demeter*, Hades is referred to as the "Host of Many," "the Son of Cronos, of many names" and "Ruler of Many."[5] Superstition about speaking the name of a powerful and possibly malevolent force or person lies behind both the figures and names of Hades and Voldemort.

A final connection has to do with one of Hagrid's pets, Fluffy. The Keeper of the Keys tells Harry that he has bought the three-headed hound at the Hog's Head from a "Greek chappie" (*SS* 192). He also says that he has revealed to a hooded stranger, who got him drunk, that the only way to get past the vicious guard is to put him to sleep with music. Fluffy is, clearly, a humorous reprise of Cerberus, the three-headed hound guarding Hades in Greek mythology.

Voldemort and Medea

The Dark Lord and Medea, the barbarian witch from the Caucasus, have much in common. They are experts at the practice of dark arts and curses. Cruelty, vengeance, a complete lack of feeling for others, and murder are essentials in their stories. Because she has fallen in love with Jason, Medea betrays her father, butchers her brother, concocts deadly potions, charms dragons, and causes the death of the king of Athens and his daughter by means of a gift.[6] She kills her own children to get revenge on her husband,

Jason, who has abandoned her, and tries to poison Theseus in order to eliminate him from being a legitimate heir to the throne of Aegeus, the king of Athens.[7] Ancient writers often associated her name [Gk *Mēdeia*] with the Greek verb *mēdesthai*, "to devise," according to Richard Hunter, who says that "she became the archetypal example of the scheming barbarian woman" (918). In the *Potter* novels, the most wicked, cunning and contriving practitioner of merciless evil, parallel to Medea, is the Dark Lord himself.

One episode in the *Goblet of Fire* offers an inviting study of the two villainous characters. The narration of Voldemort's revitalization, one of the darkest episodes of the novels, is reminiscent of one of the more gruesome scenes from classical mythology, the rejuvenating rituals practiced by the witch from the Caucasus, Medea. When she and Jason return to Iolcus, after he has obtained the Golden Fleece, his uncle Pelias is supposed to surrender the kingship to the brave young man who has risked life and limb to complete the task set for him. But Pelias refuses to fulfill the agreement. Jason's new bride, Medea, a barbarian witch, finds a way to get revenge. When Jason's elderly father, Aeson, is about to die, Jason asks her to use her magical arts to restore him. After much ritual prayer and preparation, she boils up a potion, slits Aeson's throat, and pours the potion into him. He becomes rejuvenated, just as vigorous as he was forty years earlier.

Shortly thereafter, she flees to the house of Pelias, telling them that she and Jason have had a falling out and that she has left him. The daughters of Pelias are persuaded that she tells the truth and they accept her into their household. While she is there, she tells them the story of her reviving Aeson, and they beg her to do the same for their aged father. Medea pretends to be reluctant, but finally relents. To prove to them that it can be done, she kills an aged ram and throws it into a boiling cauldron with the same magical ingredients she used on Aeson. Out jumps a lamb. The daughters of Pelias now are all the more eager to see their father similarly restored. Medea fills a cauldron with water and puts in magical ingredients, but these ingredients have no power to revitalize. She has each of the daughters stab their father, to relieve him of the aged blood, and to show their incredible love for the old man. Medea herself delivers the fatal cutting of his throat. Then she throws his body into the boiling cauldron. The witch then escapes, leaving Pelias mangled and boiled. She has gotten her revenge (*Met.* 7.159–349). The magic arts she uses—elaborate rituals and prayers, including those offered to the night (personified as Nox)—are skills she has learned from three-formed Hecate, who is associated with the souls of the dead and with Persephone, the queen of the Underworld.

In the Little Hangleton cemetery, Voldemort entrusts to Wormtail the performance of the magical process for his rejuvenation. The Dark Lord's scrawny and tiny body is lowered into the waters of a boiling cauldron. In preparation for the procedure, Wormtail "sp[eaks] to the night" (*GF* 641) and then adds the three ingredients (the bone of a father, the flesh of a servant, and the blood of an enemy). The "resurrected" Dark Lord emerges with new vitality.

While there are not one-to-one correlations between each of the details of the stories, the cumulative effect of the many similar elements begs for a comparison between the two and for a reading of each, informed by the other. These are some of those elements: death and life, fathers-sons, mortality-rejuvenation, cauldrons and supernaturally effective ingredients, revenge on one's enemies, the varying degrees on the sliding scale of "friends" and "enemies."

One of the striking differences between the two rejuvenation models contributes to the characterization of Voldemort as totally narcissistic and callous towards other people. When Aeson realizes he has been rejuvenated, he is astonished and recalls that this is the Aeson he knew himself to be forty years earlier. He is exuberant and grateful. When Voldemort emerges from his cauldron, he is obsessed with himself and his body, and pays no attention to his minister of deliverance, Wormtail, who "l[ies] twitching and bleeding on the ground" (*GF* 644). Of course, this is the wizard who obliterates the life of Cedric Diggory with a simple, "Kill the spare" (*GF* 638), and who, after dispatching Charity Burbage with the Avada Kedavra Curse, sickly announces to his snake, "Dinner, Nagini" (*DH* 12). We should not expect Voldemort to have any awareness of or concern for anyone other than himself.

Voldemort and Prometheus

What is generally known about the Titan Prometheus is that he "stole fire" from Zeus and was punished for it. But that is only short-hand for or a symbol of his defiance and his generous act. The larger story is found in Aeschylus' play *Prometheus Bound*, in which the Titan is pinned to a craggy rock for ten thousand years as punishment for his defying Zeus and giving aid to the human race. He has sided with humans at the expense of offending the chief of the gods, who does not have a high regard for humans. The victim's name means "forethought" [Gk *promētheus*]. By giving of himself to humanity, he provides the species with forethought. Aeschylus tells us that the god stole fire from an altar dedicated to Zeus and hid it in the hollow of a reed. But what the Titan delivers to the human race are self-understanding, insight, and all kinds of skills with which to create and to make progress. Before his giving these gifts to humans, they lived in caves, without self-awareness or reason. In the play, Prometheus spells out for the chorus exactly what the benefactions are: awareness of seasons, literature and math, agriculture, navigation, medicine and the healing arts, prophecy, omens and portents, hepatoscopy (discerning fate by examining animals' livers), augury, sacrificial rites, working with precious metals. He sums it up, "In one short sentence understand it all: every art of mankind comes from Prometheus" (*Prometheus Bound*, ll. 505–06; trans. Grene 1991, vol. 1, 83). Or, in unpoetic terms, all the advancements of humanity come from the gift of "forethought," personified in this god. Because of these many contributions to the human race, in some senses he could be said to have created humanity.[8]

In a sense, one could say that Voldemort is a kind of Prometheus. He takes forethought and labors to create a new nature, a new reality which excludes the one thing which defines all human beings, their mortality. When he is revitalized, he says that his followers know to what lengths he has gone to "guard [himself] against mortal death" (*GF* 648), and that he has "gone further than anybody along the path that leads to immortality" (*GF* 653). The principal difference between Prometheus and Voldemort, however, is that the Dark Lord does not undertake all the rigors of his creation for humanity (as does Prometheus), but only for himself. And, in the end, he wrecks himself upon his own efforts. The reason for his failure seems to be that he cannot understand or allow for the reality of love, which is the driving and creative force of humanity, and of course, the secret weapon which Harry possesses. Voldemort masters magic and even the darkest kinds of magic, but in his coldness and spiritual emptiness, he has nothing of a soul. He is incapable of self-examination or of having feelings for others. He desires absolute domination over all others, and he uses people as tools for his own self-preservation. Totally lacking in sympathy and empathy, feeling no emotions but anger and revenge, he demands the world to submit to him. He is the antithesis of a Prometheus prototype.

Voldemort and Zeus

In some ways, oddly, the person of Voldemort has a distant likeness to the most powerful deity of the Olympian gods, Zeus. The Greeks thought of Zeus as a god of weather, a sky-god, who gathers clouds and hurls thunderbolts. He is famed for using his lightning bolt to punish or kill his victims. One example is the story of the young man Phaëthon.[9] In his youth, Phaëthon brags that he is the son of the sun god, Helios (also called Apollo or Phoebus). Taunted by his peers that his claim is a lie, he asks his mother for evidence. She swears an oath before heaven that if it is not so, she should be blinded. Then she sends him to ask the god himself for first-hand confirmation. Helios takes precautions to protect the boy from the sun's full radiance, covering him with a most powerful "sunscreen." He swears by the river Styx that the story is true and that as a gift of good faith, he will grant to Phaëthon whatever he asks. The boy impulsively asks to be allowed to drive his father's chariot of the sun across the sky. Instantly, Helios realizes that he has promised too much and he tries to dissuade his son from the foolish attempt, for not even the king of the gods can accomplish that, unharmed. But Phaëthon, in his rash ambition and destructive youthful self-confidence, is unyielding. Helios tries to curb his son's impulsiveness and urges him not to attempt anything daring, but to keep to the middle course. The horses of the chariot are far beyond his ability to control and the result is disastrous as he flies too low and scorches the earth, immolating whole cities, causing the Ethiopians to become black, and drying up water courses. After appeals by Neptune and Earth to bring an end to this chaos, Jupiter hurls a lightning bolt at the helpless lad, killing him and rescuing the world (*Met.* 1.751–2.400). This is a story which to Romans teaches the wisdom of the Golden Mean, the value of moderation.[10]

When Voldemort attacks Harry with the Avada Kedavra Curse, a brilliant green flash is made and a lightning-bolt shaped scar is left on the boy's head. The mythological motif is reprised. This is not to say that Voldemort is modeled after or intended to be viewed as the god Zeus, only that the use of the thunderbolt as the weapon chosen for killing, reminiscent of its role in Greek and Roman mythology, suggests the enormously formidable power of Harry's enemy.

A second connection with Zeus has to do with Semele and Dionysus. The god, who is known for his many infidelities to his wife, Hera, seduces a woman named Semele. In jealous vengeance, Hera convinces the young woman that Zeus is not giving himself to her fully, that he is withholding himself from her. This rumor makes Semele think that perhaps he is toying with her and he is not a worthy partner, that she is not important to him. For whatever reason, she convinces him to disclose himself to her completely. The unbearable flash of lightning kills her. Though she is incinerated, the child which she carries, Dionysus, is rescued by Zeus. He sews the fetus into his thigh, and when it is born, Zeus commissions Hermes to transport the newborn to Nysa, there to be reared in safety by nymphs. In the two stories, supremely powerful figures (Zeus, Voldemort) wantonly kill victims (Semele, the Potters) with unbearable flashes of revealed power (lightning, the Avada Kedavra Curse), both employ the lightning-bolt as a visual manifestation of their destructive acts (Semele's incineration, Harry's scar),[11] and the two infants who survives (Dionysus, Harry) come to be viewed as "savior" figures.

Another classical legend links shooting stars with humans who have "divine" qualities. The shower of stars which occurs on the night of Voldemort's defeat, when Harry is an infant, is similar to the report that a comet or shooting star heralds the demise and deification of Julius Caesar (*Met.* 15.84ff.). In both cases, heavenly omens appear on the occasion of the demise of much-heralded and opposite types of figures—Caesar as a hero of the Roman Republic and Voldemort as the most powerful wizard of the Dark Side.

Finally, let us mention, again, one of the standard features of classical epics, the one-on-one duel. In the *Iliad*, Achilles battles *mano-a-mano* with Hector; in the *Aeneid*, Aeneas and Turnus duel. Twice, Voldemort does singular, pitched battle with Harry (in the cemetery at Little Hangleton and in the Great Hall). This type-scene takes the conflict from the universal level to a personal level, simplifies the conflict (hero versus villain), and lionizes the winner. In epic fashion, the battle between the Dark Side and the rest of the Wizarding world is pared down to the two essential figures—Voldemort and Harry, The Boy Who Lived and the monster who has always been out to kill him.

Chapter VI

Other Major Characters with Classical Kin

In earlier chapters, we looked at the triad of main characters in the *Harry Potter* novels—Harry, Albus Dumbledore, and Lord Voldemort. In this chapter, we turn our attention to eight more characters who are crucial to Harry's quest, and whose names, nature, and actions are significantly colored when viewed in connection with the classical antecedents to which they call attention.[1] Here, we shall encounter personalities who range from the humblest of Wizarding folk (e.g., Rubeus Hagrid), to the most beautiful woman in the world (Helen of Troy). In these characters we find themes and motifs such as love and hate, fire, snakes, kings and queens, oracles and prophecies, petrification, philosophical wisdom, stars and constellations, abduction, narcissism, parent-child dynamics, emperors, the Underworld, and dragons. The people we shall meet here call forth recollections of mythic and legendary figures such as Heracles, Apollo, Hermes, Tantalus, Persephone, Prometheus, Dionysus, Odysseus, Noctiluca, Zeus/Jupiter, the Sibyl, Medea, Icarus and Daedalus, Polyphemus the Cyclops, and Poseidon.

Draco Malfoy—Draconian Slytherin

The son of Lucius and Narcissa Malfoy, Draco, who is Harry's principal enemy among students, shows himself, by virtually all his behaviors, to be the complete opposite of Harry.[2] His personal name is a suitable title for the kind of person we find this snake-in-the-grass to be. The Greek word for "dragon," "snake," or "serpent" is *drakōn*. What parents would name their baby boy "the snake"? People such and Lucius and Narcissa would, magical people who are devoted to Lord Voldemort and the Dark Magic of their ancestral hero, Salazar Slytherin. The boy's name has a very negative significance, historically. "Draco" is the name of the first ancient Athenian to organize and codify written laws for his city (seventh century BCE). He went too far, however, and instituted laws so cruel (for example, the death penalty for laziness), that ever since his time, unbelievably oppressive measures or unimaginable and unreasonable laws have been called "draconian" (Howatson 214).

Draco and his family, too, have that excessively cruel trait. They have no tolerance for anyone except their own kind, "pure-bloods." And they are willing for non-pure-bloods to be put to death. When we meet Draco for the first time, even before we hear him speak or observe his behavior, his name warns us to beware that he is a sinister and rigidly self-righteous young wizard. His family name does not offer any positive counterbalance to our suspicions, either, as Rowling appears to create "Malfoy" from the French words "bad evil" (mal/mauvaise) and "faith" (foi), meaning "bad (or evil) faith." He and his family are the best examples in the series of people who fully trust in the wrong things, supremely evil things. And in the end, after all that the Malfoys have endured and despite the graciousness and toleration which they have received a number of times at the hands of kindlier magic folk, Draco and the Malfoys continue to be devoted to the Slytherin heritage and the Dark Side. Draco passes on this tradition by naming his own son "Scorpius," which in both Greek and Latin means "a scorpion"[Gk *skorpios*, "scorpion; the constellation Scorpio" > L *scorpius/scorpios*, "scorpion, the constellation Scorpius"]. The family never softens up.

Ginny Weasley—Persephone Rescued from Hades

The youngest of the Weasley children, Ginny is bewitched during her first year at Hogwarts by the enchanted diary of Tom Riddle. She is drawn under his control by his powers, manipulated to create mayhem in the school, abducted and imprisoned in an underground crypt by the most powerful Dark Wizard. Harry descends into the underground world of the basilisk (the Chamber of Secrets), overcomes Riddle, kills the monster with the Sword of Gryffindor which he pulls from the Sorting Hat that Fawkes delivers to him, and is healed by the tears of his winged savior.

We have mentioned twice the similarities between Ginny Weasley's bewitchment and abduction to the Chamber of Secrets, and the myth of the Abduction of Persephone, once to emphasize Dumbledore as a divine deliverer, and once to point out that in the stories, Voldemort/Tom Riddle has much in common with Hades. Ginny is similar to Persephone in that both young women are of super human nature, both come under the mesmerizing power of lords of death by means of fascinating items, both are abducted against their will to underground worlds inhabited by deadly monsters, both are kept there by masters who have no intention of releasing them, both are rescued by the will of "lordly" deliverers who send winged agents to effect the rescue, and both are returned to their grieving mothers to whom they tell their whole story. Fortunately, Ginny's rescue from Tom Riddle is complete, whereas Persephone's is seasonal.

In the episode of her abduction another similarity between Ginny and Persephone may be that they seem to be contradictory characters. There are positive and negative sides to their actions and behavior. In the *Chamber of Secrets* Ginny is her usual self, a normal and likeable young woman, until she becomes enchanted. Then she paints bloody warnings on the wall, and engages in very suspicious behaviors. She becomes a bewitched and sinister person, an aid to Tom Riddle. Persephone, the divine maiden who loves things of beauty (flowers), also becomes the queen of the dead in the Underworld. Both characters show opposing natures in their stories. Adrian Room points out that the goddess brings death (no crops) in the winter and life (rebirth of crops) in the springtime. He proposes that her name may mean "bringer of death" as the goddess of Hades [Gk *pherō*, "to bring" + *phonē*, "murder," "slaughter"] (239). Of course, both stories are about innocent young women who are forced to come under the influence and domination of supreme lords of evil and death. Their transitions naturally depict "before" and "after" states.[3]

A larger theme than diabolic trickery and heroic rescue of a fair maiden links these two stories. Both are part of a larger body of literature, the *Harry Potter* series and the *Homeric Hymn to Demeter*. The larger theme is the attempt to overcome human mortality, a life-and-death issue. Following the episode about Persephone in the *Homeric Hymn to Demeter*, the ancient poet narrates at length the story of the goddess Demeter's attempt to make immortal a young boy named Demophoön, who has been entrusted to her as his caretaker. Nightly, she puts him in a fire to burn away his mortality. One night, however, she is discovered by the child's mother, who brings an end to the ritual. Demeter then establishes a cult in her own honor, the Eleusinian Mysteries, in which those who fulfill certain sacred rituals will gain wealth, success, and most importantly, life beyond death. Robert J. Lenardon has written, "This is a hymn permeated by emotional longings and religious allegories about death and rebirth, resurrection, and salvation" (Morford 348).[4]

Many of the classical parallels to and predecessors of elements in this series have their significance precisely at the point of that particular theme. For example, Heracles achieves his famous record of victory in unbelievable contests because his step-mother, Hera, attempts to kill him all during his life. Medea, like Voldemort, seeks to trick death and restore youth to aging victims with her magical powers. Orpheus journeys to the Underworld to retrieve his beloved Eurydice from Hades and Persephone. Dionysus Zagreus is retrieved from death and the Underworld to renewed life.

Another item to notice is the use of or avoidance of certain names. Both of the captors in these stories are such terrifying beings that people are afraid to speak their names, lest they incur some punishment. Only Harry and Professor Dumbledore dare to speak the Dark Lord's name without fear, others referring to him as "He-Who-Must-Not-Be-Named." In classical mythology, Hades, whose name means "the Unseen," was referred to by many names, one of which is "the Son of Cronus, of many names." Both, however, are referred to as "Lord." Touching on this briefly, at this point, is worthwhile, for in the *Homeric Hymn to Demeter*, the goddess is referred to with Greek names such as Demeter ("earth-mother," "grain-mother"), Doso ("I shall give/provide"), Maia ("good mother") and Deo (a substitute for "Demeter").

The towering figures of Voldemort and Dumbledore are opposing points of orientation in the theme of life and death. Voldemort's sole passion is to become immortal, to escape death. When revitalized, he tells his Death Eaters that he has taken steps to keep from dying and claims that he has "gone further than anybody along the path that leads to immortality" (*GF* 653). Dumbledore, on the other hand shows great placidity about death. He calms Harry's anxiety about the impending death of Nicolas and Perenelle Flamel by saying, "to the well-organized mind, death is but the next great adventure" (*SS* 297). In the last advice or personal support which he gives to Harry, he shows himself to be the personification of peace about death.

The conquest of death has been one of the powerful and persistent topics of much of western tradition. Rowling often works this theme along with the concept of the presence of the dead in the hearts and lives of those who survive and who move ahead to deal with their loss. She has said that the theme of the entire *Harry Potter* series is found in the scripture quotation on Harry's parents' grave stone: "the last enemy that shall be destroyed is death."[5]

In this context, we should consider the significance of her quotation from Aeschylus in the frontispiece of *Deathly Hallows*. The passage comes from *The Libation Bearers* (ll. 466–78), the second play in the set of three plays known as the *Oresteia* (*Agamemnon, The Libation Bearers, The Eumenides*), first performed in Athens in 458 BCE. The mythic story line behind the plays includes a lengthy series of misfortunes which fall upon the "House of Atreus." For generations, the house had been plagued by tragedies because of disrespect for the gods, hubris, betrayal, murder, the heinous act of killing one's nephews and serving their cooked flesh to their father as retribution for a brother's sins, and assassination, to name only a few of the impious acts.

The *Oresteia* is concerned with the tragedies in the House of Atreus associated with Agamemnon, the king of Mycenae. At the time of the Trojan War (twelfth century BCE), when the Greek armies were about to set sail for Troy, the winds were contrary and the seas were turbulent. A prophet claimed that the goddess Artemis was angry because the commander-in-chief, Agamemnon, had offended her. A human sacrifice was needed. Agamemnon summoned his daughter, Iphigeneia, to come to Aulis, under the ruse that she would become the bride of Achilles. When she arrived, she was sacrificed to Artemis. The weather conditions improved. The Greeks sailed away. And they returned ten years later, after their victory in Troy. During all this time, Agamemnon's wife, Clytemnestra, seethed over his betrayal and the murder of their daughter.

The plays of Aeschylus pick up the story at this point. During the king's absence, his wife Clytemnestra took a lover and co-regent named Aegisthus, with whom she hatched a plot to murder the king on his return. She slaughtered Agamemnon at an unguarded moment, when he was defenseless. The remaining two children of the royal couple, Orestes and Electra, come to the fore in the story at this point. Young Orestes had been sent away from Mycenae to keep him out of the way of the queen and her lover. After Agamemnon's death, the young man returned home and conspired with his sister to take blood vengeance on their mother and Aegisthus, a deed which he was compelled to carry out by order of Apollo. Orestes had to kill something of himself, his own mother, to save the house of Atreus and the people of Mycenae. Although the act of matricide had divine sanction, the Furies, or avenging spirits of the dead, besieged Orestes relentlessly. Eventually, however, he was exonerated for the murder by the approval of Athena.

The passage which Rowling quotes comes from the chorus, as they supplicate the gods to send some children from within the royal house to remove the malady from which it suffers. James Hogan points out that the metaphor which Aeschylus used is a medical image. The dynasty of Agamemnon is portrayed as an ailing person, suffering incurably from a hereditary pain which has fallen on the house by disastrous fate. The chorus here appeals for a medical cure from within the household (124).

Perhaps the most immediate point of contact between Orestes and Harry Potter is the two youths as saviors of their people. Both young men are sons who are under divine or supernatural constraint (Apollo's order, Harry's prophecy) to avenge the murders of their fathers. Both are the only male offspring of their houses (the family of Agamemnon, the Potter family) who can remedy the cause of the plague on their people (Clytemnestra, Voldemort). Each has to assume his commission by a life-or-death act. They are constrained to bring about the death of something of themselves (Orestes' own mother, the part of Voldemort which resides in Harry). Both anguish over their task (Orestes prays to the gods and his father's ghost for their aid, Harry communicates with deceased parents and family-figures for help) (Adney 260–61).

Adney and Hassel see another connection between Orestes and *Harry Potter* in the motif of the sins of the fathers being visited on the heads of their children. The tragic cycle of the dynasty of Agamemnon is replayed in the families of Lucius Malfoy and Marvolo Gaunt. Because Lucius Malfoy failed to fulfill the murderous task which Voldemort had assigned to him, his son Draco was dragged into service to complete the job. Marvolo Gaunt's "pure-blood fanaticism" poisoned his children Morfin and Merope, leading to the birth of the Dark Lord and the meaningless deaths of his own children (325).[6]

There is more here, however, than the detection of a point-by-point parallel between Orestes and Harry. One wonders why, in only one volume, Rowling embroiders her work with a gem of an epigraph like this one. We latch onto proverbs, imagery, characters, and examples which speak to something inside of us, which draw from us a "Yes! That's it!" And when we seize these paradigms, it is because something deep inside us experiences a sympathetic surge, as if our ideas, views, or efforts and those of the well-turned phrase are in tune with each other. What makes examples from classics so precious is that in them we find ourselves in tune with the souls and experiences of people of the ages. And what Rowling says about life and death is the rediscovery of a human treasure which belongs to the ages, but which is now re-set for a new time and a new age. It is the inspiration of the Muses all over again, for the Muses are the daughters of Zeus and Mnemosyne, "Memory."

Hermione Granger—Helen of Troy, Prometheus, Medusan Victim

Hermione is the bookish and brilliant female friend of Harry Potter and Ron Weasley, whom Draco Malfoy calls a "Mudblood" (a magical person born to "Muggles," i.e., non-magical parents). Her special talent is producing portable, waterproof fire on demand. She is a perfectionist, a model student, phenomenal at insightful observation and thinking ahead, the only magical person in the series to initiate and complete time travel and be in two places at the same time, and a major source of discovery and information for Harry, Ron and the readers throughout the series. Perhaps more than any other of the main figures in the series, she exhibits noteworthy change or development in her character. At first, she seems to be a very up-tight and strict moralist, a corrector of other students. Even in her first year, though, she begins to relax her hard and fast rules-oriented ethic and saves Harry and Ron from possible expulsion from Hogwarts by falsely taking the blame for their being caught in the bathroom where the troll is, against orders from the Headmaster. The next year, she devises a deceptive plot to ferret out information from fellow students by using Polyjuice Potion, in a major disregard for numerous Hogwarts rules. In her fourth year, her genuine sense of mercy for others who suffer leads her to launch a program to improve the situation of poorly-treated elves. In her transformation, we see her growing up, not simply becoming educated or "schooled."

In several ways, Ms. Granger calls to mind elements of the legend of Helen of Troy, who is said to have been the most beautiful woman in the world. First of all, there is her name, "Hermione." That is the name of the daughter of Helen and her husband Menelaus, king of ancient Sparta.[7] Helen and her daughter have something in common with Hermione Granger—a mixed heritage. Since Helen is semi-divine (her father is the god Zeus, but her mother is the human Leda), her daughter Hermione is, at best, one-fourth divine, hardly a pure-pedigree deity. Hermione Granger's parents are both Muggles, making her a magical person without pure magical pedigree. She is the only person who is badgered frequently for not being a pure-blood witch. The irony of that criticism is that her name instantly summons up recollections of (1) the daughter of the most beautiful woman in the ancient world, and (2) the child of one of the greatest of ancient Greek rulers and warriors, and even lineage with the king of the gods. The ancient Hermione is heir to some of the most remarkable genes in the whole world—pretty amazing stock. And Ms. Granger is almost certainly the most talented student at Hogwarts, far more noble than Draco Malfoy who castigates her for her genes. Both Hermiones are extra-special, even though they are from non-pure bloodlines.

A second connection with the Hermione-Helen legacy of classical tradition has to do with the phenomenon of being two places at once. Helen of antiquity has always been the object of widely opposite opinions. Some people see her as a vile and wanton woman who abandons her husband, daughter, throne and kingdom for a fling with a Trojan foreigner, and whose behavior precipitates the ten-year long Trojan War. Others, however, view her as a victim of Aphrodite, the goddess of love. The goddess promised to give Helen to Paris, the Trojan prince, as a prize for judging Aphrodite to be the "fairest" in a beauty contest between Hera, Athena and herself. From this more forgiving perspective (made popular by the poet Stesichorus in his *Palinode*), an innocent and captive Helen goes to Egypt on her way to Troy. She stays there in Egypt for the entire duration of the Trojan War, while a phantom of her goes on to Troy. Euripides also tells this version, though as he presents it, Zeus creates an image of Helen which is taken to Troy while the real Helen stays in Egypt (*Helen*, 1275ff.).[8] So, in the classical tradition, we have Helen in two places at the same time by the intervention of the gods. Hermione Granger, too, is able to be in two places at the same time, by means of the Time-Turner which Professor McGonagall has given her.[9]

From a different angle of vision, several features of Hermione appear to justify viewing her as a female Prometheus: her talent with portable fire, her courageous stand on behalf of a whole race of beings who are considered worthless, and her capacity for being always mentally quick to draw conclusions and to think ahead of the present moment. Her skill with producing blue fire which she can transport in a jam jar keeps HH&R warm outside on a bitterly cold day. With this talent, she attempts to break a curse on Harry's broom by setting Snape's gown on fire. When the three fall into the Devil's Snare, she produces the flames from which the plant recoils, releasing Harry and Ron. And her transportable, waterproof fire makes it possible for her to brew the Polyjuice Potion in the girls' bathroom.

In mythology, the Greek Titan Prometheus steals fire from Zeus and carries it as a gift to humanity in a lowly fennel stalk. In the Greek story, the irony is that the element which is so precious for warmth, industry, arts and so much more, is hidden in material which surely would burn, and the fire would be lost ("treasure in an earthen vessel," so to speak). The broader theme at work in both stories of Prometheus and Hermione is "strength concealed in weakness," a regular topic in quest stories. In Hermione's actions, the valuable commodity which is placed in a throwaway item, a jam jar (which would extinguish the fire, except in magic, where physics does not apply, apparently), is not so much ironic as it is a humorous variant on a motif which is as old as mythology.[10]

Hermione also takes the initiative to lead a campaign to improve the welfare of elves. As an activist, not just a bleeding heart sympathizer, she organizes the Society for the Promotion of Elfish Welfare. No one seems to care about the well-being of these creatures, not even tender-hearted Hagrid. In this way, too, she emulates Prometheus. The larger context of the Titan's stealing fire for humanity is his siding with the human race against the will of Zeus himself, who places no value on the race of humans. In Aeschylus' play, *Prometheus Bound*, the god elaborates on all he has given humanity (i.e., what the "gift of fire" really is): self-awareness, intelligence, literature, agriculture, mathematics, navigation, medicine, prophecy, religious life, metallurgy, and more (ll. 436ff.). As this "creator" god gives to insensitive and ignorant humans a transformed level of being, in defiance of the wishes of the supreme god, Hermione takes on the project of uplifting the quality of life of the lowest creatures on the magical world's social ladder, with no help from friends or power figures.

This leads us to the most consistently evident "Promethean" of Hermione's traits, her thinking ahead, her foresight. As we note earlier, the name "Prometheus" in Greek means "forethought"—that is, every art of mankind comes from forethought. While Harry is very clever and ingenious at times, it is Hermione who most often thinks ahead and takes actions in advance. She hits upon a way for the three to sneak into the Slytherin common room and find out more about the previous opening of the Chamber of Secrets and the Heir of Slytherin—by using a magical potion which can transform them into the shape of other people. When HH&R have to escape the Death Eaters who burst in on Bill and Fleur's wedding, she does not have time to prepare for their forced departure, for the Death Eaters appear immediately after Kingsley's Patronus warns them. But, she has planned ahead of time, packing in her small, beaded bag everything they need: the Invisibility Cloak, their change of clothing, even Muggle money. She thinks ahead to remove the portrait of Phineas Nigellus from the wall so that he cannot tell Snape about any activities at Number Twelve Grimmauld Place. Able to hatch a plot instantly, in order to make a way out of a tight spot, she pronounces the incantation "Geminio," and reproduces a copy of a locket which Dolores Umbridge is wearing, so that the witch will not miss it when the three take the real one from her. With each of the Disapparitions of HH&R, Hermione has thought ahead about where to go to be safe, and has brought provisions for their refuge. She Disapparates them to the forest where the Quidditch World Cup is held and she begins to cast protective spells all about it. Thinking quickly and looking ahead, she allows Harry to be seen by the Death Eaters just before they Apparate from Xenophilius Lovegood's house, thereby rescuing them and protecting both Xenophilius and Ron's family. With almost instant reflexes, she takes action to save Harry by jinxing his face so that he will not be recognizable. Although Harry Potter himself is clever and ingenious at times, it is Hermione who most often grasps the larger situation, comprehends most instantly what must be done, and takes action in advance.

Earlier, we noted that Harry is the best when it comes to drawing proper conclusions from clues. This is not to take anything away from brilliant Hermione. She is very intellectual, quick of mind, disciplined in finding information, much more bookish and, at times, more observant than Harry. One might grant her, therefore, the sole right to be thought of as the "brains" of the HHR outfit. But, Harry outstrips everyone at synthesizing seemingly unrelated matters, deducing from hints or clues, seeing the bigger picture. In retrospect, it seems that Hermione's smart fore-thinking acts are examples of her traits of care-taking and safe-keeping, which reflect a conservative and responsive mentality. Harry's "Odyssean" deductions are more adventurous, risky, and generally relate to the advancement of the plot of the stories. In short, he functions with a hero's instinct, but she with brilliant caution.

We should note another classical element which surfaces in association with Hermione, her being turned to stone. The famous story of the Gorgon named Medusa has set the precedent for this motif. Anyone who makes eye contact with Medusa dies immediately by being petrified. The Gorgon is killed only by the cunning hero Perseus, who is aided by the gods. In order to get close enough to her, he wears the Cap of Invisibility and views only her reflection in his shield. Hermione appears to use the tactic of Perseus, in that she sees the basilisk only as a reflection in a hand-held mirror. The model provided by the story of Perseus is altered, however, in that she is turned to stone, but she is eventually revived from petrification by magical means.

Luna Lovegood—Prophetess, Goddess of Light

Ms. Lovegood is the daughter of Xenophilius Lovegood, the editor of *The Quibbler*, a magazine for the Wizarding public which focuses on news items and issues which are not in the mainstream of journalism. He publishes opinions which are considered by some wizards to be bizarre. Luna's fellow students consider Luna to be a crazy person or a "lunatic" (someone out of their mind and under the influence of the moon), because of her peculiar ways of dressing, speaking, and thinking. Ginny Weasley calls her "Loony" Lovegood, as an unkind play on her name. Since she is much like her father, Luna speaks about things as normal and unquestioned which others see as preposterous and unreal—the "Blibbering Humdinger," the "Crumpled-Horned Snorkack," "nargles," "heliopaths," and "Wrackspurt siphons." While all magical people are probably eccentric to some extent, Luna is unique among the Wizarding people of the world of Harry Potter.

At the same time, however, she possesses abilities or traits which link her to Harry and to Professor Trelawney. For example, when the upper-level students enter their vehicles at the train station to be transported to Hogwarts at the beginning of Harry's fifth year, Luna and Harry are the only ones who can see the winged, dragon-like thestrals which draw the carriages. They can see the creatures, because they both have seen death, whereas the other students have not. Also, of all the students at Hogwarts, Harry and Luna are often misunderstood and viewed by other students as being too eccentric or dangerous. Luna is similar to Professor Trelawney, in that while both witches appear to be very unorthodox in their social manners, they possess inner, hidden gifts of insight or foresight which make them especially helpful to others.

Luna's name fits her in many ways, evoking images of a goddess of light and clarity, a prophetess, priestess, or oracle. From the most ancient periods, the Romans worshiped the moon goddess, Luna [L *Lūna, -ae,* "moon, goddess of the moon, light of the moon"], whose name is related to *lūx,* "light, source of light" and *lūmen,* "light, radiance" (OLD 1050, 1053). In the goddess' temple, which was lighted every night on the Palatine Hill, she was called "Noctiluca" [L *Noctilūca, -ae*], or "she who shines in the night" (Bell 1991, 284).

In the Greek and Roman world, people would seek out and receive prophetic and oracular wisdom from a female prophetess-priestess such as the Pythia of Apollo at Delphi or the many Sibyls such as the Sibyl at Cumae, who spoke under the inspiration of Apollo. These women helped inquirers learn about fate, the future, and things beyond human knowledge. They would deliver their oracles and prophecies in mysterious ways and in unintelligible language (which, of course, enhanced the "divine" or "mystical" element of the communication). At Delphi, the priestess sat on a tripod and went into a trance, because of some kind of divine visitation or because she inhaled natural hallucinogens which came from a fissure in the earth beneath her tripod. During her trance, she would utter strange sounds, which her priests then translated into enigmatic and poetic Greek.

In her behaviors and persona, Luna Lovegood resembles the Roman luminary, or these goddess-priestess-prophetess figures, ironically producing light in obscurity or offering unique and enigmatic insight. Her strange speech, her gift of divination, her bizarre perspective on reality, and her puzzling answers seem to align her with these ancient seers. For example, the chiming, alliterative proverb that she speaks, which we learn is Rowena Ravenclaw's mantra, and which grows more significant with each repetition ("Wit beyond measure is man's greatest treasure") signals Luna as a unique source of wisdom. And when the students must find a way to get to the Ministry in order to rescue Sirius, she alone sees clearly and simply what is unthought-of and physically invisible to all the others, except to Harry—that they should travel by flying on the thestrals.[11] While Harry wracks his brain to figure out what item associated with Rowena Ravenclaw he is supposed to be trying to find, Luna, in a casual way, offers a suggestion which solves the puzzle. It is Rowena's diadem. And when the personified eagle-shaped knocker on the Ravenclaw common room door gives the enigmatic challenging question, "Which came first, the phoenix or the flame?" and she answers "a circle has no beginning" (*DH* 587), the door praises her reasoning and opens for her and Harry.

Probably the most telling act of Luna's which compels us to see her as an oracular source is when she helps Harry deal with Sirius' death and his struggle with his feelings of guilt and loss. He seeks guidance from the wisest living person he knows (Albus Dumbledore) and from one of the ghosts, who ought to know about life after death (Nearly Headless Nick). But neither of them can give him any real help. Ironically, the most eccentric student at Hogwarts turns out to be a source of wisdom for Harry about things feared and unknowable ... Loony Lovegood. In Harry's chance meeting with her in the hall, their conversation begins with her telling him she has lost almost all the things she owns, because other students have taken them as a cruelty to her. Harry's emptiness at the loss of the only "family member" he has known, and his desire to be away from everyone else, causes him to understand and pity Luna. She surprises him with her confidence about the return of her belongings, which sets up readers for the more crucial part of their conversation, dealing with hope on a larger scale. Like the ancient Sibyls, who did not soften their words to pacify even a desperate inquirer, Luna asks with childish directness, "That man the Death Eaters killed was your godfather, wasn't he?" (*OP* 863). No euphemisms or polite circumlocutions ... just the truth. The bond between them is set when Harry learns that she has seen her own mother die. Luna expresses her confidence that she will see her mother again and offers Harry something hopeful to which he can cling (that they both heard the voices beyond the veil there on the dais in the Department of Mysteries). Luna, alone, gives him information and hope which helps to reduce the burden of grief Harry carries. As the prophetesses or seers often helped ancient people to make some sense out of tragedy or crisis and to gain some kind of stability in the face of the unknown, Luna Lovegood becomes a source of light for Harry in his darkness, giving him direction in his search for understanding which reduces, a bit, the burden of grief he carries, and which allows him to move forward emotionally after his tragic loss. The strange girl serves as a type of "Noctiluca" for Harry.

Minerva McGonagall—Athena/Minerva Revisited

Ms. McGonagall is Professor of Transfiguration and Assistant Deputy Headmistress of Hogwarts. She is the Headmaster's right-hand assistant, an Animagus, a stern witch with a nurturing and supportive nature for students, especially for Harry Potter. With this powerful female administrator and teacher, we encounter a character whose name and role relate clearly and powerfully to her very specific ancient predecessor, "Minerva," the Roman/Italian goddess of wisdom and learning, creative arts and war, protector of school children, and uniquely trusted daughter of Jupiter. Both the professor and the goddess (who is identified with the Greek goddess Athena), are "shape-shifters," who can transform themselves into another form. The goddess has a much wider range of alternate forms, however, than the Animagus professor, whose alternate form is that of a tabby cat. Athena can assume the appearance of Odysseus' friend Mentor (*Od.* 2.268, 22.205ff., e.g.), the daughter of Dymas (*Od.* 6.22), a young girl (*Od.* 7.18ff.), a shepherd (*Od.* 13.221ff.), a tall and beautiful woman (*Od.* 13.287ff.), or an old woman (*Met.* 6.42ff.), and even a sparrow (*Od.* 22.239).

McGonagall's relationship to Dumbledore has parallels to the goddess' relationship with her father, Zeus (Jupiter). Athena is uniquely close to and trusted by the king of the gods. The ancient Greeks celebrated her as the protector of their city and culture, and venerated her for the wisdom which was hers by birthright. She was conceived by Metis, whose name means "thought, counsel," and born directly from the head (or mind) of her father Zeus, who brings order to the world. Of all the Olympian gods, Athena is the one whom Zeus allows to wear his protective aegis (a goat-skin or skin-covered shield), and she is the only deity ever allowed to wield his thunderbolt (i.e., act in his place and exercise his unique authority).[12] Similarly, McGonagall is portrayed as a wise headmistress and teacher much committed to the welfare of Hogwarts and its students, and to the good life of the Wizarding world. And it is to her alone that Albus Dumbledore, perhaps the most powerful leader in the magical world, and the most honorable defender of the good in the magical world, entrusts his authority in his absence.

Minerva's relationship to Harry Potter has parallels to Athena's relationship with Odysseus, as his protector and helper. At Hogwarts, when Harry sometimes breaks the rules, she is stern and magisterial in her manner, but flexible and temperate in her punishments. She takes steps to develop his skills at flying and playing Quidditch, comes to his aid and rescues him several times, promotes him to the Quidditch team as Seeker even during his first year, and gives him a very personal gift, a Nimbus Two Thousand broom for his sport. Professor McGonagall gives Harry the gift of knowledge about his father, that he was an excellent Quidditch player. This not only enhances his knowledge of his family; it also gives him another way of relating to them— by knowing that his skills are inherited. She is an exact opposite mother-figure to Harry than his relative, Petunia Dursley. Petunia never offers to tell him anything about his father, his family, or himself, except the lie that his parents died in an automobile crash. She tries to extinguish any dreams or ambitions Harry has, making his life miserable, even to the point of dyeing Dudley's hand-me-down clothes with grey dye. She removes any color or evidence of life from Harry's drab existence.

During Odysseus' journey home to Ithaca after the Trojan War, he suffers the wrath of the sea god Poseidon (because he has blinded the Cyclops Polyphemus, Poseidon's son). Fortunately for Odysseus, he has a divine helper in Athena. She came to his aid during the Trojan War. And on his long odyssey homeward, when he makes it to the land of the Phaeacians, the goddess becomes active again, to help him secure the cooperation of the Phaeacians in completing his homeward pilgrimage, and to begin plans for retaking his kingdom. When he arrives home, in Ithaca, after twenty years' absence, he has to rid his palace of more than a hundred suitors who daily occupy his home in an attempt to get the queen, Penelope, to choose one of them to replace the long-absent king. Athena plots out the strategy to follow. She taps him with her wand and transforms him into a haggard, unrecognizable old beggar, so that he can get into the palace undetected (*Od.* 13.429ff.). How very like Minerva McGonagall, the Professor of Transfiguration!

Ron Weasley—Shadow-Hero in His Own Right

Ronald Bilius Weasley is Harry's dearest friend and the closest thing to a brother that Harry ever has. The bond between the two boys is such that when something that Harry would greatly miss is taken from him, to be rescued from the lake as the Second Task of the Triwizard Tournament, Dobby tells Harry that Ron Weasley is "the thing Harry Potter will miss most ..." (*GF* 491). Ron, however, is not the main character in the series, but a secondary figure to the hero. He is the youngest of Arthur and Molly Weasley's six sons, the other five of whom are much smarter and more successful than he. His young sister has greater magical ability than he possesses. His family is so large that he feels himself to be an unimportant member of a group, with no sense of individual worth. He struggles within the shadow of his family's poverty. They are so poor that all he receives from their "bounty" are hand-me-down clothes, dowdy hand-made sweaters, a second-hand wand which had belonged to his older brother Charlie Weasley, for a pet, an old rat named "Scabbers," and a disgusting antique of a dress robe to wear to the Yule Ball. He is not the equal of Hermione in intellect, drive or native talent. And, of course, he is overshadowed by the principal hero of the series, Harry.

Perhaps the differences between the two boys accentuate the uniqueness of their partnership. Ron comes from a pure-blood magical family, grows up in the Wizarding world, having little real knowledge of the Muggle world, and by most measurements is a very common person. When he was a child of three, his brother Fred taunted him by turning his teddy bear into a spider. Consequently, he has an intense fear of spiders. Like many adolescent boys, he roots for a favorite sports team, the Chudley Cannons. He collects frog cards, plays wizard chess, brags about the acceleration of his broom. At first, he performs very poorly at Quidditch, though he does undergo remarkable development in the sport. And, in a very boyish gesture, when he chooses a birthday gift for Harry, it is a book about how to "make time" with girls (*Twelve Fail-Safe Ways to Charm Witches*). Even after years of maturing, when he comes into possession of Dumbledore's Deluminator, which is the instrument that will enable him to do super-human things, he childishly toys with it for three days, which greatly annoys Hermione.

Ron is so insecure and so plagued by the taunts which his family's poverty invites, that when the Slytherins invent a chant to demean him and dispirit the Gryffindor Quidditch team ("Weasley is Our King," *OP* 404), and when the Horcrux in the locket taunts him as being a nothing, the least loved by his mother and by Hermione, the torturing challenges hit their mark in the lad. Not depicted as a high intellect, he does not appreciate Dumbledore's often esoteric language and ideas, and he is usually unimaginative when called upon to work out strategies himself. For example, when HH&R ponder ways for Harry to survive the Second Task, Ron's suggestion is stunningly dull: "Harry, just go down to the lake tomorrow, right, stick your head in, yell at the merpeople to give back whatever they've nicked, and see if they chuck it out. Best you can do, mate" (*GF* 486).

Harry, on the other hand, is a half-blood wizard, reared with no awareness of the magical world. Yet, even before he has any idea that he is a wizard, strange and magical things happen to him. Demeaned and abused by all three members of his adoptive Muggle family, somehow he develops uncommon resilience and possesses super abilities of which even he is unaware. When he is finally introduced to the Wizarding world, he discovers that he is universally famous, for reasons he does not know. People whom he has never seen consider him to be The Boy Who Lived, The Chosen One. He possesses a psychic-existential quality (the capacity to get inside the mind of the Dark Lord), special skills (such as Parseltongue), and a personality trait (impulsive drive), which are uniquely his own, and which make him vastly different from his dear friend, Ron Weasley.

But the differences are not all that are to be considered. Although Ron lives in the shadow of others, he is a shadow-hero-in-the making, on his own "quest." He has passions and dreams. When he looks into the Mirror of Erised, which is much the same as looking into his own heart, he does not see the image of a loser or a dull person. He sees himself as he wants to be— an individual, not a faceless member of a crowd, a winner, Head Boy, captain of the Quidditch team, holding the Quidditch cup. He sees all this because it is what he longs for, to become the opposite of what he has come to think he is. In his deepest desires, he wants to be a winner, a remarkable individual, a recognized and heralded leader. And his deepest desires are goals he begins to achieve. In time, he becomes a Prefect and the Gryffindor team's Keeper.

While Ron often appears to be a bit dull, on occasion he exhibits a surprising practicality. For example, he is the first of his triad actually to put into practice the levitation charm (Wingardium Leviosa). But he does it in an emergency, to disarm the troll in the bathroom, not as an in-class exercise of floating feathers. And, when HH&R enter the chamber which is filled with hundreds of shining, winged keys, Ron is the one who narrows down the task of picking out the key which will open the huge wooden door by noticing that the right key would be an old-fashioned one like the handle on the door. His practicality leads him to find a way for himself and Harry to get to Hogwarts when they are shut out of Platform Nine and Three-Quarters—the enchanted, flying Ford Anglia.

More significantly for Ron's own journey as a shadow-hero, he shows increasing bravery, selflessness and courage in his companionship with Harry. He sacrifices himself at wizard chess, so that Harry can win the game and proceed to the Sorcerer's Stone. When Harry dives into the forest pool to retrieve the Sword of Gryffindor, he becomes strangled by the chain of the deadly Horcrux-locket. Ron dives into the pool and saves him. Here, Rowling repeatedly uses language which she usually reserves for Harry, terms of "saving." One of the effects of this episode is to depict both young men as heroes, saviors: Harry saves Ron from the Black Lake, and Ron saves Harry from the frozen forest pool. In this episode, Ron summons the courage to destroy a Horcrux, a part of the very soul of Voldemort. He never becomes so fearless as to be able to speak the Dark Lord's name. But in destroying the locket which plays on his deepest fears and his sense of inadequacy, he conquers his internal enemies and displays his advancement in accomplishing his own "quest."

A major development in Ron's heroic progress is brilliantly linked to the advancement of his relationship with Hermione. When she does not know how the two can destroy the cup of Hufflepuff, he comes up with the idea of using the deadly power of the basilisk's fang. To get a fang, they must open the Chamber of Secrets by speaking Parseltongue (which Ron had heard Harry using to open the locket Horcrux). This involves a number of motifs of the hero's journey, including a visit to the Underworld. In telling Harry about the success of this plan, Hermione gushes that Ron's idea was "absolutely brilliant," and that he was "amazing," which Harry echoes with "Genius!" (*DH* 622–23). The courage and maturity of this shadow-hero comes to the fore, also, with respect to the House-Elves. Although Ron has shown no compassion or concern for these oppressed magical folk (i.e., he was not willing to assist Hermione with her drive to improve their rights, and join SPEW), this changes radically during the battle of Hogwarts. He tells Harry and Hermione that they had forgotten the House-Elves. Harry presumes that Ron wants them as companions in the battle, but Ron says that they should rescue the House-Elves: "I mean we should tell them to get out. We don't want any more Dobbies, do we? We can't order them to die for us...," Hermione is stunned and kisses him passionately (*DH* 625). Along with Hermione, he rescues Vincent Crabbe from the fiery Room of Requirement. This shadow-hero becomes a savior-figure and "gets the girl," as heroes should.

In the classical tradition, a hero is often accompanied by a companion or most dependable friend. When Menelaus set out to rescue Helen, his abducted wife, and to wage war against the Trojans, he could count on his brother, Agamemnon, to assist in the adventure by leading the troops. At Troy, Achilles, the greatest of the Greek warriors, had his dear friend Patroclus to attend to him. Heracles had the assistance of Iolaüs in his battle with the Hydra. Theseus was able to make his way into the labyrinth and kill the Minotaur only with the help of Ariadne. The helpers are not down-played; but they stand next to the main heroes.

Most of the famous "pairs of friends" which we mentioned earlier include a main figure or hero and a secondary figure who is the first companion of that hero. Patroclus dies in battle while wearing the armor of the hero Achilles, who has withdrawn from the conflict because of his pride. Pylades attempts to take the place of his friend Orestes, who is on trial for murder and who is the central figure in their story. Damon jeopardizes his own life on behalf of Phintias, who has been sentenced to death. Nisus dies in an attempt to avenge the death of his friend Euryalus. While both members of the pairs are renowned for their true friendship, the sacrifice and courage of the first companions heighten their status as friends, even though they are shadow-heroes.

Rubeus Hagrid—Polyphemus, Hermes, and Charon

Hagrid is the Groundskeeper and Keeper of the Keys at Hogwarts, trusted messenger of Albus Dumbledore, good friend of HH&R. He appears to be a rough-cut, mentally-limited semi-giant, whose emotions and wisdom are much greater than his social skills. He is magical, but not a full-blooded wizard, a half-giant, a friend of students (perhaps because he never completed his own tenure as a student at Hogwarts) as well as of faculty, a warm-hearted teddy-bear of a man, who is totally devoted to Dumbledore, and who has a liking for the most bizarre and dangerous creatures. As Hagrid does not undergo character development or transformation in the series, but remains ever the same, he serves in the ever-unpredictable Wizarding world as an element of constancy and reliability.[13] His persona, however, is not simple and two-dimensional, but is richly colored with a variety of features characteristic of several classical figures. His roughness and social awkwardness are complemented by his kindness and a sweet and amorous tendency. He has a preference for all sorts of animals over the company of humans. He has a tendency to over-indulge in drinking alcoholic spirits which sometimes accentuates another trait, a proclivity to say more than he should about secrets, before catching himself. He has a liking for flutes and music. And, most specially, he serves in various ways as a unique conductor, guide, and messenger. In these respects, he recalls the mythological characters Polyphemus, Hermes, and even Charon.

Hagrid and the Cyclops

Polyphemus is the most powerful of the one-eyed, uncivilized giants called Cyclopes [Gk *Kuklōps, -ōpos < kuklos,* "in a circle" + *ōps,* "eye" (LSJ 1007, 2042)]. He falls in love with a sea nymph whose beauty is revealed in her name, Galatea, "milk-white" [Gk *gala, galaktos,* "milk, Milky Way" (LSJ 335)].[14] Although grotesque and savage (no one escapes his brutality or the threat of being eaten by him), he is overcome with longing and does his best to win over the girl by improving his appearance and singing to her songs of his love.[15] Unfortunately for him, Galatea loves another, a handsome youth named Acis, and she hates Polyphemus as much as she loves the boy. Hagrid's story and that of Polyphemus have much in common. Of course, the most immediate similarity is the motif of a "monstrous" figure seeking a love interest. At the outset, we would presume that both poor chaps are in for heartbreak. For Polyphemus, this is his only, and luckless, experience of romance. Hagrid, on the other hand, has a persistently romantic nature: he finds a wife, Mosag, for the acromantula Aragog, and tries to find a girlfriend for his monstrous half-brother Grawp. At a Christmas dinner, when everyone seems to be a bit loosened with merriment, Hagrid even dares to kiss Professor McGonagall on her cheek, which she appears to enjoy.

Apart from the broad motif of "ugly boy seeks pretty girl," (or Beauty and the Beast), there are particular similarities which compel comparison between Hagrid's courting Madam Maxime and the uncouth Cyclops' courtship of the sea nymph. Both Hagrid and Polyphemus are gigantic in size. When we first meet the Hogwarts Groundskeeper, we are told that he is enormous, both in height and breadth, that he has long and tangled hair and beard, with grossly oversized hands and feet. The Cyclops, shaggy with hair all over his body, is so huge that he uses a pine tree for a staff or wand [L *baculum, -ī*], has an eye the size of a shield, and claims that his body is as large as that of the king of the gods. Both are herdsmen or keepers of animals who offer wild animals to their females (Polyphemus proposes four bear cubs to his beloved; Hagrid shows Madam Maxime the three dragons being kept for the First Task). Both suitors fall head over heels in love and attempt to present themselves as attractive, despite their naturally homely looks: Hagrid tries to tame his hair with axle grease, Polyphemus combs his hair with a rake and shaves his beard with a scythe).[16]

Both have a fondness for wind instruments and their music: Hagrid apparently trains "Fluffy" to relax and go to sleep by the sound of music. He also makes a wooden flute as a Christmas present for Harry, who uses it to lull Fluffy to sleep in order to slip by him. The Cyclops plays on his panpipes and sings of his love to Galatea, to soften her feelings toward him. Although his appeal begins with sweet sentiments of love, he gives in to his anger about her rejecting him by slipping in his complaints that she is obstinate, unfeeling, inconsistent, unresponsive, vain and cruel. Because Hagrid is a tender-heart and not a savage, his approaches to Madam Maxime lack any such selfish taunts. His softness is highlighted by his being the opposite of his ancient parallel at this particular point. At the same time, his verbal skills do reveal his unrefined nature. For example, on one occasion he speaks complimentary words of her this way: "An' I'll tell yeh this, she's not afraid of roughin' it, Olympe. Yeh know, she's a fine, well-dressed woman, an' knowin' where we was goin' I wondered 'ow she'd feel abou' clamberin' over boulders an' sleepin' in caves an' tha', bu' she never complained once" (*OP* 424).

Another famous story about Polyphemus has to do with Odysseus' encounter with and escape from this Cyclops.[17] On his lengthy homecoming adventure, Odysseus comes to the island where Poseidon's son tends his sheep. Being curious and in need of food, the heroic warrior and his crew enter the savage's cave. When they are trapped inside by the giant, Odysseus devises an escape plan—to get their captor drunk, blind him, and slip away. Gentle Hagrid is nothing like the savage mythic figure in temperament; but his great weakness is his tendency to overdo it with alcohol. When he overindulges, he gets too talkative, and lets slip secrets which he should guard (as when Harry sets up the situation where Hagrid drinks a number of buckets of wine and passes out, allowing Harry to ferret out secret information from Horace Slughorn). In both stories, the powerful giants are bested and removed as barriers to the progression of the heroic individuals (Odysseus and Harry) by playing on the giants' same weakness, their excessive drinking.

The names of these two lovers may connect them as well. "Rubeus" is a Latin adjective which can mean "made of brambles" or "red/reddish." Hagrid surely appears to have a rough appearance, as if he is made of brambles and not fine materials. As to whether "red" is the more appropriate connotation for his name, he is said to grow redder in his face as he drinks. As to his family name, Rowling has said that the word "hagrid" is an Old English word designating someone who has had a bad night, and that since Hagrid is in the habit of drinking a lot, he had known many bad nights.[18] The name "Polyphemus" [Gk *Polyphēmos* < *polus*, "much, many" + *phēmē*, "legend, word, rumor, reputation"] can mean "wordy," or "knowing/abounding in many tales, songs" (LSJ 1445). The name can mirror Hagrid in several possible ways. First, he always knows much about things which Harry wishes to learn, and often withholds that information; but when he does tell what he knows, which is usually too much, it provides for Harry and readers a rich supply of background details. Second, Hagrid has many tales to tell, and a number of tales have been told about him during his life. It is virtually impossible not to see points of contact between the ancient stories about Polyphemus and the episodes of Rubeus Hagrid.

HAGRID AND HERMES

The second mythological figure to whom Hagrid is similar is the god Hermes, who is a god of borders and boundaries, business and trickery, bridges and intersections of all kinds, a messenger and guide to travelers, a god of music—a god who touched ancient life on many fronts. Madeleine Jost has said of him, "because he was essentially kindly, he was one of the most familiar gods in the daily lives of the Greeks" (669). Of all the Wizarding people, Hagrid seems to be the gentlest soul we meet, perhaps not unlike ancient Hermes.

The correspondences between the two are quite numerous. Hagrid is the son of a wizard and a giant; Hermes is the son of Zeus and the daughter of the nymph Maia (i.e., from super-human stock). The Greek god is the patron of shepherds and flocks, and Hagrid is the caretaker of animals and, once, Teacher of Care of Magical Creatures. Both Hermes and Hagrid are accused of horrible misbehaviors in their youth, and are spared. In his infancy the god steals some of the cattle which belong to Apollo, who finds him out and takes him to appear before Zeus for his crime. Hermes lies to Zeus's face and swears to the king of the gods that by god he has not stolen the cattle. Zeus, knowing the character of the infant god, rather than punish him, laughs at his audacious lie, overlooks the fault and gives Hermes a trusted place among the Olympian deities. During Hagrid's student days, Tom Riddle charges him with opening the Chamber of Secrets and unleashing a deadly monster on the school. Dumbledore, knowing Hagrid's character, disbelieves the charge and gives him a place of service and respect at Hogwarts.

Both Hermes and Hagrid have special connections with children. Hermes is a patron of children (Roberts 335), and Hagrid is a devoted nurturer of the students at Hogwarts, and a close friend and parental figure for HH&R. Katherine Grimes points out that in Rowling's novels, Hagrid's shepherding and nurturing of animals and youth makes him a kind of father-figure to Harry (109, 112).[19] She writes, "Hagrid reminds one of the shepherds and cattleherds who take in abandoned children throughout mythology—the shepherds who save Oedipus, find Paris ...; the cattle herder who saves Cyrus the Great; the swineherd who rears Romulus and Remus; the ox-herders who rear Hercules..." (112).

Another episode links the Greek god and the Groundskeeper, which we have mentioned earlier, the story of Zeus, Semele and Dionysus. Both are dispatched by their masters to rescue special infants and carry them to safety—Hagrid commissioned by Dumbledore to rescue Harry from his home and bring him to Privet Drive for safekeeping while he grows up, and Hermes to rescue the infant Dionysus and take him away for safe rearing. The motif which both of these stories serve is the conquest of death. Of all the Greek gods, Dionysus (known as Dionysus Zagreus) is uniquely associated with life and death ... and life again, for he had once been dismembered by the Titans and restored to life. His resurrection is celebrated in the yearly revitalization of the grape vines and the return of grapes (De Rose "Death," 2012, 21). He is predominant in ancient artistic expressions of hope for life after death. In the entire *Potter* series, Harry's epithet, The Boy Who Lived, serves to reprise a theme of hope in the face of death.

In the same way that Hermes serves Zeus as his trusted messenger to gods and humans, Hagrid serves Dumbledore, doing his bidding and communicating with students, giants, and Muggles. As a messenger, Hermes carries with him a staff or "caduceus," while Hagrid employs as his magical instrument a pink umbrella—a comical variation on the famous staff of Hermes. The god is a trickster, a "prince of thieves," the patron of trickery, deception, mischief and illusion, the god of every type of prosperity, even if the prosperity comes by gambling—as Hagrid wins the dragon's egg by playing cards. Hermes is a god of music, who invents the lyre from a tortoise shell when he is only one day old. Later, he invents the Pan-pipe [Gk *syrinx*]. One tradition has it that when he is sent to kill Argus, the hundred-eyed guardian which Hera has set over Io, he lulls the watchman to sleep with the music of his flute or pan pipes, and then kills him (Grimal 59). When Harry has to get past the watchdog "Fluffy," he uses the flute which Hagrid made for him.

Both Hagrid and Hermes are intermediaries who carry out orders, transport people, and deliver messages. Hermes is the only god who moves about freely from Olympus to Earth and even to Hades. As guide to the Underworld, he is known by the epithet "psychopomp," a guide of souls [Gk *psychopompos*]. His most famous escorting is his role in leading Orpheus and Eurydice from the Underworld upward to the land of the living.[20] Hagrid, too, is a kind of transporter of souls. Early on, he comes to escort Harry from the Muggle world to the world of magical people. He sets Harry out on his great quest to discover who he really is, where he really belongs, and where his destiny will lead him. He escorts him down into the Gringotts vaults, which is a virtual Underworld itself. He is the guide who leads students into and out of the Forbidden Forest.[21]

HAGRID AND CHARON

In a way Hagrid also has much in common with another transporter to the Underworld, the boatman Charon. Birkalan writes that "a common motif in the journey to the underworld is the crossing of a body of water" (2005, 489). When Hermes escorts the dead to the Underworld, he then turns the souls over to Charon, the ferryman who punts them across the river Styx to Hades. Hagrid performs a similar function at the beginning of every school year, when he transports the first-year students from the train station at Hogsmeade to Hogwarts by small boats across the enchanted lake. Although he does not take the students to their death in an Underworld, he does lead them at night across a dark lake which contains fearsome creatures. The boating experience is a transition from the Muggle world to the heart of the mysterious and magical Wizarding world—surely a significant rite of passage, which, in some senses, marks the termination of a life that came before (life totally outside the magical world) and the beginning of a life which lies ahead (life in the magical world).[22]

There is a striking difference between these two transporters, however, which brilliantly reveals Hagrid's character. For him, this duty is a joy, for he loves the students and the world into which he ferries them. His eyes may be said to be bright with happiness. Charon, on the other hand, appears to be depicted, primarily, with eyes glowing viciously or their being dull and dreary, reflecting his shadowy world and depressing work. The name often used for him in Greek poetry, "Charon," is a short form of "Charops," which has two meanings—"bright-eyed," "fierce-eyed," or "glazed, dull, glassy" (LSJ 1980–81).

Severus Snape—Mosaic of Classical Allusions

The Professor of Potions at Hogwarts School of Witchcraft and Wizardry (and one-time Professor of Defense Against the Dark Arts) is the most enigmatic character in the *Potter* series. Because he is so multi-faceted or inscrutable, there are several allusions to antiquity which surround his personhood and his role in the books. He stirs our suspicions about his harsh nature; he exemplifies a wizard of impure bloodline; as a potion-master, he is linked to ancient traffickers in questionable medicines; he binds himself to an inescapable social contract, like those made by the gods; he salts his rhetoric with Herculean imagery; and he suffers like mythical victims in the Underworld.

In the Latin language, from which his name comes, "severus" means "serious, strict, harsh, severe" [L *sevērus, -a, -um*]. Even pronouncing his name creates alliteration, reproducing the hissing sound of a snake (<u>S</u>everu<u>s</u> <u>S</u>nape). His name warns us ahead of time about his off-putting manner. His family name also foreshadows a dark-sided personality. "To snape" is "to be hard upon, rebuke, snub (a person)," in a sharp or severe manner, deriving from Old Norse *sneypa*, "to outrage, dishonor, disgrace."[23] His name is quite appropriate for both his personality and for a Head of Slytherin House.

As the son of Eileen Prince and Tobias Snape (who was a Muggle), he is himself not a pure-blood in the magical population, but a combination of magical and Muggle heritage. Because of his parentage, he might not be the ideal for such people as the Malfoys, but he is akin to a number of major figures in classical mythology who were born from the union of a god and a human, e.g., Achilles (whose mother was a sea nymph, Thetis, and whose father was a human, Peleus), Aeneas (whose mother was the goddess of beauty, Aphrodite, and whose father was the human, Anchises), and Heracles (born to Zeus and the human Alcmena), to name only a few.

The representations of some other ancient and famous men called "Severus," provide us with images which we might bring to the person of Severus Snape. The name is associated with several Romans who have made it immortal: Emperors Lucius Septimius Severus, who ruled 193–211 CE and Marcus Aurelius Severus Alexander, who ruled 222–235 CE; several lesser-known figures in Roman history; and the historian Sulpicius Severus (360–420 CE). The first of these men, the Emperor Septimius Severus, ruled by military might and bloodshed, and offers a special association with Professor Snape: neither is a "pure-blood." The Emperor's mother was born into an Italian family, the Fulvii, who were highly respected in aristocratic circles, making her native-born or "pure-blood." His father, on the other hand, was of Punic ancestry (Birley 1351), that is, of the heritage of the Carthaginians, who were the centuries-old enemies of the Romans. Thus, he was a powerful man of mixed race and blood. M.G. DuPree makes this insightful comment on the Emperor's situation: "he must have been aware all of his life of his own status as a kind of 'half-blood' among Rome's oldest and purest noble families" (51).[24] Although Severus Snape is menacing, cold, abusive, and nasty to people, he does not torture them with death, but with threats of harm and death.

His role as Potions-master to Dumbledore is reminiscent of antiquity as well. In ancient Greek, the word *pharmakon* meant both "drug" and "poison." Those with skills in medicine knew the uses of curative agents as well as toxic agents. It seems that people in high places in the Greek and Roman worlds often had ready access to experts with medicines and poisons. At times the mysterious deaths of potential royal successors or of political leaders turned the eyes of the public to such figures. For example, the Roman historian Suetonius claims that the Emperor Claudius was poisoned, perhaps by his official taster, Halotus, or that the Emperor's wife, Agrippina fed him poisoned mushrooms (Claudius 44). The Emperor Nero employed the services of an expert female poisoner, Lucusta, to kill Britannicus (the son of the previous Emperor, Claudius, his probable successor), and rewarded his accomplice with estates and a supply of students (Nero, 34). At Hogwarts, Severus Snape is the go-to person for help with a poisonous drink or a jinxed necklace, concocting Veritaserum, mixing up Wolfsbane Potion for Lupin's nights as a werewolf, and helping with Dumbledore's withering hand. But he also is skilled in "stoppering" death (*SS* 137) and practicing Sectumsempra. He can help or harm with his expert abilities.

The Unbreakable Vow which Snape makes with Narcissa Malfoy has a parallel of sorts among the Greek gods. They, too, are said to have a virtually unbreakable vow, whenever they swear their oaths to each other by the river Styx. If they break their vow or are untrue to their oath, they lie in a sick trance, breathless, without voice or spirit, taking no nourishment for a year and then they are cut off from the gods and their councils and feasts for nine full years (*Homeric Hymn to Apollo* 83–89; Hesiod, *Theog.* 767–806). Styx, for whom the river is named, is the oldest daughter of the gods Oceanus and Tethys, and is greatly honored because she and her children took the side of Zeus in his battle with the Titans. Because of this honored status, the gods swear their unbreakable oaths by her (Howatson 541).

When Professor Snape likens the difficulty of fighting the Dark Arts to the task of fighting a monster with many regenerating heads, he alludes to one of the twelve famous contests which Heracles endures in order to become immortal. The story goes that a monstrous, poisonous water serpent [Gk *hydra*], which has numerous heads,[25] has been ravaging the countryside at Lerna in the Peloponnese. Whenever Heracles strikes off one of the heads, two more quickly replace the one removed. In short, his task is multiplied with each seeming success. He is victorious, in the end, only because his nephew Iolaüs, who accompanies him, uses a torch to cauterize the stump as each head is removed, so that it cannot renew itself. As a side bonus to the battle, Heracles is able to use the deadly poison of the Hydra on his arrows in later encounters. Snape appears to know and appreciate the rhetorical force of the story on his students. He may be a strange character, but he and Rowling know their mythology and its usefulness.

In one of the few scenes which cause readers to have some pity for Snape, we learn something of the emptiness and emotional agony which the professor has endured for all his years. It is one of the most touching scenes in the series. There in the Shrieking Shack, Snape seems different, and not simply because he is dreadfully wounded. He seems uninterested in spouting venomous taunts or directing curses at Harry. Apparently the boundless hatred which he has for James Potter, and—by extension—for James' son, Harry, has disappeared. He makes a single request, for Harry to look at him. There is more here than exchanged glances. Their eyes have shown us who they are before. The first time their eyes meet, during Harry's Sorting Ceremony, his scar sears with pain. Snape's black eyes are cold and empty-looking. They glow, fanatically, however, when he thinks he has captured Harry, Lupin, Ron, Hermione, and Sirius Black together. One might say that Snape's eyes show his emptiness and torment. By contrast, Harry has been told, often, that the shape of his eyes and their bright green color are exactly like his mother's. In this scene, Rowling writes very poignantly, "The green eyes found the black" (*DH* 658). Now who they are may be more completely revealed to each other than ever before. It may be the first time they have really seen each other. When Snape asks Harry to look at him, he is expressing a final wish, to see once more the eyes of Lily Evans. For all his life, he has suffered the anguish of his unrequited and irreplaceable love for Lily. The loss has twisted and seared his heart and soul all his days, with no possibility of a cure. Her eyes, born into Harry, comprise her living continuation in this world, even after her death. It is Severus' devotion to her and his unending self-torture for being, unknowingly, an instrument of her death, that has made Albus Dumbledore so certain of Snape's penitence and trustworthiness. Severus' torment is reminiscent of the unremitting misery of three victims of eternal torment in Tartarus, the lowest regions of the Underworld: Tantalus, the fifty daughters of Danaüs, and Sisyphus. The irony of his torment is that he endures it not because of any evil which he has done but because of his deep and unrequited love for a wonderful person.

Sirius Black—Godfather with Various Shades of the Ancients

Black is Harry's godfather and an Animagus, whose nickname is "Padfoot," (or "Snuffles"), because he transforms into a huge, black dog. Although a dear friend of Harry's parents in his youth, and the best man at their wedding, he is charged with complicity in their murder and with killing thirteen people in a single, savage crime spree, including twelve Muggles and his supposed close friend, Peter Pettigrew. Harry believes the public opinion of the man and seeks to avenge his parents' murder. In a dramatic encounter, Harry learns the truth, that Sirius had been betrayed and was not an accomplice in the death of his parents. This recognition creates a strong bond between the two. Sirius becomes a "parent" of sorts to Harry, his confidant and the boy's sole "family" member. There are several aspects of the classical world and mythology which relate to the character we know as Sirius Black. They have to do with his name and standing in his family, several parent-child motifs, and even the blind prophet, Tiresias.

SIRIUS THE "DOG STAR"

The first link between the wizard and antiquity is his name, "Sirius," a name which has been used for the brightest star in the sky since at least the eighth century BCE (*Works* 417), and called the "Dog Star" since at least the fifth century BCE (Aeschylus, *Agamemnon* 967). The myth behind this name is that Orion, a hunter, passionately pursues the daughters of Atlas, the Pleiades, and that Orion and the girls are changed into constellations, along with his hunting dog, whose name is "Sirius" (Morford 233). The name derives from terms which denote scorching or parching [Gk *seirainein*, "to parch, scorch" > *seirios*, "hot, scorching" > *Seirios*, "the Dog Star, Sirius"].[26] The star is located in the constellation of Canis Major, the "Great Dog," and its rising in the summer in conjunction with the sun led the Romans to designate the hottest weeks of the year the "dog days."

Since Sirius' Animagus form is a big, black dog, it is quite suitable for him to bear the name of the Dog Star. And since he passionately pursues Peter Pettigrew and the Death Eaters for revenge and justice, he is indeed a hunter. In many ways Sirius is depicted as being an outstanding or very prominent person in the magical world, a unique individual. He is widely held to be a mass-murdering traitor, the most vicious of criminals, Azkaban's most notorious prisoner, the only inmate there ever to remain sane, and the only one ever to escape. And among his own family members he is unique, as the only one of them to be placed in Gryffindor rather than Slytherin House. Moreover, he is the only member of his family who fights on the side of the Order of the Phoenix against the Dark Lord and the Death Eaters, whom his family support and join.[27] In short, just as the star Sirius shines with unique brightness in the dark heavens, Sirius Black outshines many other characters in the *Harry Potter* series by his notoriety. And because of his singular commitment to defy Voldemort and the dark side of the magical world, he stands out prominently from all the rest of his family's heritage and tradition. One might say he is the brightest star in the whole "Black" sky.

In quest stories, help and rescue often are supplied by an agent who is dangerous or forbidding. The fearsome helper for Harry is a huge and terrifying black dog which appears to be spying on Harry but who turns out to be the boy's godfather and benefactor.

THREE CLASSIC
PARENT-CHILD MOTIFS

A second link to the ancient world is the presence of the three motifs familiar to readers of classics, which we have mentioned earlier: a) a parent or parent substitute (step parent or godparent) holds death over the head of the child; b) the father-figure serves as protector and advisor against the rashness and impetuousness of a son; and c) a child disposed of or exposed to death, but rescued and nurtured by animals and/or shepherds. It might seem odd that Sirius Black can serve in all these ways at once—a menacing parent, a nurturing parent, and a rescuing animal. But he is presented to readers for an extended period as a crazed and vicious killer who betrays his dearest friends, and is revealed, finally, to be completely misunderstood in that regard. And as he is both a magical human and an Animagus, these things are possible in Rowling's brilliant development of this character.

A Parent as a Threat to the Child's Existence

The first of these three motifs is the backdrop of the drama of the relationship between Sirius and Harry—the child whose life is at the mercy or whim of a murderous parent or parent-substitute. Although Sirius is Harry's godfather, all we know of him for a long time is that he is an enemy of the Potters and that he is intent on killing the boy. When Harry learns that Sirius is his godfather, he realizes that his family and his life have always been a target of murderous intent. And once Sirius breaks free from imprisonment, Harry's life seems to be in his godfather's hands.

This dramatic psychological motif is age-old, as we see in the myths of Meleager and Heracles. Meleager, the son of Ares and Althaea, is permitted to live his life only so long as his mother desires him to stay alive. She has been informed by the Fates that her son will live until a log burning in the fireplace is consumed. So she extinguishes it and preserves his life ... until years later, in a rage over his killing her brothers, she takes the log from the chest in which she has kept it and throws it onto the fire, bringing an end to her son's life. Heracles, likewise, lives his entire life trying to survive the unrelenting hatred of his stepmother, Hera. She detests Heracles because he is her husband's son by another woman, the human Alcmena. She attempts to kill him as a newborn child and puts him in situations as an adult which are intended to annihilate him (the Twelve Labors of Heracles and other life-threatening contests). So he spends his entire life in a threatening and treacherous atmosphere. Fortunately for him, he is so powerful that he can prevail in all these contests. For that reason, when he dies, his body is burned and his human part goes to the Underworld, but a part of him, the heroic part, is made immortal and taken up to Olympus.

A Benevolent Father-Figure

Transformation of a Character and a Motif

Sirius' role in the second motif, the "father" or father-figure who warns, advises, and protects the "son," emerges only as the truth about Sirius is revealed, and Harry's understanding of who the man is to him is transformed from evil to good. Harry writes to him, asks him questions, and desires to communicate with him when suspicious or terrifying things happen. Sirius gives him a knife which can open locks and undo knots and a mirror which can help the two communicate, even when they are far apart. This twist in the story is a creative alteration of the previous motif of the murderous parent, which is made possible by the recognition and reconciliation scene at the Shrieking Shack. The character of Sirius Black takes a complete reversal before our eyes.[28] When Harry knows the truth, he leaps at the opportunity to leave the Dursleys' house and live with Sirius. His anxiety that his life has hung treacherously in the balances comes to an end. And its end transforms the common motif in that it does not culminate in the death of the child (as with Meleager); rather, the model has been used and set aside for a radically different resolution—the reconciliation of the child and the parent substitute.

The Golden Mean

While Arthur Weasley, Remus Lupin, Albus Dumbledore, and perhaps even Rubeus Hagrid all serve, in part, as father-figures to Harry, Sirius is a unique type of father-figure. In mythology, which projects human experience on a cosmic screen, we find models of caring fathers who use their wisdom and experience to warn impetuous, daring, and inexperienced sons not to do things that are reckless and impossible. And the lessons are usually not heeded, making the subsequent tragedy a forceful means to drive home the point of the stories. Two of the most famous myths that come to mind, in this light, are the myths of Phaëthon and Icarus.

Phaëthon is the son of the sun god Helios, who manipulates his father into allowing him to drive the chariot of the sun across the heavens. Unable to control the horses, he wreaks havoc on the earth with his erratic driving. Both the god of the waters (Neptune), and the goddess of the earth (Earth), call upon Jupiter to stop this impetuous and destructive act. Though he has been warned by his father not to be rash, but to keep to a middle course, Phaëthon undertakes more than he can handle and perishes for it.

The other familiar myth concerns the most celebrated craftsman of the ancient world, Daedalus, and his son. In order to escape from the island of Crete and king Minos, Daedalus invents wings made of wax, feathers and string, on which the pair fly to their freedom. Icarus, however, youthful and full of longing for adventure, does not take his father's advice to keep to a course mid-way between the ocean and the sky, and in his playful flight, his wings melt, causing him to plummet to his death in the sea, which has been named for him, the Icarian sea (*Met.* 8.183–235).

Both of these myths express the ideal of "moderation" [Gk *sōphrosynē*, "avoiding excess"; *mēden agan*, "nothing too much"; L *nē quid nimis*], which is one of the principal values of the ancient Greeks. Known as the Mean or Golden Mean, it is cited or developed in the writings of Aeschylus, Pindar, Aristotle, and by the Roman poets Horace and Ovid. These stories give examples for Greek and Roman youth to seek the "middle way," the proper balance in all things, not to be rash or impetuous, because that often leads to catastrophic consequences. Sirius Black's role as godfather is a singular example of the same kind of moderation. While he himself was an impetuous youth, as an adult and as Harry's godfather, he serves as a moderating force for the boy, warning him not to jump to conclusions or to act hastily.

An Exposed Child Rescued by Animals or by a Shepherd

Sirius' capacity as an Animagus serves the third motif, a child disposed of or exposed to death, who is rescued and nurtured by animals and/or shepherds. The motif is a commonplace in classical mythology. At least six different examples spring to mind from mythology—Zeus, Telephus, Paris, Pelias, Romulus and Remus, and Atalanta. As a child, Zeus is reared not on Olympus but in a cave in Mt. Dicte on the island of Crete. His mother, Rhea, fears for his life because his father, Cronus, has swallowed all their previous children, in order to prevent their overthrowing him and taking his place. Zeus is kept on the island of Crete, hidden away from his father. He is provided milk by the goat Amalthea, whose skin later becomes his famous protecting shawl, the aegis, which he shares with Athena. Telephus, a son of Heracles, is exposed by his grandfather, suckled by a deer, rescued by shepherds, and turned over to a king who rears him (Grimal 437). Paris, the young Trojan prince who takes Helen to Troy, initiating the Trojan War, as an infant is exposed to die by order of his father Priam, the king of Troy. One tradition says that he is rescued by shepherds, and another that he is suckled by a bear for five days, then reared by the very servant of Priam who was charged with disposing of the boy (344). Pelias, one of Poseidon's sons, is abandoned but discovered by some horse dealers who care for him, or he is suckled by a mare and taken in by a shepherd (352). Romulus and Remus, the infant twin patriarchs of Rome, are taken away to be drowned in the Tiber River in order to remove all male claimants to the throne of their uncle Amulius. The men who have been ordered to do this murderous deed are prevented by the swollen river from getting out far enough in the stream to drown the boys. So, they put the children in a basket and place it in one of the shallow eddies, presuming that it will wash into the rapid main stream and the boys will die. Livy, who tells the story, says that destiny steps in and the boys are first suckled by a she-wolf, then discovered by a shepherd, Faustulus, and reared by him and his wife Larentia (*A.U.C.* 1.3.10ff.).[29] Atlanta is an example of the female exposed by her father when she is an infant. A female bear suckles and nurtures her, and she is eventually discovered and reared by hunters who educate her as a hunter (*Libr.* 3.9.2). Katherine Grimes, whom we cited as pointing out Hagrid's shepherding and nurturing of animals and youth, notes that Sirius is a kind of father-figure to Harry, reminiscent of the motif of animals who protect abandoned children, a persistent motif of mythology—"the bear who nurses Paris, the wolf who nurses Romulus and Remus and the woodpecker who guards them, the eagle who saves Gilgamesh, the doe who nurses Siegfried, and the swan who feeds Lohengrin" (112).[30]

SIRIUS AND THE
BLIND PROPHET TIRESIAS

One more suggestive parallel which deserves consideration is that between Sirius Black and the blind prophet of ancient mythology, drama and literature, Tiresias. There are two parts to their parallel. The first part has to do with their unique ability to retain their sanity and prophetic capacity in their respective hellish environments. Sirius is the only prisoner ever to be incarcerated in Azkaban who retains his sanity and reasoning ability, and who seems normal. He alone is capable of discovering that Peter Pettigrew is alive, and he alone is clear-headed enough to prophesy that Pettigrew is at Hogwarts. Tiresias is similarly unique in that when he dies and becomes just a shade or a ghost, he is the only person ever allowed to keep his intelligence and strong mental abilities in Tartarus, the lowest realms of the Underworld in mythology, comparable to Azkaban in the Wizarding world. He can even prophesy the future. All the other dead in Hades are mere flitting shadows (*Od.* 10.488–95; Lombardo 155; Callimachus, *Hymn* 5.121–30).

The second part of the Sirius-Tiresias connection has to do with their episodes of summoning and conversing with the dead. Harry's last encounter with Sirius occurs in the Forbidden Forest, when he summons Sirius Black, Remus Lupin, his father and mother. They appear to him in unique form, having bodily identity but not really physical bodies, and yet not just ghostly forms or shadows. Harry can talk with Sirius and ask him about death, and be heartened by Sirius' replies about what death will be like. This is strikingly similar to two very famous encounters with the shades of the dead in classical literature. Odysseus, weary and beleaguered from so many toils and intrusions caused by Poseidon to delay his homecoming, learns from the witch-goddess Circe that in order to get home to Ithaca, he must first consult the soul of the blind prophet Tiresias in Hades. In books ten and eleven of the *Odyssey*, the hero learns from Circe the magical rite or "nekuia" [Gk *nekuia*] for summoning the dead in order to ask about the future. With his sword he digs a cubit-square area in the sand, and pours into the sacred space wine, honey and milk, barley, and blood. When he completes the ritual, many of the dead emerge, including Tiresias, all identifiable by their form and appearance. Tiresias prophesies the future for the pilgrim, tells him how to get home to Ithaca, and informs him as to how he will die. Odysseus tries three times to embrace his mother's shade, but catches only empty air as she recedes from him.

Centuries after Homer, the Roman poet Vergil recycles this scene and makes his variations on it in the famous sixth book of his *Aeneid*, in which his hero, Aeneas, visits the Underworld. He risks his life and acquires his ticket to the other side, a golden bough, which he shows to Charon the boatman, who punts the dead across the river Styx. Aeneas meets many of the dead, who are shades and not physical bodies, but who are still recognizable and capable of communication with him. His father, Anchises, gives him a guided tour of the Underworld and prophesies to him the future of Rome and Aeneas' own destiny. Three times the visitor attempts to embrace his dead father, but catches only empty air. The common factors to all these tales are the encounter with the dead, made possible by some magical formula and words and tangible tokens; the nature of the deceased; and the summoning of the dead by all three to learn of the future and about the nature of death.

Chapter VII

Cast of Supporting Characters

Many of the proper names in the *Harry Potter* books echo names which were used in the ancient world (most of them Latin, a few Greek, several Hebrew). In sowing these names about in her magical world, Rowling draws into close proximity or even into overlapping positions three worlds—the magical world, the ancient world, and the world of her readers. In this way, her story-telling invites us to bring to the novels all the imagination and memory we have of those ancient times and tales. Sometimes a character is highlighted by his or her bearing a name or title which has become so famous that it heralds an unforgettable predecessor, or which has come to be synonymous with a function. For example, Professor Trelawney has a name that is the title of ancient and famous prophetesses, "Sibyll." And Neville Longbottom's imposing and queenly grandmother is named "Augusta," the Latin name meaning "venerable" or "honorable." This name was used for wives and sometimes grandmothers of the early Emperors of Rome. It fits her well and adds to Rowling's depiction of the grand-dame and the status of Neville's family.

At other times, a character is colored by being completely the opposite of the ancient person who has made the name famous. One example is Augustus Rookwood. His name is memorable because of Octavian, the first Emperor of Rome, who brought an end to a century of civil war, who was declared "Augustus," "the August one," by the Roman senate in 27 BCE, and who was considered to be divine because of his accomplishments.[1] Mr. Rookwood, however, is a Death Eater and a spy ... a schemer and traitor to his famous name.

Occasionally, a character's life situation is remarkably—and sometimes very subtly—evocative of an ancient person's life situation. An example of this is Severus Snape's father, "Tobias." A biblical figure named Tobias (*Tobiah* in Hebrew, *Tobias* in Greek), on his family's return to Judea after the Babylonian Exile, could not convince the puritanical Jewish priests that he and his sons were "pure" Israelites, without any taint of non–Israelite blood. Similarly, Severus Snape could not claim pure-blood status among wizards because his father was a Muggle, making him only a "half-blood" wizard. The effect and value of these classical names resides in the degree of similarity or dissimilarity between the classical models and the *Harry Potter* characters, as the names add color and interest to the stories at large.

This chapter does not list all persons or named figures in the novels, only those which appear to have some connection with or which may be informed by ancient classical literature, lore, and culture. Nor does it summarize all of the actions of the figures being introduced. The information presented is limited to aspects of the individuals which offer some type of parallel or similarity to ancient predecessors or resources. Several of the "characters" presented in this chapter are not humans. They are included, however, because they bear the identity of ancient mythological or historical figures (Brutus, Callisto, Europa, Ganymede, Io, and Hermes) or, as important "actors" in the novels, they show strong and important connections with classical prototypes (Dobby, Fawkes, Fluffy). Classes of non-human beings, such as centaurs, unicorns, and the like, will be presented in Chapter VIII. The following entries are alphabetized by first or middle name because most those included are more readily recognized by that name. And, very often, the first or middle name of a character is where the connection to ancient parallels exists.

Abraxas Malfoy

The paternal grandfather of Draco Malfoy. During a class with Professor Slughorn, Draco Malfoy, in an attempt to ingratiate himself to the teacher, says he thinks that his grandfather, Abraxas, is an acquaintance of the Professor. We learn nothing about Abraxas, except that he has died of dragon pox. So, we have no image of his character or customary behavior, and are left to envision him on the basis of his impressive and ancient name. "Abraxas" (also spelled "Abrasax") is one of the most common terms in ancient magic, mystical philosophy, and religion. It is not a personal name, but a sequence of Greek letters which add up to the numerical value of 365. On ancient amulets and charms which were worn to protect the wearers, he is depicted as having snakes for legs, a body covered with armor, and the head of a rooster (Gager 265). He is invoked in magical papyri and spells, (sometimes along with the Greek gods, the Egyptian gods, the Hebrew god Adonai, the archangels Michael and Gabriel, and other mystical powers) to make a spell or charm effective.[2]

In the second century CE, Abraxas was appropriated by Gnostic sects, which held that there were two worlds or realms: one gloriously spiritual and the other, the present material world, which is evil. For them, salvation was deliverance from the evil world by overcoming the 365 heavens or spiritual levels of power between the two worlds. Abraxas was the cosmic or solar deity over these heavens. The name has been used, also, in Jewish mysticism (kabbalah) as a charm, or as a secret term in place of the Tetragrammaton (YHWH), since the Hebrew word for "four" is *arba* (Rudolph 311).

This is no new name, invented by Rowling. And so the question arises, what difference does it make that Lucius Malfoy's father is named "Abraxas"? Draco tries to curry some favor with Slughorn, who is a name-dropper and likes to show that he is acquainted with famous and powerful people. And the student does this by an almost casual mention of his grandfather's name, which has for millennia conjured up dark, divine, cosmic associations. The appearance of the name also adds to the impression of Draco's family as having a long-standing association with the Dark Arts and their exercise of dark magic.

Agatha Timms

A witch who, during the Quidditch World Cup tournament, makes a heavy bet with Ludo Bagman on the outcome of the games. The wager is half of the shares in her eel farm. Nothing else is known of her in the novels; but her name derives from a Greek adjective [*agathos, agathē, agathon*], which means "good, noble, gentle," or "well-born" (LSJ 4). How curious it is that the entrepreneur of eels, and a gambling woman to boot, has such a refined name as "Agatha," "the noble woman."

Agnes

A patient on the closed Janus Thickey ward, whose face is covered with fur and who communicates by barking. We learn nothing of her sickness or history, or even her last name. "Agnes," however, is familiar to Catholics. Saint Agnes, a Christian martyr who lived in the fourth century CE, is venerated for her virginity and devotion to Christ. "Agnes," most likely, derives from the Greek word for "pure," "holy," or "chaste" [*hagnos*] which comes through Latin as *agnus*, "lamb." The tragedy of Agnes' ailment (caused by some spell gone wrong, as with all cases on the fourth floor of the hospital), is multiplied by the fact that it happens to someone whose name leads us presume that she must be saintly and lamb-like.

Agrippa

A wizard pictured on a Chocolate Frog card, which is apparently a rare item, as Ron has a collection of almost five hundred cards but not this one. His name is quite familiar to students of Roman history or of the New Testament. Marcus Vipsanius Agrippa (64–12 BCE) was the close friend and political associate of the Emperor Augustus, devoted to Rome and a very generous benefactor to the state. He commanded part of the fleet which defeated Mark Antony in the battle of Actium in 31 BCE (which event and date are considered to mark the transition from the Roman Republic to the Roman Empire).

Other powerful Romans bore this name, too, including the grandson of Herod the Great, Marcus Julius Herod Agrippa I (10 BCE–44 CE). He is remembered for putting to death James, the brother of John and imprisoning Peter (Acts 12:1–19). His son was called Agrippa, as well, Marcus Julius Herod Agrippa II (27–93 CE), before whom Paul defended himself (Acts 25:13–26:32). "Agrippa" signifies power, high office, authority, and perhaps elicits an element of fear or danger. Is this wizard's Chocolate Frog card a rare find because of his famous name or because of the notorious legend surrounding that name and the fatal consequences of those who appeared before the ancient Roman Agrippas?

Alastor ("Mad-Eye") Moody

A member of the Order of the Phoenix and retired Auror, usually called by the nickname "Mad-Eye" because of his magical eye, with which he can see through doors, invisibility cloaks, walls, and even the back of his own head. His personal name is a very appropriate choice for him, since in ancient Greek it designates a relentless deity or spirit, who avenges the dead in order to bring about justice [Gk *Alastōr* < *a-*, 'not' + *lanthanomai*, 'to forget, escape notice" (Room 35)]. Moody spends his life energetically and devotedly hunting down and imprisoning the Death Eaters who torture and kill innocent people for their Dark Lord. His unique, magical vision is reminiscent of the classical figure Lynceus, who was one of the original Argonauts, and who was reputed to have such powerful eyesight that he could see things at a great distance and things hidden underground (*Libr.* 3.10.3). The origin of his reputation probably stems from his gift at discovering and retrieving metals underground. In light of that, he is celebrated as the very first miner (Grimal 266). This is not to propose that Alastor is a Lynceus in modern, magical dress. It is interesting, however, to note that imaginative lore about uncommon vision has been around for millennia, and now adds to the aura of Mad-Eye Moody.

Alecto Carrow

A Death Eater, sister of Amycus Carrow, who corners Dumbledore on the tower. Under Snape's administration, she is assigned the position of teacher of Muggle Studies. She and Amycus are put in charge of severe discipline, making students practice the Cruciatus Curse on fellow students who are in detention. In classical mythology, Al(l)ecto [Gk *Al(l)ēktō* < *a-* "not" + *lēgō*, "cease," meaning she is relentless] is one of the three Erinyes or Furies [Gk *Erinyes;* L *Furia, -ae*], the mad and avenging goddesses who take vengeance for guilt, especially for murder and heinous infra-family crimes (OLD 749)]. Their names are "Tisiphone," who avenges blood crimes, "Megaera," who is contentious and argumentative, and "Al(l)ecto," whose rage for vengeance is unceasing and implacable (Brewer 466). Mythologically, they come into being as the result of a heinous crime, arising from the drops of blood spilled when Cronus (time) castrates his father Uranus (sky).

A common explanation might suggest that they are the guilt-producing and disturbing ghosts of the dead. Their accustomed dwelling is at the entrance to the Underworld, where they avenge crimes. Sometimes, however, they appear in the upper world of human existence as the avenging spirits of the dead (Howatson 258). In Vergil's *Aeneid* (7.323ff.), Alecto is the Fury whom Juno summons to create war and strife between the Trojans (under Aeneas) and the Rutuli (under Turnus), so as to prevent Aeneas from fulfilling his destiny to rule in Italy. The Fury, who has a thousand ways to wound, takes a serpent from her own head and puts it into her victim's chest to incite herself, fury, in the victim (Fitzgerald 207). She is sinister, pitiless, and masterfully efficient in stirring up hatred on both personal and tribal levels. With her violent and demonic nature, Alecto Carrow appears to be true to the name she bears.

Ambrosius Flume

The proprietor of Honeydukes candy shop in Hogsmeade. The name of the merchant of sweets and confectionary delights is perfect for him, as it is the term for the food of the immortal gods. The Olympian gods nourish their immortality with Nectar and Ambrosia [Gk *ambrotos*, "immortal, divine" > *ambrosios*, "divine, pertaining to the gods" > *ambrosia*, "immortality," "elixir of life," "food of the gods" > L *ambroseus/ambrosius*, "divine, belonging to the gods" (OLD 116; LSJ 79)]. Occasionally, in classical literature, the gods give ambrosia to humans for whom they have a personal liking. Athena gives it to Penelope as a beautifying face cream (*Od.* 18.190–94; Griffiths 69). While the gift beautifies or preserves human recipients, it does not immortalize them. Flume's family name is a proper English word, meaning "river" [L *fluō*, *fluere, fluxī, fluxum*, "to flow" > *flūmen, fluminis*, "river, stream, copious supply" > ME flum, "river" (Mish 482; OLD 716)]. Apparently, Mr. Flume is a copious supply, a river, as-it-were, of goodies which make life sweeter for Hogwarts students and residents of Hogsmeade.

Amycus Carrow

The brother of Alecto Carrow, and a violent Death Eater. In battle, he toys with Ginny Weasley, hurling Cruciatus Curses at her while he giggles. Under Snape's Headmastership, Amycus is given the post of Teacher of the Dark Arts. His cruel, taunting behavior demonstrates the foul and contemptible character of the brute, who is much like the mythological fighter who has made the name famous. Ancient Amycus [Gk *Amykos* < intensifying prefix *a-*, "very, much" + form of *mycaomai*, "bellow" (Room 46)] is one of Poseidon's sons, a gigantic man, and king of the Bithynian tribe, the Bebryces. When Jason and the Argonauts sail into the Black Sea (in search of the Golden Fleece), they encounter Amycus, who taunts all visitors to his land and forces them to box with him, the winner being free to treat the loser as he wishes. Of course, Amycus always wins, being Poseidon's son. However, one of the Argonauts, Polydeuces, famous as a boxer, fights and defeats him, either by killing him (*Argonautica* 2.1–97) or by knocking him out, binding him and making him promise never again to harm strangers (Theocritus, *Idyll* 22.³). Both of the Amycuses are brutal figures of cruel disposition and powerful fighters, who are at last rendered powerless, and made submissive to their opponents.

Andromeda Black Tonks

Born Andromeda Black, she is the sister of Narcissa Black Malfoy and Bellatrix Lestrange, and mother of Nymphadora Tonks by a Muggle, Ted

Tonks. Because of her marriage outside the Wizarding world, she is removed from the Black family tree. Her name comes from a mythological legend which reads much like her own story. The classical Andromeda [Gk *Andromeda*], is the very beautiful daughter of Cepheus, the king of Ethiopia. Her mother, Cassiopeia, makes the mistake of bragging that either the girl's beauty or her own exceeds that of all fifty or one hundred daughters of the sea nymphs, the Nereids. For this arrogance, the nymphs persuade Poseidon to punish Cassiopeia's kingdom and to send a monster against their land. Cepheus learns from the Egyptian god Ammon that the only way to prevent this disaster is to sacrifice his daughter, Andromeda, to the monster. He expels Andromeda from the family and community, tying her to a rock. She is rescued by Perseus, who convinces her father to let her marry him if he kills the monster (which he does, using the Cap of Invisibility) (*Libr.* 2.4.3–5). As the wife of Perseus, she becomes the mother of a line of Persian kings, and deserving of her name, which means "ruler of men" [Gk *anēr, andros*, "man" + *medōn*, "ruler," guardian" (LSJ 1089)].

Eventually, Andromeda and her parents and Perseus are transformed into constellations. In her constellation, the famous princess is depicted at her most critical moment, when she is chained to the cliff and awaiting her doom. So, even in her accomplishments and glory, she is remembered for her greatest peril. Similarly, Andromeda Tonks, although she escapes from the Black household and has a good life, is commemorated only by a spot where her name and image are burned from the Black family tree tapestry. The two Andromedas, Ms. Black and the Ethiopian princess, are ousted from home and family, "rescued" from isolation and dejection by a lover from outside the exclusive family, experience legendary marriages and are celebrated for the awful things they endure from their family, their home, and their public.

Antigone (Rosalind Antigone Bungs)

Hermione finds this witch when she combs the library for the names of wizards or witches who might have the initials R.A.B. No other details about Ms. Bungs are related in the series. She does, however, have a very famous classical name. Antigone is one of Oedipus' two daughters (who, incidentally, are his "sisters," since Oedipus fathers them by his own mother) [Gk *Antigonē* < *anti*, "contrary, against" + *gonos*, "child, birth," meaning her birth is an abnormal one (Room 54)]. She stands up bravely against her tyrannical uncle Creon, the new king of Thebes, and chooses to do what is right and moral, even if it leads to her death (which it does). In Greek mythology, the dramatic story of Antigone is a remarkable paradigm of feminine courage and noble principle in the face of cruel and unreasoning power (especially in Sophocles' play, *Antigone*). The name is legendary for this woman's story and in its masculine form (Antigonus) it is used for a line of Macedonian kings who succeed Alexander the Great. Ms. Bungs is fit with large shoes to fill, when she is named "Antigone."

Antioch Peverell

Original owner of the Elder Wand, who becomes drunk with the power of the wand and kills an old enemy, boasting himself to be invincible. According to Lovegood, Antioch is later himself killed, and the wand passes to successive owners by a trail of murder and blood. His name recalls Antiochus I [Gk *Antiochos*] and a number of successive rulers of the Seleucid Empire (after the death of Alexander the Great, stretching from Asia Minor to western Iran, 321–64 BCE). The name also designates other figures, such as lawyers, historians, and philosophers, down to the fifth century CE. For Jews, the name raises horrible memories. Antiochus IV (about 215–164 BCE), who called himself "Epiphanes," "the manifest god," but whom the Jews nicknamed "Epimanes," "the insane," attempted to eradicate Judaism with horrors not unlike those of the Holocaust (see 1–2 Maccabees for the history of this period). Given the abuse of absolute power, merciless killing and cruel arrogance of both Antioch Peverell and the Seleucid king, perhaps we do not go astray in seeing in Mr. Peverell something of the legendary and awful character traits of the ancient Seleucid of that name.

Antonin Dolohov

A Death Eater who tortures many people and participates in the killing of Fabian and Gideon Prewett. His personal name is loaded with contradictions. The name "Antonin" describes the Roman Emperors and some members of their families during the years 138–192 CE—Antoninus Pius, Marcus Aurelius, Lucius Verus, and Commodus (the "Antonines"). It derives from "Antonius" [L *Antōnius* > *Antōnīnus*], the designation for a group of Roman families [L *gēns, -tis*], including the illustrious statesman, Triumvir, warrior and lover of Cleopatra, Mark Antony (83–30 BCE). One expects that by his name, Dolohov should probably have some measure of greatness and nobility about him ... unless he, like Dedalus Diggle and a few others, is named for the ironic absence of what the name promises.

There is one way in which this Death Eater is quite reminiscent of Mark Antony, and that is the way in which he deals with his political enemies. Mark Antony used proscriptions as his method of removing political opposition. In proscription, a powerful leader declared his opponents to be enemies of the state and outlaws, then seized their property and displayed their names publicly as outlaws. The military which supported the powerful leader would then kill the outlaws and receive reward for their service to the state. In one of the most famous proscriptions, Mark Antony had Cicero killed, and his head and hands displayed on stakes in the forum at Rome to discourage other opponents from speaking or writing against him. Dolohov, likewise, wants to eliminate all opposition to his Dark Lord. So, ironically, both the ancient Roman and the modern wizard carry names of greatness, but practice cruel elimination of their enemies.

Apollyon Pringle

The caretaker of Hogwarts when Mr. and Mrs. Weasley were students. Apparently, Mr. Weasley received a beating by Pringle for the couple's late night stroll together (*GF* 616). His name conjures up very threatening images, for it is the name of the angel over the bottomless pit of the Underworld in the biblical book of Revelation (9:11) [Gk *Apollyon* < *apollyōn*, "destroying, ruining" < the verb *apollūmi*, "to kill, destroy"]. There must be a personality profile used to hire Hogwarts caretakers, for both Pringle and Argus Filch are frightening and loathsome characters, as their names suggest.

Arcturus (Regulus Arcturus Black)

Sirius Black's younger brother, a Death Eater, who resigns his position and is killed for disloyalty. His name may reveal something of his relation to his family and, particularly, to his brother. The name "Arcturus" is older than our earliest western literature, being an ancient designation for the brightest star in the constellation Boötes, the Ox-Herder (*Od.* 5.2783; *Works* 566, 610) [Gk *Arktouros* < *arktos*, "bear" + *ouros*, "guard," L *Arctūrus*] (LSJ 242; OLD 164; Toomer 366–68). According to astronomer James B. Kaler, Arcturus is "the brightest star of the northern hemisphere and the fourth brightest star of the entire sky."[4] As this seems relative to the *Potter* novel, Regulus disavows the Dark Lord, but only after a life of esteem by his family, which prevents his place on the family tree tapestry from being removed. Sirius Black, however, leaves the family as a teenager, and record of his existence is scorched from the tapestry. So, Sirius, the older and more profoundly rebellious son of the Black family, is more "glaring" or "pronounced" of the two who make up the family constellation of boys-gone-wrong. Regulus is a rare hero, of sorts, in the Black family. Both Sirius Black and Regulus Black are luminaries or leading stars in the night of conflict against Voldemort and the Dark wizards. See also "Regulus," below.

Argus Filch

The annoying, ever-snooping caretaker at Hogwarts, who delights in catching students in some act for which he can punish them. He has the most menial job at the school, possesses no magical talent, and appears to take out his anger over his low standing by relishing in the misfortune and difficulties of others. Two mythological types demand attention at the mention of the caretaker's name. One is the figure of a sentry, and the other is the image of a famous boatman.

First, his given name is perfect for this spy-master-guardian. "Argus" is a Latinized spelling of a Greek name which signifies "keenness" and "swiftness," and is the name of two famous guardians in mythology [Gk *Argos* < *argos*, "shining, glistening, swift"; L *Argus*].[5] One of these is associated with Zeus's womanizing tendency. The king of the gods falls in love with a priestess or princess named "Io." His wife, Hera, discovers the infidelity, and Io is turned into a heifer (either by Zeus, to cover up his deed, or by Hera, to punish both the girl and Zeus). To prevent any further trysts, Hera sets Argos as her guard to keep an eye on the cow (various versions say he has four eyes, one hundred eyes, or eyes all over himself).[6] He is very likely called "Argos" because he keeps his eyes open and bright, and his lookout is always keen (LSJ 236). Zeus sends Hermes to lull Argos to sleep with conversation and with flute or pan-pipe music, and then to kill him (Grimal 59). For his devoted service, Hera honors Argos by placing his eyes in the tail feathers of the peacock, the bird which is sacred to her (*Met.* 1.568–746).

Another guardian by the name of "Argos" is Odysseus' faithful dog. When the king of Ithaca arrives home from the Trojan War, after a twenty-year absence, his faithful watchdog recognizes him as his returning master, thus fulfilling his duty, and dies (*Od.* 17.292). These two mythic "Arguses" are very diligent and keen in the performance of their duties. And, in his own way, Mr. Filch is as devoted and unfailing in doing his duties as are Hera's sentinel and Odysseus' hound. The differences between our Squib and the mythic Arguses, however, are in their motivations and images. The honorable watchers of antiquity are about serious business and have responsible purposes. Argus Filch, however, is more of a pest and an intruder than a sentinel. His nasty spirit and evil motivations—which derive, most likely from his low self-concept and jealous desire as an underling of the magical world to retaliate against those who are above him socially—betray the dignity of his name. Yet one would be hard pressed to invent a more suitable name for the never-resting hall monitor and "evil-eye" of Hogwarts than "Argus."[7]

Second, the boatman correspondence is suggested by Filch's low station and work in the Wizarding world in general, and by one scene in particular. When Fred and George Weasley make their departure from Hogwarts, they create and leave behind a swamp in a hall on the fifth floor of the east wing. They do this to annoy Dolores Umbridge and Filch, who are unable to remove it. In sympathy with this act of protest, the teachers leave the swamp in place, forcing Filch to "punt" the students to their classes across that foul body of water (OP 676). This image echoes the work of the mythological figure, Charon, the cold and cruel ferryman who "punts" the souls of the dead across the river Acheron (or Styx) in the Underworld to Hades in his leaky little boat, and who must be paid for his lowly service (Aen. 6). Both Filch and Charon have a "hell" of a job and occupy the lowest social ranks of their respective worlds. On the social ladder at Hogwarts, Argus Filch is at the bottom, and in the Wizarding world. He is a "wannabe," a Squib, a person who has no magical powers at all. He even becomes a willing assistant to Dolores Umbridge in reinstating punishments and privations on students. Charon, too, exists at the bottom of his world, and springs from very low origins—he is a child of Night (Nox) and Erebus (Gloomy Darkness). In ancient art work he is depicted as "a disreputable, filthy old man with a straggly beard and tattered clothes who bullied souls..." (Clayton 57). Both of these "boatmen" perform menial and perhaps inglorious tasks, punting others across waters into magical realms. But there is a difference between them. Charon's name echoes what we saw above, (about "Argus" meaning "shining, bright"). In poetry, he is called Charon (Gk *Charōn*). But that name is a shortened form for Charops [< *charops, charopos*, "bright-eyed," "fierce-eyed," which was used for the eyes of vicious lions, bears, and dogs, but also could mean "glazed, dull, glassy" (LSJ 1980–81)].[8]

His surname, "Filch," is not exactly a term that dignifies his family. "To filch" means "to steal." He is not depicted as a thief, though as a Squib, he does attempt to acquire what he does not have. The name, at least, enhances the negative aspect of his character.

Ariana Dumbledore

Albus and Aberforth's sister, Ariana, was attacked by Muggle boys when she was six years old, and kept in seclusion from age seven. She accidentally killed her mother during one of her rages at age fourteen, and was herself killed, accidentally, during a fight between her brothers and Grindelwald. Her name "Ariana" was the title used to designate a region in the east of the ancient Persian Empire [L *Ariānē*]. Perhaps her name connotes an atmosphere of the "far away," the ancient, and the mysterious.

Augusta Longbottom

Neville's imposing and regal grandmother. She has a name which was used for wives and sometimes for grandmothers and other close female relatives of the Emperors of Rome, "Augusta" (OLD 214). It derives from the Latin adjective which means "solemn, venerable, worthy of honor, majestic, dignified" [L *augustus, -a, -um*]. The formidable name surely suits her. It also casts a bright light of class, dignity, and power over Neville's family, which is much needed, in light of the indignity the family endures because of the pitiful state of his parents.

Augustus

AUGUSTUS ROOKWOOD

A wizard who works in the Department of Mysteries, but who is secretly a Death Eater and a spy who gives important information about the Ministry to Voldemort. This name should call to mind an imposing male figure of power and dignity, the first Roman Emperor. The title "Augustus" ("venerable," "honorable") was conferred upon Gaius Octavius (Octavian) in 27 BCE by the Roman Senate for his bringing an end to a century of civil war. He was thought of as divine because of his great accomplishments, not the least of which was the ushering in of an era of decreased military expansion and conquest, which made for governmental strength and peace, lasting several hundred years (the Pax Augusta, "venerable peace" or Pax Romana, "Roman peace"). The honorific name was used by Emperors thereafter. With Rookwood, we have the application of a classic name which illumines the character's nature by his being a polar opposite to the values associated with the name. The Death Eater is hardly one who works to end civil war. Indeed, he plays both sides of the

Wizarding world as a traitorous spy, to help the Dark Lord defeat the very colleagues at the Ministry who trust him. Hardly deified for his labors, this wizard is vilified and is all the more memorable for his betrayal of his exalted name.

Augustus Pye

A Healer in training at St. Mungo's Hospital, who tries, unsuccessfully, to use Muggle medical methods on Arthur Weasley, on the ward for treating Serious Bites. Mr. and Mrs. Weasley, angered by the novice's experimentation, become anxious to see his mentor, Hippocrates Smethwyck. The name "Augustus" is ironic, for it suggests great esteem accorded to someone of magnificent accomplishment, applied to an inexperienced and unsuccessful novice.

Barnabas

Barnabas Deverill

The wizard who is killed by Loxias, who then takes possession of his Elder Wand. The name "Barnabas" is an Aramaic name [*bar nebū'ā*], which means "son of encouragement" or "son of (the god) Nebo" (Daniels 610). In the New Testament book of Acts, the name appears [Gk *Barnabas*] as a nickname given by the apostles to a "Joses" or "Joseph," who sells an estate and gives the proceeds to the apostles to support their work, and who becomes an associate of St. Paul in his missionary endeavors (Acts 4:36–37). The wizard and the missionary may have the same name; but their actions are quite different. Deverill is killed by a wizard whose name is an epithet of the god Apollo ("Loxias"), and his treasured wand is stolen from him. Paul's associate chooses to part with his valued property in order to give it to the work of the apostles for their God. Perhaps the irony of a magical "Barnabas" being so inconsiderately abused and killed, while his name reminds us of a model of generosity and helpfulness in a great cause, adds to the interest we might have in a Deverill by the name of Barnabas.

Barnabas Cuffe

The editor of the *Daily Prophet*, and one of the important figures with whom Horace Slughorn prides himself for being on close personal terms.

Barnabas the Barmy

Opposite the Room of Requirement hangs a tapestry with the image of this wizard, who is said to have tried to teach trolls ballet. Since the name

"Barnabas" refers to someone who literally "encourages" others, perhaps this wizard could be considered "barmy" (that is, "excitable, crazy, flighty") because he undertook the impossible task of encouraging such lumbering beasts as trolls to master one of the highest forms of art and culture.

Bartemius

BARTEMIUS CROUCH, SR.

A previous Head of the Department of Magical Law Enforcement, and slated to be made Minister of Magic, whose actions brought him public disfavor. His uncontrolled ambition to be made Minister of Magic caused him to ignore his own son, who rebelled by becoming an ardent follower of Voldemort. His mad zeal overcame sound reasoning, as he allowed Aurors to use the illegal Unforgivable Curses on his enemies to defeat the Dark Lord and the Death Eaters. And he became as violent as his enemies. His moral and mental declines show how unmeasured passion, although directed against something evil, can itself turn into an equally wicked force and can ruin even those who have the best of intentions. He even sentenced his own son to Azkaban without a trial.

BARTEMIUS, "BARTY" CROUCH, JR.

The rebel son of Bartemius Crouch, Sr., who becomes Voldemort's most faithful servant. Along with three other Death Eaters he is condemned to Azkaban by the Council of Magical Law for using the Cruciatus Curse on the Longbottoms. He serves the Dark Lord as his "mole," at Hogwarts by disguising himself as an Auror, using Polyjuice Potion to keep his game concealed. He is so characterized by his mad rage that when he kills his own father, he proudly confesses to the murder.

"Bartemius" is a modern spelling of the name "Bartimaeus" which is a Greek version [Gk *Bartimaios*] of the Aramaic name *bar timai*, "son of Timai," or "son of the unclean" (Blair 361). The biblical "Timaeus" is a blind beggar who calls out to Jesus for mercy and healing over the repeated demands of others in the crowd that he keep quiet. When Jesus calls for him to be brought forth, Bartimaeus throws off his garment and comes to Jesus, who heals him, because of his faith. Upon receiving his sight, he immediately and resolutely follows Jesus into Jerusalem (Mark 10:46–52). Might it be that with the Crouches we have here an ironic twist on this name? The biblical Bartimaeus, living in the darkness, is blessed with sight and whole-heartedly gives himself to a great cause, voluntarily following Jesus toward Jerusalem, where Jesus is headed to die. Barty Crouch, Sr., blinded by his own self-absorbed devotion to a cause and to hoped-for future personal glory, disregards everything except his mission, and in the end loses himself and all he has, rather than gain a purpose and clear-sighted perspective. And Barty Crouch, Jr., blinded by hatred, pursues a path of murder and deception, losing all sense of good and bad.

When we read that these men are called "Bartemius," we anticipate the striking elements of the famous biblical story: blindness and sight, loss and gain, devotion and unselfish commitment to a noble purpose. The Bartimaeus of the Bible is blessed by his persistence and devotes himself unstintingly and unselfishly to a grand cause. The Crouches become blinded by zealous aims of self-glory (Barty, Sr.) and bitter revenge (Barty, Jr.), which lead to madness and death for them both. The differences between these wizards and the blind man of Jericho, who makes the name "Bartimaeus" unforgettable, create a most impressive characterization of the father-son duo.

Brutus (St. Brutus's Secure Center for Incurably Criminal Boys)

The contrived name of an imaginary reformatory for incorrigible boys. In their contempt for Harry, and in an attempt to pander to Vernon Dursley's sister, Marge, who despises Harry, the Dursleys tell Marge that their strange nephew attends this reform school for delinquents. The cruelty and grotesqueness of this contrived institution is a measure of both the hatred of the Dursleys toward Harry and Marge's delight at the thought of the "idiotic" lad being treated as a vile thing.

The selection of the name "Brutus" for the institution is splendidly imaginative. First, perhaps the best-known "Brutus" in western history is Marcus Junius Brutus, the Roman general who takes the lead in the conspiracy to murder his former close friend, Julius Caesar ("Et tu, Brute?," Shakespeare, *Julius Caesar*, 3.1.77), and who ended his own life by suicide. So perhaps we are to be shocked that the patron saint for whom a school for boys is named is imagined to be something like a traitorous assassin. Second, deriving from ancient times, the name "Brutus" carries the meaning of someone who or something which is violent, severe, or grievous [Gk *barus*, "heavy, violent"], as well as "stupid" [L *brūtus, -a, -um*, "heavy, stupid, idiotic"]. It seems quite humorous, then, that there could be a Saint Brutus, i.e., "Saint Stupid," or "Saint Violent." But, this shows how much the Dursleys adore the notion of

Harry's being mistreated ... under the holy torture of those who idolize and carry on the work of a saint whose very name spells grief.

Third, for the classical reader, the name "Brutus" brings to mind the famous story about a hero from the earliest days of Roman history. Folklore is filled with the Cinderella type—the unwanted, neglected, scarcely tolerated member of a household who, in the end, becomes superior to her captors—or a Clark Kent type—the seemingly dull and awkward person, who lives a double life, concealing a super-hero identity. And "Brutus" is one of the most famous examples of this theme. In Roman history (510 BCE), a young member of the royal family, Lucius Junius Brutus pretends to be insane to avoid being killed by his uncle (Tarquin, the king) as a potential claimant to the throne. When Tarquin is unsettled by a frightening omen, he sends his sons to Delphi to inquire as to its significance. The boys, Titus and Arruns, take with them their cousin Brutus, to have an object of ridicule while on their trip. Brutus takes with him a hollow wooden stick, which he offers to Apollo as a gift. This does not seem to be odd, for a dullard such as Brutus. But what is unknown to his cousins is that inside the cheap, throw-away item is a rod of gold—which Livy says is "symbolic ... of his own character" (A.U.C. 1.56; de Sélincourt 96–97). His cover-up works. He survives to maturity. When the time is right, he heroically throws off his disguise and vows to ensure that there will never be another king over the Romans. Livy comments, "a miracle had happened—he was a changed man" (A.U.C. 1.59, 99). Brutus, whose nickname signifies "the stupid," based on his early behavior, becomes a leader of the Roman Republic and one of its first consuls. His name becomes the designation for a gēns, a group of Roman families, which lasts for centuries.

Now, as this applies to Harry. The Dursleys take Harry to be their "dull," "incurably criminal" nephew. And, in their imaginations, they relegate him to a training school for fools and dullards. The beauty of the name of this "school," however, is the irony associated with the word they think indicates the boy's nature. Beneath what is to them his "idiotic" appearance, is growing a wizard of such unique character that every witch and wizard in the world will know his name. So although Vernon Dursley would prefer to shove Harry into a school for dullards, the obvious question is, "Who is the real 'Brutus' or idiot here?" Recalling the ancient tale sheds a unique light on the use of this name. One of the standard themes of quest stories is "strength within hidden weakness," which is at work here, just as we saw it at work in Harry's drawing the ruby-encrusted Sword of Gryffindor from the tattered Sorting Hat to kill the basilisk, and in Hermione's producing fire from common items such as a jam jar.

Cadmus Peverell

The brother of Antioch and Ignotus Peverell and original owner of the Resurrection Stone. When he resurrects his deceased fiancée, he is so dejected at the state of her being that, in misery, he commits suicide in order to join his beloved in the world of the dead. The name "Cadmus" [Gk *Kadmos*; L *Cadmus*] is a name which is at least as old as the poetry of Homer (*Od.* 5.333) and Hesiod (*Theog.* 937). In myth, Cadmus is the founder of ancient Thebes, a dynasty which figures prominently in ancient mythology and legend. He is reputed to be the person who gave the art of writing to the Boeotians. His story begins when his sister Europa is abducted by Zeus from their Phoenician homeland. Cadmus is sent to bring her back home; but after lengthy attempts to retrieve her, he is directed by the Delphic Oracle to give up his pursuit and to establish a city, Thebes. His dynasty and successors become plagued with misfortunes.

In at least three ways, there are parallels between the wizard Cadmus and the ancient Greek figure. First, both engage in a fruitless pursuit of a loved one who has been taken away (Peverell for a fiancée, his predecessor for a sister). Second, the transmission of a cursed, physical token or prized possession is associated with the suffering and degeneration of the renowned tradition of both men's families. The name "Peverell" has been a touchstone of authenticity for wizards who claim family purity; however, the family falls into such deep decline that it comes to be represented by the Gaunt family, with all their dysfunction, and the greatly troubled boy, Tom Riddle, who murders his Muggle father and grandparents. The family token associated with Cadmus Peverell, the Gaunts, and Tom Riddle is the Resurrection Stone, which not only jinxes the Peverell owners, but also brings about Dumbledore's death, since he falls to the temptation to put it on so that he can recall his dead sister and parents.

In the Greek precursor, the House of Cadmus of Thebes is the citadel of culture and civilization in Greek mythology. Yet tragedy and ruin run through that family dynasty. For example, Harmonia's daughter, Agave, in drunken Bacchic frenzy wrenches from its torso the head of her own son, Pentheus, the king of Thebes. And as another example (of many which can be told), Oedipus fulfills his cursed fate of unknowingly killing his father, marrying his mother and begetting children by her. The tangible token associated with the curse on the House of Cadmus is the jeweled necklace of Harmonia.

Third, the snake motif is prominent in the stories of both men named "Cadmus." When the Phoenician founder of Thebes arrives at his destined location, he offers grateful sacrifice to Athena. Needing water, he and his men go to a spring which happens to be sacred to the god Ares and which is guarded by a powerful serpent, a son of Ares. Cadmus kills the protector of the site, offending the god. At this, he hears a voice prophesying that he, too will be seen as a snake (*Met.* 3.97–98). Years later, while reviewing his family's profound grief and misfortunes, he recalls the killing of the serpent and he prays that he, too, will become a serpent, a prayer which is fulfilled for both himself and his wife. The snake motif is quite prominent with the Gaunts, who are Parselmouths, and proud heirs of Salazar Slytherin. Their front door is decorated with a dead snake, and Morfin plays with live adders.

A final motif links this Cadmus to the *Potter* novels. The Theban king gives to his bride, Harmonia, the wedding gift of a charmed necklace made by the god Hephaestus. It is passed on to or stolen by others as time goes by, and it brings death and murder to those who receive it or are associated with it. This same motif of the cursed necklace makes its appearance in Harry's world. It appears as an item for sale in Borgin and Burkes' store window (where a warning tag notifies shoppers that it had caused the death of nineteen Muggles), and as a gift given for the purpose of its claiming a twentieth victim.

Callisto

One of the four moons of the planet Jupiter, named for some of the people whom he loved. Callisto [Gk *Kallisto,* "fairest, most beautiful"; L *Callisto*] is a beautiful girl (or nymph) of Arcadia, a devoted follower of the goddess Artemis (Roman Diana), which means she is a devoted virgin. Disguised as Diana, Jupiter tricks her, seduces her and makes her pregnant. She is transformed into a bear (either by Jupiter, to hide his affair, or by his wife Juno, to punish him and the girl, or by Diana as punishment for the girl's not being chaste). But that is only the beginning of her hardship. Years later, when her son Arcas [Gk *Arkas,* "an Arcadian," perhaps from *arkos* or *arktos,* "bear"; L *Arcas*] has grown into a young man, the two meet when he is hunting and is about to kill the bear which he has come upon. Staring in love and longing at her son, Callisto cannot run away. Her human sentiments strive within her; but her bear body prevents her from expressing them (*Met.* 2.401–530). Jupiter intervenes to save mother and son by transforming them into the constellations Ursa Major (the Great Bear with seven of its stars forming the Big Dipper) and Ursa Minor (the Little Bear whose stars contain the

Little Dipper) [L *ursa, -ae,* "bear, Bear (the constellation)"]. But his jealous wife has her revenge even then. She positions the stars in the heavens so that the constellations will never dip into the ocean, forever denying the mother and her cub water to satisfy their thirst.[9]

Professor Sinistra assigned her students the task of writing an extensive essay on the four moons of Jupiter. Hermione had mastered the names and features of the moons, but Ron labored unhappily and unsuccessfully at the task. He even considered asking Hermione to let him see her essay, a proposal which Harry saw as useless (*OP* 295).

Caractacus Burke

Founder of Borgin and Burkes' store. His personal name would be an appealing choice for a shady magical character, as the English word "caract," can designate a magical character, symbol, or a charm [Gk *character,* "mark, stamp, figure, brand" > L *character,* "stamp, impressed mark" (LSJ 1977; OLD 309), variant spelling "caract," and taking on the meaning of a spell, magical rite or sign, or charm since the early middle ages].[10]

The name, however, goes far back in British and Roman history. In 43 CE, the Romans seized the capital of the king of Britain, Caratacus [misspelled over time as Caractacus; L *Carātacus*]. He was forced to flee, and for nine years to lead military resistance to the Romans from Wales. He gained a wide reputation as a king. In 51 CE, his troops were defeated and he was taken to Rome as a captive. The Roman historian Tacitus indicates that he pled his case before the Emperor in a way which glorified himself and thus magnified the glory of the Romans' victory. Consequently, Claudius let him live rather than put him to death as an unworthy enemy (Tacitus, *Annals* 12.33–38). Perhaps the arrogance of both Cara(c)tacuses is what makes them similar. Or, perhaps it is their common trait of cleverness or shiftiness. The ancient king, with a weaker army than that of the Romans, but with lots of cleverness, kept the Romans from victory for a long time. Mr. Burke, as a business man who traffics in Dark Magic items, seems to be a shifty merchant.

The word "burke" derives from the activity of a murderer by that name who killed by suffocating or strangling his victims, in order to sell their bodies for dissection.[11] Whether Caractacus Burke ever killed anyone is uncertain. The nefarious activity of the killer who made the word famous does sound similar to the business activity of the shop owner.

Cassandra

CASSANDRA TRELAWNEY

A famous Seer, the great-great-grandmother of Professor Sibyll Trelawney, who is the teacher of Divination at Hogwarts. The mythical Cassandra [Gk *Kassandra*; L *Cassandra*] is the daughter of the king and queen of Troy, and a gifted prophetess. The god Apollo wants her love, and at first she agrees, in gratitude for which he gives her the gift of prophecy. But she changes her mind, and Apollo gets his revenge for the rejection by asking for just one kiss. When she allows him to kiss her, he spits into her mouth and thus curses her, so that although she can prophesy accurately, no one will ever believe her, thinking her prophecies to be nonsense. She is able clearly and accurately to foretell events which precipitate great misfortune: that the visit of her brother Paris to Sparta, in order to see Helen, will cause a great war (Euripides, *Andromache* 293; Ovid, *Heroides*, 16, 120); that the wooden horse which the Greeks leave on the shore will be the fall of Troy (*Epit.* 5.16ff.; *Aen.* 2.235ff.); and that both she and Agamemnon will be murdered (Aeschylus, *Agamemnon,* 957ff.). These prophecies are uttered in vain, however, as they are ignored (Howatson 522–23). The introduction of the name of this ill-fated prophetess into the tradition of Professor Trelawney is especially appropriate, as Sibyll Trelawney herself is generally dismissed as a crackpot, even though on very rare occasions she prophesies the truth.

CASSANDRA VABLATSKY

Author of the textbook *Unfogging the Future.* One expects a recognized authority and writer of a school textbook on Divination to be a most trusted resource in her field. But this author's name makes the reader question whether that author has any ability to say anything clearly, correctly, and authoritatively on things mystical.

The name "Cassandra" means "man-trapper" [Gk *kassuō,* "to stitch together, to hatch a plot" + *anēr, andros,* "man" (Room 84)]. With respect to Ms. Trelawney, perhaps the message for readers is to be aware that by her given name, she is good at intrigue even when she speaks in a matter-of-fact manner. And with respect to Ms. Vablatsky, perhaps what Rowling hints at by using this name is to warn, "reader, beware!"

Ciceron Harkiss

The man who, according to Horace Slughorn, gave Ambrosius Flume (the owner of Honeydukes candy store) his first job. The name is Spanish

(Cicerón) for "Cicero" [L *Cicerō, -ōnis,* the *cognōmen* or family name of the larger group or *gens, Tullia, -ae*]. Whether or not one needs to import any significance of the classical Roman rhetorician/politician/philosopher/lawyer Cicero to this gentleman, about whom we know next to nothing, we are at least alerted to his carrying a most famous name.

Circe

A famous witch who is honored by having her picture included among the Chocolate Frog cards (*SS* 103). She has the same name as the witch-goddess of Homer's *Odyssey* (Books 10–11), who uses a wand and drugs to transform Odysseus' men into pigs. Odysseus is prevented from being turned into a pig when he eats her poisoned food by taking an antidote beforehand, a magical herb which the god Hermes gives to him and which is called "moly"—from which we get the expression "holy moly!"[12] Odysseus compels her to transform his men back into their human state. It is she who convinces Odysseus to enter the Underworld to learn from the blind prophet Tiresias how to get back home to Ithaca after the Trojan War. Tradition which came after Homer's epics indicates that he fathered at least two sons with Circe, Agrius and Latinus (*Theog.* 1011–13). The Frog card witch appears to rely on and advance the tradition of powerful, seductive and dangerous women of magic.

Cornelius Fudge

The Minister of Magic whose performance is lackluster, and whose judgments are incredibly poor, and whom Hagrid calls a "bungler" (*SS* 65), that is, a clumsy or awkward person who does bad work. Fearful of public criticism and too eager to give a display of "leadership," he imprisons Hagrid in Azkaban, even though he appears not to believe that Hagrid is guilty. At Harry's hearing before the Wizengamot, Fudge pushes for a "guilty" verdict, rather than try him fairly. He attempts to silence Dumbledore's criticism by sentencing him to Azkaban. And when the Dark Lord appears publicly in the Ministry of Magic, befuddled Fudge is jittery, startled, and cannot get himself to believe what he has seen. But the charmed statues of the House-Elf and the goblin in the Ministry attest, unquestionably, to the appearance. And these non-human statues have to attend to the leader of their Wizarding world. Eventually, of course, he is dismissed from office.

As to there being any connection between Fudge and the dead Greeks and Romans, his personal name signals to anyone in advance of meeting the man that a "Cornelius" must certainly be someone notable, impressive, and praiseworthy. "Cornelius" is the name of a respectable Roman family and tribe [L *Cornēlius*]. Perhaps of all the ancient Corneliuses of whom we know, the one who most closely resembles Fudge in his pride and downfall would be Gaius Cornelius Gallus (69–26 BCE). This Roman noble, a trusted friend of the Emperor Augustus, is given high official rank and duties. However, he is later recalled in disgrace from his office as the first prefect of Egypt because in his arrogance he boasts of himself in inscriptions on the pyramids and has statues of himself erected all over Egypt. He is formally denounced by the Emperor and takes his own life (Courtney 378–79; Howatson 260).

Like the ancient Roman official, Cornelius Fudge fancies himself a special kind of man. He and Lucius Malfoy (whose personal name, too, is a famous and popular Roman name) share a preference for "pure" families (among whom they count themselves), and a prejudice against all who are not pure-bloods. While this trait is glaringly obvious to us in the way the Malfoys speak and act, the trait is not emphasized repeatedly in Fudge, mainly because as a paranoid public figure, his first concern is to avoid controversy and to maintain the status quo. In spite of our presumptions that anyone named "Cornelius," and chosen to be the leader of the entire Wizarding world would be a person of class, poise, dignity, and pedigree, when Fudge's guard is down, he shows that he really is a man of common material. For example, when he sees the pustules on Marietta Edgecombe's face, without catching himself, he blurts out, "galloping gargoyles!" This outburst reveals that he is really not a person of self-composure and noble bearing. It locates him, for us, among others who are from a much lower cultural stratum: Hagrid, the rough-cut groundskeeper, exclaims, "Gulpin' gargoyles" (*SS* 54); Ludo Bagman, the head of the Ministry's Department of Games and Sports, who has a problem with gambling and money-laundering, and impulsively blurts out, "gulpin' gargoyles" (*GF* 133); and the shady criminal Mundungus Fletcher, bleats, "gormless gargoyle" (*OP* 86).[13]

While the Minister of Magic has a truly noble Roman personal name, his family name is not to be envied. "To fudge" means "to cheat." Perhaps the character and fate of the ancient Roman are not without some parallel to Cornelius Fudge.

Damocles

Marcus Belby's uncle and a former student of Horace Slughorn, developer of the Wolfsbane Potion, for which he receives the Order of Merlin award. To develop that treatment, he obviously has to deal with werewolves and live in constant peril. His example of fame achieved, accompanied by the ever-present danger of catastrophe has a predecessor in the literature of the Romans. The tale of the "sword of Damocles" is the legend of a man who got what he wished for ... and more. The story goes like this. In ancient Syracuse (Sicily), the tyrannical king Dionysius declares that he is a happy man. One of the people in his court, Damocles, hears the king and tries to gain his favor by flattering him, telling him that surely Dionysius is the happiest of all men. The king, not fooled by shallow praise, turns the tables on the flatterer. He asks Damocles how he would like to live as the king does, since he thinks a king's life is so blessed. Damocles very eagerly seizes on the opportunity. The king places him on a golden couch and provides feasts for his appetite and servants to fulfill his wishes. Dionysius, however, gives him more than Damocles requests, for he wants this flatterer to know the full truth about the life of a king. To make him aware of the dangers always hanging over the head of a king, he has a sword hung from the ceiling by a horse-hair, dangling directly over Damocles' head. The ever present threat of death so terrorizes Damocles that the pleasures he thought he would enjoy have no appeal to him and he begs to be relieved of the opportunity to be as happy as the king. Cicero, who tells us this story, concludes, "Dionysius was indicating clearly enough that happiness is out of the question if you are perpetually menaced by some terror" (Cicero, *Tusculan Disputations*, 5.61, trans. Grant 85). Damocles the wizard may be praised by many people for his invention of Wolfsbane Potion, but the fact that he is called "Damocles" gives a strong impression that his path to fame, constantly experimenting with werewolves, has been paved with terrible dangers and not just joy.

Daphne Greengrass

A student who, along with Hermione, is called to take the practical portion of their O.W.L. test in Charms. "Daphne" is the name of a nymph whom Apollo pursues for love, and who rejects his advances. As the god chases her, she calls upon her father, Peneus, a river god, to save her. He rescues her by transforming her into a laurel tree [Gk *daphnē, -idis*]. But Apollo does not lose her completely, for he makes the laurel his sacred tree, which is then forever associated with him. The tale is an etiological legend, explaining why the laurel is sacred to the god. Among the Greeks and Romans individual gods came to be associated with particular trees—Athena with the olive tree,

Artemis with the myrtle tree, Zeus with the oak, Silvanus with the forest, Rumina the fig tree (Garry "Trees," 2005, 466).

Dedalus Diggle

A wizard, a member of the Advanced Guard and original member of the Order of the Phoenix who acts very unwisely and endangers the security and safety of the Wizarding world by excitedly setting off a shower of shooting stars. Professor McGonagall, critical of his carelessness, says Dedalus "never had much sense" (*SS* 10). Seven years later, he tells Vernon Dursley that he is completely at a loss as to how to operate the controls of an automobile. His mental dullness and technical ineptitude strike the reader as ironic, for he bears the name of the most famous engineer, craftsman and inventor in antiquity, the Greek "Daedalus," whose name means "cunning worker" or "artist" [Gk *Daidalos* < *daidallō*, "to work cunningly" > L *Daedalus*]. The skill of the inventor becomes the stuff of fable, even before the finalization of our earliest western literature, the *Iliad* (18.590ff). And his reputation has grown over the centuries.[14] He is renowned for designing the famous Minotaur's labyrinth beneath the palace of Knossos, and for inventing human flight by shaping wings for himself and his son, Icarus. When he wants to escape from his captor, Minos, the king of Crete, he devises wings of wood, wax and feathers in order to fly away to Sicily. He tries out unknown and untested devices, and the maiden launch of the wings can possibly lead to a tragic finale. He warns and advises his teenage son, Icarus, not to test the limits of the wings, not to go too high or too low, lest they come apart and he be killed. Daedalus is analytical, thoughtful, careful. Anticipating the possible consequences of attempting to fly, he urges his enthusiastic son to be moderate and keep to the middle course. Naturally, the impetuous boy disobeys and falls to his death in the sea which is named after him, the Icarian Sea (*Met.* 8.183–235).

Rowling's use of this name adds irony to her character portrayal of the wizard. Diggle is completely the opposite of his predecessor. Daedalus creates unimaginable inventions; the wizard Dedalus, lacking common sense, carelessly endangers the Wizarding public and is flummoxed by the simple mechanical controls of an automobile. The Greek inventor is cautious, considering consequences, avoiding excess. Mr. Diggle, however, is impulsive and lacks foresight. By adopting this name, Rowling gives us a lens through which to envision her character. At the mention of the name, we are prepared to encounter genius, to expect traits of the ancient figure in Dedalus the wizard. By the time we get to know him, however, his own distinctive character is marked by the striking and clever contrast he offers to the original "Daedalus."

Dexter Fortescue

An outspoken former Headmaster at Hogwarts whose portrait hangs in the Headmaster's office. Being a strong supporter of Harry and Dumbledore's Army, he belittles Dolores Umbridge and the authorities at the time for using spies and crooks to do their work. His name is most appropriate for this gentleman, as "Dexter" comes from the Latin word for "right, on the right-hand side, favorable, agreeable, strong" [L *dexter, dext(e)ra, dext(e)rum*]. Used for the hand which is extended to show good faith and to hold weapons, it connotes power and is the opposite of the word for "left" [L *sinister, sinistra, sinistrum*], which connotes the left hand or side, or that which is adverse, harmful or immoral. In both of Dexter's appearances in the novels, he is on the side of what is right and strong and opposed to what is wrong and immoral.

Dobby

The most prominent House-Elf in the series, and as such, he is quite fittingly named. The term "dobby" denotes a "household sprite or apparition supposed to haunt certain premises or localities; a brownie."[15] Two features of this character might be read in light of ancient models: Dobby as an oracle or prophet and Dobby as an emancipated slave. First, Dobby the seer. Prophets and oracles are often visionary and vague, whether they are House-Elves or priestesses. The first time we meet him, the strange little creature attempts to give Harry a warning that he may be in danger. He cannot be specific about the danger, so he speaks vaguely, trying to make Harry comply with his directions. When Harry cannot understand the communication, the elf abuses himself harshly, because he is torn between his passion to deliver a message which will protect Harry, whom he respects tremendously, and his fear of betraying his master's family by revealing details which are private.

When Dumbledore confronts Lucius Malfoy about the diary of Tom Riddle, Dobby points to the diary and hits himself in the head with his fist. Again, the "oracular" elf is completely unable to say what he means, leaving Harry totally confused. We eventually learn that he is trying to communicate very subtle truths. For all the guarded help he tries to give Harry, the clue is much too obscure and unclear, and the way it is presented suggests an explanation in exactly the opposite direction. The elf is a comical, tragic, and conflicted seer. He has lots to reveal, but he is constrained not to divulge any of it.

As a prophet or oracle, Dobby is not the equal of the ancient Sibyls or priestesses, whose life function was to present the concerns of people to the gods and deliver to the seekers some direction as to the will of the gods and the destiny of the inquirers. But behind the fantasy story of Dobby is the model of ancient oracles, which were notoriously ambiguous. At times, they could lead to very unfortunate outcomes, if interpreted wrongly. For example, Herodotus reports that Croesus, the king of Lydia, felt he should check the rising power of the Persians. So he sent an embassy to Delphi to inquire of the priestess of Apollo if he should wage war on the neighboring kingdom. The answer given was that if he attacked the Persians, he would destroy a great empire. Encouraged by the oracle, he marched against Persia and was soundly defeated. He destroyed a great empire, but it was his own (*Histories* 1.53).

Second, regarding the method of Dobby's gaining his freedom, he has told Harry that the only way a House-Elf can be freed is by his master's giving him an article of clothing. Harry uses that piece of information to trick Lucius Malfoy into unknowingly liberating his own House-Elf. He gives Lucius the diary of Tom Riddle, in which he has hidden a nasty sock. Angered, Malfoy tosses the article of clothing away, and when Dobby catches it, he is liberated. As remote from ancient society as this "custom" might appear, it is a humorous twist on a typical ancient Roman practice, the conferring of the cap of freedom. The emancipation of a slave in the ancient Roman world involved a master's giving of an article of clothing to the slave, but a very particular article, not just any kind. The item was a cap, a "cap of freedom" [Gk *pīlos*, "cap, helmet lining" > L *pilleus*]. It was a felt cap worn as proof of one's new status.

Each year, during the festival called the Saturnalia, in late December, Romans would celebrate the harvest by revelry and the relaxing of many of the usual business and school affairs. Slaves were freed from their usual duties and even if they were not free, during this festival they could wear the cap of freedom and enjoy privileges not available to them at any other time. It was a time of partying and laxity, not unlike Carnival today. During the French Revolution, the pilleus or cap of freedom was worn by those rising up to claim their liberty. The artwork on the inside of the dome of the Capitol rotunda in Washington, D.C., depicts "Liberty" sitting to the right of George Washington, wearing the pilleus, the cap of Liberty. In view of the history of the "cap of freedom," Dobby's catching a filthy sock takes on new, and humorous, meaning.

Doris

DORIS CROCKFORD

A witch whom Harry meets during his first visit to the Leaky Cauldron.

DORIS PURKISS

An unbalanced witch who claims, in an article in *The Quibbler*, that "Sirius Black" is an alias for a singer whose real name is Stubby Boardman, with whom she had been romantically involved at the time of the alleged crime committed by "Sirius Black" (*OP* 191–92). The name is Greek (*Doris*), and refers to someone from Doris, in northern Greece, therefore, a "Dorian." Dorians were not known to be unbalanced. Their locale, however, just may be the original source of the modern name.

Elphias Doge

Member of the Advance Guard and lifelong friend of Albus Dumbledore. He wrote the obituary for the Headmaster in the *Daily Prophet*, providing us with much background information on Albus. The two friends planned a world-tour together after their graduation from Hogwarts; however, Albus' family situation prevented him from participating. Doge traveled alone and wrote exciting reports of his experiences to his friend. Later, he felt that he may have been insensitive by writing so joyously to his friend who was suffering at home in horrible and tragic circumstances (the death of his mother and his sister).

Their relationship and his personal name compel us to consider the friends in light of a very similar and famous narrative, the biblical story of Job and his friends. "Elphias" is a variation on the Hebrew name "Eliphaz" [*'elifaz*], the exact meaning of which is uncertain, but possibly signifies "God is fine gold," or "God crushes."[16] The biblical Eliphaz was a friend of Job's during the latter's miserable and lengthy sufferings (as Elphias was Albus' supportive friend when life caved in on him). Not all the features of the biblical character are applicable to Albus' friend, but the biblical Eliphaz did try to comfort his unfortunate friend (Job 2:11; Holbert 471; Lundberg 398). In his attention to the plight of Job, at a point of exasperation over the unending woes of his friend, Eliphaz went so far as to blame the sufferer for his misery, surely a very insensitive, if well-intentioned, tactic. Similarly, while Doge enjoyed his travels and freedom, his exciting letters were focused on himself and were insensitive to Albus' confinement and suffering.

Another suggestive parallel between the biblical friends and the magical friends is that Dumbledore reached out his hand to Doge when the latter had dragon pox. In the biblical record, Eliphaz reminds Job of how the suffering man instructed many and strengthened others' weak hands (Job 4:1–2). The Elphias-Eliphaz parallels perhaps invite us to visualize Dumbledore as something of a suffering Job figure, at least in his early years, and Elphias as a good friend in bad times, but not a friend with perfect sensitivities.

Elphias' family name, "Doge," has a distant Latin origin. That was a title of chief magistrates in the old republic of Venice and Genoa in the sixteenth to eighteenth centuries [L *dux, ducis*, "leader" > It] (Neufeldt 403). The name may well direct us to picture Elphias as an outstanding person, with a significant family heritage. Altogether, these similarities suggest that one might view Doge as a wizard of noble ancestry and a serious, if imperfect, friend not unlike the friend of the most famous sufferer in western history.

Europa

One of the four moons of the planet Jupiter. The moons are named for mythical people with whom Zeus (Jupiter) was romantically or sexually involved. Europa [Gk *eurus* and *eurōpos, -ē, -on*, "wide, broad, far-reaching" > *Eurōpē* > L *Eurōpa*] (LSJ 731)] was a Phoenician princess of Tyre whom the god, either in the form of a bull or by means of a bull, abducted and took to Crete, where he made her the mother of Minos and Rhadamanthys. This tale gives a mythological explanation of Phoenician expansion around the Mediterranean, tells how the Minoan civilization came to be, and cites the origin of the name of the continent of Europe. The bull was installed in the heavens as the constellation Taurus and Europa became identified with the female goddess of Crete.[17] The moons were the subject of a long essay which Professor Sinistra assigned to her Astronomy class as homework. Hermione took the assignment with relish, but to Harry, and especially Ron, the task was pure drudgery (*OP* 295).

Fabian Prewett

Brother of Gideon Prewett and Molly Weasley and one of the original members of the Order of the Phoenix, pictured in Mad-Eye Moody's photograph of the group. Moody praises the brothers for their courageous fight to the death at the hands of five Death Eaters. The name "Fabian" is of Roman origin [L *Fabius, -a, -um*, the name of a college of priests, a tribe, and a group of Roman families > *Fabiānus, -a, -um*, a personal male name, or, as an adjective, "belonging to Fabius"]. The most famous of the Roman Fabians is probably Quintus Fabius Maximus, the general who led the Roman armies in their defenses against Hannibal in the second Punic War (218–201 BCE). His method of resistance was to avoid direct battle with Hannibal, who defeated all his enemies on his way to Italy. He impeded Hannibal's advance by following him, but avoiding pitched battle. For this tactic, he was given the nickname "Cunctator," (the "Hesitator"). His methods were eventually praised for their success and practicality, and he was called the "Shield of Rome" (Howatson 249). Fabian is an heir to a most appropriate name, one which recalls a famous leader in legendary warfare.[18]

Fawkes

Dumbledore's winged companion, a "phoenix." The mythological bird has brilliant gold and crimson coloration. According to ancient lore, it dies every five hundred years and is reborn as a new bird from its own ashes. The phoenix fable that is found in the *Harry Potter* series is an enhanced version which has the bird dying and rising more frequently, the newborn arising from the ashes of its immolated predecessor [Gk *phoinix, phoinīkos*, "Phoenician," "crimson," a color associated with ancient Phoenicia]. Fawkes also is given particular amplified abilities over the legendary phoenix, which play a significant role in the development of the plot. The power of Fawkes, in particular, benefits both Harry and Voldemort, for both of their wands have at their core a feather from Fawkes' tail.

Fawkes is a helper, a healer, and in his regeneration a symbol of continuing life through resurrection.[19] What he stands for magnifies the irony of the opposite natures of Dumbledore and Voldemort. Dumbledore does not crave life, but embraces death as "the next great adventure" (*SS* 297), while Voldemort, fixated on gaining immortality, wastes his life vainly trying to keep from losing it. The symbol of what Voldemort wants belongs to the one who has no anxiety to attain it.

Fluffy

One of Hagrid's pet creatures, a ferocious, three-headed dog which he posts as guard over a door leading to the chamber in which the Sorcerer's

Stone is hidden. As fierce as the mastiff is, he can be lulled to sleep by music, Harry's playing on his wooden flute. Anyone who has even a smattering of knowledge of Greek mythology can quickly recognize this most obvious parallel to the classics, the three-headed guardian of Hades, named "Cerberus." In re-packaging this borrowed image, the author's humor is as charming as the image is arresting, for she has Hagrid name this vicious dog "Fluffy." This is a witty reversal of the image of the dog, as well as a revelation of the character of Hagrid, who, in his innocence and kind-spiritedness, sees what is cuddly and attractive even in bizarre and vicious creatures.

In mythology, Cerberus [Gk *Kerberos* > L *Cerberus*] stands guard to prevent entrance into, as well as escape from, the Underworld.[20] His image is intended to strike terror in those who behold him, with his three heads[21] which inhibit anyone's sneaking up on him, threatening horrible attack at every angle. On a water pot dating from the sixth century BCE, Cerberus also has snakes on his heads and paws. He is said to have a serpent's tail as well (De Rose "Mythical Animals," 2005, 68). He comes by his monstrous appearance fairly enough, having been born into a family of bizarre individuals. His great-grandmother is the snake-headed Gorgon Medusa; his own parents are monstrous beings (Typhon, his father, has a hundred serpent heads and Echidna, his mother, has the lower body of a snake). His siblings are the Chimaeras (who breathe fire and have the body of a she-goat and the tail of a snake), and the poisonous, many-headed Hydra, which Heracles kills.

Cerberus is conquered only a few times, and usually by someone disabling him or capturing him by force or trickery. However, in Vergil's poem about Orpheus' descent to the Underworld to plead for the return of his lost bride, Eurydice, who has died an untimely death, the guardian is overcome in a different way. It is the stirring power of his passionate music that stills the processes of the Underworld, silencing and calming Cerberus, and persuading the deities of the dead to return to him his beloved (Vergil, *Georgics* 4.453–527). There seems to be an echo of Orpheus' musical power to soothe in Harry's lullaby to Fluffy.[22]

The broader thematic parallel, though, is between Harry's adventure and that of Heracles in the Underworld. In having to undergo the contest of getting past the three-headed guard-dog which guards the realms beneath, Harry again cuts something of a figure of Heracles. Of the Twelve Labors which he had to undergo to gain immortality, one was that he had to overcome Cerberus somehow, bring him to the upper world to show to King Eurystheus, and return him to the Underworld. The two contestants' methods are different—Heracles has to wrestle and chain Cerberus; Harry uses a flute. And their tasks differ—Harry only has to get past Fluffy; Heracles has to subdue him, take him to the upper world and return him. But their heroic, life-endangering descents to their respective Underworlds bear similarities which encourage us to bring to Harry's trial the colors and tones of the trial of Heracles, in which he survives a deadly contest.

Galatea Merrythought

The Defense Against the Dark Arts teacher at Hogwarts during Tom Riddle's student days. The mythological "Galatea" [Gk *Galatia* > L *Galatēa*] is a sea nymph who loves a shepherd boy named Acis, but who is courted by the grotesque Cyclops Polyphemus. Knowing that he is no match for handsome Acis, the giant hurls a huge stone upon him. As Acis' blood flows from under the stone, Galatea transforms the stream into the river Acis which flows at the base of Mount Aetna, thus making a river god of her lover.[23] If Ms. Merrythought is anything like her name, she probably had milky-white complexion, and was very attractive.

Ganymede

A moon of the planet Jupiter. The professor of Astronomy at Hogwarts, Professor Sinistra, required a lengthy essay on the four moons of Jupiter, which Hermione completed in short order and with mastery of the subject. Ron and Harry labored unhappily on the project until the late hours of the evening (*OP* 295). In Greek mythology, Ganymede [Gk *Ganymēdēs*; L *Ganymēdēs*] was a handsome young son of the king of Troy, whom the god abducted because of his beauty. In order to have him nearby, always, he put the boy in service to the gods forever as their cup-bearer. When the planet Jupiter was named for its commanding size, it seemed logical that the nearby, orbiting moons should be named for those mythological figures whom Zeus/Jupiter wanted to have for himself, including Ganymede.

Gideon Prewett

Brother of Fabian Prewett and Molly Weasley and one of the original members of the Order of the Phoenix, pictured in Mad-Eye Moody's photograph of the group. Moody praises the brothers for their courageous fight to the death at the hands of Death Eaters. The name "Gideon" is the biblical name of a heroic Israelite judge (a person specially appointed by God to assume leadership in restoring the community and to wage unrelenting war on the enemies of God's people). He served as leader during the period between the settlement or conquest of Canaan by the Israelites and the accession to the throne of Israel's first king. Gideon also had a gift for divination (see Judg 6–8). The similarity of the two Gideons appears to be their bravery and commitment to be leaders in a crucial fight for their causes.

Gilderoy Lockhart

Professor of Defense Against the Dark Arts at Hogwarts during Harry's second year at school. With this professor, two classical referents come to mind, Narcissus and the Roman god Janus. First, Gilderoy is a real "narcissist," a person totally fixated on his own image and self-importance (Adney 349). With Lockhart, it is all about himself. When he begins the dueling instruction, he asks if everyone can see him and hear him, not whether everyone can see and hear. But, he is even farther down the road of mental instability than the original "Narcissus," for he imposes himself on everybody else. He has the students purchase all seven of his books, apparently presuming he is giving them the most wonderful opportunity to have so much of him. He is so blind with self-love that Hermione can trick him with flattery into signing a permission slip for her to use the books located in the restricted section of the library.

His boundless ego is exemplified by the gaudy and enormous peacock-feather quill which he uses. This is quite the contrast to Harry's eagle-feather quill, which reflects his bold and courageous character. Rowling's creation of quills to reflect characters is somewhat akin to the ancients' ascribing to the gods sacred birds which characterized their nature or power (e.g., Zeus's powerful eagle and Athena's/Minerva's owl, symbolic of wisdom).

Lockhart thinks everyone else adores him just as much as he adores himself. No matter what the situation, somehow he presumes that he is the real center of interest. The "pools" in which he views his beloved (as Narcissus beholds his love object in his pool) are of various sorts: the autographed press-photos which he sends out to his fans; his five awards for his fabulous smile, conferred by *Witch Weekly*; and his photographs on the dust jackets of his books. Since these photos are magical, his moving image appears to be real.

There are a couple of variations on his likeness to Narcissus, though, which show creative use of the original model. First, unlike Narcissus, who eliminates all other people from his world, Lockhart imposes himself on everyone around him. And second, he is a fraud and he knows it. He loves to recite his credentials, but they are a sham. He is of the Order of Merlin, but only third class—bottom of the list. He is only an honorary member of the Dark Forces Defense League. And when he is called upon to apply the wondrous skills which he claims to possess, he is a shivering coward who tries to escape and to cover his exit by casting a memory charm on HH&R, who have discovered his duplicity. Narcissus is not a duplicitous fraud, only a very disturbed youth.

Second, Janus is the Roman god of gates, doorways, and beginnings, represented with two faces, oriented toward opposite directions [L *iānus, -ī,* "doorway," > *Iānus, -ī*]. He is seen as a god concerned with the beginning and ending of things, such as the beginning of a new year (hence, our month named "January"), and the start and conclusion of wars. In addition, he is the god called upon first in ritual prayers (Purcell 771). Gilderoy Lockhart is also a figure with two faces, but with a completely different meaning, that is, of being "two-faced," a phony, duplicitous, which is not at all a part of the idea of the Roman god who is concerned with looking back and forward at the same time. The god's facing opposite ways has nothing to do with deception and fraudulence.

Lockhart's hospitalization on the Janus Thickey ward at St. Mungo's suggests another feature of the Roman god worth comparing with the professor's story. The fourth floor of this hospital is allocated to long-term residents. Because the patients in this ward are so severely incapacitated, though possibly mobile, the door to the ward is locked. In ancient Rome, during times of peace, the doors to the temple of Janus were kept closed. During war-time, they were kept open. Perhaps, since the chapter in which we read about his hospitalization is entitled "Christmas on the Closed Ward," there is a hint that with Janus' doors closed, the patients housed within, including Gilderoy Lockhart, are safely tucked away, out of the fray and conflict of life.

While the name "Gilderoy" does not derive from classical languages, it does reinforce the character of the man. The legendary Gilderoy was a Scottish thief whose crimes were so much greater than those of the worst criminals, that he was hanged higher than the others.[24] The name probably derives from a combination of two words. The verb "to gild," (from an OE word *gyldan*) denotes covering something with a thin veneer of gold, or covering over something in order to conceal defects, or to make actions or words seem to be brilliant by using deceptive words.[25] The "-roy" almost certainly is from Fr *roi*, "king, of royal family." Lockhart is the superlative thief of glory, more arrogant and artificial than any other character in the series. He claims credit for marvelous accomplishments which he never did. The lauded wizard is no royalty at all, but a faker and fraud who covers his emptiness with a golden imagery to hide reality.

Gregory the Smarmy

Apparently a wizard whose life and accomplishments deserve to be remembered, as a memorial statue of him stands in a hall at Hogwarts. The function of the statue in the story is not to introduce Gregory himself, but to serve as a landmark for a secret passageway out of the school which is behind the statue. The wizard's name, "Gregory," has been famous since the early centuries CE, particularly in the Christian tradition. Numerous saints, fathers of the church, scholars, and popes have gone by that title. It has a very positive connotation, as it comes originally from a Greek verb which means "to be alert, fully awake, watchful" [Gk *grēgorein > grēgoria*, "watchfulness, alertness" > *Grēgorios* > LL *Gregorius*]. Rowling's sense of humor surfaces once again, as she tags this sentinel-statue with a most impressive and exalted name, signifying something such as "the most noble watchman," but then gives him a completely discordant nickname, "the Smarmy," i.e., one who is "flattering in an oily, insincere manner" (Neufeldt 1266). And the irony of his name and his function is that what he actually is watching is not a great hall or throne room, but a hidden passageway out of Hogwarts.

Hector Dagworth-Granger

Famous as the founder of the Most Extraordinary Society of Potioneers, mentioned only as one of the names which Professor Slughorn drops in order to impress others. The ancient "Hector" [Gk *Hektōr* > L *Hector*] is the principal Trojan warrior in Homer's *Iliad*, the son of the king of Troy (Priam), and the single most formidable foe of Achilles. The only parallel between these two "Hectors" seems to be that the founding father of an extraordinarily famous society deserves a name that rings with fame and glory.

Helena Ravenclaw

The beautiful and proud ghost who inhabits the Ravenclaw Tower and who is known to students as "the Gray Lady." She is the daughter of Rowena

Ravenclaw, one of the founders of Hogwarts. She stole her mother's wisdom-giving diadem and hid it. Unfortunately, Tom Riddle charmed the secret of its location from her with pretended, sympathetic kindness toward the young lady.[26]

The sad, perpetually youthful ghost bears one of the most famous names in history, the name of the beautiful woman whose face launched a thousand ships, Helen of Troy [Gk *Helenē,* "torch, light" > L *Helena* > Fr *Hélène*]. Since Helen's father was Zeus and her mother a human, Leda, she was half goddess. Her beauty was her glory and her undoing. When the Trojan prince Paris was compelled by Zeus to judge who was the fairest of the beautiful goddesses Hera, Athena, and Aphrodite, each of the contestants bribed the young man with her best offer (the famous "Judgment of Paris"). Aphrodite, the goddess of love, promised Paris that if he would choose her, she would give to him the most beautiful woman in the world, Helen (who happened to be the wife of Menelaus, the king of Sparta). He decided in her favor and an international conflict ensued.

Her beauty became the cause of wide-ranging opinions of this demigod. Some ancient Greeks held that she was courted by Paris (also called Alexander) and, of her own free will, abandoned her kingdom, family and home to flee with the young suitor to Troy. Thus, she was seen as a bitch of a woman who abandoned everything for a fling with a Trojan foreigner, which caused a ten-year war between her home country and Troy. Others, however, thought that she had been driven out of her senses by Aphrodite, the goddess of love, in order to deliver her to Paris as the prize which she had offered to him. In this latter version, it was said that Helen went to Egypt on her way to Troy and stayed there for the entire duration of the Trojan War, while a phantom or image of her went to Troy (e.g., Euripides, *Helen,* ll. 1275ff.). So some ancient people detested the wantonness of the beauty who appeared to trade up in her personal situation, regardless of the effect it had on everyone else, while others made excuses for her innocence, believing that the gods often played with humans' lives. In either view, she was considered the most beautiful woman in the world, and her abduction was said to be the spark which ignited the Trojan War.[27]

Helena and Helen are alike in several ways. They are the offspring of legendary parents—Helena, the daughter of a famous founder of Hogwarts (of quite noble descent), and Helen, the daughter of the king of the gods. Their striking beauty leads to tragic consequences, as desperate men long to possess them. The men act outrageously in their self-interest (as an impetuous admirer, the Baron kills Helena and then takes his own life in remorse, and Paris abducts Helen from her palace and insults her husband who has extended to him the social contract of hospitality). Both women have almost unspeakable shame mingled with their beauty. After Helena steals her mother's diadem, she flees, and her dying mother sends the Baron to summon her back. That mission results in murder and suicide. Helen of Troy is viewed, widely, as uniquely evil in caring only for herself at the expense of everyone else. Both women play significant roles in connection with and just prior to battles of Olympian magnitude. And, both are depicted (always, in the case of Helena; often, in the case of Helen), as "phantoms."

Hepzibah Smith

An elderly, dignified witch who is a wealthy heir of Helga Hufflepuff. Tom Riddle feigns interest in her to charm her, kills and robs her of the cup of Hufflepuff and the locket of Slytherin. Her name is, of course, a biblical name, the investigation of which rewards our knowledge of Miss Smith. "Hephzibah" [Heb *kheftsi-vah*], means, "my delight is in her." In the Hebrew Scriptures, the name is used for the mother of the Manasseh, the most wicked of the kings of ancient Judah (2 Kgs 21:1). While we know nothing of this mother, her son reigned for fifty-five years and reinstated pagan worship.

There are some striking parallels between these two Hepzibahs which are worth noting. Miss Smith calls Tom, "boy," several times and worries over him in a fashion that is a bizarre mixture of motherly concern and amorous attraction. And Hepzibah's "boy," Tom Riddle, surely becomes an unparalleled cause of misery for everyone, just as did Manasseh. Also, we should expect that a woman named "my delight is in her," would be the object of someone's genuine devotion and joy; but in the case of Miss Smith, the "delight" which her "boy" shows her is artificial, self-serving, and treacherous ... an ironic breach of the meaning of her name.

There is another biblical reference, however, that offers even more irony and perhaps additional perspective on the "Hepzibah" of Harry's world. The name is used metaphorically by the prophet Isaiah, to depict the glorious restoration of the fallen city of Jerusalem (Isa 62:2). In that poetic section, there is a prophecy that although Jerusalem (Zion) had fallen, she would rise again and attract all nations, and in her new and wealthy state, be united to God as a bride to a bridegroom. The motif of dejection and abandonment, followed by the joy of a bride in whom the bridegroom finds delight, is driven, in part, by the meaning of the name "Hephzibah," which the NRSV translates as "My Delight Is in Her":

The nations shall see your vindication,
and all the kings your glory;
and you shall be called by a new name
that the mouth of the LORD will give.
You shall be a crown of beauty in the
hand of the LORD,
and a royal diadem in the hand of your
God.
You shall no more be termed Forsaken,
and your land shall no more be termed
Desolate;
but you shall be called My Delight Is in Her,
and your land Married;
for the LORD delights in you,
and your land shall be married.
For as a young man marries a young
woman,
so shall your builder marry you,
and as the bridegroom rejoices over the
bride,
so shall your God rejoice over you (Isa 62:2–5, NRSV).

The irony is obvious. Miss Smith is a picture of wealth and high status, a very old, lonely and wealthy witch, a hoarder of precious antiques who is fixated on her pretended aristocratic status, while at the same time, unfortunately, smitten with Tom Riddle like a schoolgirl. Tom leads her to believe that he has feelings for her, or at least interest in her, but only because of her treasured heirlooms, not because he cares for the woman herself. And what Hepzibah gets from this "suitor" is her murder, not her marriage. The travesty of pretended "delight" in the high-born woman of impressive wealth, and the tragedy of a hopeful joining of the giddy old dame and the suave but sinister young man that ends in murder and betrayal, elicit memories of the biblical poem. At the same time, however, the story of Ms. Smith breaks the model by the reversal of the image which surfaces with the hopeful name "Hephzibah." The motif of abandonment followed by marriage (love realized), is reversed here.

We ought not to overlook, also, that Hepzibah's family name is quite common and about as ordinary as one can imagine—"Smith." It appears that Rowling has created a character that combines a dignified, legendary first name with a common family name. This combination of such widely differing elements is gently humorous. It also appears to depict some commoners (the Smiths) who name their child with a grandiose personal name, perhaps as a way of elevating the status or prestige of their family.

Hermes

Percy Weasley's screech owl, named for the Greek god who serves as Zeus's messenger to mortals and other gods. The god Hermes [Gk *hermē-* base, connoting "interpretation" > *hermēn-*, "interpret" > *hermēneus*, "interpreter" > *Hermēs*] is associated with all kinds of boundaries and intercourse, where people meet or engage something or someone other than themselves. As such, he is a messenger god (the god of roads, the god who guides souls to and from Hades), known to the Romans as Mercury. Ancient depictions commonly include his being winged or wearing winged sandals, which suggests his swiftness as a messenger. Thus, Percy's owl has the perfect name for a winged messenger. In the ancient poetry of Homer, it was customary to refer to spoken words as "winged words," because, once spoken, words put to flight cannot be retracted and have their own fortune [Gk *epea pteroenta*; see also *Homeric Hymn to Demeter*, 315, 320]. In these novels, as well, messages are "winged words" sent forth by birds, at times on the wings of "Hermes" himself.

Hestia Jones

A witch who is a member of the Advanced Guard and the Order of the Phoenix. Although her family is very ordinary ("Jones"), her personal name is that of the Greek goddess of the hearth, Hestia [Gk *Hestia*, "hearth"]. To yoke such an Olympian name with this unexceptional family name is clever and humorous, something which is interesting because of the wide gulf of connotation between the two. It appears that the Joneses may have thought quite highly of their daughter, or that giving her a divine name would add a kind of cultural or social boost to their family heritage. The yoking together of the grand and the plain in names is somewhat jarring, dare one say, a yoking of the ox and the ass [an injunction from Deut 22:10]?

Hippocrates Smethwyck

Chief Healer on the Dai Llewellyn Ward of St. Mungo's, where Arthur Weasley recuperates from an attack by a giant snake. When Smethwyck's intern or trainee Healer, Augustus Pye, unsuccessfully experiments on Mr. Weasley by using Muggle medical procedures instead of magic, Arthur calls for the Chief Healer himself. Mr. Smethwyck bears the name of the Father of Medicine, Hippocrates, the most famous physician of the ancient world (fifth-fourth centuries BCE), about whom legends and stories abound. This is a great name for one in the medical profession. However, it also promises more than an ordinary medical professional can possibly deliver. In the Chief Healer's defense, Arthur Weasley does recover from the strange and unsuccessful therapy of Augustus Pye, and Hippocrates Smethwyck fulfills the first of the promises in the Hippocratic Oath taken by physicians—to do no harm to the patient.

Horace Slughorn

The retired teacher of Potions at Hogwarts and one-time Head of Slytherin House. Of course, readers will immediately wonder if this gentleman is anything like the famous and frequently-quoted Roman poet whose name he shares, Horace (Quintus Horatius Flaccus, 65–8 BCE). As men of learning, both Slughorn and the Roman poet enjoy and nurture a circle of intellectual and political supporters and influential friends. The poet Horace was a member of the celebrated literary circle of the poet-patron Maecenas, a circle which included the successful and famous poets Vergil, Propertius and Varius, and was favored by Augustus, the first Roman Emperor. Professor Slughorn fosters his own elite circle in the exclusive "Slug's Club," and he takes pride in his personal association with renowned former students. Interestingly enough, some of his chosen students and their relatives (as well as others whose names he drops) also have famous Roman names: "Marcus Belby" and his uncle "Damocles," Cormac McLaggen's uncle "Tiberius," and "Hector Dagworth-Granger."

The similarity between the two Horaces, however, also reveals Slughorn's uniqueness. The professor's addiction to prominent personalities betrays a Narcissus complex. His name-dropping and collecting of potential celebrities reveals him to be a self-concerned man of influence, a power-broker, who establishes and manipulates associations between influential people (commonly known, today, as "networking"). He seeks to enhance his own glory and position himself as a peer of those famous people. Horace the poet, however, was invited into Maecenas' literary circle because of his genuine literary excellence. He did not foster shallow, impressive friendships as a veneer of nobility.

Here, we must return, one last time, to an episode which we have mentioned previously, Dumbledore's and Harry's visit to Budleigh Babberton to coax Horace Slughorn out of retirement, and its similarity to the Greek's commissioning three of their leaders (Odysseus, Phoenix, and Ajax) to convince Achilles to return to battle (*Il.* 9). When we first meet Slughorn, he is on the run, having spent an entire year in hiding, frequently moving from place to place, in order to avoid discovery. Dumbledore takes Harry with him, his clever young star-student wizard, to lay out two options for the recluse. Either he can spend his life hiding in fear, or he can seize the opportunity to be a respected mentor of young leaders of the future.

These two resonances from the ancient world—Slughorn's similarity to the Roman poet and to the Greek warrior—give us colors which seem to fit him and to shape our view of the man in important ways. For one thing, they show us something about his name-dropping and networking with important people that would not be quite as obvious for us if we did not compare him the Roman poet. That is, his activity is an attempt to glom on to the success and notoriety of others, not because of his own talent but because of his over-weening desire to be thought of as important himself. Also, the man who hides by turning himself into a chair is shockingly different from the famous and talented poet who did not seek to finagle his way into a literary circle, but was sought after because of his astounding talent. Finally, the similarities between the attempts to recruit Slughorn and Achilles to re-enter the struggle with their people's great enemies makes us think of the war with Voldemort in epic terms, as an epic type-scene, with fear and honor as driving factors, and Dumbledore and Harry as figures of mythic significance for the past and future of the Wizarding world.

As to his family name, Slughorn, the term means a stunted, deformed, downward-turned horn of and animal of the ox family.[28] Perhaps his collecting of important people, his name-dropping, and his "Slug Club" reveal something of the man's insecurity, divulged by his name.

Ignatius (Percy Ignatius Weasley)

The middle name of the ambitious and arrogant third son of the Weasleys, Head Boy at Hogwarts, who grows to resent his family of origin and removes himself from their circle, but returns to them in the end. Several sources from antiquity have made the name "Ignatius" famous. It may derive from the name used for one of the ancient Roman clans [L *Egnātius*], or from the name of Marcus Egnatius Rufus, who plotted to kill the Emperor Augustus (OLD 595). If one thinks of that "Egnatius," does the traitorous predecessor make Ignatius Weasley seem to have a traitorous streak in him? But the name may be derived, also, from one of the most famous early Christian martyrs,

Ignatius, the bishop of Antioch, who was put to death as a public spectacle for the Romans in 108 CE. Bad or good, the preceding people named "Ignatius" definitely made the name unforgettable.

Ignotus Peverell

The name of a deceased person inscribed on a headstone in the cemetery of Godric's Hollow, one of the three original owners of the Deathly Hallows. He possessed the Cloak of Invisibility. The personal name is no compliment to the man, for it announces him as a "nobody" or a person of low social rank [L *īgnōtus*, -a, -um, "of low birth, unknown"].

Io

One of Jupiter's four moons, named for a poor victim of Jupiter's lust. Io's story is this. Zeus (Jupiter) has a dalliance with Io [Gk *Īō*; L *Īo*], a priestess of Hera (Juno). The poor victim is transformed into a cow, either by Zeus (to hide his infidelity) or by Hera (to punish both her husband and the girl). Hera then charges a guardian (Argos) to keep an unfailing watch on her. Zeus counters by sending his messenger Hermes to put Argos to sleep by singing or by telling stories to him. When all of the guard's eyes finally close, Hermes kills the guardian. As a memorial to the service of the faithful guard who is killed in the line of duty, Hera puts Argos' eyes in the tail feathers of the male peacock. She also sends a gadfly after the poor girl, who endures extensive wanderings, trying to escape the punishing pest. Eventually, in Egypt, Io institutes worship of Isis and is herself worshiped as the goddess (Aeschylus, *Prometheus Bound*, ll. 561–887; *Libr.* 2.1.3). Her name is exclamation of strong emotion, a cry of grief and suffering [Gk and L *iō*]. As the beleaguered girl-turned-heifer tells her tale to Prometheus, and the gadfly attacks her, the chorus pities her with the words *iō, iō moira, pephrik' eisidousa prāxin Ioūs*, "Alas, fate, the fate, I shudder at seeing Io's fortune" (ll. 694f.). The moaning and the name of the girl are the same. And she bemoans her ceaseless wandering and misfortune with the words *iō moi moi· he, he*, "Oh, me ... me; woe, woe" (l.742). For Io, to exist is to suffer.[29]

The four moons are mentioned in the *Order of the Phoenix*. HH&R were directed to write extensive essays on the moons for Professor Sinistra as homework for their Astronomy class (*OP* 295). The contrast between Hermione's quick and excellent work on the assignment and the laborious progress of Ron and Harry illustrates the distinctive characterizations of the three students and friends.

Janus Thickey

A wizard for whom the fourth floor of St. Mungo's is named, the ward for long-term residents suffering from spell damage. The patients on this ward are severely incapacitated, but capable of getting out of bed, so the door to the ward has to remain locked. Rowling appears to be playing with our imagination and memory when she invents the name of the ward. Janus [L *iānus, -ī,* "doorway," > *Iānus, -ī*] is the Roman god of gates, doorways, and beginnings, being represented with two faces, peering in opposite directions. In Rome, during times of peace, the doors to his temple were kept closed; during war-time, they were kept open. Perhaps there is a hint that with the ward's doors closed, the patients within, including Gilderoy Lockhart and the Longbottoms, are out of the fray and conflict of life (i.e., in a period of "peace," from their past conflicts), or that they are now in a place where they have to deal with their past and seek a different kind of future (facing two directions at once).

Lily Evans Potter

Harry's mother, who dies trying to protect him from Lord Voldemort's Avada Kedavra Curse, when Harry is a year old. Her self-sacrifice for her son initiates the pervasive theme in the novels of "love conquers all." Prinzi notes that while there are numerous mothers and mother-figures in the novels, Lily is the only one whose character is unchangingly consistent: "She's as perfect in Harry's mind and ours at the end of the seven books as she was at the beginning" (274). She is true to her name [L *līlium, -(i)ī,* "a lily," probably like Gk *leirion,* "the white lily," "a flowery narcissus" (OLD 1030; LSJ 1036)], good and kind and pure to everyone. She is known by all for her goodness, and the most consistent focus of Harry's longing for family. One wonders if her name might suggest a contrast between Lily, the white narcissus flower, and Narcissa Malfoy, the mother of Harry's hateful enemy.

Lily's selfless act represents the classic motif of a mother or mother-substitute who attempts to save her child (either by intervening to prevent harm or death, or by attempting to make the child immortal). Her unselfish love is similar to that of the Greek sea goddess, Thetis, who attempts to protect her son, Achilles. The goddess hides him in the fire at night in order to consume his mortal qualities and anoints him with ambrosia—a process which is interrupted when his father, Peleus, catches her in the act. Another version of her love has her dipping him in the river Styx (*Libr.* 3.13.6). Despite her efforts, his heels remain his vulnerable spot, as she holds him by those tendons while she attempts to immortalize him. Another mythological mother-figure who attempts to immortalize her infant is Demeter, the goddess of grain, who nightly places the boy for whom she is in charge, Demophoön, in the fire to burn away his mortality. Her process is interrupted by the boy's natural mother and the divine protection is not completed. The result is Demeter's instituting a center of worship for herself where people could seek immortality from her.

Livius

One of the wizards mentioned in the history of the Elder Wand, who perhaps killed Loxias to obtain it. Livius [L *Līvius*] was the name of a Roman *gens* (family or clan), borne by such illustrious people as Livius Andronicus (284–204 BCE), who is sometimes called the Father of Roman literature, and Titus Livius, "Livy" (59 BCE–17 CE), the historian who wrote a history of Rome in one hundred forty-two books, covering the span of time from the founding of Rome and its mythological origins (753 BCE) down to his own time. Though Livius is only a name to readers, with no lengthy tale of his own in the *Potter* series, he shares a name with others who made history in remarkable ways.

Loxias

A wizard who kills Barnabas Deverill and takes possession of the Elder Wand. Loxias is himself defeated by either Arcus or Livius, and thus loses possession of the powerful wand. The title "Loxias" [Gk *Loxias*] was used in the ancient Greek world as an epithet for the god Apollo. The precise meaning of the name is unknown, but it refers to the obscurity or obliqueness of the god's oracles, which were notoriously vague, and open to several contradictory interpretations [Gk *loxos*, "oblique, obscure, indirect, ambiguous"]. It is interesting that Xenophilius Lovegood says of the wizard Loxias that it is uncertain which of the two (Arcus or Livius) defeated him and took the wand.

An epithet of Apollo is proper for this wizard, who is a murderer. Although Apollo is known as the god of music and poetry, he is also depicted as one who brings death and destruction. His name derives from the Greek words *apollūmi or apolluō*, "to destroy utterly, to kill" (LSJ 207). The *Iliad* opens with a lengthy description of the death and plague which the god brings to the Greek armies, and even to their animals. Another famous myth reports that Apollo kills all seven of the sons of proud Niobe because she has dishonored Apollo's mother, Leto. The aspect of his being a bringer of death was part of the ancient Greeks' rationale for untimely death. They believed that when a boy died an early and untimely death, Apollo was the cause. In the *Harry Potter* story, "Loxias" adds the unique element of an eclipse or obliqueness to the story, blurs the boundaries between reason, magic, religion, and the supernatural, and hints at the topics of death and murder.

Lucius Malfoy

Husband of Narcissa Black Malfoy and father of Draco Malfoy, a member of the Hogwarts board of governors and a Death Eater. He has a very familiar Roman name. Free-born Roman males had three names, the *praenōmen* (personal name), the *nōmen* (name of the tribe or family/clan) and a *cognōmen* (branch of a family). So, for example, Cicero's name was Marcus Tullius Cicero. If it seems odd that so many ancient Romans were named Lucius or Marcus, it is because there were only about eighteen personal names used for free-born Romans—Aulus, Appius, Gaius, Gnaeus, Decimus, Kaeso, Lucius, Marcus, Manius, Numerius, Publius, Quintus, Servius, Sextus, Spurius, Titus, Tiberius, and Vibius (Sandys 208–09). The cognomen was inherited from an ancestor who was noted for some particular physical trait, mental quality, circumstance of birth, occupation, or fauna and flora (Solin 997). Alberto Angela cites some of the more humorous examples: "Rufus (the red), Cincinnatus (curly), Brutus (stupid), Calvus (bald), Caecus (blind), Cicero (chickpea), Nasica (big nose), Dentatus (big teeth)" (131). So, for freeborn Romans there were few "proper" names, which distinguished them from freed slaves or foreigners.

Lucius Malfoy's personal name, then, is a name which in the Roman world would designate him as a free-born Roman. The oldest etymology of the name comes from Varro in the first century BCE. He writes that the people of the territory of Reate who are known as the "Lucii" are so called because they were born "at first light," that is, at dawn (*prīmā lūce*).[30] There is definite irony in Malfoy's wearing this name. It is hard to believe that he could be said in any way to be "in the light." But, the name fits the head of a family which is obsessed with purity of blood and status, and which believes that Muggle-born wizards and witches are disgusting. Their tacky egotism and cruelty do no justice to a name which had for centuries signified real class and dignity. Perhaps the "light" element in Lucius' name is more akin to the ironic name of "Lucifer," the fallen angel, the Devil, whose name means "bringer of light."

Marcus

MARCUS BELBY

One of the students in Horace Slughorn's Slug Club, a nephew of Damocles. Young Marcus gets choked while eating pheasant, and Professor Slughorn points his wand at the boy and magically clears his airway, allowing him to breathe normally again. His personal name, "Marcus," was one of the few proper, personal names [L *praenōmina*] given to free-born Romans.[31] This name set its owner apart from freed slaves or foreigners. The lofty name of young Mr. Belby suggests that we are to think of him as belonging to the category of noble individuals or, at least, of nobly-named individuals. There is a touch of humor in the gathering of students whom Professor Slughorn considers to be people on their way to importance. The boy with a well-born name in the group is introduced to readers by only one action ... his choking on his dinner.

MARCUS FLINT

Captain of Slytherin's Quidditch team. While his name would seem to announce to us that he is of good bloodline and a "quality" wizard, to Harry he appears to be of less than the best pedigree, for he looks part troll. Obviously, he is a young man who is not quite equal to his name.

Marge Dursley

Vernon Dursley's disgusting and evil aunt, whose visit to Privet Drive is given a whole chapter in *Prisoner of Azkaban*. She has such a passion for breeding her twelve bulldogs that it torments her to be separated from them. When she appears at the Dursleys' door, she carries her favorite bulldog, "Ripper," under her arm. She enjoys pampering the dog and brutalizing Harry. She sees Harry as a mongrel, bred from a bad bitch (his mother).

There are intriguing and serviceable parallels between Marge and the classical figure "Scylla," whom Robert Bell calls "perhaps the most loathsome monster in mythology" (395). At some point in her life, Scylla had been attractive, but a love triangle ruined her. A sea-god named Glaucus sought to gain her affections, but he was rebuffed. To force her hand, he went to the sorceress Circe to get magical help. The witch, however, wanted Glaucus for herself, so she made Scylla completely ugly by pouring into a pool, where the girl bathed, a poisoned potion which caused her to become deformed. When she waded into the pool up to her waist, she turned into a monster with twelve feet, with a voice that sounded like a dog's barking, and a waist of six ferocious dogs' heads, each having three rows of teeth. From her cavern at the Straits of Messina, she would snatch sailors from their ships and eat them if they sailed near to her (*Od.* 12.85–100, 245–59; *Met.* 14.1–74). The ferocious, attack-dog personality of Marge, her fixation on her bulldogs, and her sporting "Ripper" at the waist, all remind one of Scylla.

Then there is Marge's expertise on pedigree, her opinion of how the deficiencies of the bitch come out in the pup, and her obvious self-image as one of fine pedigree. If we go a bit further with the comparison of the two "dog-women," the parentage of Scylla may affect our image of the bulldog breeder. Scylla's father, Phorcys, a god of the sea, was also the father of monstrous offspring—the Graiai and the Gorgons. Her mother was Hecate, whom Greeks connected with the Underworld and Persephone, making her a divinity associated with souls of the dead. Hecate would release ghosts and demons into the world at night, her approach was signaled by the howling of dogs, and dogs were the customary sacrificial victims offered to her (Howatson 277). Scylla was born from the kind of parents who produce monsters. Does her likeness to Marge suggest questions about the quality of the parentage of Vernon's aunt … and of Vernon Dursley himself?

Marius

One of the uniformed wizards guarding the doors at Gringotts, who checks visitors with Probity Probes. He has the same name as a famous Roman military and political leader, Gaius Marius (157–86 BCE). Both are men who serve and protect the public.

Merope Gaunt Riddle

The brow-beaten and extremely humble-looking daughter of Marvolo Gaunt, sister of Morfin Gaunt, and mother of Tom Riddle. The two outstanding features of Merope's ill-starred life are her love for a Muggle (Tom Riddle, Sr.), and her tragic death, owing to complications of the birth of her son. She falls in love with Tom Riddle, Sr., but being quite unattractive and having very low self-esteem, she cannot win his attention. So, she enchants him, eventually lets the enchantment subside, and thus loses her husband. She is one of three mothers in the *Potter* novels who die for or because of their sons. The other two are Lily Potter and Mrs. Crouch (who dies in Azkaban to liberate her son, Barty Crouch, Jr.).

The name "Merope" [Gk and L *Meropē*] is found in numerous classical myths, at least nine of which we know from surviving records. Most of the occurrences are little more than names preserved almost incidentally, with no significant details about the women. Two of the "Meropes," however, are reminiscent of Merope Gaunt Riddle, in that they are ill-fated women who suffer shame because of marriage to unacceptable husbands or because of some misfortune with respect to their sons.

First, there is the Merope who is one of the seven daughters of the Titan Atlas and Pleione (who is a daughter of the god Oceanus). Six of the divine daughters mate with gods and are pursued by the giant hunter Orion. The seventh, Merope, mates with the mortal Sisyphus, who is the cleverest of all human beings (*Il.* 6.153). Her match-up with him leads to misfortune for both of the lovers. This is the tradition about Sisyphus. His sin is that when Zeus secretly abducts a girl named Aegina, and her father, the river god Asopus, is searching for her, Sisyphus tells the father what occurred, thus exposing the father of the gods. On learning that Zeus has raped his daughter, Asopus pursues the god, who uses his thunderbolts to force him to return to his own waters (*Libr.* 1.9.3; 3.12.6). Zeus sends Death to kill Sisyphus, but clever Sisyphus binds Death itself, with the result that people do not die. Finally, Ares sets Death free and turns Sisyphus over to the god. Clever Sisyphus, however, tricks Death by convincing his wife, Merope, not to perform the necessary funeral rituals that would allow him to pass over into Hades. So, he finagles Hades into letting him return, in order to compel Merope to perform these last rites. When he gets to the upper world, he does not fulfill the bargain to return to the Underworld, and he deceives Death by living to a ripe old age. When he does finally die, Zeus gives him eternal punishment in the Underworld by having him to use his hands and head to push a huge stone up a hill, only to see it roll back, forcing him to repeat his futile, penitential task forever.[32] Merope's bad outcome is that although she and her six other sisters are eventually transformed into the seven stars in the constellation of the Pleiades, which is a beneficial constellation for indicating agricultural seasons, because of her choice of such an unworthy mate, she is made the dimmest of the seven stars, as if to hide her in shame.[33]

The links between these two women are their noble ancestry, their fateful match-ups with inappropriate husbands, and their inglorious ends. They are not exactly the same, and it is the differences in their stories that make Ms. Gaunt unique and not simply a boring repetition of the goddess myth, pasted onto the *Potter* story. The goddess loses her glory after marrying a traitorous husband whose punishment in the Underworld becomes legendary, and she fades into invisibility forever. Merope Gaunt comes from "pure-blood" magical ancestors, but the decline in her family's glory has taken place long before she becomes the wife of a Muggle gentleman. And, in the end, she dies with no dignity or glory at all. She progresses not from glory to shame but from shame to even greater indignity. In fact, "gaunt" is not only a reinforcing name for the woman. The whole family, in its decline, can be viewed as haggard, greedy and hungry.

The second Merope of note from the classical world offers a different parallel for consideration, that is, the connection of the name "Merope" with an ill-starred son. Polybus, the king of Corinth and his wife, Merope, rear their adopted son, Oedipus, as their own. Unfortunately, the boy is fated by prophecy to kill his father and marry his mother, by whom he will have children. Eventually, Oedipus realizes that Polybus and Merope are his family of rearing, but not his biological parents. Unfortunately, he learns this after the prophecy which curses his family has been fulfilled. Both Tom Riddle and Oedipus, born under accursed circumstances, kill their fathers. In light of these famous, ancient women and their stories, the name "Merope" itself foreshadows for us not only expectations of misfortune for Mrs. "Merope" Gaunt Riddle, but misfortunes specifically with respect to her marriage partner and her son.

Miriam Strout

A Healer who works on the Janus Thickey ward at St. Mungo's Hospital. She is depicted as a sensitive care-giver, a "motherly looking" person, who treats her patient Gilderoy Lockhart as if he were a two-year-old (*OP* 510–12). Unfortunately, she is punished for a single, innocent oversight. She unwittingly places beside the bed of a patient (Broderick Bode) a plant which has come to the hospital as a gift, but which is in reality a deadly Devil's Snare plant, which kills Bode. The nature, fate, and especially the name of this Healer may echo elements of the "Miriam" of ancient Israelite history. When Moses' mother feared for his life, she made a water-resistant reed basket and placed him in the shallows of the Nile River. His older sister, Miriam [Heb

Miryam], stood watch to see that he would be safely discovered by someone (Exod 2:4). The daughter of the Egyptian Pharaoh came upon the child, and Miriam offered to obtain a wet nurse for the infant. She brought her own mother to serve as the caretaker of the child. Years later, during the Hebrews' journeys in the wilderness, Miriam challenged Moses' leadership, for which she was punished by God with leprosy, but was subsequently healed by Moses' prayer for her (Num 12:1–16). The similarities between these two "Miriams" are these: both exhibit caring sensitivity, seeing to the welfare and safety of their respective "children" (Moses and Gilderoy Lockhart) and both are punished for a single misdeed. If we consider the stories of the Miriams side-by-side, the biblical story suggests to us that this Healer has been named thoughtfully, and that the name itself might suggest to us something of both the character and the fate of Ms. Strout.

Mulciber

One of the wizards whom Igor Karkaroff names as being a Death Eater, in hopes of getting his own sentence to Azkaban reduced or commuted. Mulciber puts people under his control with the Imperius Curse, making them do his bidding. His name is an epithet which the Romans gave to Vulcan, the god of fire and the blacksmith of the gods [L *Mulciber, -eris*]. The name suggests rough-handling or beating in order to shape metals into a desired form [L perhaps from *mulcō, mulcāre, mulcāvī, mulcātum*, "to beat up (someone)," "to handle roughly," which would describe his tempering metals by beating and shaping them; or from *mulceō, mulcēre, mulsī, mulsum* or *mul[c]tum*, "to beguile, to charm, to quiet"]. The god was venerated mainly so that he would prevent fires or keep fires in check.[34] The connection between the Death Eater and the Roman deity is that both exercise forceful control in manipulating their objects—the Death Eater to mold and force people to do his will, Vulcan to beat and force his materials into the shapes he wishes or to subdue them by charms.

Murcus

The female chief of the merpeople[35] with whom Dumbledore confers in her language (Mermish) to find out exactly what took place underwater during the Second Task of the Triwizard Tournament. Her name is an ancient name for the Aventine Hill in Rome, beneath which there was a temple for an obscure goddess, Murcia [L *Murcia, -ae*] (OLD 1147). It was also the *cognōmen* (or family name) of Lucius Staius Murcus who, before he died about 39 BCE, issued a coin with the inscription "Murcus Imp" on one side (Murcus the Imperator) and the head of Neptune on the opposite side (Scullard 703–04). The name here may connect with the Neptune coin, since both the Roman and the mermaid are "chiefs" and both are somehow associated with water.

Nicolas Flamel

Maker of the Sorcerer's Stone, and an exceedingly old wizard. Having passed his 665th birthday, he lives to be 666 years old. He has the name of a historical person, a French alchemist of the fourteenth to fifteenth centuries, who is said to have discovered the Sorcerer's Stone and to have gained immortality. The personal name is a variant spelling of "Nicholas," the name of the patron saint of Greece and a very popular name among modern Greeks [Gk *nikē*, "victory" + *laos*, "the people, crowd" > *Nikolaos* > L *Nicolaus* > OFr *Nicolas*].

Octavius Pepper

According to the *Daily Prophet*, this otherwise unknown man mysteriously disappears after Voldemort regains his powers. Though an unknown, he shares a noble classical name with Gaius Octavius (Octavian), the first Emperor of Rome, and a number of other high-ranking noble Romans.

Paracelsus

A Swiss physician and alchemist who had interests in philosophy and magic [Philippus Aureolus Paracelsus, born Theophrastus Philippus Aureolus Bombastus von Hohenheim (1493–1541)]. Allen G. Debus, professor of the History of Science and Medicine at the University of Chicago, notes that "the scientific debates of the late sixteenth century were centered more frequently on the innovations of Paracelsus than they were on the heliocentric astronomy of Copernicus."[36] The scholar is said to have adopted the name "Paracelsus" for himself because he thought that he was superior to the famous first century medical writer, Aulus Cornelius Celsus.[37] The name means "above/beyond

Celsus" [Gk *para*, "past, beyond, over and above"]. He appears in the series only once, when Peeves, the ghost, torments students at Hogwarts by dropping a bust of Paracelsus on their heads.

Patricia Stimpson

One of the Hogwarts fifth-year students who breaks down under the stress of the O.W.L. exams. Nothing else is said of her; but her parents (or J.K. Rowling, who has created her as a character in literature) apparently want us to think of her as someone of the upper class and of noble nature, by naming her "Patricia" [L *patricius, -a, -um*, "belonging to the patricians, a patrician," that sector of the people who were a privileged and distinguished class, the Roman aristocracy].

Penelope Clearwater

The Ravenclaw student who is petrified and restored, the girlfriend of Percy Weasley. Ms. Clearwater has the same given name as the famous wife of Odysseus, who waited devotedly for her husband to return from the Trojan War for twenty years. During the last few of those years, she put off many suitors by telling them that she could not marry any other man until she completed weaving a funeral shroud for her father-in-law. This was a ruse, for each night she would unravel all that she had woven during the day, thus avoiding having to decide about marriage. From her character we derive a classic image of devotion as well as a metaphor which depicts something always being done but never being finished, "Penelope's web" (Brewer 853). The name "Penelope" [Gk *Pēnelopeia/Pēnelopē*] may derive from the verb *pēnizomai*, "to wind [thread] off a reel" (LSJ 1401), an allusion to the queen's enduring and clever stall tactic. One wonders which of these two characteristics may be applicable to Ms. Clearwater—devotion to Percy alone, like that of Penelope to Odysseus, or stalling to avoid making a decision about marriage? Or both?

Phineas Nigellus Black

Great-great-grandfather of Sirius Black, former Headmaster of Hogwarts, encountered only as his personified, magical portrait. He is stuffy and defensive of Slytherin House and the Black family. He appears to be old and crotchety, as he chides and corrects young Harry, and dislikes young people in general. He is himself chided by the other portraits for not being eager and ready to assist Dumbledore. Hermione has to blindfold his portrait once, to prevent him from seeing and disclosing their whereabouts and actions. One could not find a member of the Black family more properly named than this wizard. Both of his personal names mean "Black." "Phineas" is a biblical Hebrew name [Egyptian *pe-nehasi*, "the southerner," "[those of] dark skin," for example, Nubians > Heb *pinekhas* > Gk > LL *Phinees*]. And "Nigellus" is a Latin adjective, meaning "black, dark" [L *nigellus, -a, -um*] (Brown 1968, 810; Spencer 1992, 346–47). So all three names announce the same idea, that he is a member of the Black family, a really devoted member of the Black family, who wants to be known, for sure, as "Black," among the Blacks of the Black family.

Not only the name, but also the story of the biblical character, suits the pompous and self-important Slytherin devotee. Ancient Phineas was a model of puritanical zeal and was renowned for his "strong and sometimes violent defense of the Israelite worship of Yahweh."[38] He once killed an Israelite man and the Midianite woman whom he brought into his family by spearing them through their bodies (Num 25:6–8). He served as priest in a battle with the pagan Midianites in which the Israelites attempted to wipe out their enemy by killing all the males, all the women who had ever had sex, and all the male children, preserving only the virginal girls (Num 32:1–42). The biblical fore-runner serves as a model of self-assured, puritanical zeal and deadly pride in purity, which find repetition in the character of Phineas Nigellus.

Pomona Sprout

Professor of Herbology at Hogwarts. Her name is appropriate for her profession, "sprout" clearly mirroring her passion for growing plants. Pomona is the name of the Roman goddess of fruit trees [L *Pōmōna, -ae < pōmum, -ī*, "fruit, fruit tree." She was said to prune, graft, water, and cultivate her fruit-bearing orchard in the era preceding the birth of Romulus and Remus (under King Proca) (*Met.* 14.623 ff.)

Ptolemy

A wizard pictured on a Chocolate Frog card. He must be very famous, as his card is a rare find. Although Ron owns almost five hundred cards, he still lacks this one. This was the name used by all the Macedonian kings of Egypt during the Ptolemaic Dynasty after the reign of Alexander the Great, and the name of a second century CE scholar and writer, Claudius Ptolemaeus [Gk *Ptolemaios*] (Howatson 482f.). Claudius was a man of broad learning and a prolific writer on esoteric elements of astronomy, astrology, mathematics, and geography. The fame of Ptolemy the wizard is not only deserved because of his accomplishments, but also accentuated by the reputations of those who made the name famous before him.

(Professor) Quirrell

Professor of Defense Against the Dark Arts at Hogwarts during Harry's first year at the school. Harry and Ron feel favorably toward the timid and awkward professor, mainly because they see him as a weak fellow who is trying to foil Professor Snape's diabolical plans for the Sorcerer's Stone. Yet there is something strange about the stuttering teacher and the curious turban which he wears. It tries to lure Harry into joining the Slytherins and attracts attention for its odor. The truth of the odd man's behavior comes out in a chapter dedicated to his self-disclosure (*SS Chapter Seventeen: The Man with Two Faces*). When the professor removes his turban, Harry sees Voldemort's head which has been shielded from view by the ridiculous head dressing. In one man, Harry finds two people. Adney puts it succinctly, "Janus, the two-faced god, is alluded to in the character of Quirrell" (349).

Regulus (Arcturus) Black

Sirius Black's younger brother, a luminary in their family, and a voluntary Death Eater, he does an about-face in his commitment to the Dark Lord, hatching a plot to bring down his master. The name "Regulus" [L *Rēgulus*] recalls the *cognōmen* of several Roman families, and is associated, most famously, with a great, legendary story. Marcus Atilius Regulus was a hero of the third century BCE, a successful Roman naval commander who, along with his troops, was captured by the Carthaginians in Africa. The enemy imprisoned his men and sent him to Rome to work out a peace treaty between Carthage and Rome, or to arrange for an exchange of prisoners. They made him promise to return to Carthage if the mission failed to secure peace. When he appeared before the Senate, he made a case for not accepting any such treaty or arrangement because, he said, the Carthaginians were not trustworthy. He returned to Carthage and was tortured to death (Horace, *Odes* 3.5). His story became a national legend and the dilemma he faced became a topic of study and of rhetorical exercise in the Roman schools (Howatson 491). The Latin components of his name seem to highlight the story of the hero. "Regulus" comes from *regō, regere*, "to rule, guide [someone] in the right way" > *rex, rēgis*, "king" + adjectival suffix *—ulus*, "little" and signifying a repeated action (OLD 1601, 2087). It may mean "little king," literally; but it certainly denotes a prominent figure whose personal story stands as a model for moral action.

"Regulus" is an interesting fit for Sirius' brother. Both men are caught between a powerful enemy and loyalty to a greater cause; and both pay for their commitments with their lives. The difference between the two is that the ancient Regulus stands up for principle, for his country and cause and willingly surrenders his life. Regulus Black is not the complete opposite of the Roman hero, but the circumstances of his death allow us to see him as only partially similar to his predecessor. He makes the evil choice to follow Voldemort, and then turns against the Dark Lord, on principle. He is hunted down and murdered as a defector, a turncoat, and a coward. Both men die in their conflict between the good which they choose to follow and the enemy of that good, courageously standing up for the right. Although only the last days of R.A.B.'s life could be called "heroic," his "Roman" name directs us to recall the praiseworthy heroism of the man. His courage and exemplary commitment are championed when Kreacher leads the House-Elves into the great battle against the forces of Voldemort, shouting the rallying cry, "Fight the Dark Lord, in the name of brave Regulus! Fight!" (*DH* 734).

Remus Lupin

The teacher of Defense Against the Dark Arts at Hogwarts during Harry's third year, and close friend of Sirius Black and James Potter. As a child, he is bitten by the werewolf Fenrir Greyback, and each month, at the full moon, he transforms into his altered state as a werewolf, hence his nickname, "Moony."[39] His family name is appropriate for him, as it comes from the Latin for "wolf" [L *lupus, -ī* > *lupīnus, -a, -um,* "of or belonging to a wolf," "wolf-like"; OLD 1051]. His personal name, Remus [L *Remus*] is the same as that of one of the co-founders of Rome, Remus and Romulus. Professor Lupin is fortunate enough to be associated with the names of both of the Roman ancestors, as the code name for him on the broadcast called "Potterwatch" is "Romulus." Exposed as infants, the Roman twins were rescued, nurtured and suckled by a she-wolf. As a student, Lupin was monthly "rescued" by animals, too—his Animagi friends, James Potter (a stag) and Sirius Black (a dog).

Romulus

The code name used for Remus Lupin on the radio program called "Potterwatch." In Roman history, Romulus [L *Rōmulus*] was the legendary founder of Rome and the twin brother of Remus. It is no great stretch to link this code name to the twin's name, Remus.

Rufus Scrimgeour

The Minister of Magic who succeeds Cornelius Fudge. Before assuming that office, as head of the Auror Office, he asks Tonks and Kingsley Shacklebolt "funny questions," which make Tonks warn the members of the Order of the Phoenix to be cautious around him (*OP* 122). His personal name leads us to think of him as a red-head (and perhaps, then, of a fiery temperament) [L *Rūfus* < *rūfus, -a, -um*, "red, having red hair"]. The name was a common Roman *cognōmen*.

Scorpius Malfoy

The son of Draco Malfoy, a student at Hogwarts [Gk *skorpios*, "scorpion; the constellation Scorpio"; L *scorpius, -ī*, "scorpion, the constellation of the zodiac Scorpio"]. Apparently, Draco never softens in his devotion to dark magic and retains his identity as a Slytherin-type, because he names his child for a poisonous and threatening creature.

Sibyll Trelawney

Teacher of Divination at Hogwarts, who is considered to be a fraud and a crackpot by many (including Hermione). Readers can easily get the idea that she often invents her prophecies. For example, she divines that Harry was born in midwinter, although he was actually born in July. And, overjoyed by Harry's article in *The Quibbler*, she prophesies that Harry will not die an early death but live to a ripe old age, become the Minister of Magic, and have

twelve children. Professor Umbridge attempts to shame the professor by publicly exposing her as a fraud when she compels her to make an on-the-spot
prediction. Even Firenze, the centaur, refers to the Divination teacher as
"blinkered" and "fettered," as if she were a horse-like animal with limited
vision (*OP* 603). Professor Dumbledore considers that she has probably only
predicted the truth twice—the prophecy given years earlier to him and
recorded in the orb at the Department of Mysteries, and her entranced warning to Harry that the Dark Lord's servant would break free and seek his master
before midnight. She appears to be unaware of her real prophetic power, since
she delivers her prophecy to Harry during a mantic seizure which she cannot
recall. She is anti-social, not wanting to affect her visionary talent by contact
with others, unorthodox in her manners, superstitious, and eccentric.

Trelawney is a great example of Rowling's method of highlighting the
special nature of her characters by giving them a name which was made so
unforgettable in antiquity by a predecessor's activity, that the name has
become synonymous with a role or type. Her name comes from the ancient
Greek and Latin word *Sibylla*, a word of uncertain origin, but used generally
for local prophetesses and for the prophetic priestess of Apollo at Cumae,
who guides Aeneas on his visit to the Underworld in *Aeneid* 6. It may be
that the word is onomatopoeic, as the Latin verb *sībilāre* means "to make a
hissing sound," imitating the strange and unintelligible utterances of the
priestesses when they are in a prophetic trance or overcome by natural hallucinogens. The image conjured up by the word "Sibyl" includes elements of
eccentricity (because seers may live in caves or forests and prophesy by means
of indecipherable sounds) and a high degree of suspicion about their credi-
bility.

When an oracle or prophecy is delivered in a mantic or ecstatic state (as
Trelawney's oracle to Harry), it becomes a special kind of revelation which
tends to guarantee the authenticity of the message as not simply good advice
or opinion, but a supernatural truth. Professor Trelawney is much like the
Pythia at Delphi, who utters her oracles mysteriously and in a mantic state.

The Professor of Divination stands in and well represents the tradition
set by her forebears. And her name, with the imagery it brings, gives readers
much to work with in defining her person.[40]

(Professor) Sinistra

Teacher in the department of Astronomy at Hogwarts. For a person who
instructs about the heavens, this teacher has a very unfortunate name, which

comes from a negatively-loaded Latin adjective [L *sinister, sinistra, sinistrum,* "unlucky, on the left side, perverse"]. The word is used for the left hand or side, which denotes that which is adverse, harmful or immoral. It is the opposite of the name "Dexter," which derives from the Latin adjective for "right, on the right-hand side, favorable, agreeable, strong" [L *dexter, dext(e)ra, dext(e)rum*].

Terence Higgs

Seeker for the Slytherin Quidditch team during Harry's first year at Hogwarts. One of the earliest writers of Latin literature was Publius Terentius Afer, "Terence" (about 186–159 BCE). Born in Carthage, Egypt, he was brought to Rome as a slave, subsequently freed, and because of his literary ability, gained a reputation and stature among the elite of his day. Six plays have survived as genuine works, comedies in Latin based on Greek originals. His style and humanism[41] were quite influential on Molière, Petrarch, Boccaccio, and Erasmus (Radice 22–24). He does not offer information by which to compare him to the ancient Roman, but his name is historic.

Theodore Nott

A "weedy looking" student who associates with Draco, Crabbe and Goyle (*OP* 583). When the revitalized Dark Lord gathers his Death Eaters, the fathers of these boys are there—Messrs. Malfoy, Crabbe and Goyle. A fourth Death Eater, called "Nott," who is also there, is almost certainly the father of Theodore Nott. Young Mr. Nott has an interesting name for an aspiring worker of Dark Arts. "Theodore" means "gift of God" [Gk *Diodōrus* < *theos*, "god" + *dōron*, "gift"; L *Theodōrus, -ī*]. No particular ancient individual of this name comes to mind as an illumining parallel figure. It may be that Rowling is playing with the name by adding his family name, "Nott," as if to say this boy is a gift of God … NOT!

Tiberius

TIBERIUS

Uncle of Cormac McLaggen.

TIBERIUS OGDEN

An elder in the Wizengamot who resigns in protest when Dolores Umbridge is made Hogwarts High Inquisitor. "Tiberius" [L *Tiberēus*] is one of the few proper, personal names (*praenōmina*) given to free-born Romans and especially used of the Roman Emperor. The name elicits an image of might, power, and importance among people.

Tobias Snape

The father of Severus Snape, and a Muggle. Because the Professor of Potions at Hogwarts (Severus Snape) is born from a Muggle father and a magical mother (Eileen Prince), he is not a pure-blood wizard, but a "Half-Blood Prince." This perpetuates the theme of blood as a determiner of social acceptance in the novels.

The name which Rowling has chosen for Mr. Snape could not have been more suitably picked, for an ancient figure by this name is remembered for a very similar problem: his dubious family heritage. "Tobias" is the Greek spelling of the biblical Hebrew name "Tobiah" [*Toviyah*, meaning "the Lord is [my] good"]. Tobiah was the head of a family who returned to Judea from the Babylonian Exile (after 538 BCE). He is remembered in the Bible because he could not prove that his family was of unmixed Israelite descent; therefore, he and his sons were listed as being of dubious genealogy. And that was at a time when puritanical Jewish priests wanted to exclude anyone of non–Israelite ancestry from the "righteous remnant" of Israel [Ezra 2:60; Neh 7:62, 1 Esdr 5:37 (where he is called Baenan)] (Dahlberg 657). The biblical story of Tobiah appears to have been remembered for showing how important verifiable genealogy was for restoring the Israelite community after their great crisis (Eskenazi 584).

The motif of dubious heritage is compounded by the name which Tobias and Eileen gave to their son, "Severus," which was the name of the cruel and bloody Roman Emperor of 193–211 CE. The Emperor's mother was of Italian ancestry. The bloodline of his father was Punic, that is, from the people who were the long-standing worst enemies of the Romans (Birley 1351). The Professor of Potions and his Roman Emperor predecessor could not claim pure-blood status in their respective societies. And because of their uncertain heritage, they knew the psychological alienation which their "pure-blood" superiors created for those who were considered "lesser" in their essential nature and being.

Another ancient tale which suggests connections to Tobias Snape comes from the apocryphal book of *Tobit*. This work is the legend about a courageous youth named Tobias, who was sent by his blind father to his family's homeland to secure a financial legacy and thereby save his family. His other task was to find a suitable wife for himself. When he arrived at his destination, he learned that he had a distant relative, a beautiful young woman named Sarah, who was unmarried. When her father was thoroughly satisfied that Tobias was from the right tribe and bloodline, which was required according to the Law of Moses, a marriage was arranged for the young couple. The girl had been married seven times before, and each husband died in the bridal chamber, killed by an evil demon named Asmodeus, who was in love with her (Tob 6:13–14; 7:10–11).[42] Tobias feared that he would be victim number eight. In fact, the girl's father was so convinced that his new son-in-law would die that on their wedding night he dug a grave for the young man. On the next morning, when he learned that Tobias survived, he ordered the servants to fill in the grave quickly (a bit of humor from a second century BCE legend!). After a lengthy wedding feast, the couple returned to Tobias' family, and they lived long and happily ever after.

There are several connections between the book of *Tobit* and Tobias Snape which invite comparison. First, Tobias' wife is named "Sarah," which is Hebrew for "princess." Tobias Snape's wife's family name is "Prince," making Severus a half-blood and a member of the Prince family. Second, the matter of blood and genealogical purity is a force in both stories: Tobias the Jew is of unquestionable blood line and he, along with his sons and family, lives well and prosperously; Tobias the Muggle has a mixed marriage, which causes problems for his son, Severus, which can never be overcome, a half-wizard, half–Muggle Potions master with a life of unrequited love. Third, there is magic in both households and families. The ancient young hero survived his wedding night because his companion, Azarias, who was actually the angel Raphael incognito, advised him to keep the heart, liver, and gall of a huge fish which miraculously leaped out of the Tigris River. In preparation for the wedding night, Azarias told him to burn the heart and liver over live coals of incense in the bedroom. The smoke would, and did, dispel the demon forever. Later, the gall was used on the eyes of Tobias' blind father, Tobit, to restore his vision. Although Tobias Snape was a Muggle and had no magical powers, his son became a master of magic and Potions. The materials used to save Tobias and Sarah sound like the same kind of inventory one would find in Severus Snape's private collection of magical materials. The links are not exact, as if the old story were re-written with new names. But the comparable elements in the stories are intriguing and beg consideration. Perhaps the pieces of the old story have become so common to hero tales that they are collected here and re-situated so as to create a new mosaic which resembles the historic tale. Or, to look at it from the opposite angle, what if Tobias Snape had been named Oscar McPherson? The themes, the magic, the suggestive names which are brought to mind from the old story shine new light or a slightly different perspective on the new story.

Zacharias Smith

A Hufflepuff student who is not liked by many others. He is militant in his comments towards students who gather to learn defenses against the Dark Arts under Harry's leadership. He is cynical about reports that Voldemort has returned. He is condescending, haughty, and supercilious. His manner so annoys Ginny Weasley that one time she hits him with a Bat-Bogey Curse, and during a Quidditch match, she crashes her broom into his speaker's stand, attacking him. He is disliked, also, by George, Fred, Ron and Hermione. He is so self-centered that when the younger students are being hustled out of the school and out of harm's way, he knocks first-year students out of his way, so that he can be at the front of the line to escape danger.

Could anyone have a more "biblical" name than "Zacharias"? It is the Greek spelling [*Zacharías*] of the Hebrew name "Zechariah" [*zekharyah, zekharyahu*], which means "Yahweh remembers." The name is used for a number of biblical figures—princes and musicians, leaders of clans, court officials, the famous sixth century BCE prophet, and even the father of John the Baptist.[43] This last figure may have some curious and teasing parallels to Mr. Smith. According to the Gospel of Luke (chapters 1–2), the father of the prophet is executing his priestly duties when the angel Gabriel appears to him and announces that he and his wife Elizabeth, an elderly and childless couple, will have a son who will be great and who will be named "John." Zacharias protests and is punished for his distrust by being made mute until after the child is born. Apparently this punishment turns the father around, though. When people begin to call the child "Zacharias," after his father, the mute priest writes down that the child will be named "John." For this act of repentance and belief, miraculously, his voice returns and he delivers one of the great poetic songs of Luke, the "Benedictus." There may be other "Zachariases" in literature from which Rowling draws her image for the student at Hogwarts. But the fact that young Mr. Smith is uniformly disliked by other students, who tell him to shut up, threaten him or even attack him for his cynical and distrustful talkativeness, plus the fact that he only signs on to

Dumbledore's Army after everyone else has committed to the cause, all may suggest associations with an unbelieving, muted biblical character who takes at least nine months to come around to the belief which his wife has held all along.

One last observation, a delicious bit of humor regarding Mr. Smith, has to do with the combination of his personal and family names. On the one hand, he has a name which conjures up images of noble and famous biblical personages. On the other hand, his family name is one of the most common names in the telephone directory—"Smith." Rowling has created a lad from the common stock who is adorned with a pretentious and stunning personal name. We have seen several times, previously, that Rowling can bestow on her characters a grandiose personal name and a very common family name (Hepzibah Smith and Hestia Jones). Perhaps Rowling's aim may be to depict some families as putting on airs, in an attempt to possess an undeserved nobility.

Chapter VIII

The Two Worlds of Magic: Beings, Materials and Resources

In this chapter we shall look at some of the aspects of magic which link *Harry Potter* with the ancient, classical world. Our focus here will be on a variety of links between the two worlds, both broad and narrow, and on world conceptions which underlie magic. This will include such matters as non-human beings, superstition, fear, and religion. We shall consider some of the tangible materials and devices of magic as well as some intangible resources employed by the people of the two worlds.

In dealing with the specifics of magic and myth, such as curses, wands, amulets, magical language, and the like, we add a new sphere of information to this study: the actual practice of magic, popular religion, and superstition in the world which created and transmitted classical mythology and legend. There is an enormous body of scholarship which is now available on the topics of magic, witchcraft, ghosts, curse tablets, and the occult in the Greek and Roman world. One could spend years on the role and vitality of magic, myth, religion, and superstition of that age. Excellent sources, from which we shall draw, which are available for study of primary texts, materials, and concepts in these matters, are the works of Hans Dieter Betz, John Gager, Georg Luck, and Daniel Ogden.[1] Their scholarship reveals how the ancient people actually lived out their views of fate, nature, life, and the access to the invisible powers which affect human existence ... the very stuff of mythical lore and magic.[2]

Two Similar Worlds

The magical worlds of *Harry Potter* and Greco-Roman antiquity share at least three essential characteristics: the presumption of at least two realms

180

of reality, the seen (which is knowable) and the unseen (which is both powerful and mysterious); a spectrum of varied beings who populate those worlds; and the blurring of the distinctions of space and time.

First, in the magical and speculative worlds, the visible and experiential is always jeopardized by and subject to invisible powers, unpredictable gods, supersensory principles, or Fates and prophecies. The functions of myth or mystical lore, and the goals of magic are to try to manage the unknowable and invisible: to gain power over nature and destiny or over an enemy; to protect one's self against a condition or prophecy; to win, keep or punish the object of one's affections; to curse or bless; to heal or inflict injury, to mention only a few of many functions.

Plato spoke critically of begging priests and seers who claimed to have heavenly power to forgive a rich man's sins, or those of his ancestors, for a feast, and to be able to injure an enemy by incantations (Gk *epagōgais*) and spells (Gk *katadesmois*) (*Republic* 2.364 b–c).[3] The context in which he said this was the discussion of the gods and virtue—that often good people suffer while wicked people prosper—and how people try to alter that situation. He points out that in the *Iliad*, Homer says that when mortals commit a wrong, they can persuade even the powerful gods to grant pardon by pleasing them with sacrifices and offerings (*Il.* 9.497–501). While Plato had a low opinion of the sellers of spells and such, he did not at all exclude the reality of another world besides that which can be perceived by the senses. Robert Lenardon writes, "there is also abundant ... evidence for the nonmathematical, the spiritual, and the mystical aspects of Plato's philosophy, epitomized in his visionary Myth of Er, narrated by Socrates...."[4]

About six hundred years after Plato, people were still practicing, thinking about, and writing about the use of potions (Gk *pharmakeiai*) and magical binding spells (Gk *katadesmous*) (Artemidorus, *Onirocritus*, I. 77). The ancient Greeks and Romans lived with a sense of their being at the caprice of things beyond their power (such as the weather, health, divinities and personified forces). But they also lived with the belief that by doing something special in their own realm, they could affect the future (for good or for ill).

A second characteristic of magic, old or new, is the presumed existence of a spectrum of beings, from the lowliest to the grandest, with each type having some degree of the nature and ability of those beings at the top of this pyramid. In the Wizarding world, there are the rank and file humans with no magical capacity (Muggles). Above them are the Mudbloods, who are magical, but who are born to Muggles. Next come half-bloods who have one magical parent and one non-magical parent. Then there are the Squibs, who have magical parents, but no magical powers or magical talent. Over those lesser ranks are the pure-blood magical folk. A variation on that category is represented by magical folk whose bloodline has been altered by werewolves (Fenrir Greyback, Remus Lupin, Teddy Lupin, and Bill Weasley). Higher than the typical magical Folks are the especially talented magical individuals, such as Albus Dumbledore, Tom Riddle, and Harry Potter. Rowling's magical world also offers a range of special animals, creatures (boggarts, e.g.), and human-like beings (gremlins, House-Elves), giants, and even the dead (ghosts, Inferi, Dementors, and the epiphanies of the deceased).

The ancient world of legend and myth is populated, of course, by the rank and file humans, some of whom are craven, cruel, selfish and even bes-tial, but others of whom are noble models worthy of respect and imitation. Above humans stand the spiritual-physical beings such as classes of nymphs, then the special humans who, for whatever reason, have unique and super-human abilities, next demi-gods who are born from the union of a god or goddess and a human, then local heroes and deities, the twelve Olympians, and finally the one God as the main father or mother of the gods. Creatures of horrific or marvelous character and appearance represent the entire range of experiences and forces or Fates to which humans are exposed—frightening monsters and bizarre animals or forces of nature which have some human traits, such as hundred-handed giants, cyclopes, Sirens, Harpies, sphinxes, Scylla and Charybdis.

The third shared feature of the two worlds is the blurring or overlapping of space and time. In tales of magic or fantasy, part of the charm is the author's coloring outside the lines or breaching the walls in our minds which give everything its own place and distinctness. Such a blurring of the lines includes space and time as well—a "never, never land," or a Middle Earth or the ambiguous time of the creation myths and the sagas of ancient kingdoms.

Rowling sometimes creatively erases the lines between present, past and future. A few examples will demonstrate her technique. Early in the series, readers encounter the phenomenon as Harry has a frightening dream during his first night at Hogwarts. In the dream, recollections from his past, images from the new things he has begun to experience, and deliberations about his future whirl together in a dizzying and confusing mixture. Quirrell's absurd turban sits on Harry's head and tries to make him choose Slytherin House as his destiny (future)—as if the turban were a Sorting Hat with an evil agenda. Draco Malfoy, the arrogant student whom Harry has just met, laughs at him and then metamorphoses into sinister-looking Professor Snape, who takes up the laughter with an even more frightening tone and pitch. The burst of green light, which he recalls vaguely from his infancy, startles Harry awake.

By means of Tom Riddle's diary, Harry communicates in "real time" with the Tom Riddle of fifty years previously, who is forever sixteen years old, not the Voldemort who is decades older when Harry reads the diary. In the *Chamber of Secrets*, Tom speaks of times as if they are overlapping anatomical transparencies: "Voldemort ... is my past, present, and future, Harry Potter" (*CS* 313). And he tells Harry, "Twice—in *your* past, in *my* future—we have met" (*CS* 316).

In the *Prisoner of Azkaban*, Harry and Hermione travel in time by using the Time-Turner, which Hermione used all that year to enable her to take courses offered at the same time. In the *Goblet of Fire* and *Order of the Phoenix*, Harry enters the past, seeing it in real time, when he uses the Pensieve to enter the thoughts of Dumbledore and Snape. During the battle in the Department of Mysteries, when a Death Eater is knocked backward, his head falls into a bell jar containing Time, with the result that his body outside the jar remains the same, but his head changes repeatedly to a baby's head and then back to an adult's. And, as the bond between Harry and Voldemort strengthens, and Harry has more frequent and clearer visions of what the Dark Lord is doing, his Horcrux scar transports him into the very mind and presence of his enemy.

In myth and legend, the blurring of space and time is effected by various means, such as the intrusion of the gods into human life and by the delivery of prophecies. The poet of the *Iliad* begins his epic by describing a plague which is ravaging the camp of the Greeks. He links the misfortune to the hero of the poem, Achilles. But he does not narrate the events which have led up to this state of affairs. It is only after he has set a tone and theme for the entire epic poem that he catches readers up to speed by narrating how all this came to be. Here are the events which lead up to the plague. After a particular battle, prizes of war are distributed to the leaders. Young women are awarded to Achilles and Agamemnon as trophies. Agamemnon's slave is the daughter of the priest of Apollo, Chryses. The priest implores the general to allow him to ransom back his child, Chryseïs. The warrior refuses the request, and insults and threatens the priest, who prays to his lord for help. Angered at the disrespect of his priest, Apollo inflicts widespread pestilence and death on the army of the Greeks. The gods begin to intervene after nine days of plague. Hera, who favors the Greeks, "put it into the mind" of Achilles to call an assembly (*Il.* 1.55). Their trusted prophet, Kalchas, blames the curse on Agamemnon's treatment of Apollo's priest. Tempers flare, Agamemnon sullenly agrees to dismiss the girl, but he demands to be given the slave girl Briseïs, who is Achilles' war prize. In an honor and shame culture, this is highly insolent treatment and a major breach of societal norms. During the assembly, Achilles rages with personal anger, dishonor, and hatred for the general's shameless acts which have caused such horror. At the very moment when Achilles is battling within himself whether or not to strike Agamemnon, Hera sends Athena to give the hero her counsel. She advises him to rage at his enemy personally, but not to kill him. During their conversation, the surrounding scene and all the company of the Greeks appear to have frozen, as if the laws of physics have been broken. Their exchange completed, Athena returns to Olympus, and the action starts again: Achilles berates Agamemnon verbally, and he chooses to withdraw from the war rather than to kill the general. Space and time have been relaxed as two worlds overlap.

In the *Aeneid*, prophecy is the vehicle for the relaxation of space and time.[5] In Book 1, Juno, anxious about the fate of Aeneas, questions Jupiter as to why he and his people are having such difficulty getting to Italy their destined goal. Jupiter assures her that their fate is unchanged and he delivers to her a major prophecy which links mythology and Roman history, "Unrolling [the scroll][6] farther, I shall ponder secret things of the Fates" (*longius et volvēns fātōrum arcāna movēbō, Aen.* 1.262). He foresees a universal empire for the Trojans through their descendants, the Romans. And he traces the things that will come to pass down to the future deification of Julius Caesar (1.263–96), salting the preview of history with the legends of Romulus and Remus. In Book 6, when Aeneas journeys to the Underworld to confer with his deceased father, Anchises, he receives a preview of glorious Roman history (6.752–892). This major prophecy, too, mixes the names of heroes, generals, and Roman statesmen who will later be born, down to the age of Vergil himself, with the early mythical lore of the Romans, Romulus, Remus, and the gods. In these examples, space (Olympus, Troy, the Underworld) and time (history, the realm of the immortals, past, present, and future) are quite fluid.

Non-Human Beings

A range of beasts, monsters, and creatures which are on the edge of perceived reality is often the stock-in-trade of myth-makers and magical folk.[7]

BASILISKS

This monster features prominently in the *Chamber of Secrets*. It is an enormous snake with yellow eyes, which causes anyone to die who makes direct eye-contact with it, or to become petrified even by making indirect eye-contact. Though the creature lives for many centuries, the crowing of roosters is, for some reason, fatal to it. Its venomous fangs are lethal, even after the basilisk is dead, which comes in handy for Hermione and Ron in dealing with the cup of Hufflepuff. When Harry uses the sword of Godric Gryffindor on the basilisk, the snake's venom soaks into the sword itself. This becomes useful to Dumbledore, as he later uses the sword's toxicity to destroy the stone of the Slytherin ring.

Given our angle of investigation, there are two matters that need to be addressed regarding the basilisk—the ancient imagery of the great snake and the motif of blinding as punishment, or, more specifically, the blinding or lethal power of making eye-contact with a monstrous being. First, we should consider the ancient lore and information about this fictitious monster.[8] Karley Adney and Holly Hassel have noted this about Rowling's invented monster: "The figure of the basilisk, popularly reused in modern fantasy film, literary works, and gaming, originates in Roman mythology. Rowling draws upon the traditional associations and mythical descriptions of the basilisk as a legendary serpent whose glance is fatal" (Adney 350).

The basilisk is mentioned perhaps as early as the fifth century BCE by Hippocrates (*Epistles* 19), and described in the first century CE by Pliny the Elder, a Roman scholar of encyclopedic knowledge and a prolific writer on natural history. In his record of unique animals in Africa, Pliny lists a "basilisk" [Gk *basiliskos*, "a snake, Egyptian cobra" > L *basiliscus*, "a snake, basilisk"], a term which comes from the Greek word for "royal" [Gk *basil-*, "royal, kingly"] and could well mean that it designated the king of snakes, perhaps the Egyptian king cobra (LSJ 318). He says that it is indigenous to northern Africa, and that, according to his source, it can cause anyone to die immediately who looks into its eyes.[9] The snake which he describes, however, is much shorter than the monster of snakes depicted in the *Potter* books, as it is only about twelve inches long (or, the length of twelve fingers laid side by side[10]— *duodecim nōn amplius digitōrum magnitūdine*). A white, crown-shaped marking on its head may account for its being called a king of snakes, or that title may be derived from its reputation for its toxic venom. According to Pliny, other snakes flee from it, its touch causes bushes to shrivel, and its breath can scorch grass and crack rocks. His evidence of the snake's powerful venom is about as improbable as the existence of the snake itself. He claims that once, when a basilisk was speared by a man on horseback, the snake's poison made its way up through the spear, killing both the rider and his horse (*Natural History* 8.78). Today there are several species of "spitting cobras" in Africa, which shoot their venom into the eyes of their predators in order to blind the attackers and so protect themselves. Perhaps that is part of the natural origin of the mythic power of the basilisk. The potency and mystery of the demonic reptile have sparked imagination for millennia.[11]

The second factor that reveals a link to classical antiquity is the motif of blinding of victims either as a punishment or for one's protection. Being blinded for offending someone or something sacred or powerful is a classic and long-standing motif in legend and literature. One story about events in the life of the famous Greek prophet Tiresias states that when he was a child, he accidentally caught sight of the goddess Athena while she was bathing nude (Callimachus, *Bath of Pallas*, 5). The offended goddess punished him by blinding the boy, but she appeased his mother (who was a friend of Athena) by making him a famous seer and prophet.[12] There is also the story of the Roman Lucius Metellus, who rescued the Palladium (the sacred statue of Pallas Athena) from the burning Temple of Vesta in 241 BCE.[13] He was blinded because he saw what was not supposed to be seen.

The most obvious mythological template for the deadly glare of the basilisk, however, is the petrifying power of the stare of the Gorgon Medusa, who was beheaded by Perseus. Medusa was one of three sisters, born in the early stages of the world when offspring often emerged as monstrous beings. Their siblings included the Graiai, who were the personifications of old age, having one eye and one tooth to share among the three of them, and Ladon, a dragon who guarded the golden apples of the Hesperides.[14] All three Gorgons—"Stheno" ("mighty"), "Euryale" ("wide-wanderer"), and "Medusa" ("ruler")—are often said to have had horrifying appearance and writhing snakes for hair. Medusa, however, was the only one who was mortal.

Perseus enters the story as a semi-divine hero, a son of Zeus and Danaë. His mother became the object of love of Polydectes, the king of Seriphos. But she did not love the king. In order to get Perseus out of the way of his romantic efforts, Polydectes charged Perseus with a task intended to kill him, the retrieval of the head of Medusa. Although Perseus was a very able hero, this seemed impossible until he was aided by divine powers. The messenger god Hermes gave him wings for his feet and Athena, the god of wisdom and war, gave him a mirror or a shiny shield with which he could view the Gorgon without looking directly into her hideous eyes and thus he would not be turned to stone by her. He tricked the Graiai into telling him where the Hesperides were (from whom he would get the packet or wallet to contain the head) by snatching from them the single eye which they shared among the three old women, holding it until they gave him the information he needed.[15] Athena also guided him in his journey to the land where the three sisters lived—a land, by the way, which was littered with the petrified remains of victims who had looked directly into the eyes of Medusa. Another variant reports that Hermes gave Perseus a scimitar with a curved blade for the task, and that nymphs provided him with a Cap of Invisibility, winged sandals, and a packet or wallet in which to carry the severed head.[16]

The hero used the Invisibility Cap and crept up on Medusa as she slept, viewing her only indirectly by the image reflected in the mirror or shield, severed her head and hid it in the packet. From the blood of the Gorgon sprang the winged horse, Pegasus. As Perseus flew about, the powerful blood dripped onto the Libyan sands, creating poisonous vipers. When the head was laid, enclosed in the packet, onto soft seaweed on the shore, it turned the vegetation into coral. In his adventures, Perseus showed the head to the Titan Atlas, turning him into a mountain; he exhibited it to a group of insuperable enemies (the supporters of Phineus, a suitor of Perseus' bride, Andromeda), turning them all to stone; he turned a mythical race of men, the Hyperboreans, to stone; and finally, with the head he petrified his original enemy, Polydectes. The image of the stare of Medusa was so horrifying that Athena placed it on her breastplate or aegis, to warn others of her awesome might.

In summary, in both the ancient resources and in the *Potter* novels, the "basilisk" introduces several shared motifs: death or disaster by gazing into the eyes of a deadly monster; encounter with a viper so deadly that it can be killed only by a hero with supernatural help; and a viper's venom which remains lethal even after the snake is dead. The mythological character who personified the qualities of the basilisk was Medusa, who was dispatched only by the most heroic effort and by trickery with a sword provided by the flying messenger god, Hermes. This terrifying monster and her death are prototypes for Harry's heroic battle to death with the basilisk, which is killed with the Sword of Gryffindor that is delivered in the Sorting Hat by Dumbledore's flying messenger, Fawkes.

Birds

Varieties of birds play a significant role in the novels. They are one of the instruments with which Rowling characterizes the individuals in the stories, by subtly suggesting that readers apply general concepts associated with the nature or behavior of the birds with their human counterparts. That is, the birds are mirrors of their owners. Harry's messenger owl, Hedwig, is a snowy owl, a visually innocent companion of the boy who discovers an entirely hidden realm of reality. Draco Malfoy's owl, by contrast, is an eagle owl—quite an aggressive bird, and the same bird which, in Harry's day-dream, transports him to the Riddle House where he observes a chilling scene of murder done by Voldemort in the presence of Wormtail and Nagini. The poor Weasleys can only afford the aged and worn-out owl, Errol, who collapses sometimes during his flights. His name appears to be a playful creation based on a Latin base, which accentuates his incapacity as a messenger. Percy's screech owl is named for the Greek messenger god, Hermes, who delivers messages from Zeus to mortals or other gods. This mail carrier is put into service frequently, delivering messages of love to his master's girlfriend, Penelope Clearwater.

The peacock, a bird renowned for the showy colors on the tail of the males, brings to mind thoughts of bright hues and radiant splendor.[17] This image is contradicted by the albino peacock which guards the Malfoy's yard. The contrast between our expectations and the colorless bird compels us to apply this unexpected jolt to the people who live inside the house. Arrogant and cocky, the Malfoys consider themselves to be of pure-blood wizard stock, unstained by any Muggle blood. It is ironic that the bird which represents them is devoid —"pure," as it were— of all the colors which should make the bird special. This pallid but arrogant image is reinforced by the pale-faced portraits of the Malfoy ancestors inside their house. This family's pride in its purity is an empty boast. Their "pure" world of Dark magic, Dark Marks, and sinister power is more like the "ghostly white" peacock than the splendor which the symbol itself is supposed to display. Sirius Black shows a bit of humor when he twice uses colorful tropical birds instead of owls to deliver his messages to Harry, an act which lifts Harry's spirits about Sirius' condition on the lam and gives a hint as to where he is in hiding. And, lastly, Dumbledore's Patronus is a phoenix, symbolizing ever-renewing hope.

Even the feathers of the birds contribute identity and color to characters, in the form of their writing quills. Harry's quill is an exquisite eagle feather, the powerful and active bird. No one would be surprised that egotistical Gilderoy Lockhart's quill is a peacock feather—characteristic of his huge ego, and showiness. Dolores Umbridge makes Harry write with her long, sharp, black quills which cut into his hand as he writes, drawing blood in the shape of the message, "I must not tell lies," as she tortures him in Detention. And, of course, on Professor Dumbledore's desk resides "a handsome scarlet quill" from his phoenix.

The ancient Greeks also associated individual types of birds with deities, as a way of characterizing their nature (the birds being a kind of revelation or appearance of the deity), or their actions (as omens, messengers, intruders into the world of humans). John Pollard writes, "Almost all the gods and goddesses were believed to possess avian emblems and as time went on the list tended to expand" (16). Zeus has the eagle as his messenger and omen.[18] Athena, the goddess of wisdom, is represented by the owl. The raven, swan, and falcon are sacred to Apollo. His sister, Artemis, is symbolized by the guinea fowl. The peacock is Hera's representative. Aphrodite, the goddess of love, is symbolized by the dove, the sparrow and the swan. The Roman god of war, Mars, has the woodpecker as his sacred representative. The rooster is associated with a number of deities—Hermes, Athena, Leto, Demeter, Asclepius, Helios, and the demi-god Heracles (147–48).

As to why the ancients associated birds with gods, and specific birds with individual gods, one can only speculate. Pollard's proposals are insightful, thought-provoking and reasonable. It may be that in a specific locale where a god was honored, there may have been a plentiful company of a specific species of birds, fostering the association between the bird population and the site. Or, perhaps, since birds flock to sites of sacrifice for scavenging, the association may have been made by their presence. The nature and life of birds may have been the connection. They travel over great distances, range between two worlds (the ground and the sky), and seem to have knowledge of seasons in which to migrate, nest, mate, and fledge. The anthropomorphizing of nature (imputing human traits to animals) may have been the source of envisioned parallels between birds and the gods (who are, in mythology, humans written large).[19]

The connection between birds and gods made the study of birds for divination an important practice in the classical world. Both Greeks and Romans attempted to discover the will of the gods or to see the future by interpreting the nature and behavior of birds, particularly their flights, calls, and cries, a discipline known as Ornithomancy. The sighting of a bird or birds, their species, their flight pattern, behavior, cries, the time of their sighting, and such, as well as the appearance of their entrails during sacrifice, were supposed to have definite meanings as omens from the gods. As far back as the *Iliad*, bird omens have played a significant role. When the Trojan army was successful in advancing on the Greek forces and appeared to be winning, at the point where a decision had to be made about proceeding and fighting around the Greek ships, the Trojans saw an omen. An eagle, high in the sky, clutching a gigantic scarlet serpent in its talons flew on the left of their front lines, the side signifying misfortune. The snake struck its captor, and in pain the eagle dropped the snake into the middle of the battle as a portent of aegis-bearing Zeus [Gk *Dios teras aigiochoio,*12. 209], terrifying the Trojan soldiers. An advisor to Hector interpreted the omen as a dreadful message of danger for them if they pressed forward—as he said a seer [Gk *theopropos*] would know. An opposite bird omen appears later in the epic. Priam prayed to Zeus for a sign that he would be successful at ransoming the body of his son Hector from the irate warrior, Achilles. Zeus sent an enormous eagle flying to the right of Troy, the side signifying good fortune, for all to see, making everyone glad (24.308–21).

The most famous interpreter of the will and messages of Apollo by bird omens was the blind prophet Tiresias. Oedipus implored him not to withhold any oracles of birds as to why his city of Thebes was plagued and cursed. The prophet leveled him with the dreadful truth that the prophecy of Oedipus' fate was being worked out, that the king, himself, was the plague of the city (Sophocles, *Oedipus the King*, 300ff.). When Oedipus' successor, Creon, became tyrannical and unmovable in his reign, claiming that he was the law, and that there was no higher law than he, he set himself up for tragedy. Tiresias came to warn him that he had seen the birds savaging each other, screaming and beating their wings, and that the sacrificial parts were foul, dreadful warnings which pointed to the condition of Thebes and death and disaster approaching the house of the king (Sophocles, *Antigone*, 999ff.).

In Rome, there was an official association of priests, called "augurs," whose duty was divination by observing birds. As time passed, these seers modernized and expedited their art by sometimes observing chickens rather than unreliable wild birds, to get the will of the gods. Birds of the Wizarding world, too, come under scrutiny as omens. They are important enough that the course in divination at Hogwarts includes instruction in the branch of that discipline, known "Ornithomancy."

CENTAURS

In classical mythology, centaurs are considered monstrous beings, having origins and ancestry which are shameful and bestial. The initiator of their race is Ixion, the first Greek to commit murder (Aeschylus, *Eumenides* 717). Since this act is unprecedented, only Zeus can grant pardon for such the sin. He invites Ixion to Olympus for an interview. While there, Ixion's twisted character reveals itself when he attempts to have sex with Zeus's wife, Hera. Zeus tricks him, though, by shaping a cloud (Nephele) in the image of Hera. Ixion impregnates the cloud and the offspring of this shameless act is the monster Centaurus (Pindar *Pythia* 2; *Epit.* 1.20). This monster, in turn, mates with mares on Mt. Pelion and the offspring of those unions is the race of monsters called "centaurs," being half horse, half human. For his sins, Ixion is tied to an ever-revolving, fiery wheel in Tartarus.

The centaurs of mythology are such violent and forbidding monsters that when Aeneas visits the Underworld, he finds them in the same place as other vicious, strange-bodied monsters: Scylla (a monster with the form of a woman above, a ring of dog's heads about her waist, and a sea monster below); the hundred-handed giant Briareus; the many-headed Hydra of Lerna which Heracles killed; the fire-breathing Chimaera with its goat-head and tail tipped with a serpent's head; the Gorgons with their serpent hair and staring eyes which turn to stone anyone who looks into them; the ravenous Harpies with their bird-like bodies and women's faces; and the giant, three-bodied Geryon, another of Heracles' victims (*Aen.* 6.285–89).

In early Greek mythology, art, and sculpture, the centaurs represent the wild, uncivilized, barbarian element in the world. One of the most famous scenes depicting this concept can be traced back as far as the poetry of Homer, the Battle of the Lapiths and the Centaurs. The story goes that Pirithoüs, king of the Lapiths, invites the centaurs to attend his wedding to Hippodamia. During the wedding, the centaurs become drunk and try to rape the Lapith women, which starts an epic battle. Symbolizing for Greeks the conflict between civilization (Greek culture) and barbarism, the tale of the battle was so famous that a sculptural depiction of it adorned the pediment of the Temple of Zeus at Olympia.

Only a few mythological centaurs are known by name, the most famous of them being Pholus, Nessus, and Chiron. Pholus gives Heracles hospitality when the hero is on his way to capture the ravaging boar which came down from Mt. Erymanthus. The host provides Heracles cooked meat, but eats raw meat himself. When Heracles asks for wine, Pholus is afraid to open the special jar of wine which Dionysus had given to all the centaurs as a common gift. Heracles presses the request, and Pholus unseals the jar. The other centaurs catch the scent of the wine and attack Heracles. He kills several and chases others all the way to Malea, at the bottom of the Peloponnese. Pholus accidentally drops one of Heracles' poisoned arrows on his own foot, and dies immediately (*Libr.* 2.5.3–4).

The centaur Nessus attempts to rape Heracles' wife Deïanira and is shot with a poison arrow by the hero. As he lies dying, Nessus tells her to collect and keep some of his blood, because it has the power to keep Heracles true to her if he ever falls in love with anyone else. She keeps the magical blood for years, until Heracles falls in love with Iole. Deïanira then gives Heracles a robe smeared with the blood, not knowing that it came from an animal which was killed with a poisoned arrow. Heracles' body becomes inflamed with the poison and, in order to end the pain, he has himself burned to death.

The most famous centaur of classical mythology is Chiron [Gk *Cheirōn*]. He is different from the wild centaurs because his horse-human shape did not come from savages and criminals, but from the horse-like image which the supreme, ancient God Cronus took upon himself when he courted Chiron's mother, Philyra. Chiron is reputed to be wise and kind, gifted and trained by the gods, and entrusted with the task of educating some of the most renowned figures in Greek mythology: Asclepius (Apollo's own son and the Greek god of healing), Jason (the commander of the first sailing vessel, the Argo), and Achilles (the greatest of the Greek warriors). He is immortalized in the constellation Centaurus (Howatson 142–43).

In the *Potter* novels, centaurs enter prominently from time to time, as a reminder that there are magical communities other than simply Wizarding folk. They are creatures with the body of a horse and the upper torso of a human, which live as a herd in the Forbidden Forest where they study the heavens. Newt Scamander adds that the centaurs are mistrustful of both Muggles and magical folk and that they have skills in magical healing, divination, archery, and astronomy (2001, 6). They are intelligent, but as a whole, hostile to humans. Hagrid, usually quite fond of unique beasts, referred to them as "ruddy stargazers" (SS 254). Though they are herd animals, we come to know only a few by name: Ronan, Bane, Firenze, and Magorian. And of that set, only Firenze appears to be willing to deal with humans, though he considers them to be not as skilled or as wise as his own kind. While all the other Forbidden Forest centaurs are hostile and wild, Firenze alone allows Harry to ride on his back to escape danger and engages him in a Socratic conversation to help him come to his own conclusion as to what the killing of the unicorn in the forest means. Eventually, Firenze is invited to teach Divination at Hogwarts, where he demonstrates intelligence, wisdom, cleverness of mind, and an appreciation for one of the highest Greek ideals, moderation and humility in one's ideas and behavior. Surely Firenze is the Chiron of his herd.[20]

The presence and behavior of the centaur herd at Dumbledore's funeral appears to be a striking, artistic variation on the topic of barbarism versus civilization. Known to be hostile and uncivilized, the centaurs unexpectedly come forth in a calm manner to participate with all the other mourners in respectful observance of his funeral. They even launch a volley of arrows to salute the fallen Headmaster, and then quietly return to their forest. The backdrop for this particular narration may well be the Battle of the Lapiths and the Centaurs. What one would anticipate with the appearance of the centaurs at a solemn occasion such as the memorial service for Dumbledore would be another wild, uncivilized display. But what actually happens breaks the mold made by the mythological story. Perhaps the effect of this variation is to emphasize the enormous respect in which Dumbledore is held by all.

CHIMAERAS

These creature are mentioned only occasionally in the novels [Gk *Chimaira*, "she-goat" > L *Chimaera*]. Hagrid makes a passing reference to how interesting they are. And we learn that when Elphias Doge was traveling in Greece, he encountered Chimaeras—quite appropriately, as Greek mythology tells stories about the deadly monsters. And when Draco Malfoy's friend, Vincent Crabbe casts a spell which creates a conflagration in the Room of Requirement, it appears to possess not only the normal capacity of fire, but a degree of intelligence as well, for it pursues them as if it intended to kill them. The magical fire is more than a physical force. It has menacing will and the appearance of fiery monsters, the Chimaeras. These powerful, fire-breathing she-monsters of Greek mythology have the head of a lion, body of a goat, a serpent's tail (*Il.* 6.179–82).[21] They have the same monstrous family members as their brother Cerberus. They are such hellish creatures, that when Aeneas ventured into the Underworld, he found them in the same region as the Gorgons, the Harpies, and the three-headed giant named "Geryon" (*Aen.* 6.285–89). David Leeming points out that the only important role this animal plays in surviving ancient mythic tales is in the story of its death by Bellerophon (1997, 112).

DEMENTORS

These fiendish, hooded beings, skeletal and ghastly in appearance, serve as guards at Azkaban. They drive the inmates mad by extracting all joy from them. They thrive on sucking all happiness from a person and, finally, by administering the Dementor's Kiss or the Kiss of Death, which leaves the victim's body alive but without a soul. They may attack in small groups or by the hundreds and are capable of breeding and multiplying. The ghastly features of the Dementors are reminiscent of the divine reapers, the mythological Fates, who take their grim prey in battle. In a poem which is questionably ascribed to Hesiod, entitled the *Shield of Heracles*, the author tells of Heracles' battle with Cycnus, a son of Ares who robs travelers on their way to the Delphic Oracle. Part of the poem describes the imagery which is embossed on Heracles' marvelous shield, made for him by the god Hephaestus.[22] In a battle scene depicted on the shield, the death of warriors is portrayed as the onslaught of the Fates [Gk *Kēres*]. Lusting for blood, the grim and merciless beings fight over the wounded and dying. They hook a victim in their talons, and his soul descends to Tartarus, the lowest region of Hades. Not satisfied with their quarry, they throw the victim aside and immediately return to the battle, to satisfy their insatiable lust (ll. 248–57).[23]

DRAGONS/SNAKES

According to Peter L. De Rose, "The dragon is a nearly universal motif, a reptilian or snake-like hybrid or compound animal, covered with the scales of a fish and some-times endowed with claws and wings and the head of an eagle, falcon, or hawk" ("Mythical Animals," 2005, 67). Dragons are serpents (Birkalan "Dragon," 2005, 74). The Greek word for "dragon," "snake," or "serpent" is *drakōn*. It is often synonymous with the more specific term for "snake," "*ophis*." Hesiod says that the monster Typhoeus, born from Gaia (the Earth) and Tartarus (Hades), had a hundred heads of a snake (*ophios*), a terrible dragon (*drakontos*) which blazed with flame, licking tongues, blazing eyes, and horrifying sounds (*Theog.* 825–34).[24]

Sometimes other monsters have dragon features, as the Chimera's middle is that of a dragon (*Theog.* 322). These monsters include the following: the Hydra of Lyrna, which Heracles killed; the monster Scylla; the monstrous snake Pytho, which Apollo killed in order to take over Delphi as his holy place; the dragon-snake which guarded the Golden Fleece which Jason stole; the sea-monster from which Perseus rescued Andromeda; the monster Ladon, who guarded the apples of the Hesperides, which Heracles killed in order to get the golden apples; the serpents which Hera sent from the sea to kill the infant Heracles; and the dragon which guarded the sacred spring of Ares, which Cadmus killed in order to sacrifice a cow to Athena and establish the city of Thebes.[25] The fearsome aspect of snakes is represented in the ancient depictions of Medusa's hair, Cerberus' collar, and Scylla's midriff, all of which were ringed with snake heads. Snakes were a central feature in the healing arts of Asclepius and his center of therapy at Epidaurus, probably owing to the deep symbolism of re-vitalization which derives from snakes' shedding their skin.

Dragons appear frequently and in various ways in the Wizarding World as well. Newt Scamander introduces the entry on dragons by saying that they are "Probably the most famous of all magical beasts," and then proceeds to give six pages to the subject (10–15). They are such a regular element of Harry Potter's world that one of the passwords required by the painting of the Fat Lady for admittance to the Gryffindor common room is "Caput Draconis," Latin for "Dragon's Head."

Dragons are both valuable and dangerous. Their liver sells for fifteen Sickles per ounce at the Apothecary in Diagon Alley. And, as the result of the research of Albus Dumbledore, their blood is found to be useful in twelve different ways. On the other hand, they are the source of a disease called "dragon pox." Apparently, Draco Malfoy's grandfather, Abraxas, died of the disease, and Elphias Doge contracted the disease during his first year as a student at Hogwarts. Perhaps the dreadful and potentially deadly nature of the dragon is the reason that Horace Slughorn, in his attempts to camouflage himself as a chair and wreck his living room, spatters the walls with dragon's blood (*HBP* 65).

Dragons are the essential and critical element of the First Task of the Triwizard Tournament. They are described as fire-breathing and at least fifty feet tall. The thirty-or-so wizards who attempt to control them have to resort to casting a unified Stunning Spell on the beasts, in order to bind them with chains and leather collars. A dragon is both the impediment to and the vehicle of escape for HH&R when they invade Gringotts incognito, under the spell of Polyjuice Potion. There, they find that the deepest vaults are protected by a fire-breathing dragon, which has been chained in the dark for so long that it has lost much of its sight and pigmentation. They use incantations which release the dragon and create a hole large enough for the dragon, onto which they climb, to escape from the bank.

Our most complete source for dragons in the series is Rubeus Hagrid. While he has a tender spot for all kinds of bizarre creatures, his becoming a "mother," as it were, to his own dragon provides a perspective on the beasts which only a mother could have. He always wanted a dragon, and he finally acquired a dragon egg of his own in a game of cards. The Gamekeeper studied up on how to hatch and rear his prize. The growth pattern of his baby Norwegian Ridgeback, whom he named Norbert, was phenomenal, tripling its length in a single week. As dreadful and vicious as dragons are, Rowling interjects some endearing humor into the episode of Hagrid's caretaking of his pet. When he has to send Norbert away, he packs three things for his journey—rats, brandy and a teddy bear (*SS* 240). His unique perspective on dragons is humorously portrayed again when he takes Madam Maxime to view some vicious dragons. He presumes that this "date" will be a way to get in good with her.

Flying Horses

The ancients had myths about marvelous horses, some of whom could fly. The most widely known of these is Pegasus. He was born from the bloody body of his mother, Medusa, after Perseus beheaded her. At the time of the Gorgon's death, she was pregnant with a "child" of Poseidon, the god of the sea. Since Poseidon was associated with horses, as well as with the sea, the "child" she was carrying was a horse (*Libr.* 2.4.2). Another story about the famous horse is that when his hoof touched the surface of Mount Helicon, the home of the Muses, a new and sacred spring was created, the Hippocrene fountain (*Met.* 5.254ff.).[26]

Pegasus is also associated with the divinely-gifted hero, Bellerophon. When he was at Tiryns, the local king's wife, Anteia, fell in love with the handsome young man. But he did not yield to her charms. Either in revenge or to cover her improper behavior, she charged Bellerophon with trying to seduce her (a most serious breach of the heavy social law of hospitality). To punish the offender, King Proteus sent him to Anteia's father, Iobates, a neighboring king, with orders to have the young man killed. Consequently, Iobates sent Bellerophon on a series of deadly missions, on all of which he was successful. In one of his tasks, the killing of the Chimaera, Bellerophon flew on the winged horse Pegasus and shot the monster with arrows from above. Tragically, Bellerophon also attempted to fly up to heaven on Pegasus, who threw him to his death for such an arrogant act. The horse proceeded to the realm of the gods and was transformed into a constellation (*Il.* 6.179–82; *Libr.* 3.3.1–2; Lewis 1989, 1324). Beyond the spheres of epic, tragedy, and literature, from which most of what we have mentioned comes, Pliny, the observer of natural history during the first century CE, claimed that there were horned, winged horses in Ethiopia, which were known as "*pegasi*" (*Natural History* 8.72).

Flying horses or horse-hybrids make their appearances in Rowling's novels as well. Ranging from the least to the most bizarre, there are Madam Maxime's flying palominos, Hippogriffs, and thestrals.

Madam Maxime's Flying Palominos

The twelve fantastic flying horses which draw the carriage of the representatives of Madam Maxime's school, Beauxbatons, are unique, but hardly grotesque. As palominos, they would be golden-tan colored, with white tails and spots on their faces and legs. The spectacular difference between these powerful horses and non-magical palominos is that they are as large as elephants, have fiery eyes and wings, and drink only single-malt whiskey.

Hippogriffs

These creatures are the result of the mating of horses and griffins, having heads and wings like those of eagles, but the body of a horse (Scamander 21). The talons of the hippogriffs are six inches long. The principal hippogriff, Buckbeak, has a wing span of twenty-four feet. Because of Hagrid's affinity for bizarre creatures, he brings twelve of them from the Forbidden Forest to introduce to his class. While there are no hippogriffs in classical mythology,

Vergil speaks of griffins mating with mares *(Eclogue* 8.27) [Gk *hippos, -ou,* "horse"; on "griff," see "Griffins," below].

Thestrals

The horse-like creatures called "thestrals" perform important functions while adding a Halloween-like tone to the story. The usual function of these animals is to draw the "horseless" carriages which transport upper-level stu dents from the train station in Hogsmeade to the school. To most students they are invisible, since only those who have seen death first-hand can see them. Dwelling in the Forbidden Forest, they are not healthy-looking, well-bred beings, but appear to be cold-blooded (though they are carnivorous), reptilian, skeletal in appearance, with heads like dragons, white eyes which stare in a piercing manner, and large wings more like those of bats than of birds. Their most prominent performance, however, is to provide transporta-tion for Harry and his companions to the Ministry of Magic to help Sirius Black, who appears to be in deep trouble.

GIANTS

These extraordinary, super-human types are enormous and primitive beings, up to twenty-five feet in height, who dwell in caves in the rugged mountains away from people and from wizards, whom they dislike. Accord-ing to Hagrid, whereas there were once a hundred tribes of giants, their pop-ulation had declined severely. His own half-giant, half-brother Grawp, whom Hagrid attempts to civilize, is sixteen feet in height. When Voldemort is revi-talized, he plans to recall the giants to fight on his side, along with his Death Eaters and the Dementors. Dumbledore, however, sends Hagrid to try to get them to join his side against the Dark Lord, a mission which is futile, in part because Voldemort has already gotten to them. In light of the barbaric nature of the giants, the repeated examples of Hagrid's peculiar tenderness make him unique among his kin.

In classical lore, giants belong to the earliest and most primitive stages of the Olympian gods. The first gods to arise from Chaos ("the yawning void"), were Gaia ("earth") and Uranus ("heaven"). These two were prolific in their offspring, producing both the great gods called "Titans" and a series of monstrous and savage deities, the Cyclopes, the Hecatonchires (each with one hundred hands), and the Giants. Both the Titans and the Giants waged wars with the reigning gods to displace them—mythic battles known as the Titanomachy and the Gigantomachy. Zeus and his siblings, who had been swallowed by their father, Cronus, waged war against the tyrannical despot and defeated him and his supporters. After Zeus had assumed leadership of the gods, the Giants waged war against Zeus and his supporters. When the Giants were defeated, they were confined beneath the earth. There is an irony in their origin and final destination. Their name, "Giants," in Greek is *Gigantes*, "the great ones," who are called the *Gēgenēs*, "earth-born," because they were born to Gaia, the earth (LSJ 347–48). Born from the earth, they were restricted to realms beneath their birth mother.

These early conflicts symbolize the clash between Greek civilization and its opposite, barbarism, i.e., between good and evil. As a widely-known and esteemed metaphor for Greek superiority, the Gigantomachy was represented in reliefs on the Treasury of the Siphnians at Delphi, the Parthenon, and the Great Altar of Pergamum which has been called "the greatest monument of the Hellenistic age" (Biers 292). This mythological race came between the first gods, who began to instill order in the world, and the Olympian gods, who set and preserved order. It is interesting that the main role of giants in Rowling's novels is their being allies of Voldemort in a battle to take over the world ... shades of the Gigantomachy. In both *Harry Potter* and the ancient world, Giants represent a type of existence and being which is the opposite of that treasured by the civilized, whether Greeks or magical folk.[27]

GORGONS

When Hagrid suddenly recalls that he needs to send an owl to Professor Dumbledore, he blurts out, "Gallopin' Gorgons" (*SS* 52). In modern English, "gorgon" denotes a very ugly or frightening woman. The word comes from the mythological Gorgons, three sisters (Sthenno, Euryale, and Medusa) whose appearance is quite horrible—writhing snakes for hair, and a gaze so penetrating, that anyone who looks at them will be turned to stone [Gk *gorgos*, "terrible, wild, fierce" > *Gorgō/Gorgōn*, pl. *Gorgōnēs* "the Gorgon(s)," Medusa]. The most famous of the three is Medusa [Gk *Medousa* < participle of *medō*, meaning "she who rules" (LSJ 1089)] the only one of the sisters who is mortal. When Perseus is compelled to cut off her head and present it to Polydectes, he approaches her while she sleeps and uses a mirror-like shield to view her face indirectly. In that way, he does not suffer the fate of all others who view her face.[28]

GRIFFINS

The griffin is a mythical animal with the body of a lion and the head and wings of an eagle, signifying its power both on the ground and in the air. In the *Potter* novels, griffins do not get much mention. A stone statue of a griffin stands in one of the corridors at Hogwarts, and the door knocker on Professor Dumbledore's office is in the shape of a griffin. Gryffindor House, of course, recalls the griffin by its very name. In ancient times, griffins were said to live in the far northern land of the Hyperboreans. There, they were supposed to protect a supply of gold from the one-eyed Arimaspians. Owing to this duty, griffins came to symbolize steadfast guardians (Howatson 271). In ancient Greece, the hybrid beast symbolized "vigilant strength and an embodiment of Nemesis, the goddess of retribution."[29] At the archaeological museum in Olympia there are numerous bronze artistic representations of these "bird" creatures, dating from the seventh century BCE. One of these replicas depicts a mother griffin nursing her young [Gk *grūpos*, "hooked, curved, rounded" > *grux, grūpos*, "fabled beast, griffin" > L *grips* (or *gryps, gryphis*), "griffin"] (LSJ 61; OLD 778; Stelten 111). The connection of something "hooked" to the griffin may be its hooked beak or talons.

HARPIES

The all-female Quidditch team is known as the "Holyhead Harpies." Apparently, the players are proud of their greedy, aggressive, evil-tempered style of competition, for them to adopt that name for themselves. The term comes from violent, mythic monsters which have the faces of women and the bodies of birds, or "winged women." Whenever anyone comes to their islands they spoil the food of the intruders either by snatching it away (their name means, "snatchers") or by pooping on it. Phineus, the king of Thrace, suffered from their spoiling all his food (*Argonautica* 2.177ff.). And Aeneas and his crew suffered the same treatment from these demons (*Aen.* 3.209–77) (Howatson 275f.) [Gk *harpē*, "bird of prey" > *harpazein*, "to seize, snatch" > L *Harpyia*, "the Harpies"]. In modern usage, "harpies" are greedy, evil-tempered women.

MANTICORES

While Hermione is doing research on previous legal cases regarding magical creatures in order to save Buckbeak, she finds a notice about a manticore, a man-eating monster with the head of a man, lion's body and scorpion's tail—a creature known to the ancient Greeks as well. Pliny cites the fifth century BCE Greek historian Ctesias as his source of information and describes the fabulous manticore [Gk *martichoras/mantichoras*, "man-eater" > L *mantichoras*] as a swift, man-eating, red-colored animal with three rows of teeth, a human face and ears, grey eyes, the body of a lion, and a scorpion-like tail complete with stinger, a voice which is a mixture of trumpet and reed-pipe sounds, perhaps having the capacity to imitate human speech (*Natural History* 8.75, 107).[30] According to Scamander, manticores of the Wizarding world croon softly as they devour their prey, and have skin which repels most charms; their sting means instant death (28).

SPHINXES

The mythology of the Egyptians, Greeks, and Romans includes the sphinx, a winged creature, having the head of a woman and the body of a lion. She enjoyed toying with her victims by posing to them a riddle. If they answered successfully, they were allowed to live; but, if they failed to answer it correctly, she would kill them by hurling them from a cliff or by strangling them to death. Her name, "Sphinx," comes from the word that means "to bind tight, tie, constrict, strangle, throttle" [Gk *sphingein* > *Sphingks* > L *Sphinx*]. The sphinx which Harry encounters has the usual features, but also large claws, a yellow tail with a brown tip, and sexy-looking eyes.[31] The ancient parallel to Harry's trial, or the template for it, is the familiar story of Oedipus' trial by the sphinx which plagued the city of Thebes by eating anyone who could not solve her riddle.

UNICORNS

We meet these magical horse-like creatures in the Forbidden Forest. They have a single horn protruding from the center of their forehead. The fabulous one-horned horse of legend and mythology is to readers as peculiar as Luna Lovegood's Crumple-Horned Snorkack. But in the magical world of *Harry Potter*, while unicorns are a mystical breed, they are presumed to be as real as any other animals. Mr. Ollivander inserts a single hair taken from a huge unicorn into Cedric Diggory's wand as its core. When Harry sees a blinding light about himself (and Hermione and Sirius Black), protecting them and dispelling the attacking Dementors, and then perceives that it takes a form and gallops away, he presumes that it is someone's Patronus in the shape of a unicorn. A very important episode involving unicorns comes in *Sorcerer's Stone*. Harry sees a hooded figure in the Forbidden Forest bending over a wounded unicorn and drinking its blood to revitalize itself with the magical power of the unique creature's blood. The power of the unicorn's blood is more an extension of the motif of blood in magic and myth than of any special character of the unicorn itself. Firenze tells Harry that the unicorn's blood will keep one alive who is about to die.[32]

A creature like the unicorn was referred to as early as the fifth and fourth centuries BCE (by Ctesias and Aristotle, respectively). About the turn of the Common Era, Strabo reported that Megasthenes mentioned one-horned, deer-headed horses in India (*Geography* 15.1.56). And Pliny commented that the fierce animal called the unicorn [Gk *monokerōs,* "having one horn" > L *monocerōs*] had the body of a horse, the head of a stag, feet of an elephant, tail of a boar, a deep and bellowing voice, and a three-feet long black horn protruding from its forehead (8.76). Some commentators speculate that these ancient references are mistaken depictions of a rhinoceros. The animal does not have a large role in Greek and Roman myths that have survived through the ages, despite the several reports about their existence from otherwise responsible ancient observers. David Leeming notes that in western literature the animal's horn has the power to cure, and that the unique animal can symbolize courage, nobility, and purity, pride, wrath, and destructive forces (1997, 474; cited by De Rose "Mythical Animals," 2005, 68). Rowling embellishes this animal by adding that unicorn foals are pure gold until age two, when they become silver, and that they turn completely white at maturity, age seven.

VEELA

These beauties are the mascots for the Belgian Quidditch Team, who appear at the Quidditch World Cup match. They are not ordinary human females, but nymphs or fairy-like beings whose seductive dancing and appearance cause men to become totally fixated on them, to disregard anything else, and to make fools of themselves in their efforts to gain the veela's attention. This side of the females reprises the Sirens, the bird-like vixens with the faces of girls, whose enchanting songs lured sailors to their death on the rocks. Odysseus was warned about the Sirens and he took measures to escape their deadly beauty.[33] He had the crewmen's ears filled with wax so that they could not hear the song or any commands he might shout out when he came under the influence of their music. He had himself strapped to the ship's mast so that he could not act upon the songs as they sailed by the women (*Od.* 12.39–54, 153–200).

Veela, however, have another side which links them to the mythological Harpies. When they show their angry and ugly side, their physical appearance reflects their mood. Their heads begin to resemble birds with sharp beaks and their torsos sprout frightening wings.

Tangible Materials

In magic and mythical lore, practitioners often employ items which are the stock-in-trade for their craft: wands, items to make one invisible, amulets and talismans to protect one from harm, potion and drugs and blood, among others.

WANDS

One of the first pieces of equipment which Harry receives when he enters the Wizarding world is his own wand, an extension of the individual's power, which seems to have its own personality, both teaching its owner and learning from its master, and which is so uniquely compatible to its owner that, as Ollivander says, it "chooses the wizard" (SS 82). In the upper levels of education, the students learn to perform non-verbal spells, but many are executed with an incantation and the pointing of a wand, as when Professor Slughorn restores Marcus Belby's breathing by pointing his wand at the boy's throat and intoning, "Anapneo" (HBP 144).

While wands are not ubiquitous in classical literature, as they are around Hogwarts, they are often a part of transformations. In the early stages of the appearance of the gods, Apollo gave Hermes a golden wand [Gk hrabdos], a rod signifying his authority, which he used to herd his cattle (Libr. 3.10.2–3; Homeric Hymn to Hermes 552ff.). Hermes could use it to put humans to sleep or to wake them (Il. 24.343; Od. 5.47). As psychopompus, he led people to and from the Underworld with his golden wand (Od. 24.1ff.; Pindar, Olympia 9.35, Pythia 4.178). The wand was so closely associated with the messenger god that the Homeric epithet for Hermes identifies him with this instrument, as "(he) of/with the golden wand" (Od 5.87; 10.277, 331).

The witch Circe drugged the crewmen of Odysseus and used her wand [hrabdos] to change them into pigs, lions, asses, and wolves and to return them to their human state (Od. 10.238, 389; Epit. 7.15; Met. 14.397–415). She struck Odysseus with it as well (Od. 10.293, 319).[34] When the first king of Italy, a son of Saturn, rejected the amorous advances of Circe, she used incantations, prayers and a staff [L carmina, precēs, and baculum, -ī], to transform him into a woodpecker [L picus, -ī] (Met. 14.320–96). Vergil says she did it with her golden wand [L aureā ... virgā] and potent herbs [L venēnīs] (Aen. 7.190). Juno, in disguise as Circe, was equipped with a magic wand [L magicā ... virgā; Valerius Flaccus, Argonautica 7.212]. The goddess Athena used a wand to transform Odysseus into an old beggar and back into himself (Od. 13.429ff.; 16.172ff., 456).

INVISIBILITY EQUIPMENT

In the world of Harry Potter, secrecy is a major element of magic. One of the most useful and powerful tools for secrecy is an Invisibility Cloak, a device used by several wizards. At the Quidditch World Cup, the House-Elf Winky uses one to keep watch on Barty Crouch, Jr. Mr. Weasley and Sturgis Podmore use them when they guard the door to the Department of Mysteries on behalf of the Order of Phoenix. On one occasion, the Invisibility Cloak even provides Professor Snape cover to surprise HH&R and Remus Lupin in the Shrieking Shack. The most important of the cloaks, of course, is the Invisibility Cloak which Harry inherited from his father, who used it in his student days to sneak out of the castle every month at the full moon to visit Remus Lupin while he was being kept in the Shrieking Shack. It provides Harry the opportunity to move about undetected inside and outside the castle, and even to do mischief, as when he throws mud and slime on Malfoy, Crabbe, and Goyle at the Shrieking Shack. It comes into his possession as a gift from an anonymous sender, who turns out to be Harry's perennial support and backup, Professor Dumbledore, very much in the manner of other heroes in quest stories, who are provided swords, wings, and the like by the gods who aid the heroes in their adventures and contests.

Being able to escape the notice or knowledge of one's actions—and thus being able to avoid the consequences of those actions—is a wish that has been around since the beginnings of recorded history. The Greek gods used invisibility (as well as transformation) to intrude themselves into the situations of others. As Odysseus once mused, "Who can see with one's eyes a god moving here or there, if the god does not wish it?" (*Od.* 10.573–74). Greek mythology and philosophy record the existence of two items, in particular, which can make the owner invisible for a task or action: the mythical ring of Gyges, and the Cap of Hades, which is also called the "Cap of Invisibility."

The story of Gyges in its early form does not involve the ring itself. That is added in a later development of the Gyges legends. The early tale is about the betrayal of a queen by her husband, who exposed her private beauty, all for his selfish pleasure. Herodotus tells this tale. Candaules, the king of Lydia, related to a trusted guard the details about the extraordinary beauty of his wife. Not convinced that he had made his point convincingly enough, he even contrived to have the guard, Gyges, get a glimpse of his wife naked, without her knowing it. Fearing to disobey the king, and pressured to obey, the guard gave in, and at the moment when he saw her from the hiding place fixed for him by the king, the queen caught sight of Gyges, but she kept silent. Realizing what her husband had done, she plotted to get back at him. The next day she summoned the guard and gave him two options, either to execute her plan for Gyges to kill the king, take his throne and marry the queen, or be executed immediately. He threw in with her plot to kill Candaules. That night the guard stabbed the king to death in his bed, assumed the king's rule, and took the queen as his own (*Histories*, 1.8.1–12.2).

Plato used the myth of Gyges' criminal act to make the philosophical point that humans will do wrong if they can get away with it. In the *Republic*, Plato's brother Glaucon gives the example of the same man, Gyges, but with some variations. This version records that once, during a great storm and violent earthquake, a crevice was opened in the ground. Gyges, a shepherd, descended into the chasm and found a bronze horse, inside of which was the corpse of a human, naked except for a ring on his finger. Gyges took the ring and fled. One day he noticed that if he turned the ring on his finger so that the setting was inside his hand, he would become invisible. And when he turned it right-side up, he would reappear. The ring functioned this way consistently. Confident in its magical power, he manipulated his way into the courtly circle, seduced the queen, with whom he killed the king and stole his throne (II.359C). The point Glaucon makes with this philosophical myth is that people only do what is just when they are compelled, and that if they can do injustices and not be caught, they will.

The Cap or Helmet of Hades [Gk *Aïdos kyneē*], a helmet presumed to be made of dog-skin,[35] was said to make the person wearing it invisible. According to Apollodorus (*Libr.* 1.2.1), it was given to Hades by the Cyclopes when they fought the war against Cronus and the Titans, a great piece of equipment for close-contact battle. Since Hades' name means "the Unseen," the Cap of Hades means the "Invisibility Cap" or the "Cap of the Invisible One." Hermes wore it during the Battle of the Giants and the Olympian Gods, enabling him to kill the Giant Hippolytus (*Libr.* 1.6.2).[36] During one of the battles at Troy, Athena placed the cap on her head to make herself invisible to the god of war, Ares, as she drove the chariot of Diomedes, allowing him the freedom to fight unrestrained (*Il.* 5.835–63). The Graiai gave Perseus the cap, which he used to conceal himself when he beheaded Medusa (*Libr.* 2.4.2–3).

AMULETS AND TALISMANS

These items are charms which one wears or carries in order to avoid bad fortune or to ensure good luck [L *amulētum, ī*, an item which is used to dispel or avoid evil; Gk *telos*, "end" > *telein*, "to initiate," originally, "to complete" > *telesma*, a consecrated object which can turn evil away > Arabic *tilasm*, "magic figure, horoscope" > Fr *talisman* (Neufeldt 1365)]. Greek amulets were called "phylacteries" [*phylakteria*, "preservative" or "guardian" items]. On these items would be written or drawn special religious or spiritual or magic words, phrases, symbols and signs thought to be protective and influential for good health or prosperity. Precious jewels were sometimes worn as amulets because they were believed to protect the wearer in unique ways. The deep purple quartz stone, amethyst, for example, was worn to prevent the wearer from suffering the effects of over-drinking. The word "amethyst" itself means "not drunk with wine, not intoxicated" [Gk *methy*, "wine" > *methyein*, "to be drunk with wine" + *a-*, "without" > *amethystos*, "not drunk with wine, not intoxicated"].[37]

As far back as the *Iliad*, there is literary mention of amulets. Zeus's wife, Hera, was anxious because their forebears, Rhea and Cronus, were deeply angry with each other and had not been intimate for a long time. She believed that she would be greatly honored if she could get the two back together. So she asked the goddess of love, Aphrodite, for some help. The goddess offered her own embroidered belt which had all enticements, passion, and endearments in it. Hera was directed to put it in her bosom and was guaranteed that she would get her heart's desire *(Il.* 14.197–222).[38]

Not only the mythical gods but also the common people were disposed to use these tokens of protection and luck. It was not unusual at all for people to use magical means to prevent misfortune and illness, to win love or punish a lost lover, to affect the weather, and even to curse the dead. There were sellers of tokens, talismans and amulets, curse tablets and voodoo dolls to serve the needs and the superstitions of the public. According to Georg Luck, "Amulets, talismans, and phylakteria have been found in large numbers in the Mediterranean world," shaped like parts of the body, such as an eye with an arrow through it, representing the defeat of the evil eye, or an open hand defending against the evil eye (19). In the ancient world, amulets for children sometimes took the shape of a bell which the child could use to drive away evil spirits. Among the Romans, such a locket with an amulet inside might contain pebbles to make it sound like a bell (27). Luck says there was a story about Pericles that when he was very ill, someone came to see him and asked how he was. At this, the patient pointed to the amulets which were hung on him as a way of saying that the amulets were all he had going for him, therefore, he had very little hope, "otherwise he would not have let the women try this ultimate remedy in which he hardly believed himself" (220). The occult name "Abraxas," which we have mentioned before, was often invoked to make a curse or spell function successfully. The name is found on a number of amulets and talismans from antiquity.

There is not much mention of talismans and amulets in the *Potter* novels. "Talisman" occurs once, as a simile. After a successful practice of Dumbledore's Army, Harry feels as elated about the students as if he were blessed by some talisman. Other references to amulets and talismans occur only in contexts which associate these items with fear, superstition and the irrational. When Mrs. Norris is petrified, Gilderoy Lockhart brags that he cured a city in Africa of the problem of petrification by distributing amulets. When fear about the reopening of the Chamber of Secrets grows among the students, some of them begin to market and purchase protective amulets and talismans—behind the backs of the faculty, or course. After Diagon Alley has begun to show the ravages of the second war and many shops are closed and shuttered, some wizards on the street begin to market amulets to deflect evil. Their "silver symbols on chains" are hawked as being sure protection against "werewolves, Dementors, and Inferi" (*HBP* 110–11). Rowling notes that in some of his darkest times, Harry habitually carries with him the chain of the artificial Horcrux locket, not as a talisman for good luck but as a connection with his friend and mentor, Dumbledore. She adds a note of humor to the mention of talismans when she says that Neville Longbottom, apparently being quite fearful, secures as talismans a stinking onion, a crystal, and the rotten tail of a newt.

Travis Prinzi cites a number of items in the novels which are "amulets" (though they are not referred to by that term in the stories), magical and tangible items supplied by a mentor which aid in the hero's quest. These include the Invisibility Cloak, Fawkes, the Sorting Hat, the Sword of Gryffindor, and the items left to HH&R in Dumbledore's will (the Deluminator, *The Tales of Beedle the Bard*, and the snitch containing the Resurrection Stone).[39]

POTIONS AND DRUGS

Potions are so much a normal part of magic, that the subject is a regular course of study at Hogwarts, both on the elementary and advanced levels. These mixtures have been essential items for occultists of every age. In ancient Greek, the word for "potion" or "medicine" was the same as the word for "poison" [Gk *pharmakon*], perhaps in the same way that our term "drug" can have both positive and negative meanings, depending on the nature of the material and the dosage.

The classical world is sprinkled with experts who are renowned for their skill at concocting just the right prescription to help or harm someone. Medea gives Jason a drug (*pharmakon*) to put on the tip of his spear, which will keep him safe for one day while he plows with the fire-breathing bulls and lulls to sleep the dragon guarding the Golden Fleece (*Libr.* 1.9.23). Apollodorus suggests that she kills the giant bronze monster Talos with her drugs (*Libr.* 1.9.26). He relates that out of her contempt, she kills the bride (Glauce) of her ex-husband (Jason) and the bride's father (Creon of Corinth) by sending the girl a wedding gift of a robe she has tainted with her poison (*pharmakon*), which causes the girl to burn to death when she puts it on, and causes her father to die similarly when he tries to rescue her (*Libr.* 1.9.28). In the *Homeric Hymn to Demeter*, the grain goddess tells Metaneira, whose child she is tending, that she knows a good antidote or remedy for ruinous bewitchment, that is, how to protect her child (1.230). And, as we have noted before, Hermes provides Odysseus with the antidote moly, which counteracts the effect of Circe's bewitching powers (*Od.* 10.302–06). In the academic realm of antiquity, Pliny the Elder does not put any stock in the craft of sorcerers and their spells and recipes for cures, but he still maintains that what effect they do have is due to their skills for making poisons [L *venēficae artēs*] (*Nat Hist.* 28.4). Georg Luck concludes that "it is the drugs that really work, not so much the hocus-pocus of spells and ritual" (69).

The *Potter* novels offer a veritable pharmacy of potions for all kinds of purposes. For love there is Amortentia; for making someone stay alive but appear to be dead, there is the Draught of Living Death; for good luck, the Felix Felicis potion; for memory loss, the Forgetfulness potions; for renewed health, Madam Pomfrey's Pepperup Potion; for one's digestive track, the Scintillation Solution. The Draught of Peace is supposed to give one comfort when it is taken. Mandrake potion restores petrified victims. Wolfsbane Potion is a help for the monthly symptoms of werewolves. Veritaserum extracts the truth from those who are reluctant to give it. Dr. Ubbly's Oblivious Unction is perhaps better for mental than physical wounds. The Invigoration Draught is good for energy and strength. By far the potion which gets the most press in the novels is Polyjuice Potion, for anyone desiring an alter-ego. The unnamed, four-ingredient potion which revives Voldemort is the most sinister of them all.

Professor Snape is perhaps the most talented person at Hogwarts for potions, good and bad, as he is not only the teacher of the subject but also a "wizard" at it. In the *Half-Blood Prince*, we find that not only Snape, but also his student-turned-enemy, Draco Malfoy, becomes involved with poisons and poisoned items in the forms of a cursed necklace and poisoned oak-matured mead.

Blood

In both worlds, blood has powerful symbolism. It sparks the imagination with meanings apart from its biological signification. For one thing, in the magical world, it is a factor in defining people socially, as to whether they are considered "Muggles," "Mudbloods," "half-bloods," or "pure-bloods."

Apart from its use as a means of social ranking, however, blood symbolizes life and power. When Harry observes some creature drinking unicorn blood in the Forbidden Forest, Firenze explains to him that unicorn blood has the mysterious power to preserve a person, even if the person is about to die. When Dumbledore and Harry enter the cave by the seaside, they have to make a payment of blood to the door of the cave. Some impersonal power has to be satisfied by receiving a part of the self or life of a human.

One of the most notable roles of blood in the novels is its function in regenerating Voldemort. The Dark Lord confirms what Wormtail said at the beginning of *Goblet of Fire*, that they could have used another enemy's blood besides Harry's to revive the Dark Lord. But Voldemort picks Harry, so that in receiving his blood, he will also receive some of his mother's protective love which remains in the blood. Once Voldemort receives Harry's blood, a part of Harry leaves its mark on Voldemort. The traces of themselves which they bestow on each other highlight the difference between the two. Harry's trace on Voldemort is an element of protection that came from a mother's love; Voldemort's trace on Harry is the stain of the Killing Curse. With this new resource, Voldemort can touch Harry without being hurt. In the blood, apparently, one can retain power and protection. It, too, is a magical motif.

In ancient religion, ritual, and myth, blood was an important element. It was thought to have a reviving, even regenerative value. In his *nekuia* or conjuring of the dead, Odysseus attempts to summon Tiresias and others from the Underworld by means of a ritual explained to him by Circe. He digs a pit in the seashore sand, prays to Hades and Persephone, and pours the blood of a ram and a sheep into the pit. Walter Burkert comments on the process: "thereupon the souls (*psychai*) gather to drink the blood and so to awake to brief consciousness" (60). In the *Iliad*, for the funeral of Patroklos, many oxen, sheep, goats and pigs are sacrificed, and the blood flows with such volume that it is caught in cups (*Il.* 23.34). Burkert sees this flow of blood as intended "to reach the dead man in some way, to give him back life and colour..." (60).[40]

In the mystery cults of Cybele and Attis, initiates participated in a *taurobolium*, a ritual in which an individual would enter an underground depression or cave which was covered by a grate. A bull would be slaughtered and its blood would pour down over the initiate. Robert Lenardon interprets the significance of this ritual this way: "This baptism symbolized purification, the washing away of the old life, and resurrection to a new one; and the rebirth was further symbolized by the drinking of milk, the drink of a newborn child..." (Morford 398). In the worship of Dionysus, women revelers would engage in activity which shattered the barriers between drunkenness and sobriety, between civility and mania, between sexual propriety and unbridled lust. Part of their revelry included tearing apart a live animal and eating its raw flesh (the *omophagy*) and casting its limbs about in the fields (the *sparagmos*, or scattering of the victim's parts as fertilizer or incentive to the gods). This practice appears to have been an attempt to unite or at least merge natural opposites, gods and humans, life and death. A gruesome and dramatic depiction of the wild consequences of Bacchic worship is portrayed in Euripides' *Bacchae*. In the play, the mother (Agave) of the king of Thebes (Pentheus), in her religious madness wrenches her son's head from its torso, and runs her fingers through his bloody hair, thinking that the head is from an animal taken in Bacchic hysteria. As she cools from her blazing devotion, she slowly comes to recognize the head of her son and to realize what a horrible thing she has done.

In mythology there is a tale that involves life-and-death and the blood of a fantastic equine beast (the famous centaur Nessus); but it is the reverse of the story we find here. The power of the blood of that mythological figure is not life-giving but lethal. In the saga of Heracles, he and his wife, Deïanira, come to the river Evenus, where the centaur Nessus transports travelers across for a fee. Heracles crosses on his own power, but pays the centaur to ferry his wife across the river. During the crossing, Nessus tries to rape her. Heracles shoots him with an arrow that has on it some toxic blood from the Hydra, which he had killed. As the centaur dies, he advises Deïanira to save some of his blood because it has the power to prevent Heracles from loving any other woman more than he loves her. She does as he directs and keeps it for years. In time, she fears that Heracles loves another woman, named Iole. When he requests a garment appropriate for wearing during a sacrificial ceremony, she puts Nessus' blood on a tunic and sends it to him. She presumes that the blood will act as a love charm which will ensure his return to her. What she does not know is that the blood also has some of the Hydra's poison in it. When Heracles puts the coat on, it scorches his skin so severely that he has himself burned to death on a funeral pyre to end his agony. In remorse, Deïanira hangs herself (or kills herself with a sword) (*Libr.* 2.7.6–7). The life-giving unicorn blood in the *Goblet of Fire* is life-giving, not lethal; but life and death are close to the surface of meaning for readers today and in the ancient world when blood is mentioned.

Intangible Resources

Magical power is exercised and fabulous wonders are achieved not through tangible items and equipment alone. Much of the mystery of the two realms which we are examining is produced by invisible or unseen forces and resources: the transformation or metamorphosis of something or someone, curses, jinxes, spells, mysterious language, and the symbolic use of numbers.

TRANSFIGURATION AND METAMORPHOSIS

Transfigurations blur the lines and breach the boundaries between species and naturally unparalleled types. This phenomenon does not just invite readers or listeners to exercise a "willing suspension of disbelief" so as to enjoy the fantasy; it works a bit of magic on them by compelling them to relax the desire for certainty and the demands of crippling objectivity.[41]

The Wizarding world is so infused with transformation that one of the professorships at Hogwarts is given to Transfiguration, which studies the varieties of transformers and transformations in the magical world. There are four types of transformers to note. The Animagi have mastered the skill of mutating into an animal form—James Potter, Sirius Black, Peter Pettigrew, Minerva McGonagall, and Rita Skeeter.[42] There is one Metamorphmagus, Nymphadora Tonks, who was born with the ability to change her physical features at will. Werewolves (Remus Lupin and Fenrir Greyback, e.g.), transform at the time of the full moon, with no control over their transformation. Boggarts are beings that can transfigure themselves into whatever frightens their victims most.[43] With Horace Slughorn's transfiguration of himself into an armchair, a new wrinkle is added to the usual system of metamorphosis, a person's becoming a piece of furniture with human features, one more example of Rowling's humor.

The gods of the ancient world are known for transforming themselves into various forms, quite often as birds. Zeus transforms himself into a variety of birds in order to capture those whom he desires. He becomes a swan to seduce Leda, a cuckoo to rape Hera, an eagle to capture Ganymede and take the young man to Olympus, a pigeon to seduce Phthia, and a hoopoe to have Lamia (Pollard 160). He comes to Medusa as a winged bird to have sex with her, which union produces the magical horse, Pegasus (*Met.* 6.119). His brother Poseidon takes flight, moving like a hawk attacking another bird (*Il.* 13.62–65). Hermes resembles a sea bird when he comes from Olympus to Calypso (*Od.* 5.51f.). Apollo becomes a kite and Hermes becomes an ibis during the battle of the gods and Typhon (Pollard 161). Apollo and Athena together fly up into a tall oak tree as vultures (or eagles) (*Il.* 7.58–59). Athena addresses aged Nestor and departs, having the appearance of a sea-eagle (*Od.* 3.371f.). She chastises Odysseus and then flies up to a roof beam, assuming the appearance of a swallow (*Od.* 22.239–40). The god of sleep, Hypnos, conceals his real identity by assuming the form of a singing bird (*Il.* 14.286–91).[44]

The gods can also assume the guise of humans or other gods. Zeus transforms into the appearance of Artemis (or Apollo) to gain access to the nymph Callisto, a companion of Artemis, and to force himself on her (*Libr.* 3.8.2). He assumes the persona of a shepherd to capture Mnemosyne (personified "Memory," by whom he sires the Muses). Athena disguises herself as an old woman in order to test Arachne (*Met.* 6.26ff.). In the guise of a man named Mentes, she talks with Odysseus' son Telemachus and departs, flying upward like a bird (*Od.* 1.319f.). She comes to Nausicaä in the guise of the daughter of Dymas to arrange for her to meet Odysseus (*Od.* 6.22ff.). She assumes the appearance of Mentor to assist Odysseus against the suitors (*Od.* 22.205ff.). Iris comes among the Trojans with the appearance the voice of one of Priam's sons, Polites, delivering a message from Zeus (*Il.* 2.786ff.). Hermes, in the likeness of a young man, encounters Odysseus to give him the antidote for Circe's poison (*Od.* 10.275ff.). To have sex with Alcmena (which yields the demi-god Heracles), the king of the gods takes on the appearance of her husband, Amphitryon (*Met.* 6.112f.).

Gods can take impersonal forms as well. In his insatiable sexual appetite, Zeus/Jupiter transforms himself into a bull to abduct Europa, a shower of gold in order to slip under a locked door and impregnate Danaë, the imprisoned woman (*Met.* 4.611). According to Ovid, he becomes a flame of fire to seduce Aegina; a spotted snake to entrap Demeter's daughter, Proserpina; and a satyr to rape Antiope. Poseidon/Neptune transforms himself into various forms: a bull to capture Canace (a daughter of Aeolus, the god of wind); the Thessalian river god Enipeus to seduce Iphimedeia; a ram to trick Theophane; a horse to force himself on Demeter/Ceres, who changes into a mare in an attempt to escape; and a dolphin to seduce Melantho.[45] And he is said to assume the form of a snake when he comes to Olympias, the mother of Alexander the Great (Silver 98).

One tale claims that during the Battle of the Gods and the Giants, the Olympian deities flee in terror to Egypt and hide from their enemies by disguising themselves—Jupiter as a ram, Apollo a crow, Diana a cat, Bacchus a goat, Juno a heifer, Venus a fish, and Mercury a flamingo (*Met.* 5.315–31). To satisfy his lust, Apollo is known to go in disguise as a farmer, a hawk, or a lion (*Met.* 6.103–28). On one occasion, Zeus transforms another god, Dionysus, into a young goat, in order to protect him from Hera (*Libr.* 3.4.3). Odysseus sums up these gods' metamorphoses succinctly when he says to Athena, who has appeared to him as a young shepherd and then as a beautiful woman, "It is hard, O goddess, for even a man of good understanding to recognize you on meeting, for you take every shape upon you" (*Od.* 13.312–13; trans. Lattimore 1967, 206).

Those who can transform themselves are sometimes called "shape-shifters." The term is used in the study of classical mythology for persons or gods who can alter their form at will.[46] Some notable examples are the sea divinities Triton, Nereus, and Thetis (Achilles' mermaid mother, who can take a hundred different forms, *Met.* 11.253). Periclymenus, a grandson of Poseidon, receives the gift of transforming into any bird, beast or insect from his grandfather. Mestra, the daughter of Erysichthon, can change her form to appear as a man, bird, cow, deer and more. In order to "court" Pomona, the goddess of fruit trees, Vortumnus (or Vertumnus), the Roman god of orchards and fruit, who presides over seasonal changes, assumes the form of a field hand, soldier, fisherman, and an old woman (*Met.* 14.623–771). The sea god Proteus, the master shape-shifter, can transform himself into an animal or fire or water, shifting from one form to another in order to evade questions put to him. He is seized by Aristeas after his many changes, and by Menelaus after he has undergone elusive transformations as a lion, a serpent, a leopard, a boar, water, and a towering tree (*Od.* 4.360–459).[47] Today we use the adjective "protean" to describe someone who is versatile, who has a number of different qualities, or who can shift their views on things quickly.

The Roman poet Ovid (Publius Ovidius Naso, 43 BCE–17 CE) is the most ready source for much of what we know of Greek and Roman mythology. His poem, known as the *Metamorphoses*, relates approximately two hundred and fifty mythological stories, almost all of which include some kind of transformation. Whether Rowling intentionally imitates Ovid or just draws from the literary pool of western tradition to which Ovid has contributed so very much, there are many similarities in the way both treat transformations.

Three specific similarities between Ovid's and Rowling's transformations are these. First, at times they add an interpretation to the transformation which explains the reasonableness of the change. For example, when Hagrid makes a pig tail sprout on gluttonous Dudley Dursley, Rowling has Hagrid say, "Meant ter turn him into a pig, but I suppose he was so much like a pig anyway there wasn't much left ter do" (*SS* 59).[48] The pig tail makes externally visible the nature of the boy. He is not just like a pig … he is a pig. This story is similar to Ovid's story of the fate of the women of Cyprus. They denied the divinity of Venus, the Roman goddess of love. So she punished them by condemning them to become the first prostitutes. They polluted their divine gift (sexuality) and became so hardened and insensitive that, finally, Venus turned them into stone. Ovid comments on that transformation, "They hardened, even their blood was hard, they could not blush anymore; *it was no transition, really, from what they were to actual rock and stone*" (*Met.* 10.238–42; trans. Humphries, 241, my emphasis).

Second, the two authors are alike in the ways they describe transformations. Rowling can make short work of a transfiguration. For example, all she says about Sirius Black's turning back into himself from being a dog is, "The great black dog ... turned back into a man" (*GF* 712). But she can also dilate upon the process of transformation for dramatic effect. In describing Harry's transformation into the form of his fellow student, Goyle, she provides specific and graphic details: his insides twist and coil; he feels burning going down his limbs; his skin begins to bubble; he watches his own hands transform into Goyle's huge hands, complete with the thickening of fingers and the widening of his nails; his knuckles begin to swell; his shoulders become broader; he senses his hair mutating; his enlarging frame rips the robes he is wearing; his feet hurt as they over-swell his much-too small shoes; when he scratches his ear, the body of Goyle does it, too (*CS* 216–17). Rowling uses a simile to describe this method of depicting transformation. In the case of the mutation of Scabbers back into his human form as Peter Pettigrew, she says, "It was like watching a speeded-up film of a growing tree" (*PA* 366).

The tactic of dilating on the actual process of metamorphosis, describing the process in detail, is one of the many contributions Ovid made to the telling of myths and transformations. He could have said simply, "Daphne turned into the laurel tree," for he is, at times, that matter-of-fact in his poem. But many other times he describes the actual procedure of the change. Sometimes his preoccupation with the transfiguration is playful, sometimes pathetic and touching. In the case of Daphne, who tries to escape Apollo's loving arms and is rescued by a god turning her into a tree, he describes her legs becoming heavy and numb, her skin turning into bark, her hair transforming into leaves and her arms turning into branches, her feet taking on the shape of roots and her head becoming a tree top ... while at the same time her inner being remains humanly responsive (*Met.* 1.452–567). And when he tells of the young hunter Actaeon's being turned into a stag as punishment for catching a glimpse of Diana bathing naked in a forest pool, he gives details. Horns sprout on his head. His neck lengthens. His ears become pointed. His hands become feet. His arms lengthen. He becomes covered with a spotted hide. He surprises himself at how swiftly he can run as he flees. His face becomes a deer's face. In surprise at his new face, he attempts to cry out, but hears only groans in the place of a voice. And, finally, he is killed by the very hunting hounds which he has reared because they take him for a stag (*Met.* 3.131–252).

And, third, both authors sometimes add to the transformation of bodies the psychological element of human beings retaining their full mental and emotional humanity while being in animal or non-human forms. Rowling's Animagi retain their human faculties and emotions when they transform into animal bodies: Professor McGonagall, as a tabby cat, can read a map and a street sign; as the black dog, Sirius spies on Harry, attends his Quidditch match, and meets up with Crookshanks to work out how to catch Peter Pettigrew; Pettigrew carries on a disguise as a rat for twelve years, to evade his enemies. Their transformations do not take away their human personhood, and at any time they are able to change back into their own bodies. Even when transfiguration is made possible by Polyjuice Potion, only the physical body changes, not the mind. When Hermione's transformation goes awry and she looks like Millicent Bulstrode's cat, she feels her typical human emotion of embarrassment and wants to remain hidden. The transition for Rowling's werewolves, however, appears to involve a change of body and a change of mind. At the time of the full moon, Lupin becomes dangerous to people, even his friends, having a "wolfish ... mind" (*PA* 355). Wolfsbane Potion eases these symptoms, for when Lupin takes it properly, he keeps his mind when he transforms and is not as bestial.

Ovid's gods and "shape-shifters" can take all kinds of forms, while keeping their proper minds and emotions. However, many of Ovid's stories of transformation explore the psychological trauma of a person trapped inside another form (usually, in an animal's form).[49] For example, even after Daphne is transformed into a tree, Apollo feels her heart beating beneath the bark. He hugs and kisses her, but "the wood shunned his kisses" (*Met.* 1.554ff.). And to show his irresistible love, he makes the laurel his sacred tree [L *daphnē*, *-idis*, "laurel"], to which gesture she waves her branches and nods her face-like treetop in approval (1.567). In the case of poor Actaeon, the young man is ashamed of his appearance, and senses fear at the approach of his hunting dogs. He attempts to communicate with his hunting companions and to call off his dogs, but he can make only deer sounds, though his mind wants to speak to them as before. Their unrelenting attack kills the young man while his friends look on at the stag, wishing their friend, Actaeon, were there for the kill. One of Ovid's most touching stories of transformation is his tale of the nymph Callisto's metamorphosis into a bear. With her face reshaping into a maw and her hands transformed into bear claws, she is unable to reach up and pray to heaven for release. But Ovid includes, too, her pathos, years later, when her son corners her as prey during a hunt and is on the point of killing her. Staring in love and longing at her son, she cannot run away. Her human sentiments are working within her, but her bear body prevents her from expressing them (*Met.* 2.401–530).

Mysterious and
Powerful Language

While there are such things as "non-verbal" spells in the Wizarding world, language is extremely important for the effective performance of magic. Uttered incantations, jinxes, and prophecies are ubiquitous. In the classical world, too, language was employed in the attempt to change fate, the weather, the future, and specific circumstances, either for the better or the worse. Sometimes the words in these two worlds of magic and the occult are understandable terms, which have unique power to have an effect upon reality by their ambiguity and by the various possibilities of their interpretation. At other times special, mysterious language is invented or employed as having "other-worldly" power, adding the irrational element as a unique connection with super-sensual forces.

The Power of the Spoken Word

The unanticipated and surprising effect of spoken words has been recognized for millennia. One of Homer's figurative expressions is "winged words" [Gk *epea pteroenta*], perhaps signifying the unmanageable consequences which a word, statement, opinion, or story may have once it leaves the lips of the speaker. The ancient poet was referring to intelligible speech, not gibberish or foreign languages. There are three aspects of the spoken word to be noted: words in intelligible language, the use of unintelligible language, and language associated with snakes.

Words in Intelligible Language

The goal of the practitioner of magic is to gain some control over forces, fate, or potential circumstances which greatly affect one's life. Thus, intelligible language may be used with unique or esoteric meaning, or unique language may be created which is presumed or hoped to be mysteriously effective in influencing one's "reality." Oracles, for example, were notoriously ambiguous in their meaning, even though they were delivered in sensible terms and in language that people could understand. When the Persian king Xerxes set his sights on conquering Greece, the Athenians saved their country. They sent emissaries to Delphi to get an answer from the Pythia, the priestess of Apollo, as to their fate. A first prophecy seemed to predict sure doom and advised the Athenians to flee. A second inquiry was made, in which the Athenian leaders asked for a further response, since they intended not to run, but to die fighting if necessary. This time, and probably in light of the brave attitude of this group (as opposed to the fearful and seemingly hopeless attitude of the first inquirers), the oracle indicated that their safety in a "wooden wall" would protect them. When the envoy returned with this message, it was met with two diametrically opposing interpretations. The older men believed that the "wooden wall" referred to the hedge of thorns which had many years before encircled the Acropolis, and that only the Acropolis would be saved and the Greeks defeated at sea. Others considered the "wooden wall" to mean that they should build a fleet of ships, and thus defeat the Persians at sea ... which they did (Herodotus, *The Histories*, 7.138ff.). The language of the oracle was sensible, but puzzling, open to broad interpretations. But the fate of Greece was at stake. Absolute clarity from the Pythia would have been welcomed.

In an earlier chapter, we proposed that Luna Lovegood appears to be something of an oracle or prophetess because of her odd social mannerisms, eccentric style of communication, and unique perceptiveness. She speaks somewhat in the fashion of an oracle or teacher of Divination. While her eyes do not glaze over and she does not utter non-grammatical or nonsensical words in an ecstatic trance, like the ancient diviners, her pronouncements are enigmatic, puzzling, and offer uncommon insight and revelation. She is an unexpected source of clarity.

The Use of Unintelligible Language

Since linking the visible world with a world or with forces beyond one's control is not a science but a mysterious effort, language may be invented, or normal words altered and toyed with, in the hope of changing fate or the future. Strange utterances, unknown language, or mystic incantations fall into this category. In an earlier chapter, we noted that Albus Dumbledore practices an extraordinary type of magic to make his spells effective and to cancel spells which are in place, sometimes in unintelligible words or occult incantations. While others are stunned at the petrifying of Argus Filch's cat, Dumbledore attempts to revive the cat by using his wand, "muttering words under his breath," and declaring that she is not dead. When he and Harry approach the seaside cave in search of a Horcrux, the Headmaster recognizes the presence of some protective spells at work which Voldemort has set to prohibit anyone from entering. To cancel the spells or to make them known, Albus touches the walls and murmurs things which Harry cannot comprehend. When he and Harry fly back to Hogwarts from the cave, he cancels the defensive spells which he has set around the school by using a kind of magic unknown to Harry and by speaking in an indecipherable language. And in the Headmaster's office, the Pensieve is encircled with runes and esoteric symbols with which Harry is unacquainted, but which are, obviously, known and used by Dumbledore.

Language and Snakes

Harry finds himself associated with a special minority of the magical population, those who can communicate with serpents in their own language, Parseltongue. People fear him because that ability is associated with Salazar Slytherin. It is practiced, also, by Voldemort and the Gaunts, and is a source of pride for Dark Wizards. When Harry saves Justin Finch-Fletchley from being attacked by Draco Malfoy's serpent, the students and Professor Snape act uneasy and are wary of him because he communicates with the snake. He uses it to open the passageway to Chamber of Secrets, for example. In that scene, he does not shift into a different language, as one does who is in the process of learning elementary conversational speech in a foreign language, simply quoting memorized phrases. Rather, he assumes a way of thinking and communicating that produces the snake language. He is truly bilingual.

Speaking in snake-language adds a uniquely dark element to each episode in which it appears. It contributes to the morbid mood of the Gaunt's home, where visitors are greeted by a dead snake on their door, where Morfin plays with a live adder and intones to it a rhyming threat in Parseltongue. The alliterative words which Rowling puts into his mouth imitate the sound of a snake: "Hissy, hissy, little snakey, Slither on the floor…" (*HBP* 204). The "Halloweenesque" atmosphere of Harry's encounter with Bathilda Bagshot is amplified by the fact that they communicate in Parseltongue, the language of choice, of course, for Voldemort's messenger who occupies her dead body.

Harry's ability to speak with snakes is reminiscent of several mythological figures who were said to be able to communicate with animals or to speak their language: Melampus, Helenus, and Cassandra. The Greek seer named Melampus, who could understand the language of animals, was granted that ability because of his kindness. When his servants killed two snakes, he respectfully cremated them and reared their offspring. To show their gratitude to him, when the young snakes were mature, they stood at his shoulders as he slept and purified his ears with their tongues, granting to him the ability to understand the language of animals (*Libr.* 1.9.11). The Trojan prince Helenus is perhaps best known for his prophecy that Aeneas would conclude his search for a new homeland whenever he would see a white sow and her thirty piglets by the bank of a river in Italy. That place would be the origin of what would become the Roman world. The Trojan prophetess Cassandra, as well, was said to be able to understand the languages of animals and birds. It was reported that when she and Helenus were children, they were left overnight in a temple of Apollo; and when morning came, they were discovered with serpents licking their ears.[50] Most of the classical examples of seers communicating with animals do not appear to be malevolent or violent in their practice.

The Unique Potential of Magical Language

Prophecies and oracles are part of the field of Divination, a discipline taught at Hogwarts which concentrates on knowing the unknowable and penetrating beyond space and time into the future. And, of course, in ancient mystical practice and the Wizarding world, curses, jinxes, and spells are standard features.[51] In this section, we shall take a look at strange and powerful language common to the two worlds we are comparing, and look at the curse of curses, the Killing Curse. In the next chapter we shall examine Rowling's use of classical languages, particularly Latin, for creating her magical terminology in the world of *Harry Potter*.

Prophecies and Oracles

Prophecies and oracles are very often enigmatic, allowing for various meanings or significations. That is what differentiates them from "answers," or data. They are open to interpretation and can function as both curses and blessings, depending on the understanding of the recipient. One of the epithets of Apollo is "Loxias" [Gk < *loxos*, "oblique, obscure, indirect, ambiguous"], a term applied to him because the oracles of his priestess at Delphi were first uttered in unintelligible speech, then transformed into dactylic hexameter verse by his priests, and were always cryptic and mysterious— even in their poetic translation. So in some sense, even a divine disclosure is a concealment or riddle about the truth. Oracles which become instruments of dire fate or curses in mythology include the prediction that Oedipus would kill his father and have children by his mother, and that Acrisius would be killed by his grandson, Perseus, both of whom we have mentioned earlier.

The prophecy that hangs over the lives of Voldemort and Harry Potter gives specifications which can apply to Harry, but also, perhaps, to other young men. But Voldemort fixates on Harry as his dreaded opponent because he survived the Dark Lord's attack as a child. Even if one consults the Pensieve for an additional revelation, the device produces memories, not objective records of actual fact, but the subjective recollection of individuals as they experienced a situation originally, influenced by their private feelings, emotions, and relationships.

Curses, Jinxes, and Spells

As we noted previously, under "Invisibility Equipment," secrecy is essential in magic. It is either a feature of or the main component of many spells, charms and enchantments: the memory spell (Obliviate), vanishing spell (Evanesco), secret-keeper charm (Fidelius), Revealing charms or materials (Aparecium, Homenum Revelio, Specialis Revelio, Veritaserum, the Probity Probe), the disappearing charm (Disillusionment), stunning and confusing charms (Stupefy, Confundus), the anti-eavesdropping spell (Muffliato), the blindfolding charm (Obscuro), the charm to hide from non-magic folk (Repello Muggletum), and a silencing charm (Silencio). Secrecy is behind the use of the Marauder's Map, the Extendable Ears, and Polyjuice Potion. All the passwords which admit students to the Gryffindor common room are secretive (e.g., Quid agis?). The practices of Apparition and Disapparition, Divination, Cartomancy, Ornithomancy, Numerology, Heptomology, Legilimens and Occlumens, to name just a few, all have to do with secrecy.

Secretive magical utterances are used to affect, influence, or control something or someone which is beyond anyone's ability to influence without super-human assistance, because control is either improbable or impossible. The goal may be benign and helpful or destructive and cruel. In Rowling's narrative world some incantations are intelligible and self-explanatory to English speakers (e.g., Finite or Impervius). Other incantations have names which are playful creations of Rowling's mind, and do not reveal clearly the results they intend to produce (e.g., the Bat-Bogey Hex or Meteolojinx). She does not attempt to put in print, however, the actual or representative wording of the unintelligible charms or incantations which we mentioned as being practiced by Dumbledore.

In the ancient world, people would often mix intelligible language with strange, spiritual utterances—or use the unintelligible only—in the worship of Dionysus and in some occult practices. The powerful terms might be used in curses, jinxes, and casting spells. They might be written inscriptions on talismans or amulets. Sometimes, a person would recite an incantation to curse an ex-girlfriend, to obtain security and peace of a relative, to prevent misfortune and illness, to affect the weather, or even curse the dead. The charm might be chanted repeatedly or backwards, or spoken as gibberish, so as to trick the evil forces. There were sellers of tokens, talismans and amulets, curse tablets and voodoo dolls to serve the needs and superstitions of the public. In 1991, Christopher Faraone noted that as of that time, at least one thousand lead curse tablets had been excavated from the ancient Greek and Roman world (3). In Rowling's novels, there are no curse tablets, per se. There are, however, numerous tangible items which are carriers of a harmful or deadly curse: Professor Umbridge's sharp quill which cuts into Harry's hand as he writes for her while doing detention, the oak-matured mead which poisons Ron, the cursed necklace which almost kills Katie Bell, Tom Riddle's diary, and the Horcruxes, for example.

Perhaps the most familiar, malevolent curse in Latin literature is Dido's curse on Aeneas. After he has lived with the queen of Carthage and appeared to have settled there as her co-regent, Aeneas turns to his destined task to found a new nation and abandons her and their agreement which she considered their "marriage." She curses his betrayal, plots revenge on her lover, manipulates her own sister to build a funeral pyre, and condemns Aeneas and all the people who would come after him. She prays to Juno that there will be perpetual hatred and war between Carthage and the nation which will come from Aeneas' ventures (Rome) (*Aen.* 4). Vergil wrote this story looking back on three Punic wars which Rome had with Carthage. Projecting the curse back many hundreds of years and placing it in the mouth of the queen of the country which was a most hated enemy provided a "mythological" explanation to his readers for why relations between these two nations had lasted so long and been so irreparable.

The Killing Curse

The most pronounced kind of curse in the *Harry Potter* novels is the Killing Curse, "Avada Kedavra," which cannot be reversed or countered. This pitiless and cruel curse is accompanied by a flash of green light, which impresses itself boldly on the minds of readers all throughout the series. The phrase is obviously a variant of "abracadabra," which (in addition to its having come to mean "gibberish") is very old and at one time was a very popular formula used in magic and on amulets to cure sickness, to protect from ill fate or to strengthen the possessor of the item. Georg Luck simply defines it as a magical term, which most likely comes from the Hebrew ha-bracah-dabrah, "pronounce the blessing," or a derivative from the magical word "abrasax" (494).

DuPree traces "abracadabra" back to its earliest known source, the fragmentary extant writings of Quintus Serenus Sammonicus of the third century CE, a man of encyclopedic knowledge and a physician (46–51). In those texts there is an upside-down pyramid drawn with the letters of the incantation in this fashion:

A-B-R-A-C-A-D-A-B-R-A
A-B-R-A-C-A-D-A-B-R
A-B-R-A-C-A-D-A-B
A-B-R-A-C-A-D-A
A-B-R-A-C-A-D
A-B-R-A-C-A
A-B-R-A-C
A-B-R-A
A-B-R
A-B
A

DuPree explains that the language is a transliteration of ancient Aramaic, meaning, "I will make as I say" or "I will create as I speak." So it is a phrase which combines the act of speaking with effecting or bringing about something (49, 53 n. 19). She then demonstrates how numerology, especially the numbers four, one, and nine (which signifies the dark forces) is at work in the incantation and triangle. A citation in the OED dating from 1860 suggests that the formula "abracadabra" is composed of a repetition of the first letters of the Hebrew words "father" (*ab*), "son" (*ben*), "and holy spirit" (*ruach aca-dosh*) and would be arranged in triangular fashion for reciting or for wearing on an amulet.[52] Apparently, one would recite the formula, line for line, progressing from the full form to the "a" sound only, as a kind of magical spell or mantra. Gove defines the phrase as an incantation found in magical formulas or written on amulets to cure ills and dispel misfortune, and mentions the triangular shape of the formula (5).

When Rowling was asked in an interview about her incantation she gave this reply:

> Does anyone know where avada kedavra came from? It is an ancient spell in Aramaic, and it is the original of abracadabra, which means "let the thing be destroyed." Originally, it was used to cure illness and the "thing" was the illness, but I decided to make it the "thing" as in the person standing in front of me. I take a lot of liberties with things like that. I twist them round and make them mine.[53]

MAGICAL NUMBERS

The beginning of numbering systems which have both mathematical and symbolic meanings goes back as far as the Babylonians of the early second millennium BCE. In that civilization, religion or belief was linked to mathematical science by observation of the orderliness of the heavens and nature. O. Rühle has said that for the ancients, the stars were the Scripture of the Heavens (663). The numbers seven, nine and twelve corresponded to their observations of the planets and the signs of the zodiac and had special power. Franz Cumont has this observation about the Babylonians' regarding numbers as sacred: " here the number possesses an active force, the number is a symbol and its properties are sacred attributes. Astrology is only a branch of mathematics which the heavens have revealed to mankind by their periodic movements" (1960, 62; 18f.).

The Greek philosopher Pythagoras conceived of reality as being made of numbers. Part of the confidence he had in numbers came from the observation that the pitch of notes on a musical instrument, the lyre, can be represented by numbers, and intervals on the entire musical scale can be represented in numerical terms.[54] The material relationship between size and numbers, between music and numbers, between mathematical knowledge and numbers, led to a general conclusion that all things consisted of numbers. This observation was merged with religious intimations of wholeness and cleansing of the soul, and the philosopher became both a "scientific" inventor and a religious pioneer. The school of Pythagoras was a very influential part of early Greek thinking and religion, owing to its conception about numbers and its influence on Plato with regard to the nature of the soul and the body, as well as the transmigration of souls (philosophical and religious thinking).[55]

On the more mundane level, common people ascribed to numbers special significance beyond their literal function. In many ancient societies, alphabet letters, not numbers, were used for counting. Naturally, this gave to letters a quantitative value which everyone understood (Potter 1025). Words and, particularly, names carried the merit and meaning of the sum of the numeric value of the letters which they contained. The most famous example of this phenomenon, of course, is the number 666, found in Revelation 13:18, which is widely held to be the numeric value of the title "Nero Emperor." David Potter indicates that this title in Aramaic is "nrwn ksr," yielding the following calculation: (100+60+200+50+200+6+50=666). He adds that this method of representing emperors by number rather than by name was often used in the *Sibylline Oracles*, a diverse collection of oracles from different sources in the ancient world (1025).

In telling Harry's story in so many books, it is only natural that Rowling employs numbers simply for factual information and interesting, detailed description. There is probably no hidden meaning intended when she says that Aberforth Dumbledore was convicted of some scandal with goats fifteen years in the past. At the same time, however, she appears to incorporate into her writing style a kind of "numerology" of her own. For their special effects, she employs numerical patterns which have symbolic or magical significance as a regular feature of life in the Wizarding world. Special numbers surface in the novels with extraordinary frequency. They tease readers into wondering if there is some special meaning to their being presented so regularly. The uniquely suggestive quality of particular numbers adds tone, color, mood and atmosphere to the story. Numbers which traditionally have come to have mysterious associations (fortunate or unfortunate) are abundant. Rowling's special effects would not be the same without their presence.

Below, we shall look at some of the specific and artistic ways in which she practices her narrative numerology. The purpose of this exercise is not to show that there are classical parallels to each of her uses of specific numbers, or to prove that her individual writing techniques are derived from the Greeks and Romans (though, in one case, she does show a kind of kinship with the style of Ovid). The aim of this exercise is two-fold: first, to suggest the variety of uses she makes of special numbers; second, to illustrate, briefly, the significance of many of those numbers in the ancient world.

As a sampling of her signature style, we shall look at her use of prime numbers (especially the numbers 3, 7, 13 and 17), composites produced when prime numbers are multiplied by prime numbers (9, 14, 21, 33, 39, 49, 77, 437, and 713), and the composite numbers 4 and 12, because they are frequently employed in the novels and because of their universally symbolic significance. I shall cite only enough examples to illustrate the various uses to which Rowling has put these numbers.

Prime Numbers

A prime whole number is a number which cannot be divided by any number but itself and the number one without leaving a remainder. For example, the prime number nineteen can only be divided by the number one and itself: $19 \div 1 = 19$; $19 \div 19 = 1$. The prime numbers are 2, 3, 5, 7, 11, 13, 17, 19, 23, 29, 31, 37, 41, etc. The designation "prime" comes from the Latin superlative adjective *prīmus, -a, -um*, which means "first" (in time, in order, in a series, in importance), "most important, most notable or distinguished, of the highest or best quality or class, uttermost, foremost, extreme" (OLD 1457). Such a number is unique, most excellent, not the product of anything but itself. Prime numbers, then, have a certain perceived mysteriousness about them, a uniqueness which appeals to both the left and right sides of the brain, to calculation and to intuition.

The monetary system of the Wizarding world is strange to readers because it is based on prime numbers: 17 silver Sickles=1 gold Galleon; 29 Knuts=1 Sickle. Prime numbers appear elsewhere randomly. For example, the wands of James and Harry Potter are eleven inches long; Harry's wand costs seven Galleons; it costs five Knuts for an owl to bring the magical newspaper; wizards come "of age" at seventeen; Mr. Ollivander takes a single hair from a unicorn that is seventeen hands tall for use in Cedric's wand; Harry finds the prophecy on row ninety-seven of the shelves in the Department of Mysteries. On the presence of these prime numbers, Philip Nel comments, "Given that some consider prime numbers to be mystical ... numerical symbolism subtly introduces the novel's motifs of magic and the supernatural" (31).

The Number Three (3)

The number three can signify completeness, since it has a beginning, an end, and a middle. Some ancient people conceived of the world as having three parts—the earth, the sky above, and the Underworld. Their religious systems gave first place to sets of triads of gods: at Babylon they were Sin (the world), Shamash (the world) and Ishtar (the goddess of love); at Heliopolis they were Hadad, Atargatis and Simios. There was a triad of gods at Hierapolis, and the Assyrian mysteries taught a triple division of the world and the soul (Cumont 1960, 27; 1956, 250–51). At Eleusis the Greeks venerated three gods—Demeter, Kore and Dionysus (the Eleusinian Triad). In the temple of Jupiter Optimus Maximus at Rome, three gods were honored—Jupiter, Juno and Minerva (the Capitoline Triad) (Morford 677). The Greeks personified old age as three sisters sharing a single tooth and one eye, the Graiai [Gk Graeae, "the old women"]. They believed that the Fates [Gk Moirai < meiromai, "to have a share," thus "allotters" (Room 206)] who govern life were three: "Clotho," the spinner, who spins out the thread of life, signifying birth; "Lachesis," the apportioner, who measures out the thread of life, its unraveling; and "Atropos," the inflexible one who cuts the thread of life, bringing death (Morford 135). The Romans had three deities whom they called the "Fates" [L Parcae < pariō, -ere, peperī, partum, "to give birth, bring into being" (OLD 1297)]. These were "deities of birth," whose names relate them to the time of a person's birth: "Nona," for children born in the ninth month (in their inclusive counting, this is a month short, therefore a premature child); "Decuma" for those born in the tenth month, therefore a full-term baby; and "Morta" for children still-born.

A few examples of the significant use of three in classical literature and mythology are these. In order to strike terror in the minds and hearts of his enemies, Agamemnon (the king of Mycenae) wore a chest-protector which displayed at the opening for the neck three rising snakes on each side. On his ornate shield, which depicted the face of Medusa, there was a strap bearing the threatening representation of a single serpent turning its three heads in various directions (*Il.* 11.19–40). Like Cerberus, the three-headed guardian of the Underworld, this serpent spelled danger to anyone coming from any direction. The young man Milanion who desired to marry a skilled female hunter named Atalana had to undertake a "you-bet-your-life" contest to win the hand of his beloved. Atalanta felt so confident in her prowess, that she arranged a foot race with anyone wanting to marry her. She would allow the suitor to start ahead of her, and then she, running while suited up with arms, would start later. If she caught her competitor, she killed him. If the man won, he got to marry her. No previous suitors had won such a race, and all losers had been executed. Milanion was clever enough, however, not to trust in his speed alone. He won the race and his bride by dropping three golden apples, one at a time, during the race. When Atalanta slowed to pick them up, she fell behind and lost the race (*Libr.* 3.9.2).[56]

In telling his story of Medea's rejuvenating aged Pelias with her magical arts, Ovid relies on the general conception of three as an eerie number, using it to comic excess, as it virtually tumbles over itself in its frequency: Medea relies on the help of the "three-headed goddess" (Hecate); she waits three nights until the full moon before she does her magical work; she stretches her arms to the stars and turns around three times; she sprinkles spring water on her head three times; three times she howls aloud; she travels abroad for nine days and nine nights (3 × 3) securing the ingredients to rejuvenate Pelias; she purifies Aeson three times with fire, three times with water, and three times with sulfur; and she waits three full days before performing the ritual on Pelias (*Met.* 7.159–349).

In *Harry Potter*, Rowling uses the number three more frequently than all other numbers and for a wide range of special effects. The listing below represents only some of those effects.

To Add a Tone of Dignity, Drama, or Magic

Harry's first letter from Hogwarts is one of three pieces of mail received that day, the other two pieces being a postcard and a bill, making Harry's letter unusual and mysterious; Hagrid prepares a peculiar—and humorous—travel package for Norbert the dragon—rats, brandy and his teddy bear; the magical Knight Bus is a triple-decker; the inn located in Hogsmeade is called The Three Broomsticks; Morfin Gaunt receives a sentence of three years in Azkaban; Dumbledore cites for Harry three observations about Tom Riddle which Harry should remember (his desire to be special, his having no friends, and his collecting trophies as mementos of his bullying others); Twycross teaches the students to concentrate on three things in Apparition—Destination, Determination, and Deliberation; the members of the Order of the Phoenix who transport the "seven Potters" from the Dursleys' house to safety have three modes of transportation—brooms, thestrals, and Hagrid's flying motorcycle; the three Deathly Hallows were originally associated with three brothers—Antioch, Cadmus and Ignotus; three mothers die because of their sons—Lily Potter while protecting Harry, Merope Gaunt while giving birth to Tom Riddle, and Mrs. Crouch who exchanges places with her son in Azkaban and dies there.

To Suggest Danger or Misfortune

Professor Dumbledore warns the students not to go into the third-floor corridor unless they want to die a painful death; Fluffy is completely watchful and vicious, having three heads, three pairs of eyes, three noses, and three drooling mouths; the lethal Mandrakes and the most dangerous plants used in Herbology are kept in greenhouse number three; Harry hears a voice which no one else can hear three times; he notices spiders moving in procession three times; Tom Riddle combines all three of his names to reveal that he is Lord Voldemort; Ron's Pocket Sneakoscope warns in three ways of something untrustworthy being done—it spins rapidly, whistles loudly and glows brightly; Professor Snape tells Harry that Veritaserum is so powerful that only three drops will make him reveal his deepest secrets; when the returning Death Eaters encircle Voldemort, he sees space for six others, deducts three who had died, and speaks on the fate of the remaining three; in the Little Hangleton graveyard, Voldemort uses all three Unforgivable Curses on Harry; when Harry fails to create a proper Draught of Peace in Snape's class, it is because he skipped part of line three of the instructions (which required that he stir the potion three times counter-clockwise); in Harry's dream, a snake attacks Mr. Weasley three times; the prophecy speaks of a child whose parents defied Voldemort three times, and Professor Dumbledore tells Harry that Neville's parents had narrowly escaped Voldemort three times; under the influence of a botched Imperius Curse, Herbert Chorley strangled three Healers; Dumbledore warns Harry three times not to touch the water in the cave.

To Denote Something as "Complete" or "Full"

Before Harry learns that he is a wizard, he experiences three bizarre occurrences which, in a sense, provide a complete or full set of witnesses to his being a special person: he is required to purchase a set of three robes for school at Hogwarts; he is mentioned in three Wizarding reference books; he visits the Mirror of Erised on three nights; Firenze asks Harry three questions to lead him into a more complete understanding of what he has seen taking place in the Forest with the unicorn; Harry derives information from three sources regarding the Chamber of Secrets—a ghost, (Professor Binns), a House-Elf (Dobby), and the Headmaster (Dumbledore); the phoenix possesses three special and magical qualities; after his adventure in the Chamber of Secrets, Harry has three items in hand (the Sorting Hat, Godric Gryffindor's sword, and Tom Riddle's diary); Cornelius Fudge lays down three restrictions on Harry while he stays at the Leaky Cauldron in Diagon Alley; in her third year, Hermione has three courses scheduled at the same time, a full load indeed; the Tri-Wizard Tournament includes three schools, three champions, and three tasks; Voldemort claims to have allies in three groups (his faithful Death Eaters, the giants, and the Dementors); as Voldemort tortures Harry with Unforgivable Curses, the boy feels for the third time in his life that his mind had been erased completely; Professor Umbridge posts three course aims on the board; three wizards warn the Dursleys about the dangers which Voldemort poses for them (Professor Dumbledore, Kingsley Shacklebolt and Mr. Weasley); Professor McGonagall's Patronus is three silver cats with markings which resemble her eyeglasses, her own personal power multiplied fully; Harry commissions Neville as a backup to kill Nagini, if Hermione and Ron should not be able to fulfill the task, so that, like Dumbledore (who had left three people who would know about the Horcruxes), Neville will take Harry's place, and "There would still be three in the secret" (*DH* 696); Voldemort shows his disdain for Harry Potter by tossing the boy's body into the air three times, toying with him.

To Introduce a Set of Characters

Rowling appears to have a penchant for staffing her scenes with characters in sets of three. The infant Harry is surrounded by three devoted protectors—Albus Dumbledore, Minerva McGonagall and Rubeus Hagrid; HH&R form a constant set of three throughout the novels; Draco, Crabbe and Goyle are the evil opposites of HH&R; the trio of friends is confronted in the girls' bathroom by Professors Quirrell, Snape and McGonagall; the panel of three judges, who were the heads of the participating schools, were all injured in the fiasco which occurred during the Triwizard Tournament of 1792; Fred, George, and Lee Jordan plan to defeat the Age Line and share the tournament prize three ways; Harry's experience with Dumbledore's Pensieve involves three accused wizards appearing before the Wizarding council; three individuals disappeared mysteriously—Bertha Jorkins, Barty Crouch and Frank Bryce; when Professor McGonagall learns of Harry's vision of the attack on Mr. Weasley, she takes Harry and Ron to Professor Dumbledore, and as they leave Harry's dorm, the three pass Neville, Dean and Seamus; Harry saves three members of the Weasley family—Ginny, Arthur and Ron; on the day of the Apparition test, all the students in Potions class are absent, except for Harry, Draco and Ernie; at Aragog's funeral, three people are present—Hagrid, Harry and Horace Slughorn; on the tower, three characters are present for the first part of that episode, Dumbledore, Draco, and Harry; Hogwarts was "home" for three abandoned boys—Harry Potter, Voldemort, and Severus Snape; Harry and Ginny have three children: James, Albus Severus, and Lily.

To Single Out an Individual

In stage plays, an actor can be singled out in a variety of ways. The performer can step forward and away from the other characters. The lighting crew may turn the spotlight on the one actor while dimming the lighting on others. In films, lighting, close-ups, and change in music in tandem with the camera's shifting angle can assist in presenting an individual in contrast to the others. In the novels Rowling singles out or emphasizes a particular character by contrasting him or her to a separate set of three other characters, making the person of interest someone who is naturally not a part of the specified group, an outsider to the complete set of three.

For example, when Bob Ogden, the Head of the Magical Law Enforcement Squad, visits the Gaunts to issue a summons for Morfin to appear before the Ministry, the family becomes embroiled in arguing and demeaning each other in Parseltongue. Ogden stands aside, stunned at the dysfunctional family. Ogden is the outsider to the complete set of Gaunts. Rowling writes, "All three of the Gaunts seemed to have forgotten Ogden, who was looking both bewildered and irritated" (*HBP* 210). The stunned official and the Gaunts create two opposite sets of characters, one set containing a single, sane individual, and a second set comprised of abnormal and ill-natured "pure-bloods."

This device is used quite often to distinguish Harry from his Muggle relatives. When the Dursleys take Harry to the train station, his uncle Vernon ridicules him, and all three of the family abandon him there on the platform, laughing at him; when Harry comes down to breakfast, he finds all three of the Dursleys already at table and all ignoring him; when Harry and his family are about to part permanently, Harry is summoned by his uncle as if Harry were a dog ("Oi! You!"), and Harry comes to the living room where he finds "all three Dursleys" (*DH* 30).

This "three-and-also-the other" technique is used for more than setting

Harry opposite to the Dursleys. Petunia Dursley says that her mother and father were proud of her witch-sister, Lily, but that she knew that Lily was a freak, which set envious and sullen Petunia over against all the remaining members of her family; Ron's three older brothers had excellent academic records at Hogwarts, which put pressure on him to live up their achievements; the authors of the Marauders' Map are four Animagi—three true friends (Sirius Black, James Potter, Remus Lupin) and a traitor (Peter Pettigrew); Harry is the odd man out (the fourth) of the official set of three Triwizard Champions; Barty Crouch, Jr. is sentenced to Azkaban along with three other Death Eaters, all of whom are members of the same family; of Voldemort's reconvened Death Eaters, there are three whose names are familiar, (Malfoy, Crabbe and Goyle) and a fourth named "Nott," who is probably the father of Theodore Nott, the Slytherin student who is only rarely put in the company of the sons of the three Death Eaters, so that fathers and sons make up two sets of three insiders and a fourth outsider; three faces appear in Moody's Foe Glass (Professors Dumbledore, McGonagall and Snape), who form a united set of enemies against the imposter "Moody"; when the Dursleys fail to offer a seat to Dumbledore in their home, he uses magic to seat all three of them; at Snape's house, three characters are engaged with each other for serious and secret business (Snape, Bellatrix and Narcissa), and when Wormtail tries to join the three or at least eavesdrop, Snape dismisses him as not part of the group; Tom Riddle kills the complete set of his Muggle family members (father, grandfather, grandmother), and causes the death of a fourth person, Morfin Gaunt, who is not part of the set of Muggles; Tom is a half-blood wizard in his paternal family of the three Muggles. We learn the names of only four centaurs who come from the Forbidden Forest (Ronan, Bane, Firenze and Magorian), and one of these (Firenze) is so completely different from the others that he is shunned by the other three. And, when HH&R enter Gringotts, they have a fourth, non-wizard associate, Griphook.

Ovid has a similar way of illuminating a character by contrast to other characters, a method we might call a "contrast of the one and the many." He does not use the exact same technique as Rowling—a group of three plus an outsider. He often makes a contrast between one person and "all" others. For example, when Jupiter and Mercury visit the earth disguised as humans to see if people are as impious as they appear to be, the two are dismissed from all homes except one, the small and humble hut of the elderly couple Baucis and Philemon. Ovid writes, "they approached a thousand homes, seeking a place for rest; Bolts kept shut a thousand homes; but one cottage did receive them (*mīlle domōs adiēre locum requiemque petentēs, mīlle domōs clausēre serae; tamen ūna recēpit, Met. 8.628–29*). By the end of the story, Jupiter causes a flood and drowns all the locals for their inhospitable treatment, and transforms the pious couple into caretakers of a temple, granting their fondest wishes. In another story, when an irreligious king named Erysichthon shows disdain toward the gods and personally attacks a tree sacred to Ceres, although the tree cries out in pain, blood flows from where the axe struck the mighty oak, and a nymph of Ceres prophesies the king's doom, Erysichthon completes his selfish act and dies a miserable death. Since the point which the story is making is that one owes respect to the gods, it is important that Ovid describes all the servants who were with the king as being dumb-struck and unable, or afraid, to say anything ... except for one brave soul who tried to stop the king: "all were astonished, and someone of them dared to prevent the horror and to restrain the cruel battle axe" [*obstipuēre omnēs, aliquisque ex omnibus audet/dēterrēre nefās saevamque inhibēre bipennem* (*Met.* 8.765–66)]. In other stories, he says that all the women of the city of Thebes go out to engage in Bacchic rituals, except for the daughters of Minyas alone ("alone," *solae, Met.* 4.32); that Acrisius is the only one in all of Achaia not to reverence Bacchus (4.607); that Lycabas is the boldest of a whole group of people (3.623–24). While Rowling's formula is much more repetitive, both she and Ovid have their own ways of contrasting an individual and his or her group.[57]

To Imply Frequency, Amount or Extent

Sometimes the number three is used to indicate a limitation or a small, inconsiderable degree (as if to connote "only," "as few as," " just"). At other times, it can connote the exact opposite, a greater amount or number or extent than might be expected (e.g. "as much [or as many] as," or "as long as").

The number can designate a limit or small degree. Gilderoy Lockhart is only a Third Class Order of Merlin wizard; Moaning Myrtle was killed only three toilet stalls away from where HH&R make the Polyjuice Potion; the usual life span of a rat (Scabbers) is only three years; there were just three unregistered Animagi at Hogwarts—James Potter, Sirius Black, and Peter Pettigrew; Hagrid's mother leaves him and his father when Hagrid is only three years old; as a Prefect, Draco Malfoy begins to abuse First Years, though he has had his badge a short time (Hermione says it is three minutes); Fred and George Weasley each receive passing grades on only three of their O.W.L. exams, as opposed to Bill and Percy Weasley, who passed twelve of their O.W.L.s; Hermione succeeds in performing the Vanishing Spell quickly, on her third attempt; Professor Flitwick removes Fred and George's swamp in the school corridor in only three seconds; Horace Slughorn creates a diversionary scene in only three minutes; Ginny says that Fleur speaks to her as if she were a child of three; the Gaunts' house has only three rooms for the three occupants; Hermione becomes exasperated with Ron for toying with the lights by means of his Deluminator, having had all she could stand on the third evening of this behavior.

Rowling also uses the number to express just the opposite, with a sense of largeness, amount or surprising extent. Hagrid's dragon, Norbert, grows three times his length in one week; the longest Quidditch match of all time lasted three months; Mr. Weasley has to turn back to his house three times before the family can get underway to the train station; the pumpkins which Hagrid grows specially for Halloween are so large that three men can sit in each one; Professor Binns assigns for homework the writing of a three-foot long composition; Hermione's textbooks are so numerous that they fill up three bags; at the beginning of Harry's third year at school, he has by now faced and bested Voldemort three times; James Potter, Sirius Black, and Peter Pettigrew work for three years to become Animagi; when a spell has been cast on it, a tent can have three floors of space inside; Harry feels disadvantaged in the Triwizard Tournament because the other champions are older than he and have three years' more education; Ron is surprised that Hermione will need three hours to prepare for the Yule Ball; it takes three days to decontaminate the Blacks' drawing room; of all Hagrid's students, only three can see the thestrals, which sounds like only a few, but to Ron, that seems to be many; the receptionist-witch at St. Mungo's says that three medical problems have occurred as the result of domestic arguments in one day; no one had been admitted to the office of Auror for three years; Voldemort was on the loose for three decades before he returned to power; the Ministry of Magic makes three arrests in a couple of months, to show the public they were on the job; Luna Lovegood removes three odd items from her bag before she gets to Dumbledore's parchment for Harry; Dumbledore has been offered the post of Minister of Magic three times; with Voldemort at large, there are three Dementor attacks in one week; Harry believes that the preparation they had made to infiltrate the Ministry is as adequate as if they were to spend three more months preparing.

To Effect a Magical Occurrence

To open the way into Diagon Alley, Hagrid taps the third brick on the left, three bricks up, three times; Harry wins at Wizarding chess by moving three spaces to the left; Hermione taps Riddle's diary with her wand three times to try to make it reveal any secrets it may be hiding; to read tea leaves, one has to swirl the liquid three times with the left hand to effect the magic; Hermione turns the Time-Turner three times to take herself and Harry back in time three hours; to open the jewel encrusted casket containing the Goblet of Fire, Dumbledore taps its lid three times; the formula for Voldemort's revitalization includes three ingredients—flesh, blood, and bone; the instructions for making the Draught of Peace call for stirring the potion three times counterclockwise; to seal the Unbreakable Vow between Snape and Narcissa, Bellatrix touches their joined hands three times, once after Narcissa recites each of the services which Snape binds himself to perform for her; when Harry hits Draco with the Sectumsempra Curse, Snape performs the healing counter-curse on Draco three times; in order to open the door to the Room of Requirement, Harry has to walk by it three times; Hermione pours three drops of Dittany on Ron's gaping wound to heal it; when the second brother in the "Tale of the Three Brothers" turns his magical stone three times, his long-deceased fiancée appears before him. And when Harry turns the stone in his hands three times, the shades of the dead appear to him—Tom Riddle, Sirius Black, Remus Lupin, and his parents, James and Lily Potter.

The Number Seven (7)

This number is used very often in literature, mythology, and various expressions of culture for its symbolic value. It stands for perfection, perhaps because it is one more than a double multiple of the special number three. Or, it may summon up the combined values of completeness (3) and universality (4). Richard Reitzenstein maintains that the connection between elements of nature and divine powers has a Greek origin, that the seven elements of sun, moon, breeze, wind, earth, water and fire were associated with the soul of the primal human by theological, speculative thinking about the universe (338f.). David Potter holds that the sacred value of seven may derive from the ancient belief that there were seven planets (1025). However it came to be, the number seven has acquired a powerful symbolic aura.

The Greeks employed this symbolic number often and in a variety of ways. They developed the tradition that there were seven "sages," or wise men.[58] In their religious practice, choruses of girls or groups of priests who served in honoring of the gods often were seven in number. Some Dionysiac festivals lasted seven days. A seven day fast was part of Orphic worship. Wilhelm Roscher has amassed a vast list of examples of the use of this number in the religious life and myths of the Greeks (337–462).

In the area of literature and lore, the ancients put the number to use frequently. Many of the figures of mythology have seven sons or seven daughters.

The seven daughters of the Titan Atlas form the stars of the Pleiades. Before Theseus puts an end to the Minotaur, the Greeks have to send seven young males and seven females of noble heritage every year to be offered to the beast in Crete. Niobe, the mother of seven sons and seven daughters, makes the mistake of bragging that she deserves more honor than the goddess Leto, the mother of only one son (Apollo) and one daughter (Artemis). As punishment for her hubris (excessive pride), these two gods kill her children. In the ancient mystery cult of Mithras, there are seven grades of initiation, each stage being under the protection of a planet (Beck 964). The blind prophet Tiresias, who is said to have lived for seven generations, is transformed into a woman for seven years, making him the only human who knows fully what it is to be a male and a female (*Met.* 3.316–38). Legend has it that Rome was built on seven hills—the Capitoline, Palatine, Aventine, Quirinal, Viminal, Esquiline and Caelian hills. Sibyl, the ancient seer who conducts Aeneas on his journey through the Underworld, complains that she got her wish of longevity from Apollo, but that she forgot to ask for eternal youth. So, she has lived seven hundred years and will have to endure three hundred more to fulfill her life (*Met.* 14.144–46).

Aeschylus' play *Seven Against Thebes* (467 BCE) dramatizes the mythical conflict between the cursed sons of Oedipus, who vow to share the kingship of Thebes in alternate years. When the first year comes to an end, Eteocles refuses to yield the throne to his brother, Polynices. The latter gathers an army to help him unseat Eteocles and take the power which is being denied him. The army is led by seven heroic warriors (one of whom is Polynices), who lay siege to the seven gates of the city. One of the many tragic events in the drama is that the two brothers kill each other at one of the gates and bring to an end the dynasty which began with their grandfather, Laius. A centerpiece of the play is the exchange between Eteocles and his messenger who in his report describes the frightening imagery on the shields of the seven leaders of the assault.

In the ancient apocalyptic tradition, seven is an instrument used quite frequently for revealing divine mysteries. The book of Revelation employs the number fifty-five times to signify fullness or perfection: letters to seven churches, seven beatitudes, seven seals which are to be unrolled, the sounding of seven trumpets, and seven bowls of the wrath of God, e.g. In the Apocrypha, the book of 2 Esdras has seven visions, the seventh of which tells the amazing legend of how God put Ezra into an inspired state so that he dictated the holy scriptures to five secretaries over a period of forty days (2 Esdras 14.1–48).

In the biblical book of *Tobit*, Tobias takes a wife who has been married seven times before. All seven grooms died on their wedding night, killed by a demon which was in love with her. This legend of the cursed bride has striking parallels to Rowling's character, Blaise Zabini. His mother had been married seven times, with each of the seven husbands dying mysteriously, leaving her wealthy. The implication seems to be that either she got away with killing her husbands, or that as a bride she was perfectly jinxed.

J.K. Rowling uses this convenient number quite often for its evocative and magical significance. Tom Riddle asked Professor Slughorn, "Isn't seven the most powerfully magical number?" (*HBP* 503). Harry pays a perfect price of seven Galleons for his wand, which Mr. Ollivander says is a perfect match for him; there are seven Weasley children: Bill, Charlie, Percy, Fred, George, Ron and Ginny; there are seven players on each Quidditch team; the Gryffindor common room is on the seventh floor; Slytherin wins the house cup for seven years in a row; Nicolas Flamel is seven years older than his wife; seven of the Hogwarts faculty and staff place enchantments around the Sorcerer's Stone to give it perfect protection; one of the enchantments protecting the Sorcerer's Stone is a table furnished with seven bottles and a riddle; Gilderoy Lockhart requires the students to purchase all seven of his books; the Hogwarts system is a seven-year curriculum; during Lupin's classroom lesson, a boggart is confronted seven times; Gryffindor loses the Quidditch Cup for seven years; the Marauder's Map charts seven secret passageways to Hogsmeade; when Ron was seven years old, Fred gave him an Acid Pop which burned a hole through his tongue; in the twentieth century, the Ministry of Magic has official record of seven Animagi; there are seven people present in the Shrieking Shack when Scabbers is transformed back into Peter Pettigrew; Harry is born in July (the seventh month); unicorn colts apparently reach maturity at the perfect time, age seven; after Rita Skeeter's article about Hermione is published in the *Daily Prophet*, Hermione begins to receive hate mail, delivered by seven owls; Dumbledore cites clause seven to prove that Harry is innocent; the formula for a Draught of Peace calls for the potion to simmer for seven minutes; seven locks with seven keyholes perfectly secure the trunk in which Barty Crouch, Jr. has locked "Mad-Eye" Moody; the Room of Requirement is on the seventh floor; Professor Umbridge continually interrupts Professor Trelawney's teaching by asking questions about Heptomology (divination by means of studying the mystical number seven); the prophecy declares that the chosen boy is someone who was born as the seventh month dies; Harry's copy of *Advanced Potion-Making* has notes accompanying the directions for making the Draught of Living Death, to add one clockwise stir after every seventh counterclockwise stir; Professor Trelawney's card, the seven of spades, is one of ill omen; Tom Riddle wants to split his soul into seven pieces or parts (a perfect set); the Order members transport seven "Potters" from the Dursleys' house to safety; and Albus Dumbledore's sister Ariana disappears at age seven, the age when magic begins to reveal itself in magical children.

The Number seven is found in multiples and combinations, as well. Ron brags that his broom can go from zero to seventy in just ten seconds. There are seven hundred ways to foul in playing Quidditch. The Weasleys win a prize of seven hundred Galleons. The Triwizard Tournament has a history of seven hundred years. And the tapestry in the Black's house with the family tree has been in the family for seven centuries.

The Number Thirteen (13)

This prime number often carries a connotation of misfortune or evil. In ancient Greek lore, Pelops, the grandson of Atlas and son of Tantalus, wanted to marry Hippodamia, the daughter of king Oenomaüs. As often happens, the girl's father was an impediment to their romance. The king either had improper, incestuous desire for the girl himself, or he may have been warned by an oracle that he was doomed to be killed by a son-in-law. Whatever the reason for his actions, he made it virtually impossible for anyone to win the girl's hand. For every suitor, he presented the challenge of a chariot race across the Peloponnese to the Isthmus of Corinth. If the challenger won, he got to marry the girl. If he lost, the king would kill him. Oenomaüs was weighed down with his full armor—probably so as to be ready to murder the challenger who would lose. The suitor was accompanied by Hippodamia in his chariot. Thirteen suitors had failed in this competition before Pelops. To discourage ardent hopefuls, Oenomaüs nailed onto the door of his house (or placed on posts before his house) the heads of all the previous losers. As the story turns out, Pelops won the race and the hand of Hippodamia (Pindar, *Olympia* 1.79; *Epit.* 2.4–9).[59] Mounting and displaying of the House-Elves' heads at Sirius' family home is about as gruesome as Oenomaüs' trophies—though Rowling does not specify how many there were. But for Pelops, the thirteen heads surely got his attention.

The number thirteen possesses an element of foreboding. Since Voldemort's wand is thirteen and a half inches long, does that make his wand extra cursed or super-abundantly capable of evil? One of the fares charged for riding the Knight Bus is thirteen Sickles; Sirius Black is sent to Azkaban for killing thirteen people; Professor Trelawney joins twelve diners at Christmas table, bringing the number of up to thirteen, which compels her to pronounce that the number is unlucky and to prophesy that the first of the thirteen to arise will die; the Dark Mark appears at the time of the Quidditch World Cup for the first time in thirteen years; revitalized Voldemort tells his Death Eaters twice that it was thirteen years ago that he and Harry met, a memorable and unlucky day for the Dark Lord; he tells Avery that he will not forgive him, and he demands that Avery first repay him with thirteen years of service; Harry's summoning his Patronus in a Muggle area is a breach of section thirteen of the statutes; Betty Braithwaite's interview with Rita Skeeter concerning the lies and shadier information which Skeeter wrote about Dumbledore is fittingly located on page thirteen of the *Daily Prophet*; the group which escorts Harry away from the Dursleys' home for the last time is thirteen in number; Professor Flitwick's window is the thirteenth window on the seventh floor.

The Number Seventeen (17)

Unlike the ill-omened number thirteen, seventeen appears in quite positive situations. When Mr. Ollivander makes Cedric Diggory's wand, for its core, he takes a single hair from a unicorn that is seventeen hands tall, approximately sixty-eight inches tall—a sizeable and mature animal.

An outstanding turn-about occurs during Harry's third year at Hogwarts, when Gryffindor wins the Quidditch Cup for the first time in seven years. Their team captain, Oliver Wood, is seventeen years old and in his seventh year at the school. Of course, many students would be seventeen during their seventh year, but Rowling chooses to make a point of the fact that Wood was seventeen in the year of Gryffindor's victory.

Perhaps the most important use of the number among wizard youth is that it is the age at which young people become adults. It is such an established mark that Mrs. Weasley is surprised to learn that in the Muggle world, children come of age at eighteen. Prior to their seventeenth birthday, young people are forbidden to practice magic outside their wizard school. To make sure that they do not break that rule, the Ministry of Magic imposes on them a Trace, which alerts the Improper Use of Magic Office if there is an offense. The Trace is removed, automatically, on the seventeenth birthday of the wizard (Vander Ark 306). The reason that competitors in the Triwizard Tournament must be at least seventeen is that it is for adults only.

For Harry, there is an additional spell on him which will expire on his seventeenth birthday. Dumbledore initiated the spell when he delivered infant Harry to the Dursleys to ensure that he would be safe in the Muggle world until he would become a man. When Harry realizes that he has come of age, he immediately puts his new status to the test, joyously casting charms to see them work. Now that the Trace is removed, he may be more powerful than ever before; but he is also more vulnerable.

Two connections with classical tradition and lore resonate with Harry's transition to manhood: the coming of age rite of passage at seventeen, and a gift on the occasion. In the ancient Roman world, an underage free-born boy would wear a toga with a purple stripe on the upper border (the *toga praetexta*, "adorned toga") until he was about seventeen, at which time he would begin to wear the plain white woolen toga of adult Roman citizens (the *toga virīlis*, "grown man's toga"). The ceremony occurred annually on March 17th, during the Liberalia, the feast of Bacchus, who was also called "Liber," "he who frees (from care)," perhaps celebrating the boy's being set free for adult life (Gould 67; Granger-Taylor 488). Second, Mr. and Mrs. Weasley give Harry a very special gift for the occasion, a family heirloom, a watch which belonged to the brother of Molly Weasley, Fabian Prewett. Fabian had fought and died heroically against the Dark side. His name recalls the Roman general Quintus Fabius Maximus, who defeated Hannibal's army and saved Rome by judicious maneuvering of his troops and by delaying military engagement. He became a legend and national hero to the Romans. By receiving "Fabian's" watch, Harry is linked to a famous, wise, and legendary defender who defeated a most formidable enemy.

Products of Two Prime Numbers

Some of the most surprising and interesting numbers in the novels are the products of two prime numbers (e.g., 3 × 3). Symbolically, such composite numbers seem to magnify or complement the uniqueness and significance of each of the individual prime numbers.

<u>9</u> (3 × 3): Vernon Dursley's office is on the ninth floor; Ron is proud of the Chudley Cannons for being ninth in the league; the Weasleys' clock has nine golden hands; the Third Task begins at nine o'clock; nine members of the Advanced Guard come to the Dursley house to pick up Harry; HH&R plan to infiltrate the Ministry at 9:00 a.m.; the lift in the Ministry goes down only as far as the ninth floor; Luna Lovegood loses her mother to a tragic accident when she is nine years old; Harry's Potions book costs him nine Galleons. With Voldemort restored and wreaking havoc, horrible things begin to happen, such as a nine-year-old boy killing his grandparents.

In Greek mythology and tradition, the Muses, who were the daughters of Zeus and Mnemosyne (Memory), were the sources of inspiration for the nine arts (hence our expression "dressing to the nines"): Clio (history), Euterpe (lyric poetry, flute music), Thalia (comedy), Melpomene (tragedy), Terpsichore (choral dancing), Erato (love poetry), Polyhymnia (religious hymns and dance), Urania (astronomy), and Calliope (epic poetry) (*Theog.*

75–79; *Libr.* 1.3.1).[60] The Hydra had nine heads (*Libr.* 2.5.2). A prophecy about Achilles, that the Greeks could not defeat the Trojans without his participation, was delivered when Achilles was only nine years old (3.13.8). When pestilence and death plagued the Greeks at Troy, the gods intervened after nine days of the Greeks' suffering (*Il.* 1.53ff.). Any Olympian god who took an oath by the river Styx and broke the vow taken would be removed from the councils of the gods for nine years (*Homeric Hymn to Apollo,* 83–89; *Theog.* 767–806). When Apollo's mother, Leto, was about to give birth to the son of Zeus, Hera (Zeus's wife) spitefully interfered, causing Leto to agonize in childbirth for nine days and nine nights, a number which symbolizes the absolute completeness of her toil and travail (*Homeric Hymn to Apollo,* 91). The Cumaean Sibyl offered nine books of oracles to Tarquinius Superbus; Orpheus was said to have lived for nine generations.[61]

The number was potent in the daily lives of the Greeks and Romans as well. According to Erwin Rohde, it was a common feature of the ancients to conceive of periods of time in sets of nine. The mourning customs of Greeks and Romans gave the number a special respect. The Greeks would offer a meal to a departed person at the grave site on the third and ninth days after the funeral. Because they believed that on the ninth day after a person's death the soul of the deceased could return, they spent nine days of mourning in order to "ward off maleficent action on the part of the dead" (167, 195). The Roman custom similarly included a period of mourning until nine days after a funeral and a ceremonial feast to conclude the period formally, the *novendiālis cēnae* (Balsdon 127).

<u>14</u> (2 × 7): In doing detention, Ron has to polish a Quidditch cup fourteen times; his new wand is fourteen inches long; Professor Snape has taught at Hogwarts for fourteen years; fourteen witnesses see the Slytherin Keeper jinx Alicia Spinnet; Harry wonders what has made Voldemort happier than he has been in fourteen years; during a Quidditch match, Ron misses the Quaffle fourteen times; every summer, Harry is obligated to stay with the Dursleys for at least two weeks; Hagrid is said to have drunk fourteen buckets of wine; Ariana caused the death of her mother when the girl was just fourteen years old; Harry ponders for a fortnight the possibility of teaching the other students defenses against the Dark Arts; Cornelius Fudge tells the Prime Minister that the Wizarding public has been anxious to see him dismissed as Minister of Magic for a fortnight.

Two mythical tales which employ the number fourteen are the tale of Niobe's pride, which results in the loss of all fourteen of her children (mentioned above under The Number Seven), and the myth of Ceyx and Alcyone. There are two tales regarding the couple in which they are transformed into birds. The shorter story is that Ceyx, in his arrogance, was in the habit of saying that his wife was Hera, and Alcyone would refer to her husband as Zeus. For this proud fault, Zeus punished them by turning them into birds, the gannet [Gk *kēx=kēux*] and the kingfisher [Gk *alkuōn*] (*Libr.* 1.7.4). The longer story, a virtual love story, gives a different angle on the couple's affection. Ceyx planned to visit the oracle at Delphi about grave issues his family faced. Alcyone pressed him to travel by land and not by sea. As the daughter of Aeolus, the god of the winds, she had great fear of the sea. He chose to take the sea route and was drowned in a terrific storm. Alcyone prayed constantly to Juno to keep her husband safe, though the prayers were not heeded. In pity, Juno dispatched Iris to the god of sleep, Somnus, to show the worried queen that her husband was dead. He directed Morpheus, the god of the shape of dreams, to assume the appearance of Ceyx, and to convince her that Ceyx was dead and that he should be mourned properly. She went to the very place from which her husband set sail to take her own life. The corpse of Ceyx floated to her. In inconsolable agony, she threw herself into the sea. But before she could enter the water, wings lifted her above the surface. She touched the body of her lover and, by the pitying gods, both were transformed into birds. The ending of the story shows an etiological purpose to the tale. According to the story and ancient legend, the Halcyon bird makes its nest on the waves in the winter during a period of peaceful tides and calm weather (*Met.* 11.410–748). For seven days the halcyon bird nests, and some say for seven days before and seven days after the winter solstice. This period was known to the Greeks as the "Halcyon days" [(*alkuonides hēmerai*, LSJ 676)].

In the apocryphal book of *Tobit*, when the hero, Tobias, survived his wedding night, there was great joy. His bride had lost seven grooms before this marriage, all of whom had been killed by an evil demon. Because of magic and divine intervention by an angel, Tobias and his wife Sarah lived a long and happy life together. The joyful victory was celebrated with a fourteen-day wedding feast (Tob 8:19).

21 (3 × 7): the lacewings for the Polyjuice Potion have to brew for twenty-one days; Stan Shunpike is arrested when he is twenty-one years old.

33 (3 × 11): Harry has to regrow thirty-three bones in his arm after Professor Lockhart has removed them with his bad healing charm.

39 (3 × 13): Dudley Dursley receives thirty-nine gifts for his birthday, a triply unfortunate way to show him "love," for it feeds his greediness. Professor McGonagall tells Professor Umbridge that she has been teaching at Hogwarts for thirty-nine years.

49 (7 × 7): Broderick Bode, a patient on Ward forty-nine, dies at age forty-nine (*OP* 486, 546). Perhaps the most famous use of the number 49 in

mythology has to do with the Danaïds, the fifty daughters of Danaüs. The myth relates that two brothers of Egyptian royalty generate a formidable brood of children: Danaüs has fifty daughters and Aegyptus had fifty sons. There is a quarrel between the two brothers over their kingdom, leading to hostilities between them. The fifty young men offer to marry the fifty young women. Distrusting the proposal, with Athena's help, Danaüs builds a ship and escapes with his daughters to Greece. The young men pursue them and compel their future father-in-law to permit the weddings. Danaüs gives daggers to all his daughters for them to use to kill their husbands on their wedding night. Forty-nine of the brides comply. The only one who refuses is Hypermnestra, who spares her husband Lynceus because he protects her virginity. Eventually, all are absolved of their crime, but their punishment in the Underworld is to fill leaky jars with water for all time (*Libr.* 2.1.4–5; Horace *Odes* 3.11; *Met.* 4.462–63; Ovid, *Heroides* 14).

<u>77</u> (7 × 11): Frank Bryce is almost seventy-seven years old at the time of his death.

<u>437</u> (19 × 23): Dumbledore tells students on their first night back at Hogwarts, after dinner, that Mr. Filch's list of banned objects now numbers four hundred thirty-seven.

<u>713</u> (23 × 31): Hagrid visits Gringotts on behalf of Professor Dumbledore to secure the Sorcerer's Stone from the school's vault, number seven hundred thirteen.

Composite Numbers

Composite whole numbers can be evenly divided (leaving no remainders) by numbers other than one and itself. For example, the composite number eight can be divided by itself the number one, just like a prime number: $8 \div 1 = 8$; $8 \div 8 = 1$. What makes the number eight different from prime numbers is that it can also be divided by other numbers than prime numbers: $8 \div 2 = 4$; $8 \div 4 = 2$.

The Number Four (4)

The number four sometimes carries with it the idea of "universality" or of "a full range." The earliest Greek philosophers deliberated as to what was the essential component of all matter. Empedocles posited that there are four essences—earth, air, fire, and water. The Stoics considered there to be four basic emotions (Diogenes Laertius 7, 110). The Pythagoreans held in honor what they called the "tetraktus" [Gk *tetraktus*], which was the sum of the first four numbers: $1 + 2 + 3 + 4 = 10$, the basis of the mathematical system based on ten. The number four was used to refer to the phases of the moon, the seasons, the elements (Theophrastus, *de Causis Planetarum,* 3.3.4).[62] The Olympiads were scheduled every four years. Pindar referred to the four virtues which destiny employs to affect humans (Gk *tessarās aretās, Nemea* 3.74ff.). The common perspective of the Greeks and Romans was that there were four ages in the history of the world: the Golden Age, Silver Age, Bronze Age, and the Iron Age, representing a deteriorating pattern, but occurring in cycles, so that after the hardest kind of time, a new Golden Age would return (*Works* 106–201[63]; *Met.* 1.89–150). Odysseus had his crew draw lots to see which four of them would assist him in blinding the Cyclops. The four who were elected happened to be the exact same four whom Odysseus would have chosen (*Od.* 9.331–35). In the book of Revelation, four angels stand at the four corners of the earth, holding the four winds of the earth (Rev 7:1). In the apocryphal second century CE work *Gospel of Mary,* the community which produced that document believed that the spiritual task was to overcome four powers (Ehrman 37). We still speak, symbolically, of the four corners of the earth or the four points of the compass and the four winds.

This number occurs frequently in the *Harry Potter* novels to suggest an inclusive and full range. The entirety of Harry's formative years are spent living in the world of the Dursleys, at Four Privet Drive; in Quidditch, there are four balls in play; the First Years travel across the black lake with Hagrid in boats carrying four passengers each; Hogwarts has four Houses, founded by four of the most famous wizards (Godric Gryffindor, Helga Hufflepuff, Rowena Ravenclaw, and Salazar Slytherin); when the Chamber of Secrets is opened, four students who are Mudbloods are petrified; greedy Dudley Dursley consumes four slices of pie; the Marauder's Map is authored by four individuals who write with four different handwritings (Moony, Prongs, Padfoot, and Wormtail); on Harry's birthday, he receives four birthday cakes from his entire circle of close friends; the Death Eaters toy with the Roberts family by dangling all four of them in the air; the Sorting Hat was personified by all four of the founders of Hogwarts; the usual layout of the Great Hall is four parallel lines of house tables, providing for the entire student body; Harry has to submerge himself in the bath four times before he can memorize the Mermish poem-clue; four defendants are brought before the Council of Magical Law for trial; at the Third Task, for safety, four of the faculty and staff are positioned at the edges of the maze, that is, in all directions; Harry uses the Four-Point Spell to proceed into the maze, as it directs him to true north, giving him accurate knowledge of all directions; Professor McGonagall is incapacitated by four Stunning Spells; when Rita Skeeter writes a biography of the entire life of Albus Dumbledore, the totality of her work is completed in just four weeks; when Harry encounters the dead in the forest, he is surrounded by four "parental" figures who have given their lives to protect him (James and Lily Potter, Sirius Black and Remus Lupin).[64]

Sometimes four is squared, raising the value of the number to an even higher power—as if totality were multiplied by totality. Snape tells Bellatrix that he has sixteen years of information on Dumbledore to give to the Dark Lord; Professor Trelawney's job interview with Professor Dumbledore at the Hog's Head took place sixteen years earlier.

The Number Twelve (12)

The multiple of numbers signifying completeness (three) and universality (four), twelve is also a widely adopted number to connote "totality." The duodecimal system (based on the number twelve) originated in Babylon, owing to the ancient determination that the year was divided into twelve months. This perspective of time was adopted by Julius Caesar for the Roman calendar, which has become standard in the Western world.[65] In the Greek world, groups of community dwellers would join together to form a league or "amphictyony" which was considered a sacred union. Usually there were twelve clans or groups which comprised the league, since each group had the responsibility for their sanctuary a month each year (Rengstorf 321).

The Greeks venerated the twelve Olympian gods: Apollo, Aphrodite, Ares, Artemis, Athena, Demeter, Dionysus, Hades, Hephaestus, Hera, Hermes, Hestia, Poseidon and Zeus.[66] The principal Roman gods were twelve in number: Apollo, Ceres, Diana, Juno, Jupiter, Mars, Mercury, Minerva, Neptune, Venus, Vesta, and Vulcan (A.U.C. 22.10.9). Heracles is famous for accomplishing his Twelve Labors or contests to attain immortality. In the *Republic*, Plato narrates his Myth of Er, the tale of a warrior who was killed in battle and was permitted to see the afterlife in detail and return to tell about it. Er's supernatural experience took place during the space of twelve days, after which he awoke from his state as his body was about to be cremated. He had only appeared to be dead, but had not suffered the corruption of death (*Republic* 614b2–621d3).

The frequent use of the number in religious literature seems to connect it to divine will.[67] In the biblical tradition, the Promised Land was occupied by the twelve tribes of Israel (the sons of Jacob). Jesus had "twelve" original disciples.[68] There was an ancient Jewish apocalyptic concept that world history could be divided into twelve parts or "weeks," with the last of the twelve being the Messianic period, just before the arrival of the Kingdom of God. The genealogy of Jesus in the Gospel of Luke contains seventy-eight names, eleven sets of seven, and Jesus as the seventy-eighth, or the first one in the twelfth set, the new or messianic age.[69] The writer of the book of Revelation uses the number twelve or its adjective "twelfth" twenty-four times: from each of the twelve tribes of Israel twelve thousand are sealed for God; in a vision, a woman in heaven wears a crown with twelve stars; the heavenly city of Jerusalem has twelve gates in its walls where twelve angels stand guard; the gates are inscribed with the twelve names of the twelve tribes of Israel; the heavenly city wall has twelve foundations on which are the twelve names of the twelve apostles; the dimensions of the city walls are twelve thousand stades (units of length approximately two hundred yards each); twelve jewels bedeck the foundations; the twelve gates are made of pearl; and inside the city, the tree of fruit bears twelve different species.

In the *Potter* stories, twelve does duty as well. Most of the time the number appears to be Rowling's way of saying "many" or "much" or "as many as," without being too expansive (as with, say, "a hundred," which she also uses frequently). Numbers and amounts are often given in sets of twelve: Dumbledore magically extinguishes and re-ignites the twelve lamp lights on Privet Drive; he tells Professor McGonagall that he passed a dozen celebrations on his way to Privet Drive; his watch has twelve hands; he is famous for finding twelve uses for dragons' blood; both Bill and Percy Weasley pass twelve of their O.W.L.s; Lucius Malfoy says he had heard Draco complain about Harry at least a dozen times; during the scuffle between Mr. Weasley and Lucius Malfoy in the bookstore, dozens of books fall on their heads; when Ron and Harry crash their trolleys and cannot get through to platform nine and three-quarters, a dozen curious people stare at them; for Halloween, Hagrid grows twelve huge pumpkins; during the Deathday party, a dozen headless ghosts gallop though the room on their Headless Hunt; on Valentine's day, Gilderoy Lockhart has twelve dwarfs deliver cards throughout the school; all twelve governors of Hogwarts sign the Order of Suspension of Dumbledore; Aunt Marge keeps twelve breeding dogs; twelve of the thirteen people whom Sirius Black is supposed to have killed were Muggles; Hagrid brings twelve hippogriffs out of the forest for his lesson; when the students enter the Department of Mysteries, they are surrounded by twelve doors; in the room where the prophecies are stored, the six students face twelve Death Eaters; at Christmas the Great Hall is decorated with no fewer than twelve huge Christmas trees; on Christmas Day the Great Hall table is set for twelve diners (six students and six faculty); for Christmas Mrs. Weasley sends Harry a dozen mince pies; the Apparition course at Hogwarts lasts for twelve weeks and costs twelve Galleons; Harry's Nimbus 2000 is broken into a dozen pieces by the Whomping Willow; Harry dreads that while the students are away from Hogwarts over Christmas, Professor Umbridge will have another dozen decrees passed; Peter Pettigrew conceals himself as Scabbers for twelve years; Ron re-tells his first save in the Quidditch match a dozen times; in the cave Dumbledore has to drink twelve goblets of potion to get to the locket; Harry thinks that his dozen detentions are too many; the members of the Order of the Phoenix use a dozen houses to misdirect any Death Eaters who might attack them when they spirit Harry away from the Dursley home; Harry is put off from asking a girl to go to the Yule Ball because he finds that girls always seem to be in groups of a dozen or so; as a birthday gift for Harry, Ron gives him a book which offers twelve guidelines for dealing with females.

Twelve is used also for sizes and dimensions: the troll in the girls' bathroom at Halloween is twelve feet tall; Buckbeak's wing-span is twenty-four feet, twelve on each side; Voldemort's snake Nagini is at least twelve feet long; Mundungus Fletcher requests that the Ministry compensate him for the loss of his tent (though he actually did not have a tent at all) at the Quidditch World Cup by putting in a claim for a twelve-bedroom tent; the acromantula in the maze picks Harry up and drops him from a height of twelve feet; a twelve-foot tall boggart confronts Harry in the maze; Ron claims that Sirius' knife is twelve inches long.

While the number twelve may not have a connotation as magical as seven or three, it serves well for matters of degree, quality, and mystery: Harry tells Neville that he (Neville) is worth twelve Malfoys; the twelve who survived the journey from the Dursleys toast their deceased champion, Mad-Eye Moody; Sirius' house address is Number Twelve, Grimmauld Place; a dozen winged horses pull the Beauxbatons' carriage; the Axminster flying carpet can accommodate twelve passengers; Harry and Ron contrive astrological information, so that Harry puts Venus in the twelfth house, the mysterious house or sector; Harry's hearing at the Ministry is set for August twelfth; Bill Weasley makes twelve scrolls vanish, so that no non-members can see what the Order of the Phoenix is doing; owing to the activity of Voldemort, a dozen cars fall into a river when a bridge gives way; the Felix Felicis potion is effective for twelve hours; and, Professor Trelawney happily prophesies that Harry will have twelve children.

Rowling often varies the thematic effect of twelve by referring to "half a dozen." The Knight Bus has a half dozen brass beds; Fred and George set off half a dozen Dungbombs; at Harry's hearing before the Wizengamot, Cornelius Fudge and about half a dozen others vote to convict Harry; when drunken Winky falls off her stool, half a dozen elves rush to attend to her; the common room is almost empty, there being only half a dozen students present; at a gathering of Slughorn's students, he is surrounded by half a dozen of them; Harry tells his Uncle Vernon that they had gone over his optional proposals half a dozen times; Bill and Fleur are chased by a half dozen Death Eaters; the number of people lurking in front of Number Twelve Grimmauld Place, watching for Harry, grows to half a dozen.

Chapter IX

Classical Languages
in *Harry Potter*

Rowling's use of the Latin language (and less frequently, Greek) is evident throughout these intriguing stories in one form or another. Characters frequently have genuine, ancient Greek and Roman names. Fabulous creatures and beasts of the Wizarding world sometimes have the same names as ancient mythical animals. And spells and curses sound all the more mysterious and dramatic because of their lofty Latin terminology. We even encounter the stone head of a wizard mumbling in Latin. M.G. DuPree counts approximately one hundred forty spells in the series, seventy-two of which are "either Latin, Latin-derived, or Latin in part" (40). Rowling often amplifies her use of the classical languages, by toying with them. The languages may serve simply as an inspiration for her inventive and often sportive creation of terms, incantations, or names which mirror their inspiring linguistic models to varying degrees. She does not depict wizards and warlocks using proper classical Latin, as if they were magical monks or medieval scholars. Rather, they use the language as technical terminology appropriate to the supernatural practices of magic, or as common, everyday Latin.

The presence of Latin or Latinized words contributes special color and tone to the Wizarding world. It summons up reminiscences of ancient times and legendary, mythic figures and obscure knowledge. It creates a world of people who, despite their widely varying individual social and intellectual differences, seem to represent a culture advanced by learned people. Rowling joyfully and openly professes that she takes license with the language.[1]

The terms listed in this chapter do not include full etymological treatment of the classical roots or parallels to related terms in the *Harry Potter* novels. Our interest is not to record the full history of the classical roots and words but to offer enough information for readers to identify the origins of the terms and to show how those ancient originals relate to and shed light on Rowling's terms. She uses the languages in a variety of ways which are grouped below into four categories: first, the magical vocabulary which is based on genuine classical terminology; second, the names which are not formally, true classical names, but which are formed from creative use of classical roots; third, the magical vocabulary which Rowling has created by a very free and inventive use of classical terms or English words which derive from classical words[2]; and, fourth, English terms with Latin bases, which are re-cycled as technical terms for their magical world applications.[3]

Magical Incantations and Charms Based on Genuine Classical Terminology

Accio: the incantation which activates a Summoning Charm, meaning "I summon, call forth" [L *acciō, accīre, accīvī, accītum,* "to summon"]. With the Summoning Charm, one can cause items to come to whoever utters the charm: Ton-Tongue Toffees, a dictionary, the Marauder's Map, the Triwizard Cup, a frog, bottles of Butterbeer, a wand, pickled brains, the prophecy orb, students' parchment worksheets, their essays, and flying broomsticks.

Anapneo: the incantation by which Professor Slughorn removes the food from Marcus Belby's throat when the boy is choking, clearing his airway and allowing him to breathe, meaning "I breathe again" [Gk *anapneō,* "to breathe again, recover"].

Avis: the incantation which causes a wand to emit small birds, used by Mr. Ollivander and Hermione [L *avis, avis,* "bird"].

Caput Draconis: a password required by the Fat Lady to allow admittance to the Gryffindor common room, meaning "dragon's head" [L *caput, capitis,* "head" + *dracō, -ōnis,* "dragon, serpent" < Gk *drakōn, -ontos,* "serpent"].

Cave Inimicum: an incantation which warns one to be alert to the presence of an approaching enemy, and one of a group of spells which Hermione casts around the campsite where HH&R are hiding, meaning "beware the enemy" [L *caveō, cavēre, cāvī, cautum,* "to take heed, beware"; *cavē,* "(you, singular) beware"+ *inimīcus, -ī,* "enemy, foe"].

Confringo: the incantation which activates an Explosion Charm or Blasting Curse, which Harry uses on the sidecar of Hagrid's motorcycle, and which Hermione uses on Nagini, meaning "I shatter" [L *cōnfringō, cōnfringere, cōnfrēgī, cōnfractum,* "to shatter, break in pieces"].

Crucio: the incantation which activates the Cruciatus Curse, inflicting pain on the victim, meaning "I torture, torment" [L *cruciō, cruciāre, cruciāvī, cruciātum,* "to torture"].

Defodio: the incantation which activates a digging or gouging charm by which Hermione helps the Gringotts dragon enlarge a hole for their escape, meaning "I dig up" [L *dēfodiō, dēfodere, dēfōdi, dēfossum*, "to dig up, bury, hide"].

Deprimo: the incantation by which Hermione blasts a hole in the floor of the Lovegood's home in order to escape, meaning, "I dig deep, press down" [L *dēprimō, dēprimere, dēpressī, dēpressum*, "to depress, sink deep"].

Descendo: the incantation which causes something to fall down or descend, with which Ron makes a ladder drop down from his ceiling, allowing access to an upper room where the family ghoul lives, and with which Crabbe makes a towering pile of items stored in the Room of Requirement collapse, meaning, "I descend" [L *dēscendō, dēscendere dēscendī, dēscensum*, "to go down, come down, sink"].

Diffindo: the incantation for cutting or splitting something. Harry uses the spell several times: to rip open Cedric Diggory's book bag and spill the contents; to dislodge tough brain tentacles from Ron's face; to remove the cover from his copy of *Advanced Potion-Making*; and to crack the ice on the surface of a pool. Hermione uses it to remove the ropes with which a Death Eater had bound Ron. The word means, "I split, tear open, break off" [L *diffindō, diffendere, diffidī, defissum*, "to tear asunder, divide"].

Duro: the incantation which makes pliable material turn to stone, with which Hermione petrifies a tapestry for protection, meaning "I make (something) hard" [L *dūrō, dūrāre, dūrāvī, dūrātum*, "to make hard, to harden"].

Evanesco: the incantation which activates a Vanishing Spell, useful for hiding something from others or ridding one of something offensive, as Professor Snape did with a bad concoction of the Draught of Peace, meaning "I make (something) vanish" [L *ēvānescō, ēvānescere, ēvānuī*, "to vanish, disappear"].

Expecto Patronum: the incantation which activates the Patronus Charm, summoning an individual's personal defender, meaning, "I need (my) protector" [L *ex(s)pectō, ex(s)pectāre, ex(s)pectāvī, ex(s)pectātum*, "I await, hope for, have need of" + *patrōnus, -ī*, "protector, defender"].

Expulso: the incantation which causes something to be removed forcefully, as when a Death Eater destroys a table between himself and Harry, meaning "I knock away, drive away" [L *expulsō, expulsāre, expulsāvī, expulsātum*, "to drive out, drive back, drive away from one's self"].

Felix Felicis: the name of a good luck potion which for twelve hours causes its user to be successful in every endeavor, meaning "fortunate of fortunate," or "lucky of lucky," a way of expressing a superlative degree, "most fortunate" or "luckiest" [L *fēlix, fēlīcis*, "fortunate, prosperous, favorable, lucky"].

Ferula: the incantation which Lupin uses to create a splint for Ron's broken leg [L *ferula, -ae*, "walking stick, rod, and splint"].

Fidelius (Charm): a charm used to entrust a secret to one's most loyal friend, who then becomes a Secret-Keeper, used by James and Lily Potter on Sirius Black and by the Order of the Phoenix on Dumbledore [L *fidēlis, -e*, "sincere, faithful"; *fidēlior, fidēlius*, comparative adjective, neuter, "more trustworthy, more dependable, more sincere"].

Finite (Incantatem): the incantation which ends an active curse or spell which has been cast, with which Professor Snape cancels Draco Malfoy's Tarantallegra Spell on Harry, and Professor Lupin puts an end to Dolohov's Tarantallegra Spell on Neville Longbottom. Hermione suggests that Ron employ this incantation to make it stop raining in an office at the Ministry of Magic. Harry uses it to put a stop to an avalanche of items in the Room of Requirement. The term means "you (plural) end the spell" [L *fīniō, fīnīre, fīnīvī, fīnītum*, "cease, end"; *fīnīte*, "you (plural) finish, cease" + *incantātus*, "a spell that has been cast"; the ending applied, *-em*, is a bit playful, as the formal Latin word for "spell" is *incantāmentum*].

Flagrante: the curse which makes something burn. It makes the charmed vessels in Bellatrix Lestrange's vault at Gringotts Bank blister Hermione's fingers [L *flagrō, flagrāre, flagrāvī, flagrātum*, "to burn, glow, blaze"; *flagrāns, flagrantis*, "flaming, blazing"; possibly the Ablative case of the participle, meaning "by burning"].

Flagrate: the incantation by which Hermione produces a burning cross in the air, scorching itself onto a door, meaning, "you (plural) burn" [L *flagrō, flagrāre, flagrāvī, flagrātum*, "to burn, glow, blaze"; second person plural imperative ending, "you"].

Fortuna Major: a password required by the Fat Lady to allow admittance to the Gryffindor common room, meaning "better luck" as a kindly expression [L *fortūna, -ae*, "fortune, good luck, prosperity," also the name of the Roman goddess of chance or fortune (good or bad fortune) + *maior, maius*, "greater"; the comparative degree of the adjective *magnus, -a, -um*, "great"].

Gemino: a spell which reproduces, copies something, or doubles the power of another spell. With this spell Hermione makes a duplicate copy of the locket of Salazar Slytherin, and with it the goblins of Gringotts Bank jinx the contents of Bellatrix Lestrange's vault, causing them to multiply when touched, meaning, "I double" [L *geminō, gemināre, gemināvī, geminātum*, "to double, to join (two things)," i.e., to make them twins > *geminus, -a, um*, "double, twin, pair"]; see also Geminio on p. 261, below.

Grammatica: the study of grammar [Gk *gramma, -atos*, "letter" > L *grammatica, -ae*, "grammar, the study of literature and language"]. Hermione studies this advanced subject, which is above the talents or interest of Harry and Ron.

Imperio: the incantation which activates the Imperius Curse, giving one total control over a victim, meaning "I command" [playful variation on L *imperō, imperāre, imperāvī, imperātum,* "I command"].

Imperturbable Charm: the charm which Mrs. Weasley uses on a kitchen door to prevent any eavesdropping on the work of the Order of the Phoenix, such as Fred's and George's use of their Extendable Ears, meaning "unable to be disturbed or excited" [L *in-,* "not" + *perturbō, perturbāre, perturbāvī, perturbātum,* "to disturb, to confuse" > *imperturbātus, -a, -um,* "undisturbed, untroubled, serene" > LL *imperturbābilis*].

Impervius: the incantation which activates the Impervius Charm, used by Hermione to make Harry's glasses repel water, and by the Gryffindor Quidditch team captain, Angelina, to protect the team's glasses in bad weather [L *impervius, -a, -um,* "unable to pass through, impassible"].

Inferius (pl. Inferi): corpses bewitched to do the bidding of a witch or wizard [L *inferī, -ōrum,* "the dead, inhabitants of the Underworld"]. The Inferi were a fixture in the ancient Roman world. They included all who inhabited the Underworld, both deceased humans and gods of the Underworld or "Orcus" as the Romans called Hades (OLD 896). The Inferi included the Manes or Di Manes (the spirits of the dead, or the home of the dead, or corpses), and the Di(vi) Parentum (ghosts of ancestors). The Underworld deities were honored by sacrifices in order to appease them because they were malevolent beings who could bring misfortune or disease to the living. Curse tablets or binding spells (*defixiones*) often included an appeal to the gods Pluto or the Manes [Greek *defixiones* often addressed Hades, Hermes, Gaia, Hecate, Kore, Persephone and the Furies].[4]

Rowling has toned down her Inferi. They are not gods, or post-mortem beings who can work mischief on their own, as the ancient Inferi. Hers are zombies, the dead who are animated by magic curses performed on them as puppets. She could, however, have simply called them "the Dead." But that would not summon up the millennia-old imagery or mystery of the forces which the Romans called "Inferi."

Mandrake/Mandragora: a poisonous, narcotic herb used as a medicine to induce sleep, having a large, human-shaped root reputed to give a deadly squeal when uprooted, used to restore people from the effects of harmful spells, such as the petrified victims of the basilisk [Gk *mandragoras, -ou,* "mandrake, belladonna" > L *mandragoras, -ae,* "the mandrake plant"].

Manticore: a mythological monster with the head of a man, body of a lion, and scorpion's tail [Gk *mantichōras, -ou,* "man-eater, tiger"> L *mantichora, -ae*].

Nimbus: model name of a flying broomstick, the Nimbus Two Thousand, which Harry receives as a gift from Minerva McGonagall to help him with Quidditch, a broom named for its location of use, the clouds [L *nimbus, -ī,* "cloud"].

Nox: the incantation which puts out the light being emitted from a wand which has been activated by a Lumos Charm, meaning "night" [Gk *nux, nuktos* > L *nox, noctis,* "night"].

Obscuro: the incantation which Hermione uses to blindfold the portrait of Phineas Nigellus, preventing him from spying on her, meaning "I conceal" [L *obscūrō, obscūrāre, obscūrāvī, obscūrātum,* "to obscure, make dark, eclipse"].

Oppugno: the incantation which activates an Attacking Curse. Hermione, in a jealous rage, uses it to cause canaries to attack Ron, pecking and clawing at all accessible parts of his body, meaning "I attack, strike" [L *oppugnō, oppugnāre, oppugnāvī, oppugnātum,* "I fight against, attack, assault"].

Patronus: a conjured protection for a witch or wizard, which takes the form of someone or something very dear to the individual as the projection of one's positive feelings and emotions. The form of the Patronus is different for each person since it is the projection of the individual's hopes. This term is particularly meaningful, as Harry's Patronus, a gleaming stag, is his protective father [Gk *patēr, patros* > L *pater, patris,* "father" > *patrōnus, -ī,* "protector, defender, patron"].

Portus: the incantation which transforms an ordinary object into a Portkey, a device used to initiate magical transportation from one place to another. Portkeys may be an old boot, an old newspaper, empty drink cans, a deflated football, an old kettle, a small hairbrush, or the broken head of a golden statue of a wizard [L *portus, -ūs,* "door, refuge, port, means of escape"].

Protego: the incantation which activates a Shield Charm, which Harry uses to defend himself from Snape's Legilimens incantation, and to protect himself and the prophecy during battle in the Department of Mysteries, meaning "I shield" [L *protegō, prōtegere, prōtexī, prōtectum,* "to cover over, shield, protect, ward off"].

Quid agis?: a password required by the Fat Lady to allow admittance to the Gryffindor common room, meaning, "What are you doing?" [L *quis, quid,* "what?" + *agō, agere, ēgī, āctum,* "to do, drive, act"].

Quietus: the incantation which turns off the Sonorus Charm and makes the speaker's voice sound normal instead of its being greatly amplified [L *quies, quiētis,* "rest, quiet" > ME *quietus,* "anything that serves to quiet, curb or end an activity" (Neufeldt 103)].

Reparo: the incantation which activates a Repairing Charm. With this charm, one can fix a broken window, repair a broken bowl, restore a jar, repair a broken cup, mend a pot, affix covers to a book, fix broken scales, or attach a side car firmly to a motorcycle, meaning, "I restore" [L *reparō, reparāre, reparāvī, reparātum,* "to recover, renew, restore"].

Sonorus: the incantation which activates the Sonorus Charm, magnifying a speaker's voice as if it were broadcast over a loud-speaker, with which Ludo Bagman amplifies his voice as announcer at the Quidditch World Cup [L *sonōrus, -a, -um,* "loud, noisy, resounding"].

Tergeo: the incantation which activates a Cleansing Spell, with which Hermione removes blood from Harry's face, and with which Ron cleans the oven grease from his handkerchief which he offers to Hermione when she weeps in sadness, and with which Harry removes the dust from old photographs in Bathilda Bagshot's home, meaning "I clean" [L *tergeō, tergēre, tersī, tersum,* "to rub off, wipe dry, clean"].

Personal Names

We have seen that some of Rowling's characters have genuine classical names or names based on real Latin or Greek foundations (e.g., Minerva, Lucius, Draco, Rubeus, Albus, Severus, Ambrosius). Many names which we encounter in these novels, however, are contrived or Anglicized inventions based on some Latin (or Greek) element or component (e.g., Verity, from the Latin adjective *vēritās, -ātis,* "truth"). The names in the following list are not formal and true classical names, but are formed from Rowling's playful and creative use of classical roots, sometimes by making proper personal names from Latin words which are not names all, e.g. "Filius" Flitwick and "Ignotus" Peverell.

Algie Longbottom: Neville's great-uncle who gives him the Mimbulus mimbletonia as a birthday gift. His name appears to be a playful use of the word "algae," which designates simple plant organisms that lack root, stems or leaves, like green scum in stagnant water [L *alga, -ae,* "seaweed"].

Apolline Delacour: Fleur Delacour's mother [Gk *Apollōn,* "Apollo" > L *Apollineus* (from *Apollo* + *-eus,* adjectival suffix), "of or relating to Apollo or his worship"]. As Apollo is the god of music, youth, and beauty, she must be a striking woman.

Araminta Meliflua: a distant cousin of Sirius Black's mother, known for legalizing Muggle-hunting. Her personal name looks like a playful mixture of forms related to Greek and Latin sources. "Araminta" sounds like dog

Latin; but if there are classical bases behind the word, there has been a lot of tinkering with them. The word defies definition. Her last name may be a bit less elusive, perhaps denoting something such as "she who drips with sweetness" [L *mel, mellis,* "honey, sweetness" + *fluō, fluere, fluxī, fluxum,* "to flow, to drip,"].

Arcus: a wizard mentioned in the history of the ownership of the Elder Wand [L *arcus, arcūs,* "an arch, bow," the bow of the constellation Sagittarius; one of the five zones of the ancient sky].

Armando Dippet: Headmaster of Hogwarts School of Witchcraft and Wizardry fifty years before Harry Potter's time, during Tom Riddle's student days at Hogwarts [L *armō, armāre, armāvī, armātum,* "to arm for battle"; *armandus,* "someone who must go to war"].

Arsenius Jigger: author of the book *Magical Drafts and Potions* [playful use of Gk *arsenikon,* "yellow pigment" > L *arsenicum,* "yellow arsenic," a poisonous chemical element]. With a name which calls to mind the toxic side of the potions business, Arsenius might seem to be too much enamored with the harsher effects of his concoctions.

Avery: a Death Eater who, in vain, begs for forgiveness from Voldemort, swearing his submission to the Dark Lord when, in fact, he had escaped punishment as a Death Eater by claiming he was put under the Imperius Curse by Voldemort, and was forced to obey him unwillingly [L *ad-,* "to" + *vērus, -a, -um,* "true" > English "aver," "to claim to be true"]. His name, signifying truth, is ironic, as he is a self-serving liar.

Bellatrix Lestrange: Sirius Black's cousin, sister of Narcissa Malfoy and Andromeda Tonks [L *bellum, -ī,* "war" > *bellātrīx, bellātrīcis,* "warlike, (she who) wages war"]. She appears to delight in battle, killing, and death more than all the other Death Eaters. Her name fits her behavior well.

Bilius: uncle of the Weasley children; also, Ron's middle name [L *bīlis, -is,* "bile, anger" > *bīliōsus, -a, -um,* "full of bile" > English "bilious," "having bile, liver ailment or ill-temper"]. Of course, this may simply be a play on the English word, "bilious," which means the quality of being ill-natured, peevish, or suffering from a liver ailment (Mish 121). If uncle Bilius is anything like his name, he must be an unpleasant person to have at family gatherings. One wonders why Ron's parents would have loaded that name on his shoulders.

Celestina Warbeck: popular singing sorceress, whose songs are broadcast on the Wizarding radio [L *caelum, -ī,* "sky, heaven" > *caelistis, -e,* "heavenly, divine"]. She must have a heavenly voice.

Charity Burbage: Hogwarts teacher of Muggle Studies who is abducted by Death Eaters and killed by Voldemort [Gk *charis, charitos,* "grace, kindness" > L *cārus, -a, -um*, "dear, loved" > *cāritās, cāritātis*, "dearness, affection, love" > OFr *charite* > ME]. She is named appropriately, for she teaches and writes about Muggles in a charitable, accepting way. And her kindly character and name create the strongest contrast between herself and her cold-hearted killer.

Dolores Jane Umbridge: Senior Undersecretary to the Minister of Magic, who is installed as the High Inquisitioner over Hogwarts, bringing grief to the school [L *dolōr, -ōris*, "pain, grief"; *dolōrēs*, "sorrows, afflictions"; L *umbra, -ae*, "shade, shadow" > *umbrāticus, -a, -um*, "living (or done) in the shade." Her surname is a play on the English noun "umbrage," meaning "offense, suspicion"]. She is hated at Hogwarts by students, faculty, and staff alike (except for Argus Filch) for the grief and offense which she imposes on their lives.

Elladora Black: member of the Black family who initiates the practice of beheading House-Elves which are no longer efficient. "Ella" is a diminutive of Eleanor or Helen, and "dora" signifies gifts [Gk *dōra*, "gifts"]. If she is pretty, as her name would suggest, she has a personality disorder also. Her behavior contradicts either her name or her looks.

Errol: the Weasley's old, feeble messenger owl, who has become unreliable, sometimes collapsing during his flights [L *errō, errāre, errāvī, errātum*, "to go astray, wander, blunder" > *error, errōris*, "wandering about, going astray, mistake"].

Filius Flitwick: Professor of Charms at Hogwarts [L *fīlius, -ī*, "son"]. The professor is a little man. Perhaps the word "son" suggests to readers, subliminally, the diminutive appearance of the teacher who is, actually, a very skilled wizard. The alliteration of his name, "Filius Flitwick," also adds an element of charm to his characterization.

Florean Fortescue: owner and operator of the ice cream parlor in Diagon Alley [L *flōreō, flōrēre, flōruī*, "to blossom, be covered with flowers or ornaments" > *flōreus, -a. -um*, "flowery" + *fortescō, fortescere*, "to become strong or brave"].

Ignotus Peverell: original owner of the Cloak of Invisibility [L *īgnōtus, -a, -um*, "of low birth, unknown, ignorant"]. It is ironic that one of the three famous brothers who were the original owners of the Deathly Hallows is named "unknown," or characterized as common or dull. Perhaps there is a crafty association here between his ability to be unseen under his cloak and his name, which connotes his being unknown.

Inigo Imago: author of *The Dream Oracle* [L *inigō, inigere, inēgī, ināctum*, "I drive, I incite" + *imāgō, imāginis*, "apparition, vision"]. One wonders if an expert on dreams and their meaning who has such a name as this tends to make more out of the dreams than is warranted. Or, perhaps, as Professor Trelawney, he manufactures his oracles as the need arises.

Libatius Borage: author of *Advanced Potion-Making* [L *lībō, lībāre, lībāvī, lībātum,* "to taste, pour, make a libation" > *lībātiō, lībātiōnis,* "drink offering, libation"]. Does his name give us a hint that he enjoys drinking the potions he makes?

Ludo Bagman: once a Beater for the Wimbourne Wasps, Head of the Magical Games and Sports Department in the Ministry of Magic, one of the judges in the Triwizard Tournament [L *lūdus, -ī,* "play, game, joke"]. As a former athlete and elected official of games who appears to have an addiction to gambling and betting with unreal money, perhaps his personal name signals his character as a joke of person. His last name is as appropriate for him as his first. The term "bagman" is used for someone who pays out or collects money in illegal gambling activities.

Marvolo: Tom Riddle's middle name, the name of his maternal grandfather, Marvolo Gaunt [perhaps from L *mīror, mīrārī, mīrātus sum,* "to be surprised, to hold in awe" > *mīrābilis, -e,* "marvelous" > LL *mirabilia,* "marvels" > AFr *merveille,* "wonder, marvel, prodigy" > ME *mervel* > marvel (Mish 762)]. If there is anything surprising or "marvelous" about the father of Morfin and Merope Gaunt, it is his absurd preoccupation with his family's pure blood line ... the most recent representatives of which are quite degenerate and ignoble. To name the man "Marvolo," is another example of Rowling's humor and use of irony. Tom Riddle did accomplish extraordinary things which were something special to behold. Or, as Ollivander said of him, he "did great things—terrible, yes, but great" (*SS* 85).

Maxime, Madam Olympe: Headmistress of Beauxbatons Academy [Gk *Olympus, -ou,* "Mount Olympus" > *Olympias, -ados,* "a dweller on Olympus, a goddess"; L *maximus, -a, -um,* "greatest, largest"; *maximē,* "to the highest degree, most of all"]. Her name as well as her stature suggest that she is head and shoulders above other women and particularly superior to her suitor, Hagrid.

Miranda Goshawk: author of *The Standard Book of Spells* [L *mīror, mīrārī, mīrātum,* "to admire, to wonder at"; *mīranda,* "she who is to be admired, wonderful"]. It is quite befitting that a reliable source of instruction on spells be a woman at whom readers should be amazed.

Morfin Gaunt: Son of Marvolo Gaunt and brother of Merope Gaunt who exhibits characteristics of inbreeding and genetic degeneration. While holding to a delusion of his family's having an aristocratic pedigree reaching far back in the line of pure-bloods, he and his relatives are totally dysfunctional. His name appears to be a contrived name, perhaps a play on the name of the god Morpheus [Gk *Morpheus* < *morphē*, "shape"], the god of the shapes which he causes to come to people in dreams (LSJ 1141). The drug "morphine" derives from the name of the god because of the narcotic and dulling effect it has. Ironically, the images (or shapes) that Morfin brings to the story are quite pathetic. And if his name is supposed to make us think of someone who has lost his mental sharpness, it is a success, for he is certainly dull and doped-up. He is so thoroughly stunned and memory-altered by Tom Riddle that he confesses to murders which he did not commit, and he is sentenced to Azkaban for three years as the result.

Narcissa Black Malfoy: sister of Bellatrix Lestrange and Andromeda Tonks, mother of Draco and wife of Lucius Malfoy [Gk *narkissos*, the narcissus flower > L feminine form of *Narcissus, -ī*, the name of the young man who comes to his ruin by becoming fixated on his own image]. The arrogance and inordinate self-esteem of the Malfoys is heightened by Ms. Malfoy's personal name, which reminds everyone that she is a person of supreme self-interest.

Nigellus (Phineas Nigellus Black): former Headmaster of Hogwarts, a Slytherin devotee, and crotchety old member of the Black family. He appears only as a personified portrait. Both of his personal names (Phineas and Nigellus) mean "black" [L *nigellus, -a, -um*, "black, dark"].

Nymphadora (Tonks): daughter of Andromeda and Ted Tonks, member of the Advance Guard and the Order of the Phoenix [Gk *nympha*, "nymph, spirit, a lesser goddess" + *dōra*, "gifts"]. A beautiful and talented woman such as she is deserves to have such an endearing name.

Olympe, Maxime: see "Maxime, Madam Olympe."

Perenelle Flamel: Nicolas Flamel's wife. As her husband has lived for over 665 years and she is seven years younger than he, she is extremely aged herself, and appropriately named for a woman of virtually unending life [L *perennis, -e*, "(ever)lasting"].

Pius Thicknesse: Head of the Department of Magical Law Enforcement for the Ministry of Magic [L *pius, -a, -um*, "dutiful, religious"]. As an officer whose duty is the enforcement of the law, his name seems to indicate that he lives up to his responsibility.

Phyllida Spore: author of *One Thousand Magical Herbs and Fungi* [Gk *phyllas, phyllados*, "bed of leaves" + *speirein*, "to sow" > *spora*, "sowing of seed"]. Who but an expert on a thousand botanical items would have a name suggesting seedy and leafy imagery?

Purge and Dowse: the Muggle store which serves as a front, hiding St. Mungo's Hospital for Magical Maladies and Injuries [L *pūrgō, pūrgāre, pūrgāvī, pūrgātum*, "to cleanse"]. The name of the building is playfully suggestive of therapeutics. "To purge" is to evacuate the bowels or cleanse one of something defiling. And "to dowse" (a variant spelling of "douse") is to flood with water or to extinguish something, as to cleanse or treat an inflammation.

Quentin Trimble: author of the textbook *The Dark Forces: A Guide to Self-Protection.* His surname is a play on the verb "tremble" [L *tremō, tremere, tremuī,* "to quiver, tremble at something" > ML *tremulāre* > AFr *trembler* > ME]. Who but a man named "Quentin Trimble" would compose a work on the terrifying subject of the Dark Arts?

Sanguini: the tall vampire friend of Eldred Worple (who is a former student of Horace Slughorn's and author of a book on vampires) [L *sanguis, sanguīnis,* "blood, bloodshed" > *sanguineus, -a, -um,* "stained with blood, blood-thirsty"]. His name tells us what he is all about.

Tenebrus: Hagrid's favorite thestral, the first one to be born to his herd. He is obviously very dark in color [L *tenebrae, -ārum,* "complete absence of light, darkness"; *tenebrōsus, -a, -um,* "dark, darkness of death"].

(Professor) Vector: Professor of Arithmancy at Hogwarts [L *vector, -ōris,* "carrier," a term used in mathematics for a course or compass direction].

Verity: female employee in Fred and George's joke shop, Weasleys' Wizard Wheezes [L *vēritas, -tātis,* "truth, honesty"]. It is humorous that in a store which celebrates trickery, deception, wild joking, and sportive embarrassment, the Weasley boys hire a straight-ahead woman with a name which was common among Puritan women.

Viktor Krum: famous Quidditch player for the Bulgarian team in the Quidditch World Cup and Triwizard Tournament champion representing Durmstrang Academy [L *victor, victōris,* "conqueror"]. His name announces his prominence.

Vincent Crabbe: the thuggish companion of Draco Malfoy [L *vincō, vincere, vīcī, victum,* "to conquer, overcome, subdue"; *vincēns, vincentis,* "overcoming, conquering, defeating"]. Irony appears often in the naming of the characters, as here, designating this loser as a winner.

Vindictus Viridian: author of *Curses and Countercurses* [L *vindicō, vindicāre, vindicāvī, vindicātus,* "to take vengeance, punish"; *vindictus,* "avenged (or "vengeance," if from the proper form, *vindicta, -ae*) + *viridis, -e,* "green or bluish-green"]. The name suggests a person who is envious and budding with skills at getting even.

Xenophilius Lovegood: father of Luna Lovegood and eccentric editor of *The Quibbler,* whose passionate beliefs and theories seem bizarre to most people [Gk *xenos,* "strange, alien," + *philia,* "fondness for" > ModL *xenophilia,* "fondness for people or things alien or strange"].

Classical Language Playfully Transformed for Magical Applications

At times, Rowling uses a great degree of freedom and inventiveness with language. The following list gives terms which appear to rely on Latin and Greek bases. Even the English elements of those terms are so liberally revised that at times one can only guess at the actual source of Rowling's creations, and at a possible meaning of the final forms. It appears that her aim is not to create a new and clearly definable set of terms, but to tease the reader and to make the story interesting.

Acromantula: gigantic, flesh-eating spiders [playful use of Gk *akros*, "highest, extreme" + *mantis*, "seer, prophet"; perhaps a combination of "(praying) mantis" and "tarantula" have contributed to this term].

Aguamenti Charm: a water-producing charm which HH&R are required to practice for Professor Flitwick's Charms class and which Harry uses in an attempt to satisfy the unquenchable thirst of Dumbledore [Spanish *agua*, "water" < L *aqua, -ae* + suffix *-mentum, -ī* which transforms nouns in order to denote neuter, non-abstract objects (OLD 1097, 1101)].

Alohomora: the incantation used to open locked doors or windows [perhaps Hawaiian *aloha*, "good-bye" + L *mora, -ae*, "obstruction, hindrance, delay" meaning something roughly equivalent to "farewell, obstruction"].

Amortentia: the most powerful love potion in the world [L *amor, -ōris*, "love, affection" + *potentia, -ae*, "power, might, force"].

Animagi: magical persons who change themselves into an animal form at will [Gk *magos* > L *magus, -ī*, a Persian visionary, a magician or sorcerer + perhaps L *animal, -ālis*, "animal"].

Aparecium: a Revealing incantation which Hermione uses to make a diary disclose any secrets it may be hiding [perhaps free use of L base *aperiō, aperīre, aperuī, apertum*, "to open up, disclose" + *-ium*, neuter form of a suffix].

Apparating/Apparition: appearing in the magical process of Apparition and Disapparition (disappearing from one place and reappearing almost instantly in another place) [L *appāreo, appārēre, appāruī, appāritum*, "to come into sight, to appear" > *appāritiō, -ōnis*, "service, provision"].

Aquavirius maggots: a type of grubs which Luna Lovegood and her father believe the Ministry of Magic to be breeding. She believes that some white items floating in a tank of green water in the Department of Mysteries are such larvae, but they turn out to be brains [L *aqua, -ae*, "water," + *vīrus, -ī*, "poisonous, foul-smelling slime"].

Auror: a person whose job it is to catch Dark Wizards [L possibly play on *augur, auguris,* "prophet, seer, or interpreter of omens"]. The base of the word could be one of a number of things derived from several Latin words: *aura, -ae,* "breeze, scent" (as if an Auror can detect Dark Wizards by scent); *aurōra, -ae,* "dawn, daybreak" (as if the Auror shines the light on Dark Wizards); *auris, -is,* "ear" (as if to the Auror detects Dark Wizards by what one hears); or *aurum, -ī,* "gold, made of gold" (as if the Auror is very valuable).

Cartomancy: divination by examining cards, practiced by Professor Trelawney [Gk *chartēs,* "sheet of paper, papyrus" > L *charta, -ae,* "sheet of papyrus" + Gk *manteia,* "means of prophecy"].

Colloportus (Charm): the charm used to seal a door shut [L *colligō, colligāre, colligāvī, colligātum,* "to bind, fasten, fetter, hinder" + *portus, -ūs,* "harbor, door, means of escape"].

Confundus (Charm): a charm which confuses its victims. It is activated by the incantation, "Confundo" [L *confundō, confundere, confūdī, confūsum,* "to disorder, to perplex, mix together"]. If Rowling had wanted simply to use a ready-made word here, the Latin word *cōnfūsus,* "jumbled together" would have been handy.

Cruciatus (Curse): one of the three Unforgivable Curses which inflicts intolerable pain on the victim, used at times to control someone, but which can have irreversible effects, meaning, "tormented" [L *cruciō, cruciāre, cruciāvī, cruciātum,* "to torture"; *cruciātus, -a. -um,* "tormented, afflicted"].

Deflagration (Deluxe): a set of fireworks sold by the Weasley twins at their joke shop, charmed so as to burn with intense heat and glowing light [L *dēflagrō, dēflagrāre, dēflagrāvī, dēflagrātum,* "to consume by fire, burn down" > *dēflāgrātio, -ōnis,* "burning up"].

Deletrius: an incantation which erases an image of a charm revealed by the Prior Incantato charm [perhaps affected by Gk *dēlētērios, -on,* "noxious, injurious"; the concept appears to be more similar to L *dēleō, dēlēre, dēlēvī, dēlētum,* "to destroy, to terminate"].

Deluminator: the Put-Outer which Dumbledore uses to extinguish and then re-light the street lamps on Privet Drive and Mad-Eye Moody uses to darken the street when the Advance Guard escorts Harry to Number Twelve Grimmauld Place. It can also transmit Hermione's voice and transport Ron to rejoin Hermione and Harry [made up word from L elements *dē-,* prefix denoting the reversal of a process + *lūmen, lūminis,* "light, lamp, day (light)" > *lūminō, -āre, -āvī, -ātum* "to light up" + *-tor,* suffix designating something which does or a person who does something].

Dementor: a ghastly being who thrives on sucking all the joy from a person and, by a fatal process called the "Dementor's Kiss," extracting the soul, leaving the victim alive but soulless; a guard at Azkaban prison [L *dēmens, -entis*, "out of one's mind" > *dēmentia, -ae*, "derangement, insanity" + *-tor, -tōris*, a masculine suffix which, added to a verb stem, denotes an agent (OLD 1949); here, one who drives people out of their minds].

Densaugeo: the incantation which Draco Malfoy uses to make Hermione's front teeth enlarge and lengthen [Gk *odous, -ontis*, "tooth" > L *dēns, dentis*, "tooth" + *augeō, augēre, auxī, auctum*, "to increase, enlarge"].

Disapparating/Disapparition: disappearing in the magical process of Apparition and Disapparition [L *appāreo, appārēre, appāruī, appāritum*, "to come into sight, to appear" > *appāritiō, -ōnis*, "service, provision" + *dis-* a prefix signifying the reversal of a process].

Dissendium: the incantation which opens the old one-eyed crone's hump to admit Harry into the secret passageway from Hogwarts to the cellar of Honeydukes in Hogsmeade [L *dissentiō, dissentīre, dissensī, dissensum*, "to disagree, be unlike" > *dissensiō, -ōnis*, "disagreement" + *-ium*, neuter form of adjectival suffix; just a guess at the relation between the incantation and Latin].

Disillusionment (Charm): the charm which makes someone invisible or tricks potential viewers by the masquerading deception of blending in with a background [L prefix *dis-*, (the intensification of something) + *illūsiō, -ōnis*, "an illusion or deceit" < *illūdō, illūdere, illūsī, illūsum*, "to trick, say the opposite of what is meant; tricked"], meaning something like "a thorough deception."

Ennervate: the incantation which releases a victim from a Stunning Spell, used to revive Winky, Viktor Krum, and Barty Crouch, Jr. [L *ēnervō, ēnervāre, ēnervāvī, ēnervātum*, "to weaken, take nerve or strength from someone,"]. This term can be confusing. The incantation intends to renew one's strength, but the word means to take one's strength away. Steve Vander Ark notes that in corrections which were made to the novels in 2004, the word was changed to "Rennervate," to make it clear that the incantation restored nerve and did not weaken the person to whom the incantation was spoken (104).

Episkey: the incantation which activates a Healing Spell with which Tonks heals Harry's broken nose and Harry heals Demelza Robins' injured mouth [Gk *episkeuazein*, "to restore, repair"].

Erecto: the incantation which Hermione uses to make the materials of a tent disentangle and set themselves up properly [playful use of L *ērigō, ērigere, ērexī, ērectum*, "to raise up, set up; set up, raised"]. Rowling makes this appear to be a present tense verb, by adding the *-ō* ending, as if to make the incantation say, "I erect" or "I set up."

Expelliarmus: the frequently used incantation which activates the Disarming Charm. With it Professor Snape disarms Professor Lockhart; Harry makes the mysterious diary fly out of the clutches of Draco Malfoy and removes Professor Lockhart's wand from his hands in time to prevent his casting a memory charm; Sirius and Lupin disarm Harry and Hermione; Harry injures an acromantula and attempts to disarm Voldemort. It is such an essential element in magical craft that the students of "Dumbledore's Army" practice this skill during their first instructional meeting. The incantation means something like "we remove (your) arms" [Rowling playfully makes an artificial Latin verb out of the true Latin verb *expellō, expellere, expulī, expulsum,* "to banish, drive away," + the object being removed, "arms," from the Latin noun *arma, -ōrum,* "weapons, arms, defense" + perhaps the first person plural suffix *-mus,* "we"].

Furnunculus: the incantation which Harry uses to make boils break out on the faces of Goyle and Crabbe [play on L *fūr, fūris,* "thief" + *-unculus, -a, -um,* a diminutive suffix > *fūrunculus,* "petty thief, sucker, furuncle (boil, tumor"); perhaps only a play on the English word "furunculus," a boil].

Geminio: the incantation which activates the Gemino Spell, which creates a double of something or which doubles the power of another spell, meaning, "I double, repeat" [playful use of L *geminō, gemināre, gemināvī, gemīnātum,* "to double, repeat"].

Gernumbli gardensi (Gnomes): pesky garden dwarves, twelve inches or less in height, with an over-sized head and bony feet (Scamander 19), which may possess special magical abilities. Xenophilius Lovegood exhibits his knowledge of the creatures by calling them by this "scientific" name, "Gernumbli gardensi." This is one of the freest examples of "cod Latin" in the novels. There is no ancient basis for this terminology, only the imitative sound of modern Latin scientific terminology. The word "gnome" derives from the notion of Paracelsus, a Swisss physician and alchemist of the fifteenth to sixteenth centuries, that gnomes possess a unique kind of knowledge, wisdom or insight [Gk *gignōskein,* "to know" > *gnōmē,* "means of knowing, intelligence, thought, judgment" > L *gnōmē,* "maxim, wise saying, aphorism" > Mod L *gnomus* > Fr (Neufeldt 576–77, 978)].

Heliopaths: spirits of fire, tall and flaming, which scorch the ground wherever they go, according to Luna Lovegood [Gk *hēlios,* "sun" + *pathos, pathē,* which has a very broad range of meanings, including "that which happens," "misfortune/calamity," "suffering, disease," e.g.; perhaps < *pathein, paschein,* "to suffer, feel"].

Heptomology: divination by means of study of the mystical number seven [Gk *hepta,* "seven" + *logos,* "reason" > ModL *-logia,* "the science of"].

Hippogriff: magical offspring of horses and griffins who inhabit the Forbidden Forest [Gk *hippos, -ou,* "horse" + *grypos,* "hooked, curved, rounded" > *grips,* "griffin" > L *grips* (or *gryps, gryphis*), "griffin"] (LSJ 61; OLD 778; Stelten 111)].

Hocus-pocus: gibberish incantation used as a term for "nonsense," a fake magical phrase which derives from the medieval popularization of the Latin words of the mass, *hoc est corpus meum,* "this is (my) body." When the sentence was pronounced, the wafer was said to transform into the actual body of Christ (not in its appearance, but in its essence). The public, not speaking Latin, garbled it into "hocus pocus" because it was the magical phrase which effected the transformation.

Homenum Revelio: the incantation which Hermione uses to detect if there is anyone present in the house at Number Twelve Grimmauld Place and a Death Eater uses to certify that there is someone upstairs at the home of Xenophilius Lovegood, meaning something like, "I reveal the man" [L *homō, hominis,* "person, man"; *hominem,* the direct object form of the word + playful use of *revēlō, revēlāre revēlāvī, revēlātum,* "to uncover, to unveil"].

Homorphous (Charm): a charm which Gilderoy Lockhart claims to have used to transform a werewolf permanently back into his human nature [L *homō, hominis,* "person, man" + Gk *morphē,* "shape" + L suffix *-ōsus, -a, -um,* usually meaning "rich in, full of"].

Horcrux: Horace Slughorn tells Tom Riddle that a magical person can split his or her soul and hide part of it in an object other than the body; then if the body should die, part of the person lives on. The way to split the soul is by committing the greatest evil, murder, and then by a spell encasing the torn away part into the Horcrux [invented combination of L *horreō, -ēre, -uī,* "to have a dreadful quality," "to regard with awe or dread" + *crux, crucis,* "a cross used for death by crucifixion," "anything which causes grief or annoyance, a plague, torment, etc." (OLD 463, 804)]. Granger comments on the components of the word and its application of Rowling's creation in the narrative: "rather than finding the way to immortality in the life-saving sacrifice of Christ on the Cross, the Horcrux accomplishes the task through murder" (*How Harry Cast His Spell,* 2008, 185).

Imperius (Curse): one of the three Unforgivable Curses. It gives one total control over a victim [L *imperō, imperāre, imperāvī, imperātum,* "to command" > *imperium, -ī,* "command, authority" > *imperiōsus, -a, um,* "far-ruling, powerful" + possibly the adjective suffix, *-us, -a, -um*; perhaps only a play on the English adjective "imperious," which means "commanding, domineering"].

Inanimatus Conjurus: a spell assigned by Professor McGonagall for homework, of which only a brief mention is made [L *in*-, "not" + *anima, -ae*, "soul, vital principle" > *animō, animāre, animāvī, animātus*, "to give life; living, quickened, spirited" + *coniūrō, coniūrāre, coniūrāvī, coniūrātum*, "to swear together" (from *com*-, "with" + *iūrō, iūrāre, iūrāvī, iūrātum*, "to swear") > OF *conjurer* > ME *conjuren*, "to charge someone solemnly to do or say something]. This spell must have to do with conjuring (summoning up) the dead, those who are "inanimate."

Incendio: the incantation which Mr. Weasley uses to start a fire in the fireplace and a Death Eater employs to set Hagrid's house on fire, meaning "I kindle a fire" [playful use of L *incendō, incindere, incendī, incensum*, "to kindle, set fire to"].

Incarcerous: the incantation which casts an imprisoning spell, with which Dolores Umbridge shoots ropes from her wand, binding the centaur Magorian, and which Harry employs in an attempt to stop Inferi [ML *in*-, "in" + *carcer, carceris*, "jail, prison" > *incarcerō, incarcerāre, incarcerāvī, incarcerātum*, "to imprison, put in jail" + suffix *-ōsus, -a, -um*, usually meaning "rich in, full of"; perhaps simply a Latinizing of the English word "incarcerate," "to put in prison"].

Legilimens, -ency: the ability to extract feelings and memories from another person's mind. This activity is countered by the practice of Occlumens [L *legō, legere, lēgī, lectum*, "to read" + *mēns, mentis*, "mind, seat of intellectual activity" + suffix *-ia, -iae*, which usually forms abstract nouns from adjectives].

Levicorpus: the incantation which causes the victim to hang upside down in midair, used by Harry on Ron and by James Potter on Severus Snape during their school days, meaning something such as "light body" [L *levis, -e*, "light" + *corpus, corporis*, "body"].

Liberacorpus: the incantation which activates the counter-jinx to the Levicorpus spell, meaning something like "free the body" [L *līberō, līberāre, līberāvī, līberātum*, "to set free" > *līberā*, (imperative) "(you) set free" + *corpus, corporis*, "body"].

Locomotor Mortis: the incantation which activates the Leg-Locker Curse, causing the victims to have no more mobility than if they were dead, which Sirius casts on Snape, making him fall over [L *locus, -ī*, "place" + *mōtus, mōtūs* "motion" + *-tor, -tōris*, a masculine suffix which, added to a verb stem, denotes an agent (OLD 1949); here, something which moves or drives; English "locomotor," has to do with moving or the power to move from place to place + *mors, mortis*, "death"].

Locomotor Trunk: an incantation which helps to move items (such as a trunk) [see "Locomotor Mortis"].

Lumos: an incantation which causes a wand to produce a light at its end, somewhat like a flashlight or lantern [L *lūmen, lūminis,* "light" or *lūminō-sus, -a, um,* "full of light"; or related to It *lume,* "light," or *luminoso,* "bright, luminous"].

Metamorphmagus: a wizard or witch who is born with the ability to change appearance at will, as Nymphadora Tonks [Gk *metamorphōsis,* "transformation" < *meta-,* a preposition which in compound indicates change of condition + *morphē,* "shape, form" + Gk *magos* > L *magus, -ī,* "a Persian astrologer, diviner, magician or sorcerer"].

Meteolojinx Recanto: an incantation which changes the weather. When it rains in Yaxley's office at the Ministry, and Mr. Weasley is expected to fix the problem, Ron (incognito as Reg Cattermole) asks him if he has tried this effective spell [Gk *meteōros,* "in mid-air, in the heavens" + *logos, -ou,* "reason" > ModL-*logia,* "the science of" + English "jinx"+ L *recantō, recan-tāre, recantāvī, recantātum,* "to remove by a spell, charm away" (OLD 1578)].[5]

Mimbulus mimbletonia: Neville's cactus-like plant from Assyria which his great-uncle Algie gave him for his birthday, and which spurts foul-smelling Stinksap from its boils when it is annoyed. The only thing Latin about the name of this plant is its playful simulation of scientific Latin terminology.

Mobiliarbus: the incantation which Hermione uses to move a Christmas tree in front of a table, for concealment [L *mōbilis, -e,* "movable" + *arbōs* (OL form of *arbor, -oris*), "tree"].

Mobilicorpus: the incantation which allows one to move a body easily, with which Professor Lupin transports Snape's body out of the Shrieking Shack, as if Snape were a puppet on strings [L *mobilis, -e,* "movable" + *corpus, corporis,* "body"].

Morsmordre: the incantation which conjures up the Dark Mark summoning all of Voldemort's followers, who are called "Death Eaters" [L *mors, mortis,* "death" + *mordeō, mordēre, memordī, morsum,* "to bite, eat into" > Fr *mor-dre,* "to bite"].

Muffliato: the incantation which activates an anti-eavesdropping spell by causing a buzzing in the ears of potential eavesdroppers, allowing the one casting the spell to speak but not be understood by others nearby [perhaps English "to muffle," + a Latinized third person future imperative *-to,* used in legal contexts, recipes, etc.), giving the sense of "let it be muffled" or "(you) be muffled"].

Obliviate: the incantation which activates a Memory Charm with which Professor Lockhart attempts to make Harry and Ron forget what they have realized about his being a fraud, probably meaning, "(you) forget" [L *oblīvīscor, oblīvīscī, oblītus sum,* "to forget" > *oblīviō, -ōnis,* forgetfulness,"

+ ME -*ate*, "to cause, to be come, to produce," following a Latin second person plural imperative ending of a first conjugation verb, "you," making the English words "oblivious" or "oblivion" into a Latin-sounding verb. The correct Latin imperative would be *oblīvīsciminī*].

Obliviators: people in the Office of Misinformation whose job it is to modify the memories of Muggles who have seen things about the magical world which they should not see and should not communicate to others ["Obliviate" + L -*tor, -tōris*, a masculine suffix which, added to a verb stem, denotes an agent (OLD 1949); here, it designates those who cause others to forget something].

(Dr. Ubbly's) Oblivious Unction: a potion which Madam Pomfrey uses on Ron's arms during his recuperation from the battle at the Department of Mysteries. The potion, however, appears not to be a curative for the brain-tentacle wounds on his arms so much as a healing agent for what he remembers from the battle. "Oblivious" means "forgetful or unmindful" [L *oblīvīscī*, "to forget" > *oblīviō*, "forgetfulness" > *oblīviōsus*, "forgetful" > ME *oblivious*, "forgetful"; English "unction," meaning "ointment" or "something soothing"; L *unguō, unguere, unxī, unctum*, "to anoint" > *unctiō, unctiōnis*, "anointing, smearing"]. The name seems to indicate that the soothing potion is for mental wounds. The assonance or repetition of the vowel sounds in this potion (U̲b-O̲b-iu̲s-U̲n-io̲n) exemplifies Rowling's playing with similar sounds for fun.

Occlumency, Occlumens: the ability to close off one's mind and thoughts from anyone who might be attempting to gain access to them by Legilimens [L *occlūdō, occlūdere, occlūsī, occlūsum*, "to preclude access to by locking up, shutting up, closing" + *mēns, mentis* "mind, the seat of intellectual activity" + -y from the suffix -*ia, -iae*, which usually forms abstract nouns from adjectives]. Harry is instructed in this art by Professor Snape at the direction of Dumbledore.

Omnioculars: a magical viewing apparatus, like binoculars, but instead of designating the device by the number of eyepieces (bi-), the term designates what can be seen—everything [L *omnis, -e*, "every, all" + *oculus, -ī*, "eye"; perhaps based on the word "binoculars"].

Orchideous: the incantation which makes flowers sprout from a wand, as Mr. Ollivander experiences with Fleur Delacour's wand [Gk *orchis*, "testicle," also name of a plant with roots shaped like testicles > L *orchis*, a name for a kind of orchid, which has testicle-shaped roots > ModL *Orchideae*, coined by Linnaeus in 1751, mistaking *orchid-* as the stem which was *orchis-* + L suffix -*us* > -*ous* or -*ōsus*, meaning something characterized by (as here, flowers) (Neufeldt 952)].

Pensieve: a stone basin containing a swirling liquid used for containing memories [L *pendō, pendere, pependī, pēnsum*, "to weigh, consider, evaluate" > *pensō, pensāre, pensāvī, pensātum*, "to weigh in mind, ponder" > Fr *penser*, "to think, reflect" > Fr *pensif, -ive*, "thoughtful, pensive"].

Petrificus Totalus: the incantation which activates the Full Body-Bind spell, with which Hermione incapacitates Neville and Draco binds Harry in an upper luggage rack of the train, meaning something like "completely petrified" [Gk *petra*, rock, stone > L *petra, -ae*, "stone" + *-ficere*, "to make" + *tōtus, -a, -um*, "all, whole" > ML *tōtālis*, "all, whole"].

Piertotum Locomotor: the incantation with which Professor McGonagall makes all the Hogwarts statues and suits of armor come to life and fight for the school [perhaps Gk *petra*, "stone" > L *petra, -ae*, "stone, rock" > Fr *pierre*, "stone," + L *tōtus, -a, -um*, "whole, entire, all"].

Prior Incantato: the incantation used to cast the Reverse Spell charm which produces the most recent charm performed by a wand (the Reverse Spell effect) [L *prior, prius*, "former, previous" + *incantō, incantāre, incantāvī, incantātum*, "a spell that has been cast"; *incantātus, -a, -um*, "consecrated with a charm"].

Priori Incantatem: an incantation which produces the most recent charm performed by a wand (the Reverse Spell effect). The proper Latin word for "spell" is *incatāmentum, -ī*.

Protego Horribilis: the incantation for a type of Shield Charm, protecting Professor Flitwick from something dreadful or terrible [L *prōtegō, prōtegere, prōtexī, prōtectum*, "I protect, defend, ward off" + *horribilis, -e*, "astonishing, dreadful, terrible." If the intent is to protect against something horrible, the proper form of the object would be *horribilem*. If "protego" is intended to be a noun created from the verb, it would be a feminine noun, and the word *horribilis* would agree, grammatically, "horrible protection"—quite a playful creation here].

Protego Totalum: the incantation which creates a strong version of the Shield Charm, protecting completely the one who speaks the incantation, which (along with several other charms) Hermione uses to secure the secrecy of their hiding place [L see "Protego Horribilis" + playful form of ML *tōtālem* (accusative of *tōtālis, -e*) < L *tōtus, -a, -um*, "whole, entire, all"].

Reducio: an incantation by which something is reduced to its previous size after an Engorgement Spell has been cast. Professor Moody uses it to return an enlarged spider to its normal size. The word means, "I restore" [playful use of L *redūcō, redūcere, redūxī, reductum*, "to restore, bring back"].

Reductor Curse: the curse which reduces an obstacle, tearing it down, breaking it open or blasting it away, produced by the incantation "Reducto."

Professor Snape uses it to blasts rose bushes out of his way. Harry employs it to try to get the Blast-Ended Skrewt out of his way in the maze and to coordinate the blasting apart of shelves and exploding of glass spheres in the Department of Mysteries. A Death Eater unblocks stairs leading to the lightning-struck tower with the curse [L *redūcō, redūcere, redūxī, reductum,* "to restore, bring back" > + *-tor, -tōris,* a masculine suffix which, added to a verb stem, denotes an agent (OLD 1949); here, a curse which causes something to be smashed].

Rennervate: the incantation which revives someone from unconsciousness, as when Harry tries to revive an overcome Dumbledore in the cave [a contrived word, based on L *re-,* "again" + *nervus, -ī,* "sinew, force, strength" + ME *-ate,* "to cause, to be come, to produce," following a L second person plural imperative ending, "you," meaning something such as, "(you) become strong again."].

Repello Muggletum: the incantation which activates a Muggle Repelling Charm. With this Hermione protects their hiding place in the forest, perhaps meaning something such as "I repel (the) Muggle" [L *repellō, repellere reppulī, repulsum,* "to drive back, thrust away" + playful attempt to Latinize the word "Muggle"]. Muggle Repelling Charms are mentioned, without incantation, to make Quidditch World Cup and both Hogwarts and Durmstrang schools unrecognizable to the view of Muggles.

Rictusempra: the incantation which casts a Tickling Spell with which Harry makes Draco double over with laughter until the spell can be broken by a counter spell [L *ringor, ringī, rictum,* "to show the teeth with one's mouth wide open"; *rictus, -ūs,* "the mouth wide open" + *semper,* "always"].

Riddikulus: the incantation which activates the charm to repel a boggart by forcing it to assume the form not of what its victim fears most but of something amusing to the victim. Harry uses this in the maze to repel a Dementor which confronts him, but which he realizes is, actually, a boggart [L *rīdeō, rīdēre, rīsī, rīsum,* "to laugh, smile at" > *rīdiculus, -a, -um,* "amusing, funny"; perhaps just a play on the English word "ridiculous"].

Salvio Hexia: an incantation which sets up charms to keep one safe by making protective spells effective. This is a playful creation based on the Latin verb *salveō, salvēre,* "to be well, be sound," and a Latinized form of the English word "hex," which is a curse or magical spell, the ending (-ia) of which imitates Latin neuter plural noun endings, meaning something like "I make the hexes sound and secure."

Scabior: the name of a crude, rough Death Eater and assistant to Fenrir Greyback. The name may be a variation on the Latin comparative adjective of *scaber, scabera, scabrum,* "rough, mangy" > *scabrior, scabrius,* "scabbier, rougher," or merely a Latinizing play on the English word "scabbier." He is appropriately named, being the crude ruffian that he is.

Scourgify: the incantation which activates a Cleansing Spell which Tonks uses to clean droppings and feathers from Hedwig's cage, Ginny uses to remove Stinksap from Harry's face, and James Potter once used on Severus Snape when they were students to fill Snape's mouth with soap bubbles and choke him, meaning something like, "make clean" [LL *excurāre*, "to take care of, to cleanse" + -ify, from *faciō, facere, fēcī, factum*, "to do, to make"].

Scrofungulus: a disease which appears to have as one of its symptoms spongy lymph nodes in the neck [perhaps a play on the English word, "scrofula," which is tuberculosis of the lymph nodes + fungus"; L *scrōfa, -ae*, "sow used for breeding" + *fungus, -ī*, "fungus" (probably derived from Gk *spongos*, "spongy substance") + diminutive adjectival suffix *-ulus, -a, -um*].

Sectumsempra: the incantation which causes a victim to suffer cuts or gashed wounds which can be healed only by very strong magic. Severus Snape almost certainly once used this on James Potter when they were students, and employed it to wound George Weasley. Harry uses it to wound Draco Malfoy, and to try to stop Severus Snape [L *secō, secāre, secuī, sectum*, "to cut, wound, cleave" + *semper*, "always"].

Serpensortia: an incantation for the spell which causes a snake to appear and to attack a victim, which Draco used against Harry during their duel in the Dueling Club [L *serpēns, serpentis*, "snake, serpent" + *orior, orīrī, ortus sum*, "to rise, come forth, become visible" + suffix *-ia, -iae*, which usually forms abstract nouns from adjectives].

Silencio: the incantation which activates the Silencing Charm with which Hermione silences her croaking bullfrog in Charms class and mutes a Death Eater who yells out her location to other Death Eaters, meaning "I silence" [playful use of L *silēns, silentis*, "being still, noiseless" > *silentium, -ī*, "silence, stillness" > It *silenzio*, "silence"; perhaps nothing more than a Latinizing play on the English word "silence"].

Sopophorous bean: a bean which induces sleep, an ingredient in the Draught of Living Death which Professor Slughorn assigns the students to prepare in class [L *sopor, -ōris*, "a very deep sleep," "an opiate" + suffix *-fer*, "carrying, bringing" > mod L *-phorous* < Gk *pherein*, "to bear, bring" > L *ferō, ferre, tulī, lātum*, "to bring, carry"].

Spectrespecs: special glasses which are included, at no cost to the reader, inside the *Quibbler* magazine. Presumably they permit one to see ghosts or other frightening things [Gk *skeptomai*, "look, spy, examine carefully" > L *speciō, specere, spexī, spectum*, "to behold, view, consider" > *spectrum,*

-*ī*, "appearance" > Fr *spectre*, "phantom, ghost" > English "specter/spectre, "ghost" + English "specs," colloquial for glasses].

Specialis Revelio: the incantation with which Hermione tries to make Harry's textbook, *Advanced Potion Making*, reveal any hidden features or spells, and which Ernie Macmillan tries to use in order to create an assigned antidote, meaning, "special revelation" [L *speciālis, -e*, "special, individual, particular" + playful use of *revēlō, revēlāre revēlāvī, revēlātum*, "to uncover, unveil, reveal" + *-iō*, suffix which makes feminine nouns from verb stems].

Tarantallegra: the incantation which makes the victim's legs jerk rapidly and out of control, as in a frenzied dance. Draco uses it on Harry during their duel in the Dueling Club and Dolohov uses it to disable Neville during the battle in the Department of Mysteries [L *alacer, alacris, alacre*, "quick, excited" > It *allegro*, "merry, cheerful, bright" + *Tarantella*, a lively Italian folkdance named for Taranto, a city on the coast of Italy].

Veritaserum: a colorless and odorless Truth Potion which, when taken, forces one to tell the truth. It is so powerful that only three drops make a fully effective dose. Snape threatens to use it on Harry; Professor Dumbledore uses it on Barty Crouch, Jr.; Dolores Umbridge tries to slip it into a beverage for Harry, forcing him to tell her the truth. Rita Skeeter claims to have used it on Bathilda Bagshot to get the truth out of her about Dumbledore [L *vēritas, -ātis*, "truth" + *serum, -ī*, "whey, watery part of curdled milk"].

Wingardium Leviosa: the incantation which activates a Levitation Charm, practiced in Charms class by making feathers fly. Ron uses it to disarm a troll in the girls' bathroom and in the process of his stilling the flailing limbs of the Whomping Willow. Harry uses it to repel the brains that assault him as the result of Bellatrix's spell and to slow the descent of the sidecar which falls from Hagrid's flying motorcycle [perhaps "wing" or "wind" + L *arduus, -a, -um*, "steep, lofty" + *-ium*, a Latin-like suffix for neuter nouns or genitive plural of i-stem nouns + *levō, levāre, levāvī, levātum*, "to raise, to make light" > *levis, leve*, "light" + *-ōsus, -a, -um*, meaning "full of or rich in"].

English Terms with Latin Origins, Used as Technical Terms for Magic

The list which follows catalogs words now so much a part of regular English vocabulary that most readers will readily think of them as having little, if any, connection with classical languages (except, perhaps, for "tentaculum," which is a technical, scientific term). The uniqueness of these terms is that they are all used in the *Harry Potter* novels as technical vocabulary for the Wizarding world, and not as they are commonly used in "Muggle" English. For example, "stupefy" means "to astonish someone." In the magical world, however, it is a powerful incantation which produces a Stunning Curse. All these English words come from classical roots. English meanings will be supplied only when the term listed is uncommon or unlike its use in the novels.

Abstinence: a password required by the Fat Lady to allow admittance to the Gryffindor common room. The English word denotes one's refraining from indulging in appetites, particularly from use of alcohol [L *abstinentia, -ae,* "self-denial, integrity, abstinence"]. As a woman of large dimensions, who is suffering from a hangover, it is remarkable that the password she comes up with is a word for one's choice to avoid excesses in food and drink.

Arithmancy: divination by using numbers, and a course taught at Hogwarts [Gk *arithmos,* "number" + *manteia,* "divination, means of prophecy"].

Divination: foreseeing or foretelling events that will happen in the future, often by special means such as reading tea leaves, looking into a crystal ball and the like; also, one of the courses offered at Hogwarts [L *dīvīnō, dīvīnāre, dīvīnāvī, dīvīnātus,* "to know by inspiration, to foresee; foreseen" > *dīvīnātiō, dīvīnātiōnis,* "prophecy, foreseeing the future"].

Erumpent: an African animal similar to a rhinoceros with an explosive and very tough horn, according to Scamander (16), which Mr. Lovegood swears to be a Crumple-Horned Snorkack horn. The English word means "bursting out," or "breaking forth" [L *ērumpō, ērumpere, ērupī, ēruptum,* "to cause to burst out, break open" > participle *ērumpēns, ērumpentis,* "bursting out"].

Impedimenta: the incantation which activates the Impediment Jinx, freezing a victim temporarily. Harry uses it to stop a Blast-Ended Skrewt, to stop the Death Eaters who pursue him in the Little Hangleton cemetery, and to immobilize the Death Eater Amycus Carrow. He allows Neville to use it on him three times for practice during Christmas break. The English word denotes things which hinder or impede, such as "baggage" [L *impedīmentum, -ī,* "impediment, hindrance"; *impedīmenta,* "baggage, impediments"].

Invigoration Draught: a potion which Harry composes well and hands in to Snape, but which Draco causes to crash to the floor and to earn for Harry a grade of zero in Potions class; a medicinal or magical potion which revives the recipient with energy and strength [L *in-*, intensifying prefix + *vegeō, vegēre*, "to make active, enliven" > *vigeō, vigēre*, "to be active, 'be possessed of physical or mental vigor'" (OLD 2061) + *-tiō, -tiōnis*, noun suffix indicating a condition or state of being (made vigorous)].

Numerology: divination by the study of the mystical meaning of numbers; "the incorporation of numerical patterns in a literary work, designed to suggest certain meanings" (Quinn 226) [L *numerus, -ī*, "number, calculation" + Gk *logos, -ou*, "reason" > ModL *-logia*, "the science of"].

Ornithomancy: divination by using birds, augury. It is one of Professor Trelawney's interests [Gk *ornis, ornithos*, "bird" + *mantis*, "prophet" > *manteia*, "divination, means of prophecy" > LL *mantia* > OFr *-mancie* (Neufeldt 820)].

Potions: one of the courses offered at Hogwarts, which involves studying the formulas and procedures for preparing magical/medicinal/poisonous substances, usually in a liquid form [L *pōtō, pōtāre, pōtāvi, pōtum or pōtātum*, "to drink" > *pōtiō, -ōnis*, "a drink, a magical or poisonous mixture" > Fr *potion*].

Probity Probe: a device used, apparently, to test whether someone is being honest and true. It is used by the goblins at Gringotts Bank to prove that a patron is really who he claims to be. The English word "probity" denotes honesty, and a "probe" is a device which is inserted into something for the purpose of obtaining information [L *probō, probāre, probāvī, probātum*, "to test" > *probitās, -ātis*, "honesty, uprightness" > Fr *probité*].

Protean Charm: the charm which Hermione puts on fake Galleon coins to make them read exactly the same as Harry's master coin in order to announce to her group the dates and times of the meetings of Dumbledore's Army. The term describes the ability to change into any shape, as does Proteus, the sea-god of mythological lore, who can transform himself into the form of animals or fire or water in order to elude those who ask questions of him [Gk *prōteus* or *prōtistos*, "first of all, in first place" > L *Proteus* + English suffix *-an*, meaning "characteristic of"]. Anyone or anything may be called "protean," which is very elusive because it can appear to take many different forms or positions, quickly.

Quintessence (A Quest): the title of a book which is assigned reading for Charms class. The quintessence is the purest and most concentrated form of a thing, the most representative example of anything [ML *quinta essentia*, "fifth essence"> MF *quinte essence*, "the fifth and highest element in ancient and medieval philosophy that permeates all nature and is the substance composing the celestial bodies" (Mish 1022)].

Scintillation Solution: a potion which Madam Z. Nettles, a reviewer of the

Kwikspell course for Squibs, says has become much-requested since she has been taking and using the course. It apparently gives sparkle, elation, or relaxed bowels to the user, gauged by the meaning of the name. The English word denotes a quick alteration in brightness [L *scintillō, scintillāre, scintillāvī*, "to sparkle, to glitter, to emit sparks" > *scintillātiō, scintillātiōnis*, "an eye condition in which one perceives flashes of light, a flashing or sparkling"; L *solvō, solvere, solvī, solūtum*, "to loosen, release" > *solūtiō, solūtiōnis*, "loosening, relaxing, making fluid or soft" > ME *solucion*].

Stupefy: the incantation which produces a Stunning Curse, used very frequently in battle and by Tom Riddle on Morfin Gaunt to trick him into assuming the blame for murders he did not commit. The English word denotes the act of causing astonishment or a stunning of one's senses [L *stupeō, stupere, stupuī*, "to be astonished, to be amazed" + -ify, from *faciō, facere, fēcī, factum*, "to do, to make" > *stupefaciō, stupefacere, stupefēcī, stupefactum*, "to stun, to astonish" > Fr *stupéfier*].

Supersensory Charm: a charm which allows one to be extraordinarily perceptive, with which Ron sees what is behind and beside himself, instead of using the mirrors on his car, when he takes the test for his driver's license. The English word denotes something which is beyond the detection of the five senses [L *super*, "over, above, more than" + *sentiō, sentīre, sēnsī, sēnsum*, "to perceive, to discern" + *-orius, -a, -um*, adjectival suffix, meaning "possessing a quality of" > OFr *-oire* > ME *-orie* > *-ory* (Mish 877)].

Tentacula: a poisonous plant with tentacles, the seeds of which Mundungus Fletcher sells to the Weasley twins for their magical products, and which are kept at Hogwarts in the school greenhouses for use in Herbology [L *tentō, tentāre, tentāvī, tentātum*, "to feel, touch" = *temptō, temptāre, temptāvī, temptātum* > ModL *tentāculum*, "relating to tentacles"; plural, *tentacula*].[6]

Conclusion

We have attempted the task of surveying J.K. Rowling's seven novels in the *Harry Potter* series. Our aims have been these: (1) to identify the author's obvious application of resources from classical mythology and Greek and Roman culture; (2) to identify allusions, parallels, and similarities to that ancient tradition which seem to function without obvious sign-posts directing us to the specific sources of inspiration which have made their way through history and into the Wizarding world; and (3) to assess the function and contribution of classical mythology and culture to the novels.

The range of Rowling's use of this tradition is vast, but not surprising. Not surprising because, as I have worked on this project for some years, I have been delighted, constantly, by the fact that the more deeply and closely one looks at Rowling's novels, the more one finds how much she has borrowed, and how brilliantly she has used what she has borrowed. Her narrative formula and her presentation are classic, from the overall story form (the quest folktale) to her method of framing scenes, episodes, motifs, individual books and the widest-ranging plots (with the ancient and timeless device of ring composition). While the series is not an actual, ancient epic, it is epic-informed or a modern epic in the many ways we have enumerated. The characters often have the exact names of ancient persons, shining a light for us in only one direction, toward the classics to "get" the allusion. And even when we know virtually nothing about some of Rowling's characters except that they died of dragon-pox, are authors of textbooks, or grandparents of students, the striking and sometimes playful names given to them bring to the larger story the limelight of attention and a tone of the sensational or mysterious. Characters repeat legendary adventures and contests made famous millennia ago by our forebears. The social and family dynamics of the ancient houses and dynasties, with all their glory and dysfunction, provide templates for renewed and revised communication of ageless realities.

The ancient world offers unchanging models which inspire creative persons to re-mythologize their message in terms and deeds which make the endeared message accessible for a new public. The characters, themes, motifs, adventures, and even the language of the culture which birthed and perpetuated the classical tradition all add color, atmosphere, drama, mood, and power to her stories. And often, what Rowling adds to these choice selections of materials from ages past is irony and humor, sportiveness, playfulness, variation, and accessibility. Not all the characters, dynamics, and episodes of the series have distinctive or strongly suggestive classical antecedents. However, very many of them do. To read the novels without recognizing the formidable contribution of that resource in general and the particular contributions from the resource is to miss a great part of the genius, the artistry, and much of the purpose behind Rowling's apparent intention.

It is impossible to read *Harry Potter* without some awareness of the classical tradition there. But when we appreciate more fully the influence it has had on J.K. Rowling and her writing, as well as how she has made us mindful of the timeless value and applicability of the tradition by delivering it to readers of today in her stories, both Rowling's writing and our treasured tradition are elevated to the highest levels of appreciation. The phenomenal public response to this seven-novel work and the level of accessible, if unconscious, identification with it in so many and such meaningful ways, justify our calling the series a modern epic.

Appendix

"Ring Composition" in Classical Sources and in *Harry Potter*

Ring composition is a rhetorical and literary device which creates a frame for the contents between two verbal or written signals. In its simplest form, it presents a word, phrase or motif at the beginning of a topic and repeats or unambiguously reiterates that same word, phrase, or motif at the point where the treatment of the topic ends. The purpose of the ring may be simply to initiate and conclude a topic, or to stress the content of the topic, or to summon the hearer or reader to assess the movement or contrast disclosed within the framed material, or simply to alert the recipient that the topic is finished. The device contributes unity to the theme, structure and movement to the topic, and recapitulation for the recipient.

This feature is not exclusive to classical literature, but it is very widely practiced there, and that is the focus of our attention. Extensive studies have been published on the presence, style and function of ring composition in Homer's poems and Herodotus' *The Histories*.[1] It is found in the extant writings of Tyrtaeus, Semonides, Hippocrates, Vergil, Juvenal, Ovid, and Catullus, just to cite a few. Cedric Whitman has said ring composition in Homer's oral poetry is similar to Geometric art: "The very name, 'ring composition,' arises because such enclosure by identical or very similar elements produces a circular effect, the acoustical analogue of the visual circle..." (253). He creates a schematic model illustrating how the entire *Iliad* is geometrically arranged with ring composition in an even more elaborate system which is called chiasmus."[2]

Two examples of ring composition which Whitman cites from the *Odyssey* are the scene in which the elderly servant Eurycleia recognizes Odysseus by the scar on his knee and the episode of Odysseus and Telemachus' hiding the suitors' weapons (252f.). When Odysseus arrives at his palace, Athena has disguised him as an old man. Even his wife Penelope cannot recognize him. As a noble and hospitable queen, though, she directs her aged and trusted servant, Eurycleia, to bathe and prepare their guest for entrance to her home. As the servant washes the stranger, she catches a glimpse of a scar on his thigh and knows immediately who he is, for she tended him as a young man when he got the scar. Between Homer's statement that she recognizes the scar, dropping his foot in surprise, and the time the foot hits the water, the poet inserts seventy-five lines which detail how the scar came about. Homer closes the episode with the same words with which he opens it: "she recognized the scar" (*Od.* 19.392 and 468).

In the second example, Athena directs Odysseus to disarm and kill the more than one hundred suitors who occupy his palace. Odysseus follows the plan. Telemachus plays his part in explaining to the suitors that the weapons are being locked away to keep them safe and in good order, and to prevent any mishaps, should any drunken scuffles break out. Eurycleia bars the doors, so that the suitors cannot leave. And they await the morning for the kill. The episode begins with "Now, *great Odysseus still remained in the hall, pondering how, with the help of Athena, he would murder the suitors* (*Od.* 19.1–2). It concludes with a reprise: "*great Odysseus still remained in the hall, pondering how, with the help of Athene, he would murder the suitors*" (*Od.* 19.51–52).[3]

Vergil and Ovid employ the device in their respective versions of the story of Orpheus and Eurydice. Orpheus, the most marvelous poet and devoted lover of all time, loses his bride to untimely death on their wedding day. The mournful poet endures his suffering until he dares to descend to the Underworld to persuade the gods there to give her back to him. His appeal and songs are so effective that they concede to his request, with one condition: that as the two ascend to the world above, he not look back until they arrive in the world of their previous life. Unfortunately, just before they arrive, he looks back at Eurydice, either because he has forgotten the agreement (Vergil), or because he is afraid that he may fail and because he is so eager to see his beloved (Ovid). The agreement is broken, and his dear bride tumbles, irretrievably, back to the lower regions. Vergil creates a ring beginning with the lovers' unbelievable reunion and blissful hope. He closes it with Orpheus' lament over losing his bride the second time, this time, forever. The link between the opposites of gain and loss, joy and lament, is the echoing of the name "Eurydice" in both members. Pathos is accentuated in the closing, as her name is called out by the severed head of Orpheus as it floats on the Hebrus River, and echoes back by the banks of the river:

|== *Georgics* 4.485–86 "And now, retreating he had escaped every misfortune /
‖   and Eurydice, regained, was coming to the upper airs...."

|‖__ *Georgics* 4. 523–27 "Even then when the Oeagrian Hebrus was carrying his
         head, / wrenched from his marble neck in the midst of its
         stream, / the head would roll, and the voice itself and the
         cold tongue / with fleeting breath would call, 'Oh, poor
         Eurydice!' / The banks echoed back, 'Eurydice' all along
         the stream."

Ovid uses the device to create a different focal point, not the loss of Eurydice but the pitiful anguish of the poet, in both the opening and closing of the ring. With artistry and a bit of cheeky lampooning of his predecessor, he encloses the myth with the two terms designating a mountain range in Thrace (L *Rhodopēius; Rhodopēn*):

|== *Met.* 10.11–12   "When the Rhodopeian poet had mourned for her enough
‖   in the upper Airs...."

|‖__ *Met.* 10.76–77   "Complaining that the gods of Erebus are cruel he took
                         himself to lofty Rhodope and to Haemus beaten by the
                         north winds. "

In the preceding example Ovid uses the device to bracket a partial section of one of his myths. But, he can use it to bracket his entire collection of hundreds of myths. He both begins and concludes his massive collection with personal and philosophical words:

|== *Met.* 1.1–4   "*My mind moves me to sing of* forms changed into new
‖   bodies. Gods, inspire my undertaking (for you have
‖   changed it, too) *and draw down my epic song from the
                     origin of the world to my own times.*"

|‖__ *Met.* 15.871–79   "And now I have completed a work that neither Jupiter's
                         anger, nor fire, nor iron, nor hungry time can obliterate.
                         Let that day, which has jurisdiction over nothing but
                         this body, end the uncertain space of my life whenever
                         it desires. Still, with the better part of me, I shall be
                         carried forever above the stars and my name will be
                         indestructible, and where Roman power extends over
                         conquered lands—if the predictions of seers have any
                         truth—I shall live."[4]

J.K. Rowling uses ring composition very often in every one of the novels for a variety of effects. Sometimes, it is a simple device to round out a part of the story and to help readers reflect back for a moment on the theme, scene or motif which the ring encloses. At other times, it connects something which appears in an earlier book with a similar (and sometimes creatively varied) motif in a later novel, drawing together a wide range of narrative. The following is a selective, visual summary of some of the many ring compositions she creates.

In *Sorcerer's Stone*, Rowling brackets off Harry's entire first eleven years of life by having Hagrid bring the infant from the Wizarding world to Four Privet Drive, and having him return ten years later to take the boy from his Muggle home back into the Wizarding world:

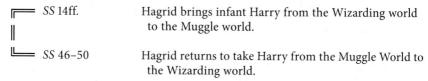

SS 14ff.   Hagrid brings infant Harry from the Wizarding world
                  to the Muggle world.

SS 46–50   Hagrid returns to take Harry from the Muggle World to
                  the Wizarding world.

Harry's deepest desire, to be able to see his family, is bracketed by his encounter with their images in the Mirror of Erised (which is taken away and hidden), and Hagrid's kindly gift to Harry of a photograph album which includes pictures of his parents. With Hagrid's gift, Harry once again has access to the images of his mother and father, but this time without the destructive element of the enchanted mirror and with the benefit of being able to take them with him. There is an important difference between the first member of this ring and the second. The Mirror does not show images of things as they are in themselves, but as the viewer very deeply wishes them to be, projections of anguished longings, illusions. The Mirror skews reality and can seduce the viewer psychologically. The picture album gives real photos of his real parents in form which will not drive him to ruin but which he can look at forever. The album is a memento, not a mesmerizer:

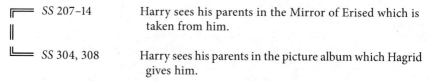

SS 207–14   Harry sees his parents in the Mirror of Erised which is
                  taken from him.

SS 304, 308   Harry sees his parents in the picture album which Hagrid
                  gives him.

The first few novels begin with Harry's unhappy life on Privet Drive with the Dursleys, and end with his having to return from his chosen world to the home of the Dursleys. For example:

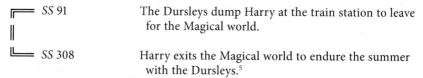

SS 91   The Dursleys dump Harry at the train station to leave
                  for the Magical world.

SS 308   Harry exits the Magical world to endure the summer
                  with the Dursleys.[5]

Rowling frames *Chamber of Secrets* with the appearance of the tortured and enslaved House-Elf Dobby in chapter two, and his reappearance in the last chapter, in which he is freed from the cruel Malfoys and is joyous about his new life:

CS 12ff.   CS Chapter Two: Dobby's Warning

CS 327ff.   CS Chapter Eighteen: Dobby's Reward

She hints that Percy Weasley is reclusive and busy writing letters during his summer off from school. She reveals the truth about the secretive behavior on the last page of the book:

CS 30   Percy, acting secretively, sends many letters by Hermes.

CS 341   Ginny discloses to whom Percy had been sending letters.

In the *Prisoner of Azkaban*, when Professor Lupin gives the students a practical introduction to boggarts, the first and last student to confront them is Neville. At first he is quite afraid, but by the time he takes his last turn, he is bold and courageous. In this way, the classroom scene is framed by Neville's quick growth of confidence:

PA 134   Neville is chosen as the first student to try to repel a
                   boggart.

PA 139   Neville is chosen as the seventh and last student to try
                   to repel a boggart.

The motif of a chance passing cloud which causes important results creates a ring:

PA 380   A shifting cloud reveals the full moon, making Lupin
                   transform and run off.

PA 415   A drifting cloud hides the moon as innocent Sirius and
                   Buckbeak get away.

The entire book is bracketed with a ring:

PA 1ff.   PA Chapter One: Owl Post

PA 416ff.   PA Chapter Twenty-Two: Owl Post Again

The *Goblet of Fire* echoes at the end a scene reminiscent of the beginning:

⌐═══ *GF* 15	Harry is awakened by Voldemort's killing an innocent bystander two hundred miles away, in Little Hangleton.
∥	
╚═══ *GF* 636ff.	Harry is transported hundreds of miles to Little Hangleton to face murderous Voldemort, who kills an innocent bystander.

Rowling uses the weather conditions during the students' travel to and from Hogwarts to significant effect:

⌐═══ *GF* 158–70	The weather during the trip to Hogwarts is dark, gloomy and very rainy.
∥	
╚═══ *GF* 726	The weather during the return trip is completely different than before, providing a kind of reverse parable: the weather goes from bad to great, but circumstances for the Wizarding world have deteriorated horribly.

The character of Ludo Bagman, as a respected official of the Ministry who has a problem with gambling, is exposed by circular treatment:

⌐═══ *GF* 126, 444–45	Bagman appears to be quite anxious for some reason.
∥	
╚═══ *GF* 732	The reason is revealed—a consequence of his bad habit of gambling.

The *Order of the Phoenix* is replete with ring compositions. At the beginning of the book, Harry is bullied by the Dursleys so that he cannot even enter the house to listen to the news on television. The last scene of the book shows a drastic alteration of roles and a shift in power as a self-assured and independent Harry leads the way out of the station, with all three Dursleys following behind him:

⌐═══ *OP* 1ff.	Harry hides from the Dursleys to listen to the news report through a window.
∥	
╚═══ *OP* 870	He boldly strides ahead of the three Dursleys, unafraid of them.

At the beginning of his school year, students are uneasy about Harry, apparently having believed the reports of the *Daily Prophet* that he is a crazy show-off. At the end of the year, students who are reading the *Sunday Prophet* call out to him and wave eagerly, apparently now wanting to show him that they believe the more recent reports about him in the newspaper and now consider him a hero:

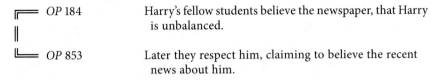

OP 184		Harry's fellow students believe the newspaper, that Harry is unbalanced.
OP 853		Later they respect him, claiming to believe the recent news about him.

On the trip to school, aboard the Hogwarts Express, Cho Chang stops to speak to Harry just when he is covered with Stinksap, embarrassing her and humiliating him. On their return trip, Harry sees Cho, which makes her blush a bit. He is surprised that he is not hurt when he learns that she now has another boyfriend. The budding romance has run its course:

OP 187	Burgeoning feelings for each other cause Harry and Cho to feel emotional.
OP 865	Their feelings in each other's presence are resolved.

On their way to Hogwarts, Neville proudly shows off his plant, the Mimbulus mimbletonia, and Harry wonders why Neville would want *such* a stunted plant which expels Stinksap. At the end of their eventful year, on their trip home, Neville strokes his plant (not poking it with a quill as he did at the beginning of the year), which now makes crooning noises when touched (as opposed to shooting out foul liquid), and he comments on how much it has grown during that year—a useful parable of the growth of the students themselves:

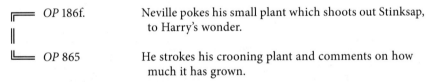

OP 186f.	Neville pokes his small plant which shoots out Stinksap, to Harry's wonder.
OP 865	He strokes his crooning plant and comments on how much it has grown.

In the *Half-Blood Prince*, there are important thematic applications of ring composition. When Harry and Dumbledore enter the cave, blood has to be offered in order to cancel the protective curses and to permit passage through the narrow entrance. Dumbledore insists that they use his own blood, since Harry's blood is more valuable. When they leave the cave, the Headmaster is so debilitated that Harry uses his own blood to gain their exit. This reversal reinforces the shift that is taking place in the roles of the two:

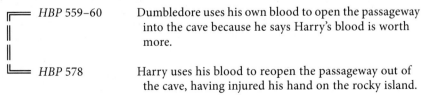

HBP 559–60	Dumbledore uses his own blood to open the passageway into the cave because he says Harry's blood is worth more.
HBP 578	Harry uses his blood to reopen the passageway out of the cave, having injured his hand on the rocky island.

In *Deathly Hallows*, the obituary of Albus Dumbledore is framed by a ring. The writer recalls the friendship which Dumbledore showed to him when he contracted dragon pox early in his first year as a student at Hogwarts. He concludes the article by affirming that Albus remained the kind of person who would befriend someone whom others would alienate:

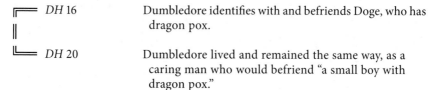

DH 16		Dumbledore identifies with and befriends Doge, who has dragon pox.
DH 20		Dumbledore lived and remained the same way, as a caring man who would befriend "a small boy with dragon pox."

Some of the ring compositions extend over several novels. In the examples which follow, I arrange them according to the order in which the rings close, rather than when they begin.

The theme of the eyes of Harry and his enemy:

SS 126		The first time Harry's and Snape's eyes meet, his scar burns with hot pain.
GF 658		As Snape dies, he asks Harry to look at him and Harry's green eyes meet Snape's black eyes, no longer causing his scar to burn.

The theme of Draco's unchangeable mentality:

SS 109		Draco warns Harry that it is not good or safe to associate with riffraff.
GF 729		Draco warns Harry that his riffraff friends will be killed first.

The theme of The Boy Who Lived:

SS 17		Surviving Voldemort's Curse makes Harry famous as The Boy Who Lived.
OP 846–47		Again, Harry lives up to the title The Boy Who Lived in his greatest combat.

The theme of Dumbledore's deep personal trust of a rugged friend, Hagrid:

SS 14		Dumbledore tells McGonagall he would trust Hagrid with his life.
HBP 643		At the funeral, Dumbledore has been entrusted to Hagrid in his death, as he carries the Headmaster's remains.

The theme of Harry's experience of Godric's Hollow:

⌐—	*SS* 12	Voldemort first attacked Harry and his parents in Godric's Hollow.
└—	*HBP* 650	Harry plans to return to Godric's Hollow, where his story began.

The topic of Harry and Dedalus Diggle:

⌐—	*SS* 10	Dedalus Diggle celebrates Voldemort's apparent defeat; Harry is entrusted to the Muggle Dursleys.
└—	*DH* 36ff.	Dedalus Diggle coordinates the final parting of Harry from the Dursleys.

The motif of Hagrid as a flying "Hermes" who rescues Harry:

⌐—	*SS* 14–16	Hagrid flies Harry on Sirius' motorcycle from the danger of his magical home to the Muggle Dursleys' home.
└—	*DH* 54ff.	Hagrid flies Harry on Sirius' motorcycle from the Muggle Dursleys' home to safety at the Weasley's magical home.

The theme of innocents always at the mercy of "pure-bloods":

⌐—	*CS* 12ff.	Dobby is an abused slave of the "pure-blood" Malfoys.
└—	*DH* 474ff.	Though freed, Dobby sees his end at the hands of the "pure-blood," Bellatrix Lestrange.

The role of Griphook the goblin:

⌐—	*SS* 73ff.	Griphook conducts Harry and Hagrid to their vaults in Gringotts to do business.
└—	*DH* 533ff.	Griphook conducts HH&R to Bellatrix's vault in Gringotts, to steal a Horcrux.

The motif of the deadly green flash and murderous attempts on Harry's life:

⌐—	*SS* 29	Harry's earliest memory is of a deadly green flash, associated with Voldemort's curse.
└—	*DH* 704	The last thing Harry sees is the flash of green light, associated with Voldemort's curse.

The tale of Harry Potter as a survivor and savior extends over the entire series. Chapter One of *Sorcerer's Stone* is entitled The Boy Who Lived. In the last chapter of *Deathly Hallows*, the clamoring public press toward Harry to touch The Boy Who Lived. Harry's first and last encounters with his arch-enemy form a ring to the "quest."

	SS Chapter One	Harry miraculously survives and becomes known as The Boy Who Lived.
	DH 744	Harry is received as a savior and all want to touch The Boy Who Lived.

Chapter Notes

Introduction

1. Text according to Coury 45.

2. A few times reference is made to Newt Scamander 2001 (J.K. Rowling) for details about the beasts of the Wizarding world.

3. For more on these criticisms, see monomyth (2014, December 17). In *Wikipedia, The Free Encyclopedia*. Retrieved 20:36, January 5, 2015, from http://en.wikipedia.org/w/index.php?title=Monomyth&oldid=6384 35265.

4. On the hero myth, see Leeming 1998. He presents primary texts and summary, arranged by the major themes of the universal story of the hero (monomyth). See Segal 1990 for the history of the study of the hero myth.

5. On archetypes and motifs in folklore and literature, see Garry 2005, which contains sixty-six essays on some of the motifs and Jungian archetypes of world literature.

Chapter I

1. Nel 42, 47, 49.

2. These motifs are very much in line with Propp's thirty-one functions. They are also, probably, informed by the proposals of Joseph Campbell's work, especially *The Hero with a Thousand Faces* (1968).

3. The theme of searching for one's father is found also in Sophocles' play *Niptra* and in Eugammon of Cyrene's *Telegonia*, in which Telegonus, the son of Odysseus and Circe seeks his absentee father (Barta 1143).

4. In many places I have indicated the classical sources of the materials cited. The range of resources and ancient records is vast. For those who are interested in pursuing further the location of the classical materials, the following are most helpful: Price and Kearns (2003), López-Ruiz (2014), Roman (2010), Robert Bell (1991), the *Oxford Classical Dictionary* (Hornblower 2012), and the incomparable *Brill's New Pauly: Encyclopaedia of the Ancient world. Classical Tradition* (Landfester, 2006–).

5. Trans. Lattimore 1967, 72.

6. Thompson classifies the wooden horse as a motif of the category Deceptions, "Capture by Deception" (K754.1). All designations by Thompson of folktale types and motif types in these notes come from his book *The Folktale* (1977).

7. Thompson calls the Odysseus-Polyphemus episode an Ordinary Folktale of the type "Tales of the Stupid Ogre," the ogre blinded (1137). The tale employs three motifs, two under the category Deceptions, "Escape by Deception": Noman (K602) and escaped under ram's belly (K604); and one under the category "Deception into Self-Injury," eye-remedy: dupe blinded (K1011).

8. Trans. Grene 1991, vol. 3, 49.

9. Later, her exuberance over Harry's finding a way to succeed in the Second Task of the Triwizard Tournament all by himself puts a strain on Harry's status as an Odyssean figure, for all the credit actually is owed to Dobby.

10. There is a clearly defined literary type of homecoming story from the ancient world, called a "nostos" [Gk plural, *nostoi*], of which the *Odyssey* is the most famous. The tales of the homecoming of a number of the Greek heroes following the Trojan War survive in fragments, which are available in West 2003.

11. According to Thompson, the Siren belongs to the motif of "Mythical Animals" (B53).

12. See Bell 1991, 216–17 and 400–01 for details and specific classical sources.

13. According to Hesiod, Odysseus and Calypso had two children, Nausithoüs and Nausinoüs (*Theog.* 1017–18).

14. Gods visiting mortals incognito belong to the category of motifs Deceptions, "Deception by Disguise or Illusion": Gods (saints) in disguise visit mortals (K1811), according to Thompson.

15. Trans. Lattimore 1967, 206.

16. Thompson classifies stories about such transportation in the category Ogres, "Kinds of Ogres": witch rides through air on broomstick (G242.1).

17. Since antiquity, there have been speculations as to the origins, meaning and significance of names and titles. The options which have been offered as possible linguistic parallels or connections between a story or a legend associated with the name. Etymology is an informed art, not a science. In Room's dictionary, the author often gives as many as three possible options for the source of a term. I do not offer all the options, only those which seem to have a sound degree of probability, and which have meaningful connection with parallels in Rowling's novels. Room has a helpful introduction to the craft of etymology of ancient names. For etymologies and sources of many of the ancient terms and names we introduce, see Maltby.

Chapter II

1. For a thorough treatment of Christian themes and symbolism in the series, see Neal 2008 and Granger *How Harry Cast His Spell*, 2008. On the savior theme in young adult literature, as it relates to the social-sexual-psychological development of the hero, see Saxena 103ff.

2. According to Thompson, trolls belong to the motif Marvels, "Marvelous Creatures" (F455).

3. Harry's challenge was to rescue Ron. He went beyond his duty and risked losing the Second Task. Murcus reported that Harry's delay was because of his "determination to return all hostages to safety, not merely his own" (*GF* 507).

4. The dual nature belongs to the theme "birth of the hero." Other classical figures of human and divine parentage are Theseus (of Aethra and Poseidon), Persephone (of Demeter and Zeus), Dionysus (of Semele and Zeus), Achilles (of Peleus and the sea goddess Thetis), and Aeneas (of Anchises and Aphrodite). See Foster 176.

5. Pindar, *Nemea* 1.33ff.; Theocritus, *Idyll* 24.

6. An interesting sidelight on the Hera-Heracles conflict has to do with the origin of the word "galaxy." Mythology offers several explanations for why there is a Milky Way. One story is that Hermes disguises Heracles when he is a suckling infant and lays the child at Hera's breast while she sleeps. She awakes and throws Heracles away from her, and the milk which comes from her breast creates the starry Milky Way (Grimal 183). According to Thompson, the story of the Milky Way belongs to the set of Mythological Motifs, "Cosmogony and Cosmology" (A778).

7. Karley Adney and Holly Hassel comment that the myth of the Twelve Labors of Hercules "bears some relation to Harry's own struggle against the many tasks throughout the series. Hercules was half-god and half-mortal and completed the Twelve Labors in order to help humanity. Harry's own defeat of a number of challenges … is undergirded by his responsibility for saving wizard-kind from the evil machinations of Lord Voldemort" (349).

8. This incident suggests several other classical parallels. Orpheus, the incomparable poet and singer, can produce music so powerfully effective that it causes stones and trees to move toward him to hear it, and the inhabitants of the Underworld to weep at its tones. Hermes uses a flute to put to sleep the hundred-eyed guardian Argus, and then kills him (Grimal 59).

9. In mythology, poor Cerberus is drugged by the Cumaean Sibyl, who helps Aeneas to enter the Underworld (*Aen.* 6.417–25), and by Psyche, who goes to the Underworld to get Persephone to give her a fragment of her beauty (Apuleius, *Metamorphoses* 4.28–6.24) (Morford 219–21). In a somewhat similar vein, Jason uses drugs or potions to enchant the never-sleeping dragon which protects the Golden Fleece, in order to steal that prize (*Met.* 7.149–58). A mythological tradition maintains that Dionysus also goes to the Underworld, to retrieve his mother, Semele (Henrichs "Dionysus," 2012, 463).

10. Morford comments that the episode has been quite influential on western art, represented in a famous painting by Annibale Carracci (1596, *The Choice of Hercules*), and in Handel's oratorio (1750, "The Choice of Hercules"). In antiquity it was told as a parable by Prodicus of Ceos (Xenophon, *Memorabilia* 2.21—34 and Cicero, *De Officiis* 1.118) (Morford 582–83, and 588 n. 24). See also Howatson 285.

11. Andrew Brown says that the name "Achilles" may be of Mycenaean Greek origin, meaning "a grief to the army" (2012, 6).

12. *Libr.* 3.13.6. The word "ambrosia" is a Greek word meaning "immortality" [*ambrosia, -as* < *ambrotos*, "immortal" < *a-*, "not" + *mbrotos*, "mortal"], often translated as "the elixir of life."

13. The surviving ancient sources of myths, legends, sagas and folktales about heroes and gods offer numerous variations, as they derive from different ages and cultures, and they serve a wide range of purposes.

14. Thompson cites this as a motif in the category Unique Exceptions: "Vulnerability in one spot" (Z311).

15. There is a humorous tale about Achilles and his mother Thetis, which circulated widely in the ancient world. It portrays her as a woman who would do anything to protect her son. But the demi-god does not seem so glorious in this myth. When he is nine years old, a prophecy decrees that the Greeks will not conquer Troy without Achilles' presence. Since Thetis knows that he will die if he goes to war, she dresses the boy as a girl and has Lycomedes, the king of Scyros, hide him among his numerous daughters (*Libr.* 3.13.8).

16. Gould 79.

17. Mary Pharr draws parallels between Harry and Achilles when it comes to Harry's experiencing the death of Sirius and Achilles' reaction to the death of his dear friend, Patroclus, in that they both "learn to accept the inherent confines of mortality" (64).

18. This type scene occurs, also, in the duel between Dumbledore and Gellert Grindelwald, and in the Headmaster's battle with the Dark Lord in the Ministry of Magic.

19. Thompson classes such stories as a type of the motif Unnatural Cruelty: "Children abandoned or exposed" (S301) and the motif Ordaining the Future: "Vain attempts to escape fulfillment of prophecy" (M370). The Oedipus story as a whole is an "Ordinary Folktale Novelle" or romantic tale (931). He comments that this is the sort of story which begins as a popular Greek form of a folktale which becomes well established and is transmitted by dramatists and poets (278).

20. For more on Harry and Oedipus, see Vandana Saxena's socio-psychological treatment of Harry, Oedipus and the Oedipus complex, using traditional, gender, and queer theory analysis (35ff.).

21. See, for example, Agnes Michels, "The Many Faces of Aeneas," *The Classical Journal* 92.4 (1997): 399–416.

22. Thompson classifies journeys to the world of the dead under the category Marvels, "Otherworld Journeys" (F81).

Chapter III

1. Philip Nel sees the literary model for the Mirror of Erised in Lewis Carroll's *Through the Looking Glass* (31). Our study is not of parallels and allusions in modern western literature, but of similarities between Rowling's novels and the Greek and Roman era.

2. On Narcissus' peculiar type of coming to know himself, see Anderson 1997, 374.

3. Another high point in Harry's self-realization occurs when he realizes that the figure whom he sees on the opposite shore of the lake, which looks like his father, is himself. Then he knows that it will be up to him, not his father, to rescue himself, Hermione and Sirius. As Rowling puts it, "he had seen himself" (*PA* 411). In Greek literature and Hellenistic philosophy the mirror was often used to symbolize self-knowledge (Spicq 162–63).

Chapter IV

1. "dumbledore | dumble-dore, n." *OED Online.* Oxford University Press, December 2014. Web. 17 December 2014.

2. One might also think of his speaking Mermish, but that is the common language of the whole community of mermaids and mermen. The strange utterances mentioned here seem to be mystical incantations, not a public system of communication.

3. Another version of his punishment reports that just over his head hang limbs full

of fruit. When he reaches up to pick some to satisfy his unending hunger, the boughs withdraw from his reach (*Met.* 4.459). Yet another story claims that Tantalus is granted a wish by Zeus. Because of his offer, Zeus has to permit his wish, to live like the gods. Because Tantalus shows such hubris in his request, however, the gift is spoiled by his having to sit at banquet with a huge boulder hanging precariously above his head, causing him such terror and distress that he cannot enjoy his food (Pindar *Olympia* 1.35–64; *Epit.* 2.1). Stenger, Jan (Kiel). "Tantalus." *Brill's New Pauly*. Antiquity volumes edited by: Hubert Cancik and Helmuth Schneider. Brill Online, 2014. Reference. Appalachian State University. 17 December 2014 http://0-referenceworks.brillonline.com.wncln.wncln.org/entries/brill-s-new-pauly/tantalus-e1200290.

4. This etymology comes from Plato, *Cratylus* 395d-e. In that same text, another option is given, that "Tantalos" may derive from the word *tantaleia*, "balancing," a reference to the stone which is over his head.

5. Two others who employ a "Socratic" kind of dialogue with Harry, in the attempt to get him to come to his own conclusions, are Firenze and Mad-Eye Moody.

6. It is also interesting to note that Dumbledore is the aged visitor to Slughorn's hideout, as Phoenix is the oldest and wisest ambassador to Achilles.

7. *History*, 4.2 (Lewis 1955, 565–66).

8. Saxena sees "no God-like figure or a divine representative in the series" (172). While there is not a sovereign, almighty and perfect deity comparable to the Christian God in the series, there are parallels to and echoes of Zeus and other ancient, supernatural beings, "gods."

9. Cunliffe 317.

10. Thompson has a category of motif for witches riding on broomsticks (G242.1) and one for witches riding unusual animals (G241.1). Rowling's humorous invention of flying motorcycles is a novel reinvention of that category.

11. On prophecy and futures in the *Aeneid*, see Mack, 1978.

12. The ruby-encrusted sword produced from a tattered old hat by magical power belongs to the theme of "strength concealed in weakness," which is a regular component of quest stories.

13. The Romans call the mother Ceres, the daughter Proserpina, the lord of the Underworld Pluto, and the chief of the gods Jupiter.

14. This is an etiological legend explaining why there are growing seasons and fallow seasons.

15. Thompson classes Perseus' winning of the princess Andromeda under the category Sex: "Princess offered as prize" (T68.1).

Chapter V

1. Another famous example is recorded by the historian Livy. According to him, the last king of Alba Longa, Amulius fears that he will be dethroned (since he himself has deposed his brother Numitor and murdered his nephews). To prevent any further male competitors, he makes his niece, Rhea Silvia, become a Vestal Virgin, so that she can never give birth to a rival. But a miracle-story gets passed around that the god Mars raped her and she bore the twins Romulus and Remus. To rid himself of any threat from the boys, Amulius orders that they be drowned in the Tiber River. The boys survive, miraculously, and become the ancestors and founders of the Roman world (*A.U.C.* 1.3.10ff.).

2. Adney remarks, "Voldemort is the dark god-like force of Mars or Hades" (349).

3. The motif of fearing to speak the name of a dreadful opponent appears, also, in the *Chamber of Secrets*, when Aragog refuses to speak of the basilisk, but calls it "The thing that lives in the castle," and tells Harry, "We do not speak of it…. We do not name it! I never even told Hagrid the name of that dread creature, though he asked me, many times" (*CS* 278).

4. Henrichs "Hades," 2012, 640, and Morford 382. Since death finally consumes all mortals, it is not surprising that Hades is perceived as eating corpses. Clytemnestra refers to the human sacrifice of her daughter Iphigenia by her husband this way, "had the God of Death some longing to feast on my children…?" (Sophocles, *Electra*, 542–43; trans. Grene 1957, 146).

5. ll. 18–19, 32–33. See Evelyn-White 291. In Jewish culture, there is a ban on speaking the holy name of God (the Tetragrammaton). In modern translations of the Bible, scholars use the word LORD for that name instead of

the name itself. In the place of that name, Jews use circumlocutions such as "the name" or "Adonai." One of the Ten Commandments demands that no one should take the name of God in vain. At the other end of the religious spectrum, there have been many names used for the supremely evil one, such as Scratch, Nick, the Devil.

6. Thompson classes Medea's helping her lover under the category Ordinary Folktales, "Tales of Magic": supernatural adversaries (type 313), the girl as helper in the hero's flight.

7. Euripides' *Medea*, Apollonius of Rhodes' *Argonautica*, Seneca's *Medea*, and *Met.* 7.1–452

8. Mary Shelley's novel about the scientist who attempts to create a new kind of human being is entitled *Frankenstein, or The Modern Prometheus*.

9. According to Thompson, the story of Phaëthon is a Mythological Motif, of the category "Cosmogony and Cosmology" (A724.1.1).

10. Another assault by Zeus, using his thunderbolt, is against Charybdis, the daughter of Poseidon. She steals cattle from Heracles, and is punished by being driven into the sea by Zeus's thunderbolt. The monster becomes the personification of currents, tides and whirlpools on the Sicilian side of the Straits of Messina. Three times each day she sucks in so much of the sea that it exposes the sea floor. Then, three times a day she suddenly spurts the waters back out, making for treacherous sailing. In mythology, Odysseus and Aeneas face this monster as they sail on their quests. This myth is the source of the expression, "Between Scylla and Charybdis," which means being in a situation between two unpleasant or dangerous options (Bell 1991, 117–18, 395–96).

11. As in almost all cases of mythological stories, there are alternative versions, for example, that the birth was a normal one or that Semele's sister Ino, not nymphs, reared Dionysus (Schachter 1343).

Chapter VI

1. This chapter includes only names which appear in the novels, not those added in other sources, even if they are from Rowling herself (e.g., "Scorpius *Hyperion* Malfoy" is only "Scorpius Malfoy" in *DH* 756).

2. Their difference extends even to their respective owls. Harry's owl is a snowy owl.

Draco's is an eagle owl. If birds are reflective of or representative of one's character (as the sacred birds assigned to the ancient gods [e.g., the owl sacred to Athena, goddess of wisdom]), Rowling's choice of birds assigned to Harry and Draco mirrors their opposite natures.

3. For a brilliant and insightful treatment of the psychological, sexual, and social aspects of the Persephone model in the story of Ginny Weasley, see Holly Virginia Blackford, *The Myth of Persephone in Girl's Fantasy Literature* (New York: Routledge, 2012), especially chapter seven, "The Riddle of Féminine Écriture in J.K. Rowling's *Harry Potter and the Chamber of Secrets* (1998)," 181–98.

4. Stories of other mythical heroes' encounters with the dead or journeys to and from the Underworld have survived; for example, Heracles, Theseus, and Orpheus, each risking his life for a significant cause. Two outstanding and lengthy narratives of encounter with the dead of the Underworld are Odysseus' summoning the dead in the *Odyssey* (Book 11) and Aeneas' journey to the Underworld in the *Aeneid* (Book 6).

5. In an article in *Time Magazine* of December 19, 2007, by Nancy Gibbs, entitled "Person of the Year 2007: Runners-Up: J.K. Rowling." Web. 25 Nov. 2014. http://content. time.com/time/specials/2007/personofthe year/article/0,28804,1690753_1695388_16954 36,00.html. The verse on the Potters' headstone is from 1 Corinthians 15:26, King James Version.

6. John Granger makes insightful observations on the matter by citing the common factors between the quotation from Aeschylus and the other quotation which follows it in the frontispiece, a passage from William Penn, the seventeenth-century Quaker and founder of the colony of Pennsylvania. He proposes that Rowling aligns the two quotations because the pacifist (Penn) and the tragedian who fought in the battle of Marathon, and perhaps also at Salamis (Aeschylus), are similar in their opposition to tyranny and oppression, though different in their methods. In addition, both quotations speak about the issue of life after death and "both the reality and accessibility of those who are dead that we have loved" (*The Deathly Hallows Lectures*, 2008 244).

7. Rowling has said that she patterned Hermione's character after herself, but that

the name is derived from a character in Shakespeare's *A Winter's Tale*. The poet took the name for his Hermione from the mythological figure (Dresang 212). The name itself appears to have some relation to the god "Hermes," who is the god of intersections, cross-roads and communications between Zeus and other gods and humans. It seems to be a feminine form of that name, and would apply to Ms. Granger as a good interpreter and mediator between clever Harry and somewhat dull Ron.

8. Morford 476f.; 522 n. 4.

9. The parallel suggested here may be a stretch, because according to the ancient tale, the Helen who was in Egypt for a decade was Helen herself, and a "phantom" of her resided in Troy for that period. In Hermione's case, it was the real person who was in both places. The parallel is not exact, but at least thought-provoking and worthy of consideration. I have not found any tradition that the Helen who was in Troy for ten years was perceived of as being anything other than the real person, even if she were a phantom. So, both "Helens" were taken to be the real Helen.

10. Prometheus' transporting fire in a narthex or fennel stalk is found in *Theog.* 567 and Aeschylus, *Prometheus Bound*, 109. According to Thompson, the story of Prometheus' deeds belongs to the set Mythological Motifs, "Creation and Ordering of Human Life": theft of fire (A1415).

11. Thompson would probably class this as belonging to the motif set Ogres, "Kinds of Ogres": witch rides an unusual animal (G241.1).

12. See Euripides, *The Trojan Women*, 80; *Aen.* 1.42; and Aeschylus, *Eumenides* 827f., "I alone among the gods know the sealed chamber's keys where Zeus's thunderbolt is stored" (Vellacott 175). Robert Lenardon says that Athena is close and warm in her relationship with her father Zeus, "but also in her devout loyalty and steadfast protection of more than one hero (e.g., Telemachus and Odysseus, Heracles, Perseus, Jason, and Bellerophon)" (Morford 190).

13. At the very beginning of the series, Dumbledore tells Professor McGonagall that he would trust Hagrid with his life. This initiates a ring composition, which is concluded with the Headmaster's being entrusted to Hagrid in his death.

14. See Theocritus, *Idyll* 11 and *Met.* 13.738–897.

15. According to Thompson, Polyphemus is a typical giant. His story in the *Odyssey* is an Ordinary Folktale of the class which includes Tales of the Stupid Ogre: the ogre blinded (1137). He is depicted with the motif in the category Marvels, "Marvelous Creatures": giant with one eye in middle of forehead (F 531.1.1.1).

16. Hagrid's best dress is horrendous, a hairy brown suit with a garish, mismatching tie.

17. See *Od.* 9.145–542.

18. J.K. Rowling interview transcript, *The Connection* (WBUR Radio), 12 October 1999. Web. 25 Nov. 2014. http://www.accio-quote.org/articles/1999/1099-connectiontransc2.htm#p3.

19. See also, "Hermes" in Roberts 335–36 and Jost 668–69.

20. A marble relief, which is a copy of an original Greek relief, which was associated with the Altar of the Twelve Gods in Athens, depicts Orpheus and Eurydice attended by Hermes, the psychopomp, at the crucial moment of their ascent from Hades to the upper world (see Morford 393).

21. There are other mythic elements which come to mind, worthy of attention, but which cannot be pursued here at length. For example, Socrates was said to practice the art of midwifery (Gk *hē maieutikē technē*), in a spiritual sense by helping others to "deliver" the ideas which they were thinking about, but which they had not yet produced fully-formed (Plato, *Theaetetus* 151c; LSJ 1072). In a sense, Hagrid delivers Harry from the dark world in which he has been living and growing. And in the process, he asks the Socratic question which sends Harry "into mental labor": e.g., "Not a wizard, eh? Never made things happen when you was scared or angry?" (*SS* 58). Harry then recalls some strange and confusing things which he had done, but which he had never connected and understood. The "delivery" is complete when Hagrid then says, "See?" (*SS* 58).

22. The term "psychopomp" was used for Charon, as well as for Hermes.

23. "snape, v.1." *OED Online*. Oxford University Press, December 2014. Web. 16 December 2014.

24. Snape's Muggle father, Tobias, also

bears a name which conjures up the ancient story of a member of an exclusive community who cannot prove to puritanical priests his unmixed ancestry.

25. Ovid (*Met.* 9.71) has Hercules report that the Hydra has one hundred heads. The customary version of the tale supplies it with eight heads which are mortal and one which is immortal (Morford 566).

26. Astronomer Jim Kaler notes that since the star "shines at the bright end of the 'minus-first' (-1.47) magnitude," it is quite appropriate that the Greeks named it for its "scorching" or "searing" appearance. Web. 25 Nov. 2014. http://stars.astro.illinois.edu/sow/sirius.html.

27. Of course, his brother, Regulus Black, changes his mind and vows to defeat Voldemort, but only after having been one of his Death Eaters.

28. The dramatic reversal of character, of fortune, and of an entire plot line as the result of a recognition or reconciliation scene is a regular feature of Roman comedy.

29. According to Thompson, the story of the twins' being cared for by the wolf belongs to the set of Animal Motifs, "Friendly Animals": animal nurse (B354).

30. Harry is nurtured and rescued by other "animals," too—Minerva McGonagall (a tabby cat), Remus Lupin (a werewolf), and James Potter (a stag).

Chapter VII

1. He was counted among the gods [L *dīvōs*] by Vergil (*Eclogue* 1.40ff.).

2. See Betz 331 for more information on Abrasax/Abraxas. For examples of ancient texts, see Ogden 2009, 207 (divination by observing the flame of a lamp), 247ff. (a love spell using voodoo dolls), 268 (protection for a little girl from illness, ghosts, and demons), and 269 (protection from hailstones and snow).

3. Rose "Amyeus," 2012, 76.

4. Web. 25 Nov. 2014. http://stars.astro.illinois.edu/sow/arcturus.html.

5. In classical mythology, a person named "Argos" was the builder of the famous ship, the Argo, constructed under Athena's instruction and sailed by Jason and the Argonauts to get the Golden Fleece. It was called "Argo," which means "Swift," because of its seagoing worthiness.

6. The epithet for him, relating to the notion of his having eyes all over his body, is the "all-seeing" [Gk *panoptēs*] (*Libr.* 2.1.2f.).

7. His pet, Mrs. Norris, appears to be an extension of the vigilant employee, as she has "bulging lamplike eyes just like Filch's" (*SS* 132).

8. Recall that Filch's predecessor as caretaker at Hogwarts, Apollyon Pringle, has the personal name of another Underworld figure, the angel over the bottomless pit.

9. According to Thompson, the story of the origin of the Great Bear belongs to the set of Mythological Motifs, "Cosmogony and Cosmology" (A771).

10. "charact, n." *OED Online.* Oxford University Press, September 2014. Wed. 23 November 2014.

11. "burke, v." *OED Online.* Oxford University Press, December 2014. Web. 16 December 2014.

12. Thompson classifies Circe among the motifs of Ogres, "Kinds of Ogres": witch transforms lovers into animals (G263.1).

13. Even Professor Tofty, in surprise, bolts out a similar expletive, "Galloping gargoyles" (*OP* 721). Such blunders appear to emerge under duress and to expose one's less polished tendencies.

14. For much more on Daedalus, see Stewart 409f.

15. "dobby | dobbie, n." *OED Online.* Oxford University Press, December 2014. Web. 17 December 2014.

16. Hicks 91.

17. Morford 415ff. and Bell 1991, 196–97.

18. Prinzi compares Albus Dumbledore to Quintus Fabius Maximus at the points of the Headmaster's confidence in himself and his patient program to win not a quick and temporary victory over Voldemort but a decisive defeat. He calls Dumbledore "Fabius Maximus of the Wizarding World" (229ff.).

19. Adney 350.

20. Room proposes that the name "Cerberus" comes from Gk *kēr berethron*, "evil of the pit," *kēr* being a female spirit of death (88, 178).

21. According to Hesiod, Cerberus had fifty heads (*Theog.* 312).

22. The motif of subduing a vicious guardian beast is reminiscent of Jason's drugging and enchanting the never-sleeping dragon with its three-forked tongue, which

protected the Golden Fleece (*Met.* 7.149–58). Thompson classifies Orpheus' Underworld visit in the category Marvels, "Otherworld Journeys" (F81.1).

23. Howatson 259; Bell 1991, 207.

24. "Gilderoy, n." *OED Online.* Oxford University Press, December 2014. Web. 16 December 2014.

25. "gild, v.1." *OED Online.* Oxford University Press, December 2014. Web. 16 December 2014.

26. He also used his feigned interest in Hepzibah Smith to steal from her the cup of Helga Hufflepuff and the locket of Salazar Slytherin.

27. An ancient legend holds that the lyric poet Stesichorus (early sixth century BCE) wrote a poem about Helen in which he presented the story that the woman eloped with Paris, and for that slight to her character the "goddess" Helen blinded the poet. He then wrote another poem retracting the first version by portraying Helen being whisked off to Egypt by the gods, her phantom convincing everyone in Troy that she was truly there—for which retraction Helen restored sight to Stesichorus (West 1999, 204).

28. "slug-horn, n.2." *OED Online.* Oxford University Press, December 2014. Web. 16 December 2014.

29. The same cry was used in the worship of Bacchus to invoke the god or divine power (LSJ 847; OLD 963).

30. Varro, *De Lingua Latina* 6.5. See Maltby 348–49.

31. An ancient etymology of the name "Marcus" suggests that the people who were called the Marci (i.e. the Marcuses) were born during March, which was named for the god Mars (see Maltby 368).

32. See Sourvinou-Inwood 1373 for summary and sources.

33. See Bell 1991, 303–04; Rose "Merope," 2012, 936; and Price 345. Frazer cites several ancient explanations for the virtual invisibility of the star Merope, and says this about the embarrassment option: "Merope, who had married a mere man, Sisyphus, was so ashamed of her humble, though honest, lot by comparison with the guilty splendour of her sisters, who were all of them paramours of gods, that she dared not show herself" (2002=1922, Vol. 2, 3, n. 1). According to Thompson, the story of the Pleiades belongs to the set of Mythological Motifs, Cosmogony and Cosmology: origin of Pleiades (A773).

34. See Rose "Volcanus," 2012, 1563 and OLD 1140.

35. According to Thompson, the mermaid and the merman belong to the motif of Mythical Animals (B81, B82).

36. http://www.nlm.nih.gov/exhibition/paracelsus/index.html "Paracelsus"

37. "Paracelsus". *Encyclopædia Britannica. Encyclopædia Britannica Online.* Encyclopædia Britannica Inc., 2015. Web. 14 Jan. 2015. Article by John G. Hargrave. http://www.britannica.com/EBchecked/topic/442424/Paracelsus.

38. Spencer 1992, 346.

39. According to Thompson, the werewolf belongs to the set of Magic, "Transformation" (D.113.1.1).

40. See Adney 349.

41. A famous and influential maxim of Terence's sums up his humanistic perspective: *homō sum; hūmānī nīl ā mē aliēnum putō,* "I am human. I consider nothing human to be foreign to me" (*Heauton Timorumenos,* "The Self-Tormenter," 77).

42. The story of Tobit and his son Tobias is an example of the Ordinary Folktale of the monster in the bridal chamber (507B), according to Thompson.

43. Boda 965–67.

Chapter VIII

1. Hans Dieter Betz (ed.), *The Greek Magical Papyri in Translation: Including the Demotic Spells* (Chicago: University of Chicago Press, 1986); John G. Gager (ed.), *Curse Tablets and Binding Spells from the Ancient World* (New York: Oxford University Press, 1992); Georg Luck, *Arcana Mundi: Magic and the Occult in the Greek and Roman Worlds, A Collection of Ancient Texts.* 2nd ed. (Baltimore: Johns Hopkins University Press, 2006); Daniel Ogden, *Magic Witchcraft, and Ghosts in the Greek and Roman Worlds.* 2nd ed. (New York: Oxford University Press, 2009). These sources deal with witchcraft, sorcery, texts from amulets and talismans, and Greek magical papyri from the eighth century BCE down to the fifth century CE and even later, in some instances.

2. Christopher Faraone has noted that the boundary between religion and magic

and superstition is debatable, but certainly at least semi-permeable (3). On magic and the occult in Roman Religion, see Warrior 93–104.

3. Faraone 3.

4. Morford 83 n. 20. The passages mentioned are Plato *Republic*, 7.527b and 614b2–616b1.

5. On time and prophecies in Vergil, see Mack 1978.

6. For the image of "Unrolling [the scroll]," to translate "volvēns," see Pharr 1964, 40.

7. For a thorough study of texts regarding dragons, serpents, and other ancient, deadly beasts, see Daniel Ogden, *Dragons, Serpents, and Slayers in the Classical and Early Christian Worlds: A Sourcebook* (New York: Oxford University Press, 2013). For an expansive treatment of mythological and legendary creatures throughout history and literature, a number of which are introduced in this section, see Malcolm South (ed.), *Mythical and Fabulous Creatures: A Source Book and Research Guide* (New York: Greenwood Press, 1987).

8. For a thorough study of the serpent in the classical world, see Daniel Ogden, *Drakōn: Dragon Myth and Serpent Cult in the Greek and Roman Worlds* (New York: Oxford University Press, 2013).

9. One legend has it that when a basilisk was killing many of his soldiers, Alexander the Great had the animal killed by getting it to look into a mirror! (Rowland 28, cited by De Rose 68).

10. The word "digitus," here, can mean finger or toe, or the breadth of a finger as a measurement (OLD 542).

11. The term is used in the Septuagint (the Greek translation of the Hebrew Scriptures which began to appear during the third century BCE) for the very dangerous adder or viper from which God's angels protect one who trusts in him (Ps 90/91.13). In a very different context, the prophecy in Isa 59:5 describes the existence of the unrighteous who would smash the egg of a spider and find in it a basilisk.

12. As we have mentioned in another context, the poet Stesichorus was said to have been blinded by Helen because he spoke critically of her in a poem, but given his sight back when he wrote another poem about her, retracting the previous one.

13. "Lucius Caecilius Metellus." *Ency-clopaedia Britannica. Encyclopaedia Britannica Online Academic Edition.* Encyclopædia Britannica Inc., 2014. Web. 24 Nov. 2014. http://academic.eb.com/EBchecked/topic/378091/Lucius-Caecilius-Metellus.

14. According to Thompson, the motif of a dragon guarding treasure belongs to the motif of "Mythical Animals" (B11.6.2).

15. Thompson categorizes the motif at work here as belonging to the group Deceptions, "Thefts and Cheats": theft from three old women with a single eye among them (K333.2).

16. The Cap of Invisibility is also said to have been given to Perseus by Hades, the god of the Underworld.

17. According to John Pollard, in the ancient world people would keep peacocks, a very costly enterprise, for their beauty, and the very word "peacock" had assumed "an aesthetic connotation for something outlandish and beautiful" (92). He quotes Aelian on the colorful glory of the bird: "It resembles a flowery meadow or a picture embellished with every variety of colour and artists have to sweat blood to do justice to its true beauty" (92; Aelian, *De Natura Animalium* 5, 21).

18. The eagle is a most appropriate representative of the king of the gods. Pollard writes, "They are superior to other birds, are high flyers and endowed with such sharp eyesight that they can descry even the smallest victims when pressed by hunger.... They live and nest among the mountains and rarely descend to the plains" (23). He quotes Aristotle: "It perches on high places because it is slow to rise from the ground. It flies high in order to obtain the most panoramic view. That is why alone among birds men term it divine" (78, citing Aristotle, *History of Animals*, 9, 619 A 14).

19. Pollard 17, 110–13, 159.

20. Adney summarizes very insightfully, "Rowling draws upon this historical association as the centaurs in Harry Potter's world are both defined by a complicated moral structure (for example, a doctrine of noninterference with nature, the ethical consequences of spilling innocent blood) and a kind of violent brutality epitomized by their exiling of Firenze when he decides to assist humans and their attack on Dolores Umbridge" (350).

21. Hesiod claims that the Chimaera had three heads (*Theog.* 320–21), as if one were

attached to its neck, one to its back and one to its middle (see Caldwell 48). Apollodorus says that the middle head breathes out fire (*Libr.* 2.3.1).

22. This is, of course, a reprise of Homer's famous descriptions of the shields of Achilles (*Il.* 18.478–607) and Agamemnon (*Il.* 11.32–40) (Barron 103).

23. Greek *kēr* was a goddess of death or doom (LSJ 948). The word is often found in the plural, *Kēres*, "the Fates."

24. *Il.* 11.39, 12, 202. In *Nemea* I, Pindar refers to the two terrible dragons (*drakontas*) which Hera had sent to kill the infant Heracles (l.40), and then comments that the child strangled each of the serpents (*ophias*, l.45), and that his mother herself fought against the arrogance of the monsters (*knōdalōn*, l.51). Another tale is that dragons/snakes came into being from the drops of the blood of the Titans (Malkin 1377). According to Thompson, stories about learning to speak animal language by having one's ears licked by a serpent belongs to the motif of Magic Animals (B165.1.1).

25. According to Thompson, giants belong to the motif of Mythical Animals (B11).

26. Birkalan comments, "Both the Greeks and the Romans attributed a prophetic power to springs, such as the ancient one at Delphi" ("Water," 2005, 491).

27. According to Thompson, giants belong to the motif of "Marvelous Creatures" (F531).

28. Thompson classifies the Medusa story under the category Magic "Transformation": petrification by glance (D581).

29. Birkalan "Mythical Birds," 2005, 82, citing Bies 1027.

30. Pliny cites this last feature from Juba, king of the Numidians at the time of the turn of the Common Era.

31. On Magical world sphinxes, see Scamander 39.

32. One may recall the Hebrew assertion that "the blood is the life" (Deut 12:23).

33. According to John Pollard, the Sirens signify doom (189).

34. A red-figure bowl dating from about 440 BCE depicts Odysseus threatening Circe with a sword as she drops her bowl of drugs and wand (see Morford 531).

35. Cunliffe 241.

36. See http://www.perseus.tufts.edu/cgi-bin/image?lookup=Perseus:image:1990.01.1415. Web. 25 Nov. 2014.

37. See Luck 218–19.

38. This story and examples of many other amulets to cure impotence, prevent pregnancy, promote healing and exorcism, cure a headache, bring good luck, et al., are available in Ogden 2009, 261–74.

39. Prinzi 176–78. He relies on Campbell 72 for this perspective on the amulet.

40. The most detailed description of Greek animal sacrifice is given by the chorus in Euripides' play *Electra* (ll. 774–843). See Parker 1306.

41. A most informative study of the subject of transfiguration and metamorphosis is P.M.C. Forbes Irving, *Metamorphosis in Greek Myths* (Oxford: Clarendon Press, 1990).

42. Thompson would classify the Animagi under the category Ogres, "Kinds of Ogres": witch in animal form (G211).

43. Since boggarts are immediately associated with one's strongest fears and can be dispelled only by one's happiest thoughts, they appear to project the individual's most intense conflict with self-doubts and self-esteem, a regular feature of quest stories.

44. Pollard 16–17, 159, 195–96 (notes 64–69). He proposes: "Since the Cretans and Greeks of the Bronze Age appear to have regarded birds as epiphanies of deities, it is not surprising that divine bird transformations should occur in literature which is nearest in time to the Bronze Age ... the epics of Homer" (155).

45. Ovid lists these transformations of Jupiter and Neptune as needlepoint depictions done by Arachne in her weaving contest with Minerva (*Met.* 6.103–28). The specific identities of the women, who are sometimes identified not by their names but as daughters of their named fathers (patronymics), are from Anderson 1982, 166–67.

46. Forbes Irving distinguishes between the transformation of gods, who use magic to assume a temporary disguise, and the metamorphosis of birds, stones, plants, islands, rivers and humans, which undergo a more complete shifting of their nature and being. The gods, transformed, remain and act as gods, while "the shape-shifter completely submerges his personality in the thing he becomes. Whereas too the gods generally become only living creatures and advanced forms of life, the shape-shifter may turn himself into the lifeless elements of fire or

water" (171). Prinzi uses the term broadly, including the Animagi, Quirrell, and users of Polyjuice Potion (195–96). The term will be used here with the general denotation of one who has the capacity to transform into another form.

47. Thompson classifies the story of his successive transformations under the category Ogres, old man of the sea (G31).

48. Mary Pharr comments on this bit of magic, "Dudley has for years quite literally thrown his weight around, regularly beating up his smaller cousin simply for meanness. No wonder that an exasperated Hagrid casts a spell that leaves Dudley with a pig's tail, the implication of poetic justice clear even to the rustic gamekeeper" (56).

49. See Spencer 1997, 20ff.

50. See Frazer 2002=1922, Vol. 1, 86–87, n. 2.

51. We noted that G.S. Kirk cited oracles, prophets and seers, communication with animals, and riddles as examples of themes which are common to heroic myths.

52. *The Compact Edition of the Oxford English Dictionary*. New York: Oxford University Press, 1971. Vol. 1, 31.

53. J.K Rowling at the Edinburgh Book Festival, Sunday, August 15, 2004. Web. 25 Nov. 2014. http://harrypotter.wikia.com/wiki/Avada_Kedavra.

54. See Copleston 49.

55. For an encyclopedic analysis of number and numbers from a psychological and symbolic perspective, see Lance Storm, *The Enigma of Numbers* (Pari, Italy: Pari Publishing, 2008).

56. According to Thompson, the story of Atalanta's race belongs to the motif of Tests, "Marriage Tests": apple thrown in race with bride (H331.5.1.1).

57. On contrast of the one and the many in Ovid, see Spencer 1997.

58. The seven are Solon, Thales, Pittacus, Bias, Cleobulus, Myson, and Chilon (Gould 72).

59. Thompson places the motif under the category of Tests, "Marriage Tests": suitor contest: race with bride's father (H331.5.2) and the posting of the heads under "Tests of Prowess": heads placed on stakes for failure in performance (H901.1).

60. See Schiesaro 974.

61. For a compendious review of the number nine in the religious life and myths of the Greeks, see Roscher 337–462.

62. For much more on the number four and its many significances in the ancient world, including a reference for the Demiurge, or the visible God, see Balz 127–39.

63. To the traditional four ages, Hesiod added a fifth age, the Age of Heroes (of the time of the Trojan War) because of the marvelous nature of those warriors.

64. Rowling has said she wanted there to be four, all of whom were parental figures for Harry in one way or another, in a Time Magazine article entitled, in "Person of the Year 2007: "Rowling Answers 10 Questions About Harry." Web. 25 Nov. 2014. http://content.time.com/time/specials/2007/personofthe year/article/0,28804,1690753_1695388_1695 569,00.html.

65. Rengstorf 321.

66. This list includes fourteen names. As Robert Lenardon points out, Hades was eventually eliminated from the list of Olympians, as his dwelling is in the Underworld, and Hestia was replaced by Dionysus (Morford 117). This preserved a set of twelve.

67. Rengstorf 324.

68. After Judas defected from the twelve, Matthias was elected to take his place and to complete the number of chosen witnesses to Jesus' life, from the beginning of his ministry to his resurrection—twelve. See Acts 1:21–6.

69. See Schweizer 36. See also 4 Ezra (2 Esdras) 14:11.

Chapter IX

1. She has commented, "My Latin is patchy to say the least, but that doesn't really matter because old spells are often in cod Latin—a funny mixture of weird languages creeps into spells. That is how I use it. Occasionally you will stumble across something in my Latin that is, almost accidentally, grammatically correct, but that is a rarity. In my defence, the Latin is deliberately odd. Perfect Latin is not a very magical medium, is it? ... I take a lot of liberties with things like that.... I twist them round and make them mine." J.K Rowling, at Royal Albert Hall (London, June 28, 2003). Cited in Beahm 178.

2. See DuPree 39–53, for an excellent treatment of a few of the magical terms in an-

cient tongues from the perspective of an historian.

3. Rowling also plays with other languages: French [*Beauxbatons*, "lovely wands," *Fleur Delacour*, "flower of the court," *Malfoy*, "bad (or evil) faith," *Toujours Pur*, "forever pure," *Voldemort*, "flight from death"]; German [e.g., *Durmstrang*, a play on the phrase *Sturm und Drang* (Storm and Stress), which is the term given to a literary movement in Germany during the 1770s and 1780s, whose most influential adherent was Goethe]; and Italian [*Firenze*, the Italian name of the city of Florence, *Relashio*, an incantation causing boiling water to spurt from Harry's wand, burning the grindylow and making them release him, (perhaps based on *relascio*, "to release," < L *relāxō, relāxāre, relāxāvī, relāxātum*, "to relax, to set free"), *Silencio*, the incantation which activates the Silencing Charm, with which Hermione quietens her croaking bullfrog in Charms class and mutes a Death Eater who yells out their location to other Death Eaters, meaning "I silence" (playful use of L *silēns, silentis*, "being still, noiseless" > *silentium, -ī*, "silence, stillness" > It *silenzio*, "silence"; or, maybe a play on the English word "silence" to make it sound like a Latin word)].

4. Gager 12. See *Thesaurus Linguae Latinae*. Leipzig: B.G. Teubner Verlagsgesellschaft, 1971.

VII, 1, Fasc. IX, 1390; Schilling, 133–34; "Di Inferi." *Encyclopedia Mythica*. 2014. Encyclopedia Mythica Online. 08 Dec. 2014 http://www.pantheon.org/articles/d/di_inferi.html.

5. M.G. DuPree says this particular formula, "wins the prize for 'most languages in a single spell,' for combining Greek, English, and Latin in only two words" (42).

6. "tentaculum, n." *OED Online*. Oxford University Press, September 2014. Web. 25 November 2014.

Appendix

1. Van Otterlo 1944; Pohlenz 1937; Immerwahr 1986; Whitman 1963.

2. An extensive body of material now exists on "chiasmus" in rhetoric and literature from antiquity to modernity. John Welch edited an entire volume on it (1981) and subsequently complemented the volume with another work given entirely to bibliography of works on the subject (1998).

3. Trans. Lattimore 1967, 282f.

4. Except for italicized portion, which is mine, trans. Sara Mack 1988, 99, 143–44. See also Williams 1978, 246–47.

5. This pattern of "off to school" and "back from school" is an organizing frame in all of the novels through the *Half-Blood Prince*.

Bibliography

Aarne, Antti. *The Types of the Folk-Tale: A Classification and Bibliography.* Trans. and enlarged by Stith Thompson. Helsinki: Suomalainen Tideakatemia, Academia Scientarum Fennica, 1928.

Adney, Karley and Holly Hassel. *Critical Companion to J.K. Rowling: A Literary Reference to Her Life and Work.* Facts on File Library of World Literature. New York: Facts on File, 2011.

Alton, Anne Hiebert. "Generic Fusion and the Mosaic of *Harry Potter.*" In *Harry Potter's World: Multidisciplinary Critical Perspectives.* Elizabeth E. Heilman, ed. New York: Taylor and Francis Books, 2003: 141–62.

Anatol, Giselle Liza. *Reading Harry Potter: Critical Essays.* Westport, CT: Praeger, 2003. *Reading Harry Potter Again: New Critical Essays.* Santa Barbara, CA: Praeger, 2009.

Anderson, William S., ed. *Ovid's Metamorphoses: Books 6–10.* Norman: University of Oklahoma Press, 1982. *Ovidius: Metamorphoses.* Leipzig: Teubner. Bibliotheca Scriptorum Graecorum et Romanorum Teubneriana, 1993. *Ovid's Metamorphoses: Books 1–5.* Norman, OK: University of Oklahoma Press, 1997.

Angela, Alberto. *A Day in the Life of Ancient Rome.* Trans. Gregory Conti. New York: Europa Editions, 2009.

Bagg, Robert, trans. *The Oedipus Cycle.* New York: HarperCollins, 2012.

Baggett, David, and Shawn E. Klein, eds. *Harry Potter and Philosophy: If Aristotle Ran Hogwarts.* Chicago: Open Court, 2004.

Balsdon, J.P.V.D. *Life and Leisure in Ancient Rome.* London: Phoenix Press, 1969.

Balz, Horst. "tessares, tetartos, tetartaios." In *Theological Dictionary of the New Testament.* Gerhard Friedrich, ed. Trans. Geoffrey W. Bromiley. Grand Rapids: Wm. B. Eerdmans Publishing Company, 1972: VIII: 127–39.

Barratt, Bethany. *The Politics of Harry Potter.* New York: Palgrave Macmillan, 2012.

Barron, J.P. "Hesiod." In *The Cambridge History of Classical Literature. I: Greek Literature.* P. E. Easterling and B.M.W. Knox, eds. New York: Cambridge University Press, 1987: 92–105.

Barta, Peter I. "Search for Father." In *Dictionary of Literary Themes and Motifs.* Ed. by Seigneuret, Jean-Charles. Vol. 2: 1141–48. New York: Greenwood Press, 1988.

Bassham, Gregory, ed. *The Ultimate Harry Potter and Philosophy: Hogwarts for Muggles.* Hoboken, CT: John Wiley and Sons, 2010.

Beahm, George. *Fact, Fiction, and Folklore in Harry Potter's World.* Charlottesville, VA: Hampton Roads Publishing Company, 2005.

Beck, Roger. "Mithras." In *The Oxford Classical Dictionary.* 4th ed. Simon Hornblower and Antony Spawforth and Esther Eidinow, eds. New York: Oxford University Press, 2012: 964–65.

Belcher, Catherine L., and Becky Herr Stephenson. *Teaching Harry Potter: The Power of Imagination in Multicultural Classrooms.* New York: Palgrave Macmillan, 2011.

Bell, Christopher E., ed. *Legilimens! Perspectives in Harry Potter Studies*. Newcastle upon Tyne, UK: Cambridge Scholars, 2013.

Bell, Luke. *Baptizing Harry Potter: A Christian Reading of J.K. Rowling*. Mahwah, NJ: Hidden Spring Publisher, 2010.

Bell, Robert E. *Women of Classical Mythology: A Biographical Dictionary*. New York: Oxford University Press, 1991.

Berndt, Katrin, and Lena Steveker, eds. *Heroism in the Harry Potter Series*. Farnham; Burlington, VT: Ashgate, 2011.

Betz, Hans Dieter, ed. *The Greek Magical Papyri in Translation: Including the Demotic Spells*. Chicago: University of Chicago Press, 1986.

Bice, Deborah, ed. *Elsewhere: Selected Essays from the "20th Century Fantasy Literature: From Beatrix to Harry" International Literary Conference*. Lanham, MD: University Press of America, 2003.

Biers, William R. *The Archaeology of Greece*. Ithaca: Cornell University Press, 1987.

Bies, Werner. "Phönix." In *Enzyklopädie des Märchens*. New York: Walter De Gruyter, 2002: 10:1022–35.

Birkalan, Hande A., and Jane Garry. "Water." In *Archetypes and Motifs in Folklore and Literature: A Handbook*. Jane Garry and Hasan El-Shamy, eds. Armonk, NY: M.E. Sharpe, 2005. "Mythical Animals: Dragon." In *Archetypes and Motifs in Folklore and Literature: A Handbook*. Jane Garry and Hasan El-Shamy, eds. Armonk, NY: M.E. Sharpe, 2005.

Birkalan, Hande A., and Millicent Lenz. "Mythical Birds." In *Archetypes and Motifs in Folklore and Literature: A Handbook*. Jane Garry and Hasan El-Shamy, eds. Armonk, NY: M.E. Sharpe, 2005.

Birley, Anthony R. "Septimius Severus, Lucius." In *The Oxford Classical Dictionary*. 4th ed. Simon Hornblower and Antony Spawforth and Esther Eidinow, eds. New York: Oxford University Press, 2012.

Blackford, Holly Virginia. *The Myth of Persephone in Girl's Fantasy Literature*. New York: Routledge, 2012.

Blair, Edward P. "Bartimaeus." In *The Interpreter's Dictionary of the Bible*. Nashville: Abingdon Press, 1962.

Boda, Mark J. "ZECHARIAH." In *The New Interpreter's Dictionary of the Bible*. Katharine D. Sakenfeld, et al., eds. Nashville: Abingdon Press, 2009.

Bonnefoy, Yves, ed. *Roman and European Mythologies*. Trans. Wendy Doniger, et al. Chicago: University of Chicago Press, 1991.

Brewer, E.C. *The Wordsworth Dictionary of Phrase and Fable*. Rev. ed. London: Wordsworth Reference, 2006.

Brown, Andrew L. "Achilles." In *The Oxford Classical Dictionary*. 4th ed. Simon Hornblower, Antony Spawforth and Esther Eidinow, eds. New York: Oxford University Press, 2012. "Odysseus." In *The Oxford Classical Dictionary*. 4th ed. Simon Hornblower, Antony Spawforth and Esther Eidinow, eds. New York: Oxford University Press, 2012.

Brown, Francis, Driver, S.R., and Charles A. Briggs, eds. *A Hebrew and English Lexicon of the Old Testament with an Appendix Containing the Biblical Aramaic*. Oxford: Clarendon Press, 1968.

Bryfonski, Dedria, ed. *Political Issues in J.K. Rowling's Harry Potter Series*. Detroit: Greenhaven Press, 2009.

Burkert, Walter. *Greek Religion*. Trans. John Raffan. Cambridge: Harvard University Press, 1985.

Buttrick, George A., et al., eds. *The Interpreter's Dictionary of the Bible*. 4 Volumes. Nashville: Abingdon Press, 1962.

Caldwell, Richard S. *Hesiod's Theogony*. Cambridge: Focus Classical Library, 1987.

Campbell, Joseph. *The Hero with a Thousand Faces*. Princeton: Princeton University Press, 1968.

Clayton, Peter. *Great Figures of Mythology*. New York: Crescent Books, 1990.

Copleston, Frederick. *A History of Philosophy. Volume I: Greece and Rome: Part I*. Rev. ed. Garden City: Image Books, 1962.

Courtney, Edward. "Cornelius Gallus, Gaius." In *The Oxford Classical Diction-*

ary. 4th ed. Simon Hornblower, Antony Spawforth and Esther Eidinow, eds. New York: Oxford University Press, 2012.

Coury, Elaine M., ed. *Phormio: A Comedy by Terence*. Waconda, IL: Bolchazy-Carducci Publishers, Inc., 1998.

Cumont, Franz. *Oriental Religions in Roman Paganism*. New York: Dover Publications, 1956 [republication of 1911 publication by G. Routledge & Sons]. *Astrology and Religion among the Greeks and Romans*. New York: Dover Publications, 1960 [republication of 1912 publication by G.P. Putnam's Sons].

Cunliffe, Richard John. *A Lexicon of the Homeric Dialect*. Norman: University of Oklahoma Press, 1986.

Dahlberg, B.T. "Tobiah." In *The Interpreter's Dictionary of the Bible*. George A. Buttrick, et al., eds. Nashville: Abingdon Press, 1962.

Dandy, Heidi Howard, et al., compilers. *Selected Papers from Nimbus—2003 Compendium*. Houston, TX: HP Education Fanon, Inc., 2005.

Daniels, Jon B. "Barnabas." In *The Anchor Bible Dictionary*. David Noel Freedman, et al., eds. New York: Doubleday, 1992.

De Rose, Peter L. "Mythical Animals." In *Archetypes and Motifs in Folklore and Literature: A Handbook*. Jane Garry and Hasan El-Shamy, eds. Armonk, NY: M.E. Sharpe, 2005.

De Rose, Peter L., and Jane Garry. "Death or Departure of the Gods." In *Archetypes and Motifs in Folklore and Literature: A Handbook*. Jane Garry and Hasan El-Shamy, eds. Armonk, NY: M.E. Sharpe, 2005.

de Sélincourt, Aubrey, trans. *Livy: The Early History of Rome*. New York: Penguin Books, 1971.

Dickerson, Matthew T. *From Homer to Harry Potter: A Handbook on Myth and Fantasy*. Grand Rapids, MI: Brazos Press, 2006.

Douglas, Mary. *Thinking in Circles*. New Haven: Yale University Press, 2007.

Dresang, Eliza T. "Hermione Granger and the Heritage of Gender." In *The Ivory Tower and Harry Potter: Perspectives on a Literary Phenomenon*. Lana A. Whited, ed. Columbia: University of Missouri Press, 2002.

DuPree, M.G. "Severus Snape and the Standard Book of Spells: Ancient Tongues in the Wizarding World." In *Harry Potter and History*. Nancy R. Reagin, ed. Hoboken, NJ: John Wiley and Sons, 2011.

Ehrman, Bart. *Lost Scriptures: Books that Did Not Make It into the New Testament*. New York: Oxford University Press, 2003.

Ernst, Elizabeth, and Jane Garry. "Chance and Fate." In *Archetypes and Motifs in Folklore and Literature: A Handbook*. Jane Garry and Hasan El-Shamy, eds. Armonk, NY: M.E. Sharpe, 2005.

Eskenazi, Tamara C. "Tobiah." In *The Anchor Bible Dictionary*. David Noel Freedman, et al., eds. New York: Doubleday, 1992.

Evelyn-White, Hugh. G., ed. *Hesiod: The Homeric Hymns and Homerica*. Cambridge: Harvard University Press, 1921. Loeb Classical Library; repr. 1982.

Faraone, Christopher A. "The Agonistic Context of Early Greek Binding Spells." In *Magika Hiera: Ancient Greek Magic and Religion*. Christopher A. Faraone and Dirk Obbink, eds. New York: Oxford University Press, 1991.

Faraone, Christopher A., and Dirk Obbink, eds. *Magika Hiera: Ancient Greek Magic and Religion*. New York: Oxford University Press, 1991.

Fenske, Claudia. *Muggles, Monsters and Magicians: A Literary Analysis of the Harry Potter Series*. New York: Peter Lang, 2008.

Fitzgerald, Robert, trans. *The Aeneid*. New York: Vintage Books, 1990.

Flotmann, Christina. *Ambiguity in* Star Wars *and* Harry Potter: *A (Post) Structuralist Reading of Two Popular Myths*. Bielefeld: Transcript, 2013.

Forbes Irving, P.M.C. *Metamorphosis in Greek Myths*. Oxford: Clarendon Press, 1990.

Foster, Leslie D. "Birth of the Hero." In *Dic-*

tionary of Literary Themes and Motifs. Ed. by Seigneuret, Jean-Charles. Vol. 1: 175–91. New York: Greenwood Press, 1988.

Frankel, Valerie Estelle, ed. *Teaching with Harry Potter: Essays on Classroom Wizardry from Elementary School to College.* Jefferson, NC: McFarland, 2013.

Frazer, Sir James George, trans. *Apollodorus: The Library.* Two volumes. Cambridge: Harvard University Press. Loeb Classical Library, 1961. *The Golden Bough: A Study in Magic and Religion.* Basingstoke: Palgrave, 2002. Fifteen volumes. Originally published 1922.

Freedman, David Noel, et al., eds. *The Anchor Bible Dictionary.* New York: Doubleday, 1992.

Freud, Sigmund. *The Interpretation of Dreams.* Trans. A.A. Brill. New York: Modern Library, 1978. Original pub. 1900.

Gager, John G., ed. *Curse Tablets and Binding Spells from the Ancient World.* New York: Oxford University Press, 1992.

Garrett, Greg. *One Fine Potion: The Literary Magic of Harry Potter.* Waco, TX: Baylor University Press, 2010.

Garry, Jane, and Hande A. Birkalan. "Trees." In *Archetypes and Motifs in Folklore and Literature: A Handbook.* Jane Garry and Hasan El-Shamy, eds. Armonk, NY: M.E. Sharpe, 2005.

Garry, Jane, and Hasan El-Shamy, eds. *Archetypes and Motifs in Folklore and Literature: A Handbook.* Armonk, NY: M.E. Sharpe, 2005.

Glare, P.G.W., ed. *Oxford Latin Dictionary.* Oxford: Clarendon Press, 1983.

Gould, H.E., and J.L. Whiteley. *Cicero: De Amicitia.* Chicago: Bolchazy-Carducci, 1999.

Gove, Philip B., ed. *Webster's Third New International Dictionary of the English Language Unabridged.* Springfield, MA: G. & C. Merriam Co., 1971.

Graf, F. "Zeus." In *The Oxford Classical Dictionary.* 4th ed. Simon Hornblower, Antony Spawforth and Esther Eidinow, eds. New York: Oxford University Press, 2012.

Granger, John. *The Deathly Hallows Lectures.* 2nd ed. Allentown, PA: Zosima Press, 2008. *Harry Potter's Bookshelf: The Great Books Behind the Hogwarts Adventures.* New York: Berkley Books, 2009. *How Harry Cast His Spell: The Meaning behind the Mania for J.K. Rowling's Bestselling Books.* Updated 3rd ed. Carol Stream, IL: Tyndale Momentum, 2008. *Unlocking Harry Potter: Five Keys for the Serious Reader.* Allentown, PA: Zosima Press, 2007.

Granger-Taylor, Hero. "toga." In *The Oxford Classical Dictionary.* 4th ed. Simon Hornblower, Antony Spawforth and Esther Eidinow, eds. New York: Oxford University Press, 2012.

Grant, Michael, ed. *Cicero: On the Good Life.* New York: Penguin Books, 1986.

Graves, Robert, trans. *Suetonius: The Twelve Caesars.* New York: Penguin Books, 2007.

Greimas, A.-J. *Structural Semantics: An Attempt at a Method.* Trans. Daniele McDowell, Ronald Schleifer, and Alan Velie. Lincoln: University of Nebraska Press, 1983. Orig. published 1966.

Grene, David, and Richmond Lattimore, eds. *Greek Tragedies: Volume 1.* 2nd ed. Chicago: University of Chicago Press, 1991. *Greek Tragedies: Volume 3.* 2nd ed. Chicago: University of Chicago Press, 1991. *Sophocles II.* Chicago: University of Chicago Press, 1957.

Griffiths, Alan H. "Ambrosia." In *The Oxford Classical Dictionary.* 4th ed. Simon Hornblower, Antony Spawforth and Esther Eidinow, eds. New York: Oxford University Press, 2012.

Grimal, Pierre. *The Dictionary of Classical Mythology.* Trans. A.R. Maxwell-Hyslop. Oxford: Blackwell Publishers, 1996.

Grimes, M. Katherine. "Harry Potter: Fairy Tale Prince, Real Boy, and Archetypal Hero." In *The Ivory Tower and Harry Potter: Perspectives on a Literary Phenomenon.* Lana A. Whited, ed. Columbia: University of Missouri Press, 2002.

Gupta, Suman. *Re-Reading Harry Potter.* New York: Palgrave Macmillan, 2003.

Guttfield, Dorota. "Lewis, Le Guin, and Rowling on the Inhumanness of Immortality." In *Towards or Back to Human Values? Spiritual and Moral Dimensions of Contemporary Fantasy.* Justyna Deszcz-Tryhubczak and Marek Oziewicz, eds. Newcastle: Cambridge Scholars Press, 2006.

Hallett, Cynthia Whitney, and Debbie Mynott, eds. *Scholarly Studies in Harry Potter: Applying Academic Methods to a Popular Text.* Studies in British Literature, vol. 99. Lewiston: The Edwin Mellen Press, 2005.

Hallett, Cynthia J., and Peggy J. Huey, eds. *J.K. Rowling: A Collection of All New Critical Essays by Contemporary Authors.* New York: Palgrave Macmillan, 2012.

Hammond, N.G.L., and H.H. Scullard, eds. *The Oxford Classical Dictionary.* 2nd ed. New York: Oxford University Press, 1984.

Harvey, D.W. "Hephzibah." In *The Interpreter's Dictionary of the Bible.* George A. Buttrick, et al., eds. Nashville: Abingdon Press, 1962.

Heilman, Elizabeth E., ed. *Critical Perspectives on Harry Potter.* 2nd ed. New York: Routledge, 2009. *Harry Potter's World: Multidisciplinary Critical Perspectives.* New York: Taylor and Francis Books, 2003.

Henderson, A.A.R., ed. *Ovid: Metamorphoses III.* Bristol: Bristol Classical Press, 1981.

Henrichs, Albert. "Dionysus." In *The Oxford Classical Dictionary.* 4th ed. Simon Hornblower, Antony Spawforth and Esther Eidinow, eds. New York: Oxford University Press, 2012. "Hades." In *The Oxford Classical Dictionary.* 4th ed. Simon Hornblower, Antony Spawforth and Esther Eidinow, eds. New York: Oxford University Press, 2012.

Hexter, Ralph. *A Guide to the Odyssey: A Commentary on the English Translation of Robert Fitzgerald.* New York: Vintage Books, 1993.

Hicks, R. Lansing. "Eliphaz." In *The Interpreter's Dictionary of the Bible.* George A. Buttrick, et al., eds. Nashville: Abingdon Press, 1962.

Highfield, Roger. *The Science of Harry Potter: How Magic Really Works.* New York: Viking Press, 2002.

Hogan, James C. *A Commentary on the Complete Greek Tragedies: Aeschylus.* Chicago: University of Chicago Press, 1984.

Holbert, John C. "Eliphaz." In *The Anchor Bible Dictionary.* David Noel Freedman, et al., eds. New York: Doubleday, 1992.

Hornblower, Simon, and Antony Spawforth, eds. *The Oxford Classical Dictionary.* 3rd ed., revised. New York: Oxford University Press, 2003.

Hornblower, Simon, Antony Spawforth, and Esther Eidinow, eds. *The Oxford Classical Dictionary.* 4th ed. New York: Oxford University Press, 2012.

Howatson, M.C., ed. *The Oxford Companion to Classical Literature.* 3rd ed. New York: Oxford University Press, 2013.

Huey, Peggy J. "A Basilisk, A Phoenix, and a Philosopher's Stone: Harry Potter's Myths and Legends." In *Scholarly Studies in Harry Potter: Applying Academic Methods to a Popular Text.* Cynthia Whitney Hallett and Debbie Mynott, eds. Studies in British Literature, vol. 99. Lewiston: The Edwin Mellen Press, 2005.

Humphries, Rolfe, trans. *Ovid: Metamorphoses.* Bloomington: University of Indiana Press, 1983.

Hunter, Richard L. "Medea." In *The Oxford Classical Dictionary.* 4th ed. Simon Hornblower, Antony Spawforth and Esther Eidinow, eds. New York: Oxford University Press, 2012.

Immerwahr, Henry R. *Form and Thought in Herodotus.* Atlanta: Scholars Press, 1986.

Jones, Peter V. *Homer's Odyssey: A Companion to the Translation of Richmond Lattimore.* Carbondale: Southern Illinois University Press, 1988.

Jost, Madeleine. "Hermes." In *The Oxford Classical Dictionary.* 4th ed. Simon Hornblower, Antony Spawforth and Esther Eidinow, eds. New York: Oxford University Press, 2012.

Jung, Carl G. *Man and His Symbols.* Trans. M. L. von Franz, et al. New York: Dell Publishing, 1968.

Kern, Edmund. *The Wisdom of Harry Potter: What Our Favorite Hero Teaches Us About Moral Choices.* Amherst, NY: Prometheus Books, 2003.

Killinger, John. *God, the Devil, and Harry Potter: A Christian Minister's Defense of the Beloved Novels.* Edinburgh: St. Martin's Press, 2002. *The Life, Death, and Resurrection of Harry Potter.* Macon: Mercer University Press, 2009.

Kirk, G.S. *Myth: Its Meaning and Function in Ancient and Other Cultures.* Cambridge: Cambridge University Press, 1973.

Kuhn, Sherman M., ed. *Middle English Dictionary.* Ann Arbor: University of Michigan Press, 1963–1983.

Kurath, Hans, ed. *Middle English Dictionary.* Ann Arbor: University of Michigan Press, 1952–1962 .

Lackey, Mercedes, ed. *Mapping the World of Harry Potter.* Dallas, TX: BenBe Books, 2006.

Lacoss, Jann. "Of Magicals and Muggles: Reversals and Revulsions at Hogwarts." In *The Ivory Tower and Harry Potter: Perspectives on a Literary Phenomenon.* Lana A. Whited, ed. Columbia: University of Missouri Press, 2002.

Landfester, Manfred, et al., eds. *Brill's New Pauly: Encyclopaedia of the Ancient world. Classical Tradition.* English edition. Francis G. Gentry, Managing ed. Leiden, Boston: 2006–. Five vols. plus index vol.

Lattimore, Richmond, trans. *The Iliad of Homer.* Chicago: University of Chicago Press, 1951. *The Odes of Pindar.* Second Edition. University of Chicago Press, 1976. *The Odyssey of Homer.* New York: Harper and Row, Publishers, 1967.

Leeming, David A. *From Olympus to Camelot: The World of European Mythology.* New York: Oxford University Press, 2003. *Mythology: The Voyage of the Hero.* 3rd ed. New York: Oxford University Press, 1998. *The Oxford Companion to World Mythology.* New York: Oxford University Press, 2005. *Storytelling Encyclopedia: Historical, Cultural and Multiethnic Approaches to Oral Traditions Around the World.* Phoenix, AZ: Oryx Press, 1997.

Lewis, Charlton T. *A Latin Dictionary: Lewis and Short.* Oxford: The Clarendon Press, 1989.

Lewis, Naphthali, and Meyer Reinhold, eds. *Roman Civilization: Sourcebook II: The Empire.* New York: Harper and Row, Publishers, 1955.

Lewis, Robert E., ed. *Middle English Dictionary.* Ann Arbor: University of Michigan Press, 1984–2000.

Liddell, Henry George, and Robert Scott. *A Greek-English Lexicon.* 9th ed. Rev. by Henry Stuart James. Oxford: Clarendon Press, 1940; repr. 1968.

Lombardo, Stanley, trans. *Homer: Odyssey.* Cambridge: Hackett Publishing Company, Inc., 2000.

López-Ruiz, Carolina, ed. *Gods, Heroes, and Monsters: A Sourcebook of Greek, Roman, and Near Eastern Myths in Translation.* New York: Oxford University Press, 2014.

Luck, Georg. *Arcana Mundi: Magic and the Occult in the Greek and Roman Worlds: A Collection of Ancient Texts.* 2nd ed. Baltimore: Johns Hopkins University Press, 2006.

Lundberg, Marilyn J. "Eliphaz." In *Eerdmans Dictionary of the* Bible. David Noel Freedman, et al., eds. Grand Rapids: Wm. B. Eerdmans, 2000.

Mack, Sara. *Ovid.* New Haven: Yale University Press, 1988. *Patterns of Time in Vergil.* Hamden, Conn.: Archon Books, 1978.

Malkin, Irad. "snakes." In *The Oxford Classical Dictionary.* 4th edition. Simon Hornblower and Antony Spawforth and Esther Eidinow, eds. New York: Oxford University Press, 2012.

Maltby, Robert. *A Lexicon of Ancient Latin Etymologies.* Cambridge: Francis Cairns Publications, 2006.

Markell, Kathryn A., and Marc A.Markell. *The Children Who Lived: Using Harry Potter and Other Fictional Characters to Help Grieving Children and Adolescents.* New York: Routledge, 2008.

Mayes-Elma, Ruthann. *Females and Power: Not All That Empowering.* Lanham, MD: Rowman and Littlefield Publishers, 2006.

Michels, Agnes. "The Many Faces of Aeneas." In *The Classical Journal*. 92.4 (1997): 399–416.

Miller, Frank Justus. *Ovid: Metamorphoses*. Cambridge: Harvard University Press, 1984. Loeb Classical Library.

Mish, Frederick, et al., eds. *Merriam Webster's Collegiate Dictionary*. 11th ed. Springfield: Merriam-Webster Inc., 2008.

Morford, Mark P.O., Robert J. Lenardon, and Michael Sham. *Classical Mythology*. 10th ed. New York: Oxford University Press, 2014.

Morgan, Jeff. "The Heroic Quest: Harry Potter and Myth." In *Selected Papers from Nimbus—2003 Compendium*. Heidi Howard Dandy, et al., compilers. Houston, TX: HP Education Fanon, Inc., 2005.

Morner, Kathleen, and Ralph Rausch. *NTC's Dictionary of Literary Terms*. Lincolnwood, ILL: National Textbook Company, 1991.

Morris, Thomas V. *If Harry Potter Ran General Electric: Leadership Wisdom from the World of the Wizards*. New York: Currency/Doubleday, 2006.

Mulholland, Neil, ed. *The Psychology of Harry Potter: An Unauthorized Examination of the Boy Who Lived*. Dallas, TX: BenBella Books, 2006.

Murray, A.T., trans. *Homer: The Odyssey*. 2nd ed. Rev. by George E. Dimock. Two volumes. Cambridge: Harvard University Press. Loeb Classical Library, 1995.

Natov, Roni. "Harry Potter and the Extraordinariness of the Ordinary." In *The Ivory Tower and Harry Potter: Perspectives on a Literary Phenomenon*. Lana A. Whited, ed. Columbia: University of Missouri Press, 2002.

Neal, Connie. *The Gospel According to Harry Potter: The Spiritual Journey of the World's Greatest Seeker*. Rev. and expanded ed. Louisville, KY: Westminster John Knox Press, 2008. *Wizards, Wardrobes and Wookies: Navigating Good and Evil in Harry Potter, Star Wars and the Chronicles of Narnia*. Downers Grove, IL: IVP Books, 2007.

Nel, Philip. *J.K. Rowling's Harry Potter Novels: A Reader's Guide*. New York: Continuum International Publishing Group, 2001.

Neufeldt, Victoria, and David B. Guralnik, eds. *Webster's New World Dictionary of American English: Third College Edition*. New York: Prentice Hall, 1994.

Nexon, Daniel H., and Iver B. Neumann, eds. *Harry Potter and International Relations*. Lanham, MD: Rowman and Littlefield, 2006.

Nilsen, Alleen P., and Don L.F.Nilsen. "Latin Revived: Source-Based Vocabulary Lessons Courtesy of Harry Potter." In *Journal of Adolescent and Adult Literacy*. 50.2 (2006): 128–34.

Ogden, Daniel. *Dragons, Serpents, and Slayers in the Classical and Early Christian Worlds: A Sourcebook*. New York: Oxford University Press, 2013. *Magic, Witchcraft, and Ghosts in the Greek and Roman Worlds: A Sourcebook*. 2nd ed. New York: Oxford University Press, 2009. *Drakōn: Dragon Myth and Serpent Cult in the Greek and Roman Worlds*. New York: Oxford University Press, 2013a.

Parker, Robert. "sacrifice, Greek." In *The Oxford Classical Dictionary*. 4th ed. Simon Hornblower, Antony Spawforth and Esther Eidinow, eds. New York: Oxford University Press, 2012.

Patterson, Diana, ed. *Harry Potter's World Wide Influence*. Newcastle upon Tyne: Cambridge Scholars, 2009.

Pharr, Clyde. *Vergil's Aeneid: Books I–VI*. Rev. ed. Boston: D.C. Heath and Co., 1964.

Pharr, Mary. "In Medias Res: Harry Potter as Hero-in-Progress. In *The Ivory Tower and Harry Potter: Perspectives on a Literary Phenomenon*. Lana A. Whited, ed. Columbia: University of Missouri Press, 2002.

Pohlenz, M. *Herodot der erste Geschichtschreiber des Abendlandes*. Neue Wege Zur Antike II, 7–8. Leipzig, 1937.

Pollard, John. *Birds in Greek Life and Myth*. Plymouth: Thames and Hudson, 1977.

Potter, David. "Numbers, Sacred." In *The

Oxford Classical Dictionary. 4th edition. Simon Hornblower, Antony Spawforth and Esther Eidinow, eds. New York: Oxford University Press, 2012.

Powell, Barry B. *Classical Myth.* 7th ed. New York: Pearson, 2012.

Price, Simon, and Emily Kearns, eds. *The Oxford Dictionary of Classical Myth and Religion.* New York: Oxford University Press, 2003.

Prinzi, Travis. *Harry Potter & Imagination: The Way Between Two Worlds.* Allentown, PA: Zosima Press, 2009.

Propp, Vladimir. *The Morphology of the Folktale.* 2nd ed. Ed. Louis A. Wagner. Trans. Laurence Scott. Rev. reprint of 1928 original. Austin: University of Texas Press, 1968.

Purcell, Nicholas. "Janus." In *The Oxford Classical Dictionary.* 4th ed. Simon Hornblower, Antony Spawforth and Esther Eidinow, eds. New York: Oxford University Press, 2012.

Quinn, Edward. *A Dictionary of Literary and Thematic Terms.* New York: Facts on File, 1999.

Race, William H., trans. and ed. *Apollonius Rhodius. Argonautica.* Cambridge: Harvard University Press, 2008. Loeb Classical Library.

Radice, Betty, trans. *Terence: The Comedies.* New York: Penguin Books, 1976.

Rank, Otto. *The Myth of the Birth of the Hero.* New York: Alfred A. Knopf, 1959.

Rank, Otto, Lord Raglan, and Alan Dundes. *In Quest of the Hero.* Princeton: Princeton University Press, 1990.

Reagin, Nancy R., ed. *Harry Potter and History.* Hoboken: John Wiley and Sons, 2011.

Reitzenstein, Richard. *Hellenistic Mystery-Religions: Their Basic Ideas and Significance.* Trans. John E. Steely. Pittsburgh: The Pickwick Press, 1978.

Rémi, Cornelia. *Harry Potter Bibliography.* 17 September 2014. Web. 23 December 2014. http://www.eulenfeder.de/hpliteratur.html.

Rengstorf, Karl Heinrich. "dōdeka." In *Theological Dictionary of the New Testament.* Vol. II Gerhard Friedrich, ed.

Trans. Geoffrey W. Bromiley. Grand Rapids: Wm. B. Eerdmans Publishing Company, 1964.

Roberts, John, ed. *The Oxford Dictionary of the Classical World.* Oxford: Oxford University Press, 2005.

Rohde, Erwin. *Psyche: The Cult of Souls and Belief in Immortality among the Greeks.* Vol. 1. Trans. W.B. Hillis. New York: Harper and Rowe, 1966.

Roman, Luke, and Monica Roman. *Encyclopedia of Greek and Roman Mythology.* New York: Facts on File/InfoPublishing, 2010.

Room, Adrian. *Room's Classical Dictionary: The Origins of the Names of Characters in Classical Mythology.* Boston: Routledge and Kegan Paul, 1983.

Roscher, Wilhelm Heinrich. *Beiträge zur Zahlensymbolik der Griechen und anderer Völker.* New York: Georg Olms Verlag, 2003. Repr. of 1917 original.

Rose, Herbert J. "Amycus." In *The Oxford Classical Dictionary.* 4th ed. Simon Hornblower, Antony Spawforth and Esther Eidinow, eds. New York: Oxford University Press, 2012. "Merope." In *The Oxford Classical Dictionary.* 4th ed. Simon Hornblower, Antony Spawforth and Esther Eidinow, eds. New York: Oxford University Press, 2012.

Rose, Herbert J., and John Scheid. "Volcanus." In *The Oxford Classical Dictionary.* 4th ed. Simon Hornblower, Antony Spawforth and Esther Eidinow, eds. New York: Oxford University Press, 2012.

Rowland, Beryl. *Animals with Human Faces.* Knoxville: University of Tennessee Press, 1973.

Rowling, J.K. *Harry Potter and the Chamber of Secrets.* New York: Scholastic Inc., 1999. *Harry Potter and the Deathly Hallows.* New York: Scholastic Inc., 2007. *Harry Potter and the Goblet of Fire.* New York: Scholastic Inc., 2000. *Harry Potter and the Half-Blood Prince.* New York: Scholastic Inc., 2005. *Harry Potter and the Order of the Phoenix.* New York: Scholastic Inc., 2003. *Harry Potter and the Prisoner of Azkaban.* New York:

Scholastic Inc., 1999. *Harry Potter and the Sorcerer's Stone*. New York: Scholastic Inc., 1997.

Rudolph, Kurt. *Gnosis: The Nature and History of Gnosticism*. Trans. and ed. by R. M. Wilson. New York: Harper and Row, 1983.

Rühle, O. "Astralreligion." *In Die Religion in Geschichte und Gegenwart*. 3rd ed. Ed. by Kurt Galling. Vol. 1: 662–64. Tubingen: J.C.B. Mohr (Paul Siebeck), 1957.

Sakenfeld, Katharine D., et al., eds. *The New Interpreter's Dictionary of the Bible*. 5 vols. Nashville: Abingdon Press, 2006–09.

Sandys, Sir John Edwin. *Latin Epigraphy*. 2nd ed. Rev. by S.G. Campbell. Chicago: Ares Publishers, 1974.

Saxena, Vandana. *The Subversive Harry Potter: Adolescent Rebellion and Containment in the J.K Rowling Novels*. Jefferson, NC: McFarland, 2012.

Scamander, Newt. *Fantastic Beasts and Where to Find Them*. London: Scholastic Press, 2001.

Schachter, Albert. "Semele." In *The Oxford Classical Dictionary*. 4th ed. Simon Hornblower, Antony Spawforth and Esther Eidinow, eds. New York: Oxford University Press, 2012.

Scheid, J. "Jupiter (Iuppiter)." In *The Oxford Classical Dictionary*. 4th ed. Simon Hornblower, Antony Spawforth and Esther Eidinow, eds. New York: Oxford University Press, 2012.

Schering, Linda S. "Hephzibah." In *The Anchor Bible Dictionary*. David Noel Freedman, et al., eds. New York: Doubleday, 1992.

Schiesaro, Alessandro. "Muses." In *The Oxford Classical Dictionary*. 4th ed. Simon Hornblower, Antony Spawforth and Esther Eidinow, eds. New York: Oxford University Press, 2012.

Schilling, Robert. "The Manes." In *Roman and European Mythologies*. Compiled by Yves Bonnefoy. Trans. Gerald Honigsblum. Chicago: University of Chicago Press, 1991.

Schweizer, Eduard. *Luke: A Challenge to Present Theology*. Atlanta: John Knox Press, 1982.

Scullard, H.H. "Murcus." In *The Oxford Classical Dictionary*. 2nd ed. N.G.L Hammond and H.H. Scullard, eds. New York: Oxford University Press, 1984.

Segal, Robert A. "Introduction: In Quest of the Hero." In *In Quest of the Hero*. By Otto Rank, Lord Raglan and Alan Dundes. Princeton: Princeton University Press, 1990.

Seigneuret, Jean-Charles, ed. *Dictionary of Literary Themes and Motifs*. Two volumes. New York: Greenwood Press, 1988.

Silver, Carole G. "Animal Brides and Grooms: Marriage of Person to Animal." In *Archetypes and Motifs in Folklore and Literature: A Handbook*. Jane Garry and Hasan El-Shamy, eds. Armonk, New York: M.E. Sharpe, 2005.

Simpson, J.A. and E.S.C. Weiner, eds. *The Oxford English Dictionary*. 2nd ed. Oxford: Clarendon Press, 1989.

Solin, Heikki. "names, personal, Roman." In *The Oxford Classical Dictionary*. 4th ed. Simon Hornblower, Antony Spawforth and Esther Eidinow, eds. New York: Oxford University Press, 2012.

Sourvinou-Inwood, Christiane. "Sisyphus." In *The Oxford Classical Dictionary*. 4th ed. Simon Hornblower, Antony Spawforth and Esther Eidinow, eds. New York: Oxford University Press, 2012.

South, Malcolm, ed. *Mythical and Fabulous Creatures: A Source Book and Research Guide*. New York: Greenwood Press, 1987.

Spencer, John R. "Phinehas." *The Anchor Bible Dictionary*. David Noel Freedman, et al., eds. New York: Doubleday, 1992.

Spencer, Richard A. *Contrast as Narrative Technique in Ovid's Metamorphoses*. Studies in Classics, vol. 6. Lewiston, New York: Edwin Mellen Press, 1997.

Spicq, Ceslaus, O.P. *Agape in the New Testament*. Volume 2. Trans. Sister Marie Aquinas McNamara, O.P. and Sister Mary Honoria Richter, O.P. St. Louis: B. Herder Book Co., 1965.

Stelten, Leo F. *Dictionary of Ecclesiastical Latin*. Peabody, MA: Hendrickson Publishers, 1997.

Stenger, Jan (Kiel). "Tantalus." *Brill's New Pauly*. Antiquity Volumes ed. by Hubert Cancik and Helmuth Schneider. Brill Online, 2014. Reference. Appalachian State University. 17 December 2014 http://0-referenceworks.brillonline.com.wncln.wncln.org/entries/brill-s-new-pauly/tantalus-e1200290.

Stewart, Andrew F. "Daedalus." In *The Oxford Classical Dictionary*. 4th ed. Simon Hornblower, Antony Spawforth and Esther Eidinow, eds. New York: Oxford University Press, 2012.

Storm, Lance. *The Enigma of Numbers*. Pari, Italy: Pari Publishing, 2008.

Sullivan, J.P., trans. *Petronius*: The Satyricon; *Seneca;* The Apocolocyntosis. New York: Penguin Books, 1986.

Thomas, Jeffrey E., and Franklin G. Snyder, eds. *The Law and Harry Potter*. Durham, NC: Carolina Academic Press, 2010.

Thompson, Stith. *The Folktale*. Berkeley: University of California Press, 1977 Repr. of the ed. published in 1946 by Dryden Press (New York). *Motif-Index of Folk Literature: A Classification of Narrative Elements in Folktales, Ballads, Myths, Fables, Mediaeval Romances, Exempla, Fabliaux, Jest-Books and Local Legends*. Rev. and enlarged ed. Bloomington: Indiana University Press, 1993, original 1955–58, Electronic resource by InteLex Corporation.

Thury, Eva M., and Margaret K. Devinney. *Introduction to Mythology: Contemporary Approaches to Classical and World Myths*. 3rd ed. New York: Oxford University Press, 2013.

Toomer, G.J. "Constellations and Named Stars." In *The Oxford Classical Dictionary*. 4th ed. Simon Hornblower, Antony Spawforth and Esther Eidinow, eds. New York: Oxford University Press, 2012.

Tracy, Stephen V. *The Story of the Odyssey*. Princeton: Princeton University Press, 1990.

Uther, Hans-Jörg. *The Types of International Folktales: A Classification and Bibliography Based on the System of Antti Aarne and Stith Thompson*. Helsinki: Suomalainen Tiedeakatemia, Academia Scientiarum Fennica, 2004.

Van Otterlo, W.A.A. *Untersuchungen über Begriff, Anwendung und Entstehung der griechischen "Ringkomposition": Mededeelingen der Kon. Nederlandse Akademie van Wetenschappen*. Afd. Letterkunde, nieuwe Reeks, Deel 7, No. 3. Amsterdam, 1944.

Vander Ark, Steve. *The Lexicon: An Unauthorized Guide to Harry Potter Fiction and Related Materials*. Muskegon, MI: RDR Books, 2009.

Vellacott, Philip, trans. *Aeschylus: The Oresteian Trilogy*. New York: Viking Penguin, 1986.

Warrior, Valerie M. *Roman Religion*. New York: Cambridge University Press, 2006.

Weidhorn, Manfred. "Mirror." In *Dictionary of Literary Themes and Motifs*. Ed. by Jean-Charles Seigneuret. Vol. 2: 850–59. New York: Greenwood Press, 1988.

Welch, John W., ed. *Chiasmus in Antiquity: Structures, Analyses, Exegesis*. Hildesheim: Gerstenberg, 1981. *Chiasmus Bibliography*. Provo, UT: Research Press, 1998.

West, M.L., trans. *Greek Epic Fragments: From the Seventh to the Fifth Centuries BC*. Cambridge: Harvard University Press, 2003. Loeb Classical Library. *Greek Lyric Poetry*. New York: Oxford University Press, 1999.

Whited, Lana A., ed. *The Ivory Tower and Harry Potter: Perspectives on a Literary Phenomenon*. Columbia: University of Missouri Press, 2002.

Whitman, Cedric. *Homer and the Homeric Tradition*. Cambridge: Harvard University Press, 1963.

Whittaker, C.R., trans. *Herodian*. Volumes I–IV. Cambridge: Harvard University Press, 1969. Loeb Classical Library.

Willcock, Malcolm M. *A Companion to The Iliad: Based on the Translation by Richmond Lattimore*. Chicago: University of Chicago Press, 1976.

Williams, Gordon. *Change and Decline: Roman Literature in the Early Empire*. Berkeley: University of California Press, 1978.

Williams, R.D., ed. *The Aeneid of Virgil: Books 1–6.* Edinburgh: St. Martin's Press, 1992.

Winstead, Antoinette F. "The Heroic Journey: An Examination of J.K. Rowling's Use of the monomyth in the Harry Potter Series." In *Selected Papers from Nimbus—2003 Compendium.* Houston, TX: HP Education Fanon, Inc., 2005.

Witzel, E.J. Michael. *The Origins of the World's Mythologies.* New York: Oxford University Press, 2012.

Index